Black Earth, White Bread

BLACK EARTH, WHITE BREAD

A Technopolitical History of Russian Agriculture and Food

Susanne A. Wengle

THE UNIVERSITY OF WISCONSIN PRESS

The University of Wisconsin Press
728 State Street, Suite 443
Madison, Wisconsin 53706
uwpress.wisc.edu

Gray's Inn House, 127 Clerkenwell Road
London ECIR 5DB, United Kingdom
eurospanbookstore.com

Copyright © 2022 by Susanne A. Wengle

All rights reserved. Except in the case of brief quotations embedded in critical articles and reviews, no part of this publication may be reproduced, stored in a retrieval system, transmitted in any format or by any means—digital, electronic, mechanical, photocopying, recording, or otherwise—or conveyed via the internet or a website without written permission of the University of Wisconsin Press. Rights inquiries should be directed to rights@uwpress.wisc.edu.

Printed in the United States of America
This book may be available in a digital edition.

Library of Congress Cataloging-in-Publication Data

Names: Wengle, Susanne A., 1977- author.
Title: Black earth, white bread : a technopolitical history of Russian agriculture and food / Susanne A. Wengle.
Description: Madison, Wisconsin : The University of Wisconsin Press, [2022] | Includes bibliographical references and index.
Identifiers: LCCN 2021015818 | ISBN 9780299335403 (hardcover)
Subjects: LCSH: Agriculture and politics—Soviet Union—History. | Agriculture and politics—Russia (Federation)—History. | Agriculture and state—Soviet Union—History. | Agriculture and state—Russia (Federation)—History. | Food—Political aspects—Soviet Union. | Food—Political aspects—Russia (Federation)
Classification: LCC HD1992 .W46 2022 | DDC 338.10947—dc23
LC record available at https://lccn.loc.gov/2021015818

ISBN 9780299335441 (paperback)

For my parents.
And for Jay, Oren, Artur, Aino, and Alex,
my sweet loves.

CONTENTS

List of Illustrations	ix
Acknowledgments	xiii
Note on Transliteration, Translation, and Place-Names	xvii
Introduction: *Setting the Table*	3
1 Governance; or, How to Solve the Grain Problem	38
2 Production	84
3 Consumption; or, Perestroika of the Quotidian	136
4 Nature	177
Conclusion: *Vulnerabilities*	212
Notes	227
Bibliography	269
Index	291

ILLUSTRATIONS

Figures

Figure I.1 Soviet poster on science and farming, 1977	13
Figure I.2 Bread and worker at the Dagpotrebsoyuz Bread Factory, 1981	15
Figure I.3 President V. V. Putin, official visit to Samara Bread Factory, March 2018	16
Figure 1.1 Nikita Khrushchev visits fields of the Moskovsky State Farm, Kazakh SSR, 1964	53
Figure 1.2 Russian grain loaded for export, Rostov-on-Don, August 2012	70
Figure 2.1 Collective farm workers during harvest, 1944	95
Figure 2.2 Sprats and workers at the S. Kirov Fish Collective Farm, Estonian SSR, 1972	101
Figure 2.3 Backyard plot, Petropavlovsk-Kamchatskii, Kamchatka, October 2007	105
Figure 2.4 Abandoned greenhouse of a former kolkhoz, Village of Krasnoye, Grachyovsk district, Stavropol Krai, 2014	110
Figure 3.1 Ice cream vendor, Leningrad, July 26, 1978	145
Figure 3.2 Fresh berries, outdoor market, Petropavlovsk-Kamchatskii, Kamchatka, October 2007	148

Figure 3.3 Kosmos Café, Moscow, July 1966 — 157

Figure 3.4 Kitchen in a communal apartment, St. Petersburg, 1997 — 158

Figure 3.5 Pensioner's meal, Anna Ivanovna's kitchen, Vladivostok, October 2007 — 169

Figure 4.1 Mironovskaya winter wheat and bread baked from this variety, July 30, 1984 — 192

Maps

Map 1.1 Food imports to the Soviet Union, late 1980s — 65

Map 1.2 Export destinations: Russian wheat, 2019 — 73

Map 2.1 Agricultural production in Soviet Republics, 1980s — 94

Map 2.2 Agroholding activity: south and west, 2019 — 116

Map 2.3 Agroholding activity: Siberia and Far East, 2019 — 117

Map 2.4 Origins of technology and financial investment in Russian agriculture, 2010s — 122

Tables

Table 1.1 Russia's five largest landowners and land holdings, 2020 — 78

Table 2.1 Timeline of changing production technologies and global integration — 88

Table 2.2 Share of Soviet food production from household farms — 107

Table 2.3 Fixed capital investment in Russian agriculture and food processing, 1994–2016 — 112

Table 2.4 Partial list of imported agrifood technologies, 2010s — 121

Table 2.5 Yield gains, Russian wheat, 1992–2019 — 126

Table 2.6 Russian wheat exports, 1993–2019 — 127

Table 2.7 Employment in agriculture and food processing, 1998–2017 — 129

Table 2.8 Pork output from household farms, 2000–2018 — 130

Table 3.1 Meat consumption, Soviet Union and Russia, 1950–2015 — 152

Table 4.1 Wheat yields, Soviet Union and the US, 1961–1991 — 185

Table 4.2 Seed varieties for main Russian grain crops developed and sold by Russian seed breeding institutes, 2020   195

Table 4.3 Russian and foreign patent holders for seed varieties registered with Gossortkommissiia, 2020   196

Table 4.4 Soviet pig breeds   202

Table 4.5 Russian imports of live cattle for purebred breeding, 2011–2016   204

Table 4.6 Breeding aims maximized in Libra/Svinka F-1   205

ACKNOWLEDGMENTS

I began writing this book in Berkeley, where food culture is alive, agricultural production is close, and nearly everyone is both a critic and a beneficiary of industrial agriculture. I finished in Chicago, as we sheltered in our homes in 2020 and 2021 during the COVID-19 pandemic. As I finalized the book in August 2021, the virus that causes COVID-19 had killed more than 4.5 million people globally and constrained the movement of most of the world's population. The virus is a nonhuman, technically even nonliving, force of nature. Its lethality revealed that twenty-first-century humans were still vulnerable to such forces, even if they seemed to have momentarily forgotten this simple truth. The unfolding of the pandemic has also again made clear that privilege and inequality are manifested as patterns of ill- and well-being, some of which revolve around food. Like many others lucky enough to have time at home, I spent numerous lockdown hours baking bread and trying (unsuccessfully) to grow vegetables. I had the good fortune of having a small home office off the kitchen with a door that could technically be closed but was mostly open, as I went back and forth between writing and cooking. I would cut an onion, start sautéing it, and then go back to finish a sentence with its scent on my fingers. I could smell when the onion was done and hear the kids rummaging through the fridge.

Overall, it was an immense privilege to be able to research and write this book. A sizable and amazing group of scholars and friends supported the project over the years in uncountable ways. I thank Jenny Leigh Smith, Oane Visser, Aaron Hale-Dorrell, Irina Olimpieva, and two anonymous reviewers for reading all or large chunks of the book; their thoughtful and detailed feedback have made this a better book. Over the years, Rudra Sil, Peter Rutland, Gary Herrigel, Doug Rogers, James Scott, David Engerman, Vladimir Gelman, Jazmin

Sierra, Karrie Koesel, Jaimie Bleck, Susan Osterman, Natalia Mamonova, Carol Leonard, Yoshiko Herrera, Scott Gehlbach, Andrew Barnes, Bob Orttung, Ilya Vinokovetsky, Brian Kuns, Stefan Hedlund, Laura Henry, Christy Monet, Andrey Indukaev, and many others read and commented on parts of the book, and I am grateful for the invaluable substantive input that helped me understand and improve the narrative. I thank the economic and agricultural historians whose work I rely on for the Soviet-era portion of the narrative, as well as the agroholdings representatives, scholars, policy analysts, and journalists who agreed to be interviewed for this project and helped me understand the brave new world of contemporary agroholdings. Natalia Shagaida, Vladimir Uzun, Eugenia Serova, and Alexander Nikulin all generously shared their tremendous expertise and insights on Soviet and Russian agriculture.

I wrote the bulk of the first draft at the Swedish Collegium for Advanced Study (SCAS) in Uppsala. I am indebted and grateful to Christina Garsten and Björn Wittrock for the invitation to spend a year at SCAS, where I could write in the wonderful surroundings of Carl Linnaeus's Botanical Garden and was introduced to the practice of fika. The encouragement and company by the other SCAS fellows—especially Jenny Larson, Wendy Espeland, Bruce Carruthers, Ben Madley, Jenny Anderson, Sofia Loden, Ekaterina Mouliarova, Sohini Ramachandran, and Jeremy Mumford—contributed immensely to turning an idea into a book. A special thank you also to Pia Hultgren, Maria Odengrund, and Ulrika Anderson for the roles they played in making SCAS fikas and lunches possible for all of us.

I would like to acknowledge the generous support by several institutions. The Swiss National Science Foundation funded a postdoc at the University of Chicago that allowed me to start the research on Russian agriculture. The University of Notre Dame has been superbly supportive, providing two indispensable resources for research: time and funding. Notre Dame's Department of Political Science (with Dave Campbell at the helm) and the dean's office approved research leaves, and several institutes contributed funding for fieldwork trips to Russia and for a book workshop (the Institute for the Study of Liberal Arts, the Helen Kellogg Institute, and the Nanovic Institute). I am also grateful for the support by the Neubauer Collegium for Culture and Society at the University of Chicago, the Östersjöstiftelsen, and Södertörn University for their support at various stages of the research. At the Neubauer Collegium, I thank Jonathan Lear and Elspeth Carruthers for creating a welcoming environment that allowed me to think through big questions about industrial agriculture, markets, and sustainability and for supporting a workshop on Agricultural Transition that Gary Herrigel and I convened in December 2020. Julie Guthman, Debra Fitzgerald, Jess Gilbert, and Shane Hamilton made comments that helped crystallize some of the main claims of the book just in time for the final revisions.

I thank Katherine Mansourova for dedicating so many hours of her years at Notre Dame to expert research assistance for this book. I thank Amber Cederström and her team at the University of Wisconsin Press for their efforts in turning the manuscript into an actual book. I thank Yuri Slezkine, Steve Vogel, Ruth Abbey, James McAdams, Ricardo Ramirez, Amitava Dutt, Juliet Johnson, Allan Mustard, Christine Evans, Faith Hillis, Victoria Smolkin, Evgenia Olimpieva, Zhivka Valiavicharska, Monica Nalepa, Natalia Forrat, Jennifer Dixon, Jennifer Brass, Jody LaPorte, Regine Spector, Tarini Bedi, Jessica Jerome, Michele Friedner, David Herne, Alexey Klaptsov, and Chris Rogers each for the support they provided in their own ways, through words of wisdom, with their friendship or with practical advice.

The premise of the book—that politics, technologies, and daily meals are all connected—draws on my earliest memories of my own *byt*. I grew up with home-cooked meals, assembled over countless hours by my mom. The book is dedicated to my parents and my family. The value my parents placed on cooking, good food, and small farms was something they passed on to me and my siblings. For this I am truly thankful. Last but not least, I am deeply grateful to Jay, Oren, Artur, Aino, and Alex, who sustain all my days with their sweet love and joy.

NOTE ON TRANSLITERATION, TRANSLATION, AND PLACE-NAMES

Original Russian sources are transliterated using the ALA transliteration scheme. Following established conventions, I depart from ALA transliterations for names and words that are well known in English, for example, Boris Yeltsin (rather than El'tsin). Cities and places are referred to by their official Soviet names, for example, Tselinograd (rather than Nur-Sultan). All translations from Russian and German are my own.

Black Earth, White Bread

Introduction
Setting the Table

Bread to the people!
—Revolutionary slogan, 1917

Those who want to see socialism at work, go visit a bread factory.
—*Ogonek*, 1952

The Promise of Plenty

In 1998 Boris Yeltsin and his team of liberal reformers faced a problem: the price of bread was rising, and with it, the government's hold on Russia's economy and the country's future was slipping. Bread is so central to the Russian diet and cultural identity that Yeltsin's reformers excluded Soviet-era bread factories (*khlebozavody*) from the extensive privatization in the early 1990s. Municipal authorities continued to operate bread factories and tried to control bread prices while hyperinflation wreaked havoc across other sectors of the economy. In the fall of 1998, however, rising prices for key ingredients collided with price controls, causing sleepless nights for Sergei Ivanov, chief engineer of Moscow's city-owned bakeries. Ivanov's biggest job now wasn't blending and baking bread, something that his khlebozavody had done for decades. He now had to balance the competing imperatives of market forces, politics, and compassion. Russian grain harvests were meager that year, as they had been for several preceding years. The flour used in Moscow bakeries was made from wheat grown in Kazakhstan and Ukraine. When the ruble collapsed in August, the crisis confronting Ivanov became acute. Currency devaluation meant that imported wheat and flour suddenly became a lot more expensive. Meanwhile, stockpiles of flour at Moscow's four large flour mills dwindled, and by late August, only a few days' worth of flour—and bread—remained. The fallout of Yeltsin's liberal reforms threatened to derail Russia from the promised path toward a prosperous and democratic future.

Rising prices for food staples were among the most tangible signs that something was going wrong. To forestall catastrophe, Moscow's mayoral office issued new price caps for bread baked by city-owned bakeries, along with stern warnings to private producers and retailers to refrain from increasing prices. The mayor, Yuri Luzhkov, a powerful populist, was well aware that bread was political. One contemporary commentator pointed out a truth evident to every Russian citizen and politician:

> Bread seems to be just a regular product. In actual fact, it is a special, political one. Insufficient bread in the city immediately affects every family. A price increase is a hit on every wallet.[1]

Would there be enough bread for Muscovites? If so, how, and at what cost? As Sergei Ivanov tells it, his bread factories pulled through the crisis in 1998 by negotiating with suppliers and the mayor's office. Luzhkov played a key role: emergency loans underwritten by city authorities paid for the expensive, imported wheat and flour. Moscow's bread factories had a long-standing reputation for baking "the world's best bread," known proudly as *stolichnyi*. That year, they had to learn to find flour to bake in a volatile, new, and globally connected market economy. In subsequent years, local and federal authorities learned from the troubles of 1998. They stockpiled wheat during harvests to stave off future crises and eventually developed a metropolitan food security plan.[2] When Vladimir Putin became president, his government designed policies and deployed support to farmers to revive and strengthen Russian wheat production on Russia's fertile soil.

The concerns of Ivanov, the mayoral office, and poor Muscovites in the late nineties reflect the momentous change that had occurred in Russia since the collapse of the Soviet Union in 1991. Had collective farms in Ukraine and Kazakhstan still been part of the Soviet-era food procurement system, none of these actors would have had to worry about the ruble exchange rate. In the late Soviet period, shortages of all kinds were pervasive, and grain imports were necessary to feed livestock. But Muscovites had been at the apex of the Soviet political hierarchy and could largely take for granted that the capital city would always be well supplied with fresh, high-quality bread. By 1998, much indeed had changed in a few short years.

Black Earth, White Bread is about change in the Russian agrifood system. The shift from the Soviet planned economy to the post-Soviet market economy is central, but twenty-first-century changes owe much to radical top-down campaigns of the twentieth century. The book also suggests a new way to think about the political economy of food and agriculture more generally, providing answers to two deceptively simple questions: what are food systems, and how do they change?

The transformation of agriculture and food production from the Soviet to the post-Soviet period in the 1990s was just one of several dramatic episodes of change that form a distinctive arc in Russia's history. Prerevolutionary Russia was predominantly rural; at the beginning of the twentieth century, most subjects of the Russian empire farmed the land. Grains and bread were the basis of daily meals, and during times of war and crises, many went hungry. The imperial order was overturned in part because it failed to feed urban citizens during World War I. Lenin promised bread and land, and he gained support for the Bolshevik Revolution because of the resonance of this promise. Conventional wisdom has long regarded the Russian countryside as perennially backward and thought of the Russian economy as inherently different and less efficient than the capitalist economies of the industrialized West. Yet Russian history is marked by several high-stakes rural transformations. Each episode of change was marked by important technological shifts, many with technologies adopted and adapted from industrial agriculture in the West.[3] Joseph Stalin collectivized and mechanized farms—at an enormous human cost. Nikita Khrushchev brought thousands of hectares of marginal steppe under cultivation during the Virgin Lands campaign—with disastrous environmental consequences. Boris Yeltsin decollectivized and privatized land. During Vladimir Putin's presidency, oligarchic agrifood conglomerates gained ownership of vast tracts of Russia's most fertile farmland and imported Western technologies.

Each rural reform brought about new social, economic, and political realities—not once but several times over the last hundred years, and not only in the countryside but in cities as well. The ongoing crisis in food provisioning and Lenin's promise of plentiful bread were central to the collapse and reconstruction of authority in the fateful years 1914–21.[4] Although grain was grown across the Soviet Union, in fertile and stingy soils alike, the Black Earth region, or Chernozem, epitomizes the possibility of abundance in Russia's agriculture.[5] Food and agriculture were central aspects of political power and legitimacy for the nearly eight decades of Soviet rule that followed, and they remain so to this day.[6] Successive Soviet governments worried about grain and the provisioning of staples to all—in other words, about "food problems" (*prodovol'stvennye problemy*)—and they all promoted their own "food plans" (*prodovol'stvennye programmy*). Putin made these kinds of problems and the economic recovery of domestic agriculture central priorities of his presidency from his earliest days in office.[7]

The chapters that follow retell the arc of change drawn by the recurring transformations of the Russian food system. We will see how Soviet and post-Soviet governments defined new policies to feed citizens while responding to the failures of their predecessors and drawing on emerging technological innovations. These transformations are historically contingent and rooted in Eurasian soil, but elements of the story about agriculture, food, politics, and technology are relevant beyond Russia. The book emphasizes a tight connection between political change, technological change in food systems, and the transformation of everyday lives (*byt*)—a connection that we can grasp and understand through the lens of *technopolitics*.

A first key prerequisite to understanding food systems and how they change is an awareness of food's multifaceted existence: it is at once deeply personal but also has a social life and a cultural and political career. Every meal tells a story, and each field has a history. Eating is an intrinsic element of the quotidian of all citizens, and the "transformation of the everyday" (*perestroika byta*) was a central concern of Bolshevik revolutionaries. Not only in Russia are diets part of daily life and a vital element of thriving or suffering. Eating habits and tastes also serve as artifacts of social, economic, political, and cultural orders everywhere. Food, with its symbolic meaning deeply embedded and constitutive of changing culture, is involved in constructing identity and status. Yet only physically available foods can be eaten. The material reality of food matters just as much as its symbolic properties. What is produced, imported, and sold affordably in an area determines the local diet. Agriculture, food production, and processing are organized in particular ways (with distinct owners, management structures, labor conditions, etc.) and employ a set of increasingly complex technologies. Finally, agriculture is also at its core a form of domestication, a process that inextricably links humans with nature and thereby changes both. These facts make food a unique and compelling tool with which to track profound transformations across different realms of collective human life.

All of this also makes agriculture and food eminently political issues. Sergei Ivanov's conundrum and Mayor Luzhkov's response reveal the political dimensions of the Russian food system at a particular time—in this case, in the early post-Soviet period, marked by the economic turmoil that resulted from Yeltsin's liberal reforms. In the late Soviet period, long lines and empty shelves signified a profound crisis of the planned economy and in no small measure contributed to the sense that the Soviet Union was unable keep its promise of plenty. In each period of Russian history, elites have had access to particularly prized foods, while marginalized groups have experienced shortages. Soviet nomenklatura always had much better access to imported food than anybody else. Russia is hardly the only country where inequalities and food shortages have helped to precipitate political unrest: from the 1918 Rice Riots in Japan to the Arab Spring in 2011, food has played a central role in crystallizing public anger. Because food is political, governments everywhere have shaped rural production. James Scott notes in *Against the Grain* that "no institution has done more to mobilize technologies of landscape modification in its interest than the state."[8] As the most important product of these modifications, food directly and viscerally exposes citizens to the state's political projects. This is obvious in the case of paternalistic governments such as those of the USSR and post-Soviet Russia, but it is no less true for market economies. All varieties of capitalist countries have supported, protected, and shaped agricultural production in pursuit of political aims, such as rural modernization, urbanization, or conservation.[9] States pick winners among farms, enlisting them for political goals by smoothing their path to success, supporting the technologies they need to operate profitably, subsidizing their inputs, and keeping foreign competitors at bay.

Political projects, promises, and utopias shape agriculture and food production, and hence people's diets and everyday lives, in important ways. This part of the story is intuitive. What needs more attention is the fact that political projects flounder or fail as often as they succeed in their efforts to shape production and diets. Change is a consequence of both intended success and unintended failure—it results from multivocal responses by political, economic, and social actors to policies, initiatives, and campaigns. Failures are important elements of agricultural histories, and the list of vulnerabilities of industrial agriculture, in Russia as elsewhere, is long and growing. Political schemes to modernize agriculture go up against nature, and nature isn't always pliable and amenable to human wishes. Soils and organisms often comply and produce abundance, but at other times they do not, and together with precipitation and climate, they resist political schemes to produce certain types or quantities of crops. Consumers and their desires, too, are forces of change that often resist top-down attempts to define and satisfy human needs.

Technologies involved in agriculture and production are a critical element of success and failure. Throughout the twentieth century, agricultural production and livestock rearing became ever more closely linked to material technologies and the science of producing food and commodities. Tractors, center-pivot irrigation systems, and biotechnology are but three examples of these trends. We will see that many different types of technologies were important over time; for now, we can think of technologies as machines and techniques that amplify human power to shape nature. Evolving agricultural technologies define human interactions with nature over time. But technologies are also instruments in the hands of political actors who select, support, and favor particular tools, techniques, and forms of domestication. A Stalin-era eulogy to the tractor illustrates well how this particular machine was seen as a political instrument as much as a form of motorized horsepower: "Tens of thousands of tractors plow the fields, cutting off the roots of the kulak exploitation with sharp plowshares, erasing boundaries, uprooting capitalism in the village."[10] Today, Russian authorities think of CRISPR-Cas 9 genome editing techniques in political terms, viewing CRISPR as a technology that Russian scientists need to master in order to reduce the country's dependency on foreign (Western) powers. A central argument of this book is that politics and technologies together drive change in food systems and that we should think of food systems as technopolitical regimes. *Technopolitics* refers to the support of and reliance on agricultural technologies—from tractors to CRISPR techniques—in policy regimes that seek to realize particular political goals and utopias. A technopolitical regime is forged by privileged agents of change and the technologies they employ to grow crops and raise animals.

Technopolitical regimes in agriculture deserve attention because they have far-reaching and important consequences: they define diets, byt, and patterns of privilege; imply a particular type of interaction with nature; and align a domestic food system with a pattern of integration into the global economy. Successes and failures of agro-technopolitical regimes also have political repercussions. Success tends to generate respect, acquiescence, and approval for political projects. Failure is more complicated. It may lead to a revaluation of existing technologies, or it may trigger social critiques of the dominant technopolitical regime. Failure and glaring vulnerabilities may also be largely ignored, especially by actors who are financially and ideologically invested in existing orders. Yet, when the costs of failing technopolitical regimes mount, alternative ways of farming receive more attention, by consumers, policy makers, and farmers themselves. Change occurs if groups of actors modify dominant technopolitical regimes in response to failure, vulnerabilities, social critiques, or shifting global technological frontiers. The main components of food systems—politics, production, diets, and nature—are all interrelated, and a change in one realm affects the others.

Black Earth, White Bread makes the claim that technopolitics is a compelling conceptual device for the study of agrifood systems in Russia and elsewhere because it can reveal these dynamic relationships. For one, it links technologies and political outcomes. It can draw attention to very material and biophysical aspects of food systems, from tractors to refrigeration to agricultural biotech. Technological solutions are essentially machines that can function well, or, conversely, can malfunction and fail for any number of reasons. Technopolitics helps us understand how technologies are produced by the social and political contexts while also shaping them as they are employed. Finally, a technopolitical lens reveals how agricultural technologies embroil humans with nature in codependent relationships. Agricultural technologies are always a form of domestication of biophysical realties, and as such, they are at the core of human endeavors to make nature useful. Grains are grasses, pork and poultry are animals, and sweetness is derived from plants—in the Russian case, from sugar beets. In cultivating land and rearing livestock, humans transform nature to make it more palatable and desirable for themselves, but they also make themselves covulnerable with the natural environment they are part of. Agro-technopolitical regimes unfold and are conditioned by complex and fragile webs of mutual sustenance.

Food systems deserve attention precisely because grains and meat are not just the carbohydrates and proteins that sustain us. Daily meals are both *materials* and *symbols*. This is true for many foods, but it is particularly so, in the Russian case, for bread. Yuri Lotman, a Russian sociologist and public intellectual, made this observation about bread in 1994:

> Let's think about something as simple and familiar as bread. Bread is real and visible. It has weight, form, and one can cut it and eat it. But when we say "give us our daily bread," the word "bread" does not mean just a thing. . . . It has a broader meaning, as "the food that is necessary for life."[11]

Agro-technopolitics is a concept that can reveal how the material and symbolic aspects of food together drive change. A framework that grasps these connections between political, economic, social, and environmental change is especially important for understanding periods of radical transformations, of which Russia has undergone several over the last hundred years. Social science inquiry that specializes in documenting change in one realm of life (political institutions, economic orders, social organizations, or cultural life) often misses how changes in these spheres are intricately interconnected. The chapters that follow answer a series of questions about Russian history that arise if complexity of change in the agrifood system is taken seriously: How has the modernization of agriculture transformed Russian society? What were the drivers of change in agriculture and livestock domestication? How did change connect Russia with the West? And how did human interactions with nature change as the agrifood system evolved? The stakes in answering these questions are high, and new ways of thinking about the politics, technology, and nature involved in agricultural production are urgently needed.

CHANGE IN THE SOVIET AND RUSSIAN FOOD SYSTEM

In the Bolshevik slogan "Bread to the people" (*Khleb narodu!*), a loaf of bread's importance far exceeded its "weight and form," as Lotman put it. Lenin's promise was an incandescent moment in Russian history: it shed light on events that preceded the revolution and followed long after. Its resonance reflected the misery of hunger and poverty that encouraged support for the Bolshevik project. "Bread to the people" was a powerful idea that stood for the provisioning of all citizens with the "food that was necessary for life." It was also, at the same time, a formidable logistical challenge that preoccupied the Bolshevik government for decades. Successive Soviet governments needed to find a way to solve what was called the "grain problem"—that is, to convince or coerce peasants to grow more grain to feed urban workers, or, metaphorically, to coax white bread from Russian soil. Though Lenin's promise was essentially symbolic, it spurred into action numerous and diverse actors to help realize this goal and make food staples and small luxuries broadly available. Even if the groups who were actually receiving the goods were initially limited, and even if the planned economy fell short at times, the promise of plenty acted as a commitment on the part of Soviet and Russian governments to provide for citizens' basic needs. That commitment continues to steer Russian politics to this day.

Soviet modernization created and sustained a rapidly growing army of urban workers who had an adequate diet most of the time. This was a feat made possible by the rural policies of the socialist state. Russian peasants, meanwhile, toiled for decades with few rewards. Collectivization and the famines that followed took an enormous human toll: millions of peasants in Ukraine, Kazakhstan, and elsewhere perished.[12] Collective farms removed meaningful control of the land from rural workers, and at least initially, few benefits of Soviet modernization reached the countryside. Yet collective farms remained the backbone of Soviet industrial agriculture for the rest of the twentieth century. Decisions about types of crops and how to plant them and about livestock breeds and how to raise them were placed under the auspices of the party and planning bureaucracy and reflected political priorities. Through these mechanisms, Soviet governments brought enormous change to the Russian countryside. While this book focuses on food crops, Soviet farms also produced a lot of valuable non-food products—cotton, flax, and wool, for example. Deeply enamored with science and modernization, successive governments pursued the newest technologies and methods to spur collective farmers to produce more.[13] The technologies used to farm and produce food changed radically over the course of the twentieth century, starting with mechanization during the Stalin years and expanding to capital-intensive irrigation projects and research-intensive livestock and plant breeding.

For the most part, Soviet production made bread and basic staples available to all, while meat and other desirables remained in short supply for everyone except the party elites in urban centers. While the reach of the state-directed industrial food system was extensive, it was far from universal. Away from the centers of power—the larger cities in European Russia and the capitals of the Union Republics—and away from politically privileged industrial towns and military installations, the supply channels of the planned economy petered out. With few items for sale in village stores, shortages meant that many citizens grew their own potatoes, vegetables, and fruits; many kept a cow or goats, pigs, rabbits, or hens on small rural household farms (*ogorody*) or suburban garden plots (*dacha*). This type of farming has been known in US scholarship as "private," household or subsistence farming; the official Soviet terminology for it was "private subsidiary agriculture" (*lichnoe podsobnoe khoziaistvo*, or LPKh). The term LPKh refers to the growing of food on small plots by rural residents and city dwellers. Throughout the Soviet period, authorities considered this kind of private, small-scale production economically inefficient and politically problematic.[14] The designation itself implies that LPKh is subordinate to collective farming (*lichnoe* means personal, and *podsobnoe* means subsidiary), thus minimizing its economic relevance.

Not only homegrown but also wild-growing foods such as berries, mushrooms, and herbs played a relatively large role in the Soviet Union, for many of the same reasons subsistence farming did.[15] The imperfection of planned food provisioning mirrors what economic historians have found across the planned economy more generally: "the Soviet economy was neither adequately planned nor well controlled."[16] As this kind of private, small-scale food production and gardening essentially grew in the spaces that the state did not reach, it also relied on very different technologies, knowledge, and skills than the collective sector did. The state's efforts were focused on machines, tools, and the knowledge needed for large-scale farming, whereas the production on ogorody and dacha plots was labor intensive and largely dependent on hand tools and local knowledge.[17] The highly capitalized farming technologies and large-scale operations were significant but not the single defining feature of Soviet agrotechnopolitics. In response to the state-supported industrial agriculture system's shortcomings and failures, rural and provincial city residents, and even many Muscovites, supplemented their diets with homegrown and gathered starches, proteins, vitamins, and other nutrients. In the most general terms, Russian consumption was shaped by the availability, access, and allure of products from state-run industrial farms, tiny subsistence plots, and forests and steppes.

After the collapse of the Soviet planned economy in 1991, collective farms struggled to adjust to skyrocketing prices for inputs and fierce foreign competition in food commodity markets. Domestic agricultural production on state farms collapsed, and a decade-long, dire crisis followed. As Grigory Ioffe, Tatyana Nefedova, and Ilya Zaslavsky have pointed out, at that time, despite decades of urbanization, Russia still remained a "rural country." A large part of the population worked the land, and millions of families (around a quarter of the population) survived on food they grew and gathered themselves.[18] At the start of the new millennium, many Russian farms were undergoing rapid change, and today agrifood corporations employ fewer people to produce more grain, sugar beets, milk, and meat than ever before. Although changes in production happened primarily in Russia's more fertile areas—especially the Chernozem, where large agrifood corporations acquired control of vast land assets and introduced cutting-edge technologies—it transformed Russia's food system as a whole.[19] As agroholdings have risen, household farms are disappearing and agricultural employment has dwindled to less than 8 percent of the labor force.[20]

Whereas the Soviet Union increasingly relied on imported grains and proteins beginning in the early 1970s, with the emergence of agroholdings, Russia started producing grain surpluses and became globally competitive. Russia is now the world's largest wheat exporter. President Putin celebrates this achievement as a victory of his political and economic vision that combined market forces with extensive state support. One feature of the Putin-era agricultural agenda is his regime's 2014 ban on Western food imports in response to Western sanctions imposed after Russia's annexation of Crimea.[21] The ban on Western imports was a tremendous boost for domestic processors and producers, helping them regain a sizable share of domestic food consumption. At the same time, the post-Soviet technopolitical regime also relies on foreign investment, incentivizes technology transfers, and has been careful to exclude live purebred animals and seeds that serve as technological inputs from the broader food ban. Post-Soviet diets have evolved along with political goals, changing technologies, and forms of domestication. The Russian food system is rapidly globalizing, and food items in Russian stores resemble those in Western supermarkets. Meanwhile, authentically Russian, locally grown, and home-processed (*domashnie*) and "our" (*nashi*) foods are valued and marketed as desirable products. The allure of these foods reveals an interesting paradox: on the one hand, it aligns with the rising tide of patriotism and a romanticization of the past in other areas of Russian culture over the last decade or so. On the other hand, it also mirrors consumers' yearning for authenticity and embrace of local foods, sentiments that have gained strength worldwide at a time when actual food commodity chains are increasingly global and opaque.

For each of these momentous changes in Russia's agrifood system over the last hundred years, science and technology played an exceedingly important role. In agriculture, as in other areas of Soviet and Russian life, technology and applied science were celebrated as singularly important motors of socioeconomic change. Starting with the industrialization of agriculture in the early twentieth century, advances in farming methods were premised on the use of science and machines in the service of the socialist project: science would revolutionize the Russian economy and the modernization of agriculture would showcase this grand experiment.[22] Russian agriculture was thus always an eminently political and technological project, resting on an idealized alliance between collective farms and scientists (biologists, plant and animal breeders, agrotechnical engineers, chemists and others) who provided the necessary technologies for the many aspects of industrial food production. The plentiful, socialist future was what Sheila Jasanoff would call a techno-scientific imaginary.[23] A poster designed in the 1970s advocates for the success of this pact between scientists and farmers, displaying a joint pledge that together they "care about every field" (figure I.1). A microscope and tractor adorn the corners of the poster, an iconography that anchors the message that these two tools are essential for the care of fields and for agricultural progress. Technology and science remain central in Putin-era farming as well. A nearly identical stylized microscope is featured in the logo of the All-Russian Poultry Science Research and Technology Institute (Vserossiiskii nauchno-issledovatel'skii i tekhnologicheskii institut ptitsevodstva), a state-funded research institute dedicated to developing a Russian high-performance broiler that we will encounter in chapter 4.

Figure I.1 Soviet poster on science and farming. Izdatel'stvo Plakat, 1977.

The types of technologies, the goals that the tools were meant to accomplish, and the metrics that were deployed to measure them changed greatly over the course of the twentieth and twenty-first centuries. In the early twentieth century, standardization, mechanization, and scale—the main aims of agricultural progress—mirrored the goals of Taylorist industrialization in manufacturing.[24] The quality and types of agricultural food products soon became just as important as the quantity, though what precisely counted as part of a high-quality and appropriate diet changed over time. Yet throughout the period under discussion, political goals of governing elites, technological change in agrifood systems, and the transformation of Russian diets and byt were always tightly connected.

These connections become visible in two historic visits to bakeries, or rather bread factories, by two prominent Russian political actors. The two visits, separated by ninety years, illustrate the state's reliance on technologies to realize political promises, thereby also demonstrating the usefulness of technopolitics as a framework for understanding change in Russia's food system from Lenin to Putin. The first one involved a 1928 visit by Maxim Gorky, one of revolutionary Russia's most celebrated writers, to a Leningrad industrial bakery. As a young man, Gorky had worked in a bakery, and one of his first novels concerns the life of a baker. These facts presumably qualified him as a credible voice in bakery-related matters and were likely considerations by Soviet authorities who sent him to the bread factory. Following the visit, Gorky praised the bread factory's modern machines and argued that they should be seen as one of the achievements of the Bolshevik Revolution: "Nothing speaks more forcefully about the improvements of every-day life," he proclaimed.[25]

The twenties were a time when hunger and bread shortages were still fresh in the minds of Russian citizens. Against this backdrop, bread factories' ability to scale-up and automate the production of bread mattered profoundly, both symbolically and materially. Bread factories provided more bread for more people, but their success was also a kind of symbolic down payment on the realization of a new, socialist reality that promised so much. Bread factories were a symbol of the promise to revolutionize the everyday life (the perestroika byta), not only providing bread but also liberating women from "kitchen slavery." For decades thereafter, bread factories were seen as an essential manifestation of Soviet socialism: "those who want to see socialism at work, go visit a bread factory," suggested an *Ogonek* author to Russian audiences in 1952.[26] Not surprisingly, then, authorities paid close attention to the quality and quantity of bread produced at bread factories (see figure I.2), and recurring surveys sought to solicit consumers' apperception of these efforts.[27]

Figure I.2 Bread and worker at the Dagpotrebsoyuz Bread Factory, 1981. Rudolf Dik/TASS.

Many technologies involved in agriculture and food processing became political in this way. "Corn, comrades, is a political crop" was a well-known maxim of the Khrushchev years, when this so-called miracle crop imported from the US was the Soviet state's chosen technology to solve agricultural problems.[28] Corn was to solve many problems, but in particular it was meant to alleviate persistent shortages of high-calorie animal feed, which in turn would help put meat on Russian tables. Today, different technologies are privileged in policies and political visions of a better life in Russia: agricultural biotech has transformed field crops and animals used in livestock production, and precision agriculture relies on data-driven targeting of valuable inputs. A Russian textbook on agricultural technologies noted in 2018 that "agriculture is undergoing a technological renaissance," and one observer opined optimistically that Russia is now "dramatically ahead of America" in terms of farm technology.[29] This most recent technological revolution and the rise of agroholdings have been supported and encouraged by the Putin government with a cornucopia of policies and programs. New technologies have brought meat to stores at lower prices, making it much more readily available to Russian citizens—a direct material effect of technological change on everyday lives. Just as in the 1920s, high-quality food was clearly marked as symbolic and material down payments on Putin's promise of a better life.

This brings us to the other bookend to Gorky's bread factory visit: ninety years later, in 2018, Vladimir Putin also visited a bread factory (see figure I.3), this time in Samara, where he received a detailed briefing and inspected the contemporary technologies used to produce bread and other baked goods. The message that the state-dominated media projected was the government's continued concern for the quality of the nation's bread.[30]

Not only did the technological frontier of agriculture move dramatically, but the political imagination concerning what exactly "plenty" meant—and what diets would be required for a "good life"—changed over time. These changing norms fueled political and cultural debates and presented a technocratic challenge. Initially, during the early years of the Bolshevik experiment, the promise was enough grain and bread for all. Later, "plenty" came to mean more abundant proteins and "common luxuries," such as sparkling wine and chocolates for special occasions.[31] Anastas Mikoyan, Stalin's commissar for trade and food supplies, wanted to supply workers with white bread, not rough black

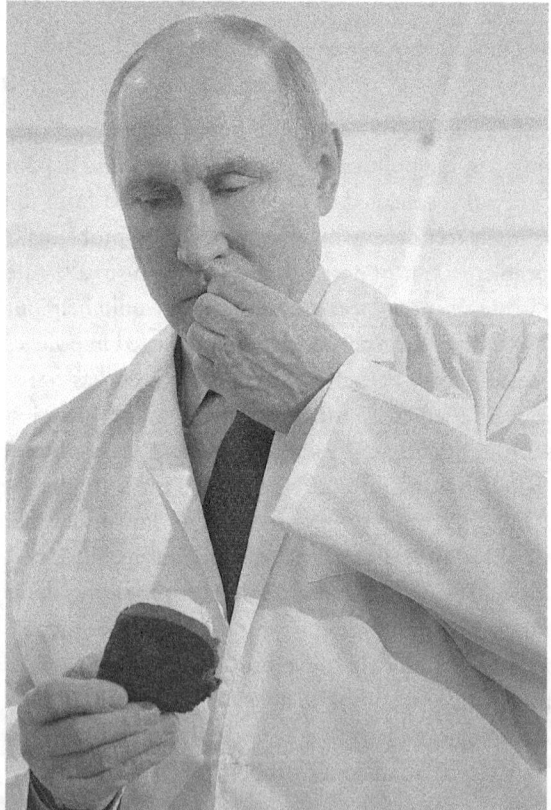

Figure I.3 President V. V. Putin, official visit to Samara Bread Factory, March 2018. Alexei Druzhinin/TASS.

bread, as a reward for having supported the revolution: "Before, we ate black bread, and now we are eating white bread. We made the revolution in order to eat more than just black bread."[32] White bread, in Mikoyan's mind, stood for the achievement of higher living standards. More meat was the promise made under Brezhnev and Putin, both times a response to growing consumer demands. Democratizing meat consumption had long been part of the vision of the good life, in Russia as elsewhere. Agriculture was also always a domain in which Soviet governments saw the need to improve on the abysmal failures of their immediate predecessors. In both the Soviet and post-Soviet periods, efforts to increase yields and production volumes were never ends in themselves: the goal was to produce more in order to keep citizens happy, thereby demonstrating the superiority of the country's political and economic order to them and the rest of the world. This goal was an integral part of the socialist modernization project. While the idealized urban life at the core of modernization is well documented, the focus here is not on industry and the cities, but on agriculture, the countryside, and food consumption.[33] Of course, many actors in Soviet and post-Soviet agricultural economies were adopting technologies for purely economic reasons—to improve efficiency and cut production costs. But even these actors were operating within a political context in which decisions followed from a broad set of political priorities, within a cultural context that shaped desires, and within a natural environment.

Food Systems as Technopolitical Regimes

Lenin's promise of bread and land, Gorky and Putin's visits to bread factories, and Sergei Ivanov's conundrum in the early nineties are all distinctly Russian incarnations of the relationship between technology, politics, food, and agriculture. Yet the concept of technopolitics can broaden our understanding of how they interact to bring about change in agriculture food systems more generally. Strictly speaking, technopolitics is not a causal theory but an analytical tool that reveals crucial relationships between diverse and changing groups of actors in the four realms of food systems—politics, production, consumption, and nature. Many of these relationships are obscured by theoretical approaches that single out one realm as the main stage and one set of actors as protagonists of historical change. Agro-technopolitics brings to the fore the connections between the triad of *politics—technology/production—agriculture/nature*, treating them as reflexive and reciprocal, often even symbiotic, relationships. There are several thriving debates and well-established intellectual traditions that speak to the role of private capital, technology, and the state in agricultural modernization. Risking an undue simplification for heuristic purposes, approaches to understanding rural transformations tend to single out either economic and material forces or the state as the dominant drivers of change. In both economic and statist approaches, some strands use deterministic theories to stabilize the relationship between protagonists, while other strands document historical particularities. Technopolitics is a concept that does not a priori single out either economic actors or the state as the dominant force that always determines outcomes. Instead it reveals the contingent, novel, and unforeseen histories that exceed the predictive power of any theory.

The Role of Capital, Technology, and Economic Dynamics

Agricultural modernization was at the core of the writings of classical political economists, including Karl Marx, Karl Kautsky, Alexander Chayanov, and Karl Polanyi.[34] For these theorists, questions related to the future of the peasantry were acutely relevant: especially in Russia, but also elsewhere in Europe, smallholding farmers made up a large share of the population, and whether they would side with the cause of the urban workers or with reactionary bourgeois nationalism was an important political conundrum. For Karl Marx and later for generations of scholars influenced by Marxist-Leninist theory, agricultural modernization was a necessary stage of industrialization. Peasants, or smallholders and subsistence farmers, were subject to expropriation by capitalists—separated first from control over commonly held land, then from all fruits of their own labor as wage laborers on fields and later in factories. Both processes were inevitable and necessary conditions for the creation of a labor class, land as a commodity, and capitalist accumulation. Politics, in the Marxist view, was only a reflection of the interests of landed elites and factory owners, and the state abetted the process of relentless expropriation of peasants.[35] Peasants, then, were likely or "natural" allies of the urban proletariat.[36] Kautsky, Chayanov, Polanyi, and others responded to Marxist historical materialism and the view that capital—and the embodied capital of machines and factories—was the driving force of industrial and rural change. Although Kautsky is better known for siding with Marxists in political struggles, in his study of the "rural problem" (*die Agrarfrage*), he treated the future of the peasantry as an open question that needed to be answered through detailed historical study. He also argued that we should not assume that Marx's template of change in manufacturing also applies to agriculture.[37] Alexander Chayanov broke more decisively with the Marxists-Leninist take that small peasants were doomed, presenting a theory of rural change that justified the utility of rural production at different scales based on his observation of an array of varied farms that had formed in the Russian countryside by the 1920s.[38] (We will see in the next chapter how these intellectual debates shaped struggles between Bukharin and Stalin in their respective solutions to the peasant problem, and how Chayanov's departure from Marxist-Leninist views cost him his life.) Karl Polanyi, in the 1940s, also departed from the determinism of historical materialism, theorizing social embeddedness as a countervailing force capable of protecting society from the destructive logic of capitalist accumulation. He was just as deeply impressed as Marx had been by the apparent power of machines to turn humans and nature into "fictitious" commodities that fueled factories. Nevertheless, drawing on classical ethnographies, he saw more contingency, agency, and possibility in economic history. In his reading of the British enclosure of the commons, political forces had the potential to tame, respond to, and shape market dynamics and material forces unleashed by technological change.[39]

These tensions between Marxists and followers of Chayanov and Polanyi continued to inform debates about rural change for the remainder of the twentieth century. As questions about the trajectory of economic development in the Global South came to preoccupy social science in the postwar decades, they informed debates about economic development, the global division of labor, and colonial rule. Harriet Friedmann and Philip McMichael have argued that rural change must be observed not as separate national trajectories but as a global process intertwined with the emergence of the modern state system.[40] They coined the term *global food regimes*, arguing that British and later American hegemony were codependent with the emergence of global economic exchange between regions reliant on industrial wage labor and regions focused on agricultural production. While Friedmann and McMichael see the political and economic spheres as mutually conditioning and reinforcing of each other during the one hundred fifty years of industrialization, they also argued that by the late twentieth century, the power of transnational capital had grown so much that it had put into question "the capacities of states and the state system for further regulation."[41] In other words, states had weakened, while capital has gained strength.

Polanyi and others tended to see technologies and factories as part of the exploitative nature of capital: factories were "satanic mills" in Polanyi's Great Transformation. North American scholarship on rural modernization during the Cold War drew on the Smithian positive valiance of machines and technological innovation as forces of progress and urbanization. Meanwhile, landmark economic and environmental histories that were not focused on deterministic theorizing highlighted both the constructive and destructive forces of technological change, and the role of both economic actors and the state. William Cronon's *Nature's Metropolis* documents how railroads and the industrialization of pig slaughter transformed the Great Plains. The invention of the refrigerated rail carriage in the 1890s gave rise to slaughterhouses in Chicago, spurred cattle herding in the American West, and greatly affected meat consumption in New York. While these changes were at the time conceived as progress and achievements of modernization, Cronon also shows how they contributed to the demise of bison that had sustained Native American life.[42] New technologies and innovations feature as key drivers of change in Cronon's masterful account: these are material forces and they are directed by railroad barons and other corporate actors, whose actions in turn are driven by the logic of private profits. At the same time, the federal government also played an indispensable role, by granting land for railroad construction, for example.

The State and Political Dynamics of Change

Marxist studies have long been criticized for their failure to acknowledge the role of a powerful, autonomous state. Stalin's collectivization via the authoritarian state that expropriated Russian peasants is the proverbial elephant in the room for Marxist modernization theory. Theodor Shanin and Henry Bernstein have pointed out that for decades Marxist scholars studiously avoided Stalin's role in Soviet rural change.[43] Many histories of Russian agriculture, including work by Zhores Medvedev, Karl-Eugen Wädekin, and Jenny Leigh Smith, afford a much greater role to the party, state ministries, and planning bureaucracy, and the account in the chapters that follow also draws attention to the role of the state in rural modernization. In agricultural histories of the US, congressional committees, the bureaucrats of the United States Department of Agriculture (USDA), and agronomists employed by public land grant universities play a very important role. Deborah Fitzgerald stresses the role of both the USDA and Wall Street in the industrialization of farming in the early twentieth century, drawing attention to a new cadre of college-educated agricultural experts, financiers, and business owners that spread across the country proselytizing for new, capital-intensive farming methods. Alan Olmstead and Paul Rhode trace the transformative effect of a particular type of technology—the improved seed and breed varieties that improve yields across much of the world, or what they call biological innovations—at the core of technological change of agricultural industrialization. But they push against a market-based logic of innovation that suggests that economic demand for this kind of technology spurred its rise. Instead, they highlight how government agencies, government-funded research, and extension programs supported and promoted biological innovation for decades in the nineteenth century.[44] In these economic histories, material technologies were indeed powerful engines of change, but agents of the state gave direction to the changes, and outcomes were neither predictable nor predetermined.

In political science studies of agriculture and rural modernization, governments and bureaucrats take center stage. Robert Bates's study argues that agricultural politics, rural economies, and agricultural production are shaped by politicians who seek to appease urban constituencies and rent-seeking bureaucrats.[45] Studies of food politics and agricultural policies in the US have focused on either political institutions or interest groups, emphasizing either the autonomy of the former or the lobbying power of the latter to shape outcomes.[46] The food movement and Michael Pollan's mantra of "voting with your fork" emphasize consumers as powerful political actors. Although the emphases on the dominant political actors vary, these contributions to the political economy of food and agriculture coalesce around a notion of food systems created and changed through the actions of particular groups of rational actors (governments, greedy corporations/capitalists, or citizens) who influence agricultural policies in accordance with their interests.[47] In studies of developing and developed countries alike, agency and politics are conceptualized in the familiar terms of political science: political elites make rules, and citizens and corporations either express their approval through the ballot box or lobbying, or conversely express their disapproval through protest or efforts that can threaten the political elites' hold on power. In Bates's theory, citizens are sensitive to price signals and, pursuant to their interests, engage in political activity as citizens—acquiescing, voting, or protesting. While these actions are no doubt important, they also have obscured the role of other actors and forms of agency.

Agro-technopolitics

Technologies, machines, and factories feature prominently in economic theories of agricultural change but are largely absent in the political science studies that focus on interests or institutions. Yet, at least since the Neolithic period, technologies have been a key determinant of agriculture and food production. Fernand Braudel thinks of technology as one of the main components of the material of everyday life, considering, for example, how particular types of ovens and alcohol stills structure life before the industrial revolution.[48] In studies of technology's link to politics, theorists often either identify stable ties between the two forces or concentrate on historical specificities in how political actors rely on technologies. At the height of the Cold War, Lewis Mumford posited two types of technologies, one of which was linked to democratic political projects and the other tied to authoritarianism.[49] Langdon Winner opposed this dichotomy and argued that we should "attend more closely to technical objects themselves," scrutinizing how technologies function and serve particular political ends.[50] Susan Buck-Morss's work accomplished this: scrambling the neat distinction between the presumed democratic West and the authoritarian East, she showed that the fetishization of the industrial machines that seemingly allow humans to master nature appeared in both the Soviet socialist and capitalist versions of modernity.[51]

In the debates about elements of the *agriculture—technology—politics* triad, what stands out is that within each, there are some strands that veer toward deterministic theorizing and demonstrating unchanging underlying logics of these relationships, while other strands are keen to grasp the complexity and uniqueness of new reconfigurations or hybrids. Technopolitics is a concept that lends itself to the latter kind of intellectual project. Gabrielle Hecht's formulation of technopolitics is a particularly promising starting point: technopolitics in her account refers to the "strategic practice of designing or using technology to constitute, embody or enact political goals."[52] Hecht defines technology as "artifacts, as well as nonphysical, systematic means of making or doing things," going beyond material technologies to include types of knowledge. A second important element of technopolitical regimes is that they link diverse sets of actors, practices, political programs, and ideologies; in Hecht's words, they "act together to govern technological development and pursue technopolitics."[53] Much like political regimes, technopolitical regimes are modes of governance that exercise power but are also subject to contestation and resistance and are affected by successes and failure. Hecht indeed stresses that technopolitical regimes are "neither static nor permanent."[54] Technopolitics grows out of thriving debates on the coproduction of science and society; in Sheila Jasanoff's broad terms, coproduction holds that "knowledge and its material embodiments are at once products, as well as constitutive of social life."[55] Technopolitics, then, helps to bridge the capital- and state-centric approaches outlined above, as it starts from the premise that the state-driven projects to provide abundant food for citizens (a social construct) and the capital-intensive industrial agriculture (the "knowledge and material embodiments") emerged together. The actors associated with the state and those associated with capital and technology in agriculture were all embroiled in these projects, shaped by their relationships and mutual dependency. States have not realized the goal of providing plenty without agro-scientific knowledge and material agro-technologies; for states to maintain authority, they have needed to coerce or coax the actors that controlled capital, land, and technology. These actors, in turn, existed, thrived, and faltered in the symbolic space defined by the state's political promise and its ability to support and promote particular technologies and actors as it sees fit.

Coproduction is a remarkable paradigm because it can address theoretically important questions that economic and statist theories of rural modernization have long debated, but it is a priori analytically agnostic about how these forces interact in particular historical contexts. In studies that have employed technopolitics, the state and political forces manifest themselves in complex and varied utopian projects: postwar French nationalism for Gabrielle Hecht, British imperialism for Timothy Mitchell, and Cold War geopolitics for Chris Sneddon and Coleen Fox as well as for Saara Matala.[56] In each of these accounts, the construction of ambitious, capital-intensive, technological utopias—nuclear technology in Hecht's case, large-scale irrigation in Mitchell's and Sneddon and Fox's, and ship-building in Matala's—hinged on the state's resources and on the political power of actors to marshal them. In each of these accounts, economic or corporate actors were indispensable but their ability to act and thrive was inextricably linked to the power and consent of the state. Government agents played capacious, active, and varied roles in each of these technopolitical projects, but they also could not execute their plans without capital-intensive tools and technologies, often wielded by private actors. Finally, and perhaps most importantly, given that coproduction is a historical and nondeterministic framework, it can grasp the limits of state capacity and control, and the unanticipated failures of technopolitical projects that ensue from these limits. The agents of the state did not always dominate and prevail. In the Russian and Soviet contexts, this is particularly important: paternalistic and controlling state projects were strong and grand in scale at some points in time and in certain places, but in other sites of these large and unruly territories, the power of the Soviet and Russian ultimately petered out or failed.

Technopolitics sheds light on the state's agency and its unintended effects as important triggers of change not only in Russia but also more generally in complex, global, and fragile agrifood systems. Sneddon and Fox point out that research on technopolitical projects is attuned to the "practical difficulties surrounding technocratic projects of natural resource governance." They draw on James Scott's observation that state-sponsored schemes were often "undone by a host of contingencies beyond the planners' grasp" as well as Timothy Mitchell's emphasis on the "continuous practical difficulties" that impeded the achievement of planning goals. Thus, they make the claim that a particularly important aspect of technopolitics is that it sheds light on "the recalcitrance of both nonhuman and human actors in willfully submitting to the novel configurations of technical expertise."[57] Given the speed of change and the complexity and uncertainty that are hallmarks of late-modern capitalism, a framework that can account for the unpredicted and unpredictable outcomes of policies and technological change, and of the failures and externalities of market economies, is a valuable tool. Technopolitics (and coproduction more generally) has been used to elucidate many aspects of technological change, but it is still largely and curiously absent from research on food and agriculture. Susanne

Freidberg's study on live-cycle analysis and footprinting, two technologies commonly used in contemporary food supply chains, is an exception.[58] A technopolitical lens, then, is this book's theoretical contribution to broader debates about contemporary food and agriculture: it allows us to address two important questions—*what are food systems, and how do they change?*—in a novel way.

Black Earth, White Bread argues that food systems are agro-technopolitical regimes that bring together disparate and evolving groups of actors who are connected through the challenge of food provisioning and deeply involved in forging change. Given how dramatically the technological edge in agriculture has shifted over the twenty-first century, and given how the types of technologies have proliferated across the world, we need conceptual tools that reveal the unforeseen consequences of practices across the different realms of food systems—governance, production, consumption, and nature. Technopolitics allows us to rethink the relevant actors, the connections between them, and how their agency matters in the politics of food and agriculture. For now, the remainder of this discussion introduces two specific conceptual levers that we gain by employing a *technopolitical lens*: the first is how this lens allows us to rethink actors and agency, and the second is how it opens up the possibility to think about connections between realms.

Technopolitics and Agency in Agrifood Systems

A technopolitical lens brings to the history of agriculture and food systems two types of actors that have played an important role in causing change, even though they are seldom considered in the debates outlined above: consumers and nature. In statist and political approaches, consumers are either irrelevant or act as citizens, voters, and activists via the channels of democratic interest representation. Seen through a technopolitical lens, consumers cause change through desires and expectations as well. We will see in the chapters that follow that Russian consumers were not satisfied with affordable staples alone and that tastes, culture, and longings have stubbornly evaded political elites' attempts to define them.[59] Russian citizens have always engaged in self-provisioning and have therefore been producers themselves; any policy that affected producers affected a large group of citizens and consumers.[60] A further vital actor involved in agriculture is the natural environment. The biophysical realities of agriculture are myriad, and there are countless examples of how nature defied human plans for agricultural progress: arid soil and recurring droughts are the challenges that come to mind first, but there are many others. Soviet environmental historians have stressed that utopian schemes to control natural forces have never quite succeeded; their analyses have contributed to an emerging consensus that we neglect the agency of "natural," material, nonhuman forces at our own peril.⁶¹ We will see in later chapters, for example, that the perishable nature of fruits challenged Soviet planners, defying the state's plans to transport and process fruit for public consumption.

Debates about the political economy of contemporary agriculture have recently started to address nature and the biophysical aspects of agriculture and food, inquiring how they can exercise a kind of agency. Mark Tilzey argues that the analytical separation between the human and the nonhuman realm— what John B. Fosters calls the metabolic rift—is unwarranted: "social systems are, to a significant degree, constituted by, and dependent on, biophysical affordances and constraints," but "these affordances and constraints are always mediated and in fact partly constructed, by human social relations and power structures that are specific in time and space."⁶² Examining such "social natural hybrids" is a crucial contribution toward a better understanding of contemporary food systems. While bringing biophysical reality to the politics of agriculture, Tilzey remains committed to the Marxist approach, arguing that the underlying or "real" logic of economic change is "the drive to maximize profit, to accumulate, to compete with other capitalists . . . , and to keep social and environmental costs to a minimum."⁶³ Here too, the history of Soviet agriculture suggests that this view might underestimate the role of the state and its agents, who were just as capable of separating the economic from the ecological as capitalist corporations. Given the environmental damage caused by Soviet planned agriculture, the metabolic rift was not an exclusively capitalist sin.

A technopolitical lens sheds light on the connections between human and nonhuman forces as contingent on historically specific political projects, without singling out particular actors and rationales—governments seeking to stay in power or greedy private producers forging a system that serves only themselves—as the ultimate drivers of historical change. Perhaps even more importantly, technopolitics allows us to think of agency not just as rational, deliberate action but also as accidental, unintended, contingent, and informal practices that elude planners and bureaucrats. Informal practices always played an important role in studies of the Soviet Union and the planned economy. A group of rural sociologists who work on post-socialist agriculture has recently argued that Eastern Europe "harbors 'implicit,' 'quiet' alternatives [to industrial agriculture] that do not result from intentional, individualised behaviours motivated by environmental and social responsibility."⁶⁴ Borrowing loosely from John Dewey's notion of publics, we could think of technopolitical regimes as forged by groups of political actors who come together through the consequences of their actions. Although Dewey arguably undertheorized the role of power, the Deweyan public helps us think of collectives that are constituted through practices and their consequences, and hence are continuously reconstituted by the effects of past practices.[65] Agency is not necessarily, or not primarily, interest-driven and defined by the boundaries of rational actors' interests but instead resides in a wide range of practices that make up agricultural food systems. Of course, rational, goal-directed agency by powerful actors has mattered crucially at times. When Brezhnev succeeded in expanding the Soviet fishing fleet in search of ways to boost the production of proteins, for example, more fish ended up on Soviet tables. When Vladimir Putin heavily subsidized high-efficiency poultry broilers, the amount of chicken in the Russian diet increased. Chicken, very hard to find in Soviet stores, became the most widely consumed meat in contemporary Russia, largely because it easily turned into a highly processed, low-cost meat item served in fast-food restaurants.

At the same time, there are just as many instances when agrifood systems changed through unintentional consequences of agency. Consider this sequence of change in the Russian food system: the increasing use of combine harvesters in the post–World War II decades contributed to the decline of land under cultivation with rye and barley, two traditional winter crops that were too tall for combine harvesters and had been harvested with either hand-held sickles or horse-driven mowers. Yet bread wheat is also less rich in protein, amino acids, and vitamins than rye; hence, as Russian black rye bread was replaced by white wheat bread, the nutritional quality of bread diminished.[66] There was very little group interest in the changing nutrient content of bread—it certainly was not the intended outcome of intentional, rational action. Once the problem was recognized, Soviet planners poured resources into developing new wheat varieties with higher protein content, yet rye never recovered its role as Russia's primary grain crop.

In sum, political interests and goals, the economic motives of producers, and consumer experiences all play important roles in changes within agrifood systems, but none of them alone have brought about the large-scale transformations of food systems over the last hundred years. No single protagonist of the four domains—the state, producers, consumers, and nature—can claim dominance or autonomy in relation to the others. They are interdependent and vulnerable, in the sense that the dynamics of change in one domain are always affected and altered by change in the others. This is not to say that in-depth studies of any of these domains and their specific dynamics are not also valuable. Yet, if we care to understand and possibly steer change in contemporary food systems, we need to depart from isolating one arena as the dominant site of change and singling out one set of actors. Food systems evolve through interlocking steps and recursive action in which change in one domain is triggered by dynamics that are either intrinsic or set about by changes in any of the other domains. Analyses and frameworks that track these connections between policies, production, diets, and environmental sustainability are important and needed.

Connections between Realms and Unintended Consequences of Agency

Change can result from unforeseen consequences, failures, and vulnerabilities—not just the ex-ante motivations of actors and the rational agency of particular groups. A focus on the unintended, accidental, and misunderstood consequences of rational agency allows us to see connections across realms of politics, production, consumption, and nature that are often considered separately. Three such connections are defining features of agro-technopolitical regimes; later chapters of the book document their appearance and role in Russian and Soviet history. First, the connections between politics and consumption are evident in the success of technopolitical regimes in making the consumption of certain foods possible, thus shaping diets. Russian and Soviet diets have changed with every success and failure of technopolitical regimes, although these changes have not affected all citizens uniformly. The workings of agro-technopolitical regimes have also created political feedback loops either challenging or affirming governing regimes. The failure of the Virgin Lands campaign in the early 1960s contributed to Nikita Khrushchev's fall from power. Conversely, Putin's success in bringing more meat to Russian tables earned him approval. Masha Gessen has argued that Russians were willing to "forfeit significant amounts of freedom if this coincided with gaining access to delicious meals in increasingly pleasing surroundings."[67] Second, the success and failure of technopolitical regimes connected domestic production with the global economy and with global food regimes in particular ways. Brezhnev-era policies led to dependence on American grains to feed expanding Soviet livestock herds. Vast quantities of US corn ended up in Russia, connecting the two countries in a highly political relationship that mattered for farmers and consumers in both countries. As the technologies of producing wheat improved over thirty years, Russian farms became leading global suppliers of wheat, creating a link between Russian farmers and consumers in the Middle East and Africa. Agricultural imports and exports are direct results of successes and failures of domestic agro-technopolitics. Third, the environmental impacts of industrial farming have created a whole set of connections between all four realms of the agrifood system that urgently demand attention, in Russia and elsewhere.

Failures of industrial agriculture could be seen as one particular subset of unforeseen consequences of technopolitics. Some of the vulnerabilities and failures of Soviet agricultural technologies are widely known. Historical accounts of Stalin's brutal collectivization emphasize its tremendous human and social costs. The environmental costs of other Soviet agricultural policies were staggering: the Aral Sea has virtually disappeared as a result of ambitious irrigation schemes to expand cotton production in Central Asia, to mention just the most obvious example. More generally, by most accounts Soviet agriculture was nearly always in a state of crisis, plagued by chronic shortages and inefficiencies. Long lines in front of stores were one of the main vulnerabilities of Soviet planned agriculture. However, there were also successes that are far less noted in Western histories.[68] Aggregate output increased in the postwar period, though at significant cost to the public budget. Ever-larger capital, land, and labor resources were allocated to collective farms, while consumer prices were capped. One of the poignant ironies of the history of the Russian food system is this: while the persistence of small-scale household production was long considered a sign of failure by Soviet authorities, today precisely this kind of simple, hearty, domestic food is most valued, even as subsistence farms are being increasingly displaced by successful agroholdings.[69]

The failures of industrial agriculture are usually interpreted in one of two ways. Proponents of markets as the ideal mechanism to allocate scarce resources think of problems associated with industrial agriculture as "market failures." Critics of market forces think of these failures as evidence of the inherent problems of capitalist modes of production that externalize costs. Both of these perspectives neglect the fact that similar (and different) failures also happened in the planned economy, and in different types of market economies. It was often industrialization and technological change in agriculture that shaped outcomes, pushed ahead either by the socialist state in the Soviet Union, or by other varieties of state-corporate, or state-farm alliances in the US, Western Europe, or post-Soviet Russia. In all these contexts, in the US, Russia, and many other parts of the world, industrial agriculture made many promises and kept some of them but also failed spectacularly. Many of the pathologies and problems of industrial food systems are by now well known.[70] Jenny Leigh Smith calls them the "gap between plans and reality."[71] These gaps in the American, Russian, and global technopolitical regimes are all worth considering; vulnerabilities are inevitable by-products of all socioeconomic systems, certainly of both markets and planned economies. In this technopolitical history of Russian industrial agriculture, vulnerabilities and hidden costs of agrifood systems will appear as triggers of change rather than as line items in a grand accounting of the merits and perils of the Soviet socialist or market economies.

The Post-Soviet Economic Transformation: Does Russia Have a "Normal" Capitalist Economy?

While this book traces evolving technopolitics, production, and consumption of Russian food over the twentieth century, the focus is in particular on the shift from the Soviet to the post-Soviet socioeconomic order. A central question that academic and public debates ask about the shift is this: what kind of capitalism has been constructed in Russia? Just as the book abstains from assessments of the planned and the market-driven food systems as superior or inferior in any absolute sense, it does not seek to evaluate the shift from a planned agrifood system to a capitalist one over the last twenty years, as successful, partially successful, or failed.[72] Rather, it documents the ways in which Soviet and post-Soviet agro-technopolitics have changed production systems, consumption, and the human-nature nexus and how these changes have introduced new vulnerabilities. When Boris Yeltsin and his group of liberal reformers initiated market reforms in the early 1990s, they meant to create a new stratum of private yeoman farmers. At the time, privatization and marketization were seen as removing the state from the realm of private commercial activity. It turned out that marketization in essence gave the state a new role rather than a diminished one.[73] Just like earlier episodes of top-down reforms, these changes had far-reaching social, economic, and political consequences—many of them unintended. Privatization was meant to distribute land broadly to rural residents, thus giving rise to a new class of independent family farmers to work Russia's fertile land. In reality, after the first two decades of market reforms, land assets ended up being more concentrated than before. New, corporate agroholdings are now the dominant actors in Russian agriculture, and they own and operate land assets that are many times larger than Soviet collective farms. They now produce more grain, sugar beets, and meat than ever on less arable land, employing intensive and global agro-technologies. Post-Soviet yield gains have meant that Soviet-period grain shortages have given way to abundant production.

All of this was encouraged and supported by the Putin regime, as his administration saw agroholdings as the actors that could deliver on the political promise of more domestic production and less dependency on imports. For some time at least, the success of import substitution and the domestication of food production have buttressed the approval and legitimacy of the Putin regime. At the same time, technological changes have introduced new vulnerabilities and costs of food production, which have not been systematically identified or tracked. While the Putin government is focused on geopolitical vulnerability that stems from import dependence, new economic and biological vulnerabilities have been created. Some rural residents are employed by booming agroholdings, but many others have struggled to get by in the last thirty years as agricultural employment has continued its steady decline. Despite intensive cultivation in some regions, millions of acres of farmland have been abandoned as rural residents have migrated to cities. Increasing dependence on genetically identical crops and livestock meanwhile increases the biological vulnerability of food production to pathogens, such as H5N8, which causes Avian flu, and the Asfivirus, which causes African Swine Fever. Far from a complete accounting of all the problems of the old and new systems, a technopolitical history observes and tracks how such vulnerabilities shift as technopolitical regimes and modes of domestication change.

The post-Soviet political and economic order defies simple characterizations by public and academic observers and continues to present a moving target. How the "big" institutional changes are reflected in the lived experiences of individuals is often especially hard to grasp. As Russia abandoned planning, privatized state-owned assets, and integrated into global markets, economic practices, everyday lives, and institutions adapted together in complicated ways. While Soviet agriculture was closely scrutinized during the Cold War, after the collapse of the Soviet Union, only a handful of observers kept track of changes in Russia's agrifood system.[74] This is a missed opportunity, precisely because food systems reveal connections between quotidian realities, on the one hand, and changing political, social, economic, and natural orders, on the other. Interlocking changes in governance, production, and consumption of food conjure an original picture of changing everyday lives at a time of global integration, addressing two broad questions about post-Soviet Russia. First, what is the nature of the economic system forged in post-Soviet Russia? And second, what does the rise of inequality look like from the vantage point of the country's changing food system?

Most observers of the Russian economy stress distance and differences between mature capitalist and post-Soviet economies, highlighting corruption, rent-seeking, and insecure property rights. The question of whether Russia now has a normal market economy echoes earlier historiographic debates about economic development in Eurasia and the West.[75] Throughout the twentieth century, scholarship has generally described food systems in Russia and the US as fundamentally different, mirroring views that market and planned economies have little in common. The US agrifood system is seen as the model of a liberal market that supplies consumers with a number of affordable choices. Studies of Soviet and post-Soviet economies, conversely, tend to focus on shortages and scarcity in the Soviet period. Accounts of the 1990s have stressed rural poverty and the failure of market reforms.[76] Yet we will see in the chapters that follow that there were many remarkable similarities as well as many influential interactions between the three economic systems that appear in this book: the Soviet planned economy, post-Soviet statist capitalism, and liberal market economies of the West. James Scott highlights the "belief in huge, mechanized, industrial farms" as a key point of convergence between American and Soviet high modernism.[77] Despite the differences in the way food was produced in the US and the Soviet Union throughout the twentieth century, both countries enthusiastically endorsed industrial agriculture. The political goals for agriculture were remarkably similar in both countries, as they turned farms into factories in order to bring more animal proteins to their nations' tables at lower cost. The rival states each played an outsized role in shaping modes of production and consumption. In both countries, then, agricultural production became increasingly divided between very large and very small units of production. The technopolitical regimes consistently helped large actors at the expense of medium and small producers. In Russia, the "middle" was eliminated swiftly and brutally during collectivization and has not reemerged. In the US, agriculture in the middle is disappearing more gradually.[78] While the Soviet and post-Soviet economies take center stage in this book, the agricultural order in the US played an integral role throughout the twentieth century—as exporters of grain, capital, and knowledge.[79] The chapters that follow thus provide a window on the much larger story of how Russian and Western technopolitical regimes were interconnected and mutually entangled.

Judgment calls about what qualifies as the success or failure of the Russian and Soviet state's efforts to modernize the countryside are the conjoined twin of East-West comparisons. From Stolypin to Putin, Russian rural reforms were judged for their efforts at catching up with the "West" (the US or Western Europe), measured along indices imported from abroad. The capitalist system produced abundance and virtually unlimited choices among consumer goods, while the Soviet system undoubtedly suffered from shortages. At the same time, and ironically, a handful of the failures of the Soviet systems were in the end advantages rather than shortcomings. The simplicity and scarcity of processed food, for example, along with a lower prevalence of purebred livestock herds, may have been assets of the Soviet food system rather than shortcomings. Today, most Russian supermarkets look nearly identical to those in Western capitalist economies. Shelves are stacked high with brightly packed and highly processed food items. These are products of technologies, formulas, and additives developed in the West. Agricultural and food processing developed in Western advanced industrial economies, sectors that have been highly competitive for decades, help Russian agrifood companies minimize costs. Other aspects of the contemporary Russian food system also seem to be imported from the US: in the realm of consumption, for example, Melissa Caldwell has shown how Russians "incorporated McDonald's into their daily lives," making it part of "family celebrations, cuisine and discourses about what it means to be Russian today."[80] Obesity has doubled in Russia over the past fifteen years, mimicking a trend that became apparent in the US a few decades earlier.[81] As introduced above, the chapters that follow track these trends, not as a failure of the Soviet system and victory of markets and the American model but as features of particular, post-Soviet technopolitical systems. In the agro-technopolitical regime of the Putin-era, various imported technologies—from combines to plant genetics to marketing concepts—play an exceedingly important role. Yet, even as these technologies replicate features of the American and West European agriculture and food systems, they are the consequences of Russian political dynamics, domesticated by Russian actors, and grown on Russian soil. Post-Soviet french fries and Russian obesity are at once global and idiosyncratically Russian, effectively blurring the boundaries between foreign and native.

Post-Soviet Inequality

One of the most striking but least understood aspects of the post-Soviet transition is the staggering rise of inequality.[82] We could think of unequal access—to food, to land, and to income—as a vulnerability of particular agro-technopolitical regimes. Income inequality, relatively low in the Soviet Union, has nearly doubled since 1991 and now approximates that of the US.[83] Despite this rapid change, Filip Novokmet, Thomas Piketty, and Gabriel Zucman find that the "distribution of income and wealth of the dramatic transformations that occurred [in Russia] since 1989–1990 are not very well documented and understood."[84] Post-Soviet inequality is made up of a number of factors; income is only the most commonly tracked indicator. Similarly, aggregate data on Soviet-era shortages and Russia's new abundance tell us little about the everyday lived experience of poverty and wealth. A history of how unequal access to food changed between the Soviet and post-Soviet technopolitical regimes throws new light on the nature of contemporary inequalities. Food-related inequality mirrors trends elsewhere but in the end is shaped by local history, culture, and politics. A single-serve container of flavored yogurt, a new product of Russia's post-Soviet food system, illustrates this point. Soviet food provisioning made an assortment of soured milk products readily available (e.g., *tvorog*, a type of curd cheese; kefir; sour cream, and a fermented milk product known as *ryazhenka*), but these were all unsweetened and usually available in larger containers or in bulk. They could be store-bought or homemade by a family member or acquaintance. The new kind of flavored and single-serve yogurt changed the texture and taste of everyday life in Russia, and if we are to believe the marketing campaigns of agroholdings, they came to represent the post-Soviet "good life" (or perhaps just the new "normal" life). Either way, not all Russian citizens and consumers have access to this kind or normalcy or quality of life. Market reforms of the 1990s created new forms of stratification, but diets remain a marker of status and wealth. As income disparities now shape access to the products of the post-Soviet technopolitical regime as never before, access to good and healthful food is less equally distributed, and for some, far less attainable, than it once was.

The chapters that follow reveal an uneven topology of abundance and scarcity in the Soviet and post-Soviet period, with evidence from meals and dinner tables. What was and is abundant, and what is scarce for whom? What forms do proteins and delicious sweetness take? Who eats freshly made tvorog, covered in raw and bitter-sweet honey, and who eats strawberry-flavored Dannon yogurt by the single-serve container? How do social values shape consumption? Answers to these questions draw up changing maps of inequality, distribution, and unequal byt in the relatively equal (Soviet) society and the newly stratified (post-Soviet) society. They also connect these maps with larger patterns of economic change and global integration in the Soviet and post-Soviet periods. Soviet and post-Soviet food systems each have characteristic features of unequal distribution, manifested in unequal access to nutritious meals versus low-quality, cheap food. Soviet society was comparatively equal, but the Soviet agro-technopolitical regime provided for a relatively limited range of foods. In the early decades, many went hungry. At times of war and crisis, and again by the late 1980s, equality existed as the absence of choices. "Kasha is really all there was," remembers a Berliner who visited Moscow in the eighties. Though the Soviet planned economy meant to erase class distinctions, political elites, the nomenklatura, always had far better access to the well-stocked stores and privileged foods. Various prized delicacies, including products of Western food systems, were available for a select few, mediated through workplace hierarchies, informal networks, and special stores. Unequal access to valued and even basic food items mapped closely to political hierarchies that privileged certain geographic sites and professions.[85]

Availability and access to various types of foods—those that secured survival and others that were considered delicious, healthy, and part of a good life—shifted as Yeltsin introduced markets and integrated Russia into the global economy. New forms of stratification were created, and elites identified new products as the markers of social class. The new privileged class was now the oligarchy, often the sons of the Soviet urban intelligentsia. In the early post-Soviet period, they had access to information, the corridors of power, and foreign-currency bank accounts, which they mobilized to accumulate wealth.[86] As members of a relatively privileged group that was already established in the late Soviet period, successful oligarchs were crafty, entrepreneurial, lucky, and not overly principled. This group acquired the most valuable assets of the post-Soviet economy and has had virtually unlimited access to prized foods at a time when many more Russian citizens became virtually impoverished. With unpaid salaries and skyrocketing inflation, many families and individuals experienced, often for the first time, anguish and anxiety about how to pay for basic food items. The most unfortunate were the families least able to navigate the requirements of the new capitalist era. Caroline Humphrey named this group "the dispossessed"—a designation that captures two aspects of their new, post-Soviet existence. The dispossessed were Russians who were deprived of property in the cutthroat struggles for ownership in the post-Soviet period. They were also no longer part of, or "possessed by," the collective domains that conferred status and basic means in the Soviet period.[87] The dispossessed included pensioners without family members caring for them, migrant workers and refugees from former Soviet countries, war veterans with disabilities, the homeless, those who were unemployed or underemployed, and many single-parent families. We will see that urban and rural dispossession and access to food looked different throughout the twentieth century. In post-Soviet Russia, rural villages have been undersupplied, with aging populations often left to fend for themselves. In cities, a retired teacher with a small pension, for example, could not easily afford flavored single-serve yogurt as a daily breakfast. Yet, if social networks of production and exchange still functioned in the old way in her neighborhood, she may receive homemade tvorog thanks to ties to another economy of highly prized goods.

Synopsis

Each of the chapters of *Black Earth, White Bread* focuses on a different group of actors: governments, bureaucrats and political leaders (chapter 1), producers (chapter 2), and consumers (chapter 3). The final substantive chapter gives voice to nature via two model organisms, wheat and pigs (chapter 4). These chapters are internally coherent histories of consumption, production, governance, and environmental change. They are linked through the conceptual framework of technopolitics as well as through multiple points of empirical connections that speak to the book's broader themes. Readers are encouraged to read the chapters in whatever order they prefer. The order in which the chapters are read matters less than in a chronological history and less than in a typical social science study that proposes a strong causal argument.

Chapter 1 details the agricultural modernization projects that Soviet and post-Soviet leaders pursued. Providing "plenty" was a central political goal of Soviet and post-Soviet regimes. These goals were to be reached through a series of ambitious modernization projects that dramatically changed the social organization and technologies of production not once, but several times over the last hundred years. The Bolshevik government had what it called a "grain problem"—Russian peasants, who made up the largest group of citizens of the overwhelmingly rural country, were reluctant to grow and hand over grain to state-procurement agents. The market mechanisms introduced during the New Economic Policy (NEP) in the 1920s failed to solve the grain problem. Stalin's collectivization increased and modernized production, but at a staggering human cost. Khrushchev's Virgin Lands campaign greatly expanded acreage, but with disastrous environmental consequences. Yeltsin decollectivized and privatized land but did little to address the devastating output collapse during the early years of market liberalization. Under Putin, oligarchic agrifood conglomerates gained ownership of vast tracts of Russia's most fertile farmland—with consequences that are only gradually becoming apparent. Each of these revolutions was motivated by the goal of introducing new modes of production and cutting-edge technologies to wrest more from Russia's abundant land. For both Soviet and post-Soviet governments, yields and production volumes were never ends in themselves; they were meant to demonstrate the viability or superiority of the Soviet and Russian political and economic order to their citizens and the world. The chapter shows that ideological agendas and political projects that legitimize governance, rule, and control of the population were reflected in food and agriculture.

Chapter 2 explores production and technologies. Technologies of crop production and livestock rearing are key determinants of what, where, and how much is produced. The Soviet approach to agriculture was a project of technological and scientific modernization, not unlike that of capitalist countries. Soviet and post-Soviet agro-technological regimes succeeded and failed in myriad remarkable ways, and this chapter argues that these successes and failures of agricultural technologies are fundamentally important for understanding Russian foodways. They resulted in particular diets and connected Russia with the rest of the world. Their successes and failures had repercussions for the legitimacy of successive governments. The chapter traces the shifts in technologies that underpin the Russian food system, from Stalin's mechanization to Putin's efforts to foster biotechnology. Each technological shift meant that a particular group of actors, seen as the most promising agents of change, was supported and allowed to thrive, while others were sidelined as either marginal or harmful to the realization of political goals.

Chapter 3 tracks diets. Daily meals are deeply personal; they are a vital part of everyday life. We eat what tastes good to us, but also what is available, what we can afford, and what we think we should eat, given social norms about healthful and appropriate meals. Healthfulness and quality, in turn, are complex and reflexive social and cultural facts, reflecting personal choices and cultural appeal. The chapter traces how the availability, access, and appeal of different types of products changed over the decades. The Soviet food system overall gave individuals relatively few choices, and scarcity shaped consumption for most. However, agency didn't disappear altogether, and consumers' desires still played an important part in determining what citizens ate. Post-Soviet markets now produce many more choices; most retail stores are fully stocked with a variety of food items. But choice is still not a straightforward determinant of consumption. It is now curtailed by cost because many items are too expensive for those at the margins of the post-Soviet economic order. Consumption is also shaped by changing food culture, which in turn is affected by patriotic sentiments stoked in other spheres of life. Russian consumers now sometimes long for types of products that were available in the past but are no longer among the range of choices. The romanticization of the past and nostalgia for Soviet-period products, like fizzy lemonade or Soviet-era ice cream, today shape consumption patterns in important ways, even as the Russian system is increasingly globalized. In evolving food consumption, we see how availability, access, and appeal together shape byt.

No account of change in food systems can omit food as a range of biophysical products, or products of nature. This aspect of food systems is the focus of chapter 4. In the Soviet period, nature—soil conditions and precipitation patterns in particular—was most often thought of as limiting output. Planners and politicians thought of technologies and science as weapons in the fight against nature. In the post-Soviet period, new technologies were imported and harnessed in new ways to study and alter nature. Plant and livestock breeding strategies are the focus of the chapter, which centers on wheat and pigs as two model organisms. Breeding strategies and genetic technologies directly affect biodiversity, targeting and promoting different traits in crops and animals. The chapter tracks changes in how geneticists and breeders valued economically desirable traits in plants and livestock vis-à-vis traits that relate to local adaptation. We do not see uniform change: pork and wheat breeding changed in different ways between the Soviet and post-Soviet periods, with important implications for biodiversity in both cases. The chapter shows how plant and livestock breeding transforms nature—animals and seeds, in this case—but also reveals changing covulnerabilities of humans and nature. The conclusion summarizes some of the themes that run through the account—with special attention to vulnerabilities, Westernization, and inequality—in light of the evidence presented in earlier chapters.

Perhaps because of the rural sector's declining importance as a source of employment, agriculture has received attention only at the margins of many of the social science disciplines—in rural sociology or agricultural economics, for example. Only a small handful of political science studies have been interested in the political economy of agriculture and food systems.[88] Unlike finance, with its recurring and urgent crises, or manufacturing, where globalization and vertical disintegration have undone whole towns, change in agriculture has been more dispersed, less recent, and less noticed. Political economy has also largely remained loyal to frameworks that consider governments, corporations, or citizens as the protagonists of politics.[89] Technopolitics not only reveals the agency of consumers and of biophysical realities in agrifood systems; it also shows how unintended and contingent consequences of policies play an exceedingly important role in how food systems change.

Black Earth, White Bread claims that agro-technopolitical histories shed new light on late-modern capitalism, in Russia and elsewhere, and that they present political science with compelling opportunities. Food systems can be a lens to track interactions between domains of life that are too often seen as discrete and disconnected, such as rural production and urban consumption. They can also tell us about interactions between human realms and the nonhuman realms of crops, livestock, climate, and soil conditions. This kind of research brings into focus two actors—consumers and nature—that are often neglected in political science. Environmental history, geography, and anthropology have led the way in theorizing consumers and nature as actors in their own right, and there is no reason why political science cannot follow. By conceptualizing food and agricultural systems as technopolitical regimes, this book opens the door to a novel understanding of political, economic, and social change, in the hope that future research will explore similar questions in new sites.

I

Governance; or, How to Solve the Grain Problem

The bread question is the most difficult problem of the revolution.... The great problem facing us is how to provide towns with the necessaries of life. In our country the workers are hungry because the exchange of goods between town and country is paralyzed.
—Nikolai Bukharin, 1925

You all know that recently the government has returned regularly, I want to emphasize that—regularly, to the problems of agriculture.... And we both know that the main problem faced by agriculture is, of course, most of all the lack of technology.
—Vladimir Putin, 2000

Solving the Grain Problem

Who has shaped Russian agriculture over the course of the twentieth century, and how? Russia's political landscape changed radically over the last hundred years, not once, but several times, and so did the politics of agriculture. The Bolshevik government was a group of urban revolutionaries with a vision to rapidly modernize a predominantly rural empire. In the Marxist-Leninist rendition of economic change, rural modernization was a necessary prerequisite for the construction of socialism, and a large share of Russia's peasantry had to abandon the land and join the industrial workforce. Yet even the most ardent proponents of this view soon realized that Russians peasants were not likely to spontaneously upend their lives and work, and that revolutionizing the countryside was a thorny problem rather than a forgone conclusion. Nikolai Bukharin argued that the solution to rural development was an improvement of urban-rural relations and a gradual approach to the conversion of the peasantry. Joseph Stalin's solution, notoriously, was the opposite—a violent war on peasants who refused to modernize. This was clearly a political project as it entailed the eradication of *kulaks*, well-off peasants and class enemies of workers. Yet modernization was also conceived as a technological revolution that would transform backward ways of growing crops and raising livestock. Decades later,

Nikita Khrushchev, followed by Leonid Brezhnev and later Vladimir Putin, also pursued specific political goals that they tried to solve by bringing new technologies to the countryside, though, of course, the technological edge moved light-years in the intervening decades. What the tractor was for Stalin, biotech is for Putin.

In each period, the political goals for agriculture and the socio-technical utopias that guided them were central to the way in which rural production changed. Initially, the primary aim of Bolshevik leaders was to extract grain from the countryside to feed urban workers and the army. Over the decades after World War II, Soviet planners and party elites tried to put meat on the table, and occasional sweet treats too. Putin wanted to grow more commodity crops and livestock to enrich domestic diets. He also wanted Russia to once again serve as the world's breadbasket, resuming grain exports that had dwindled a hundred years prior. While these were goals for agricultural production, increasing yields and overall volumes of grains and meat were never ends in themselves for the Soviet and post-Soviet governments. Plentiful harvests and satisfying meals were the material down payments that the paternalistic state defined as fundamental elements of the good life. They were meant to legitimize its control of populations and demonstrate the competence of Soviet socialism and Putin's economic nationalism to Russia's citizens and the world.

The campaigns, plans, and policies devised by the state to realize political goals during the Soviet and post-Soviet periods were important drivers of change in the rural economy. Despite significant political change over the decades of Soviet and post-Soviet rule, governments faced a remarkably similar challenge: how to realize these goals. This challenge was a version of what was known as the "grain problem" in the early years of the revolution, closely linked to the "peasant problem" that Marxist theorists had been discussing for quite some time.[1] In Russia, industrialization required that a large group of peasants become factory workers and be provided with plentiful diets. It would also be helped by imported machinery, paid for with the proceeds and the hard currency earned by exporting grain. This plan hinged on agriculture becoming more efficient and more productive in short order, freeing up labor and increasing production with fewer bodies working the fields. Urban workers would flourish if they could count on nutritious, varied, and low-cost food produced by efficient farms and farm machines. How to usher along rural modernization, increasing production and converting peasants to this cause, was widely seen as the most fundamental problem that the young Bolshevik regime had to overcome. Solving it became essential for the whole enterprise of socialist construction; it was "the problem of the revolution." In James Heinzen's assessment, it was also "the most complicated, enormous and disorganized affair" that the revolutionary government in Moscow faced.[2]

The Russian peasantry was not easily enlisted for the cause of modernization, enlightenment, and political mobilization, and getting peasants to eagerly embrace the workers' state as an ally against feudal landlords was a hard sell.[3] Confronted with Bolshevik officials who forcibly and brutally requisitioned grain during the Civil War and then returned as missionaries of modernization in the 1920s, peasants resisted conversion attempts and tried to hold on to hard-won rural autonomy and assets. These officials, in turn, realized that convincing peasants to grow large amounts of cereals, industrial crops, and livestock feed, rather than just producing enough for their own subsistence, was going to be no small feat. Throughout the early Soviet decades, the Bolshevik government largely failed to convince peasants; they did not "spontaneously" consolidate farms and hand over ever-larger quantities of grain to state procurement agents. State officials blamed the peasantry for their political recalcitrance, their unwillingness to be converted to the benefits of modern agronomy, and for their perceived backwardness in many other matters.[4]

The "grain problem" was never quite solved during the eight decades of the Soviet modernization experiment. The promise of plenty remained a promise never quite fulfilled. While radical change was brought to the Russian countryside and Soviet society urbanized, successive Russian political elites and bureaucrats were faced with a version of this same problem. They needed to find a new answer to a very basic question: how could rural production be governed in such a way that agricultural output would align with political goals?

State Campaigns and Failures

This chapter is about the political solutions sought by successive Soviet and post-Soviet regimes to the grain problem. It is also about resistance to these solutions and the problems encountered by state campaigns. Many of these difficulties will be described in more detail in later chapters. In other words, the narrative here outlines the "politics" part of the technopolitics of Russian agriculture. The state is an important actor, but not the only one. Though powerful and authoritarian at times, the state ultimately proved to have limited control that at times either petered out or ran into various obstacles in its attempt to forge change. We will see how successive policy shifts and new campaigns and schemes were always adopted in response to these perceived successes and failures of previous reforms. Sometimes new policies brought only gradual changes; sometimes they radically departed from their predecessors. There were two formidable and persistent adversaries that repeatedly foiled attempts by Soviet and Russian governments to solve the grain problem. One was nature, or, more precisely, a combination of stingy and thin topsoils, not enough precipitation, the lack of what was considered optimal livestock feed, and other problems related to the biophysical nature of farming. Though Soviet industrial farming succeeded in growing more grain and speeding up technological progress, nature was never fully conquered in the ways that agronomists and Soviet missionaries hoped for. A bad harvest, soil erosion, or a drought, to name just a few calamities, often devastated the best-laid plans. The second adversary, nearly as fickle, was society. Social actors at times followed state directives, either because they had no choice or out of shared convictions. But at other times, social actors eluded the paternalistic state's control, defying directives and prescriptions. Social resistance played out in the realms of both production and consumption. Soviet women continued to garden and grow their own food, preparing and processing it at home. And consumer tastes evolved faster than the procurement system could deliver. Resistance by nature and society will take center stage in later chapters, where we will see how actors in other realms—producers, consumers, and nature—responded to the state policies outlined here, at times forcing the state to change course.

Well aware of this resistance, successive Russian governments came up with plans to either coerce or co-opt nature and social actors. Starting in late 1929, Joseph Stalin forced peasants to join collective farms, after several years of frustrated attempts to convince them to join the Bolshevik cause voluntarily. Resistance to collectivization was met with terror in a campaign that cost the lives of millions of peasants. The Stalinist state did gain control of grain production and harvests, and procurement grew more abundant over the course of the thirties.[5] Yet it largely failed to win peasants over to the communist cause, and nature was only somewhat more amendable to being transformed. Production plummeted during World War II and the immediate postwar years. By the end of the Stalin era, too little grain was still being produced, even as an expansive and expensive Exhibition of Agricultural Achievements in Moscow proclaimed otherwise.[6] Coercive measures were loosened under Nikita Khrushchev's leadership (1953–64) as the new general secretary, in Aaron Hale-Dorrell's words, finally "began to react to conditions down on the farm."[7] As part of a broader shift to realize a new communist utopia where people would live well and consume more, Khrushchev devised new and ambitious campaigns to boost production by cultivating large areas of Siberia and Central Asia and by promoting corn—a miraculous crop in terms of its capacity to generate calories.[8] Yet Khrushchev also ran into problems, both with his attempt to overcome climatic constraints and with efforts to satisfy the growing appetites of urban consumers.

Leonid Brezhnev's reforms from 1964 to 1982 were an effort to provide plenty by pushing back against the apparent limits on agricultural yields imposed by soil conditions and precipitation. While Khrushchev had focused on quantity—more hectares sown, more tons harvested—Brezhnev wanted to increase output by wresting more crops from every hectare.[9] Intensive farming required more inputs, however. Brezhnev-era policies thus doubled down on programs to strengthen agrochemicals, machinery and equipment repair services, large-scale irrigation projects, and processing facilities. New investments in agricultural research were made to reach ambitious output targets. The enormous state resources being poured into agriculture during the Brezhnev era were made possible by export earnings from the sale of hydrocarbons at a time of booming global oil markets. By the end of the Soviet experiment, state investments in agriculture had become a vast and ever-larger share of state spending—a black hole, as many called it. Some of these resources were not well spent, or even failed to reach their intended destination, and the party leadership became increasingly concerned about waste.

In a break with sixty years of top-down reforms, Mikhail Gorbachev tried to decentralize decision-making to improve how these massive flows of valuable resources were used in the years between 1985 and 1991.[10] Planners finally explicitly recognized that agriculture is utterly dependent on local conditions and that the overly centralized decision-making, characteristic of the Soviet planned economy, was perhaps detrimental to increasing yields. Gorbachev thus embarked on reforms that were meant to place more responsibility and decision-making authority in the hands of farmers than they had had since the 1920s. As in other spheres of economic reforms, these efforts were overtaken by political events that ushered in the collapse of the Soviet Union in August 1991. Boris Yeltsin and his team of young reformers took up Gorbachev's initiative in the radically transformed economic context of the 1990s and privatized land ownership. Russian peasants were finally to receive the autonomy that Pyotr Stolypin, late imperial Russia's most well-known modernizer, had promised before the revolution. Yet with few resources, aging machinery, and a national economy in free fall and faced with a flood of cheap imports, Yeltsin's plan to create a class of Russian free yeoman farms was doomed.

Vladimir Putin, who was elected president of Russia in 2000, jettisoned the idea of small, private farming and has relied exclusively on private agribusinesses—the agroholdings—as agents of change. What came to be known as Putin's food sovereignty agenda was dominated by a focus on reducing dependence on foreign food imports and boosting domestic production. Under Putin, agricultural reforms returned to the Soviet-era preference for large-scale production. Policies now encouraged the creation of large, capital-intensive, vertically integrated industrial facilities to grow more food, though of course this time relying on private, profit-driven actors. In the contemporary Russian political context, the terms food security and food sovereignty diverge significantly from how they are used by global food activist groups, such as La Via Campesina. In the Russian context, food sovereignty is defined in statist and paternalistic terms and refers to the security of the national economy as a whole rather than nutritional security at the level of individual citizens and the rights of small-scale farmers to make sovereign decisions about their livelihoods. Putin was committed neither to saving state farms (as Gorbachev had been) nor to creating private yeoman farmers (as Yeltsin had been). What mattered now was the ability of domestic producers to harvest more, thus helping wean Russian processors and consumers from foreign imports. Private agroholdings were the only actors that could make significant capital investments to realize the productivity and production increases that the food sovereignty agenda envisaged. (A number of large publicly owned companies, such as Rosselkhoz, Rosleasing, and the United Grain Company, also played an important role, yet even these companies have private minority shareholders.) Small farmers, including subsistence and household producers, were either largely ignored or pushed out as obstacles in the way of the food sovereignty goals.[11] After nearly two decades, the food sovereignty agenda has profoundly reshaped domestic food systems: agroholdings have thrived with government support, while small-scale household producers have been increasingly unable to compete.

Policies on Price, Land Use, and Trade

A defining feature of agro-technopolitics, in Russia as elsewhere, is the flow of state-controlled resources to particular, favored rural actors and technologies. Russian and Soviet officials have used three broad types of policy tools to channel public resources in their efforts to shape agricultural production, many of them mirroring the policies and practices that governments across the world have used. The first type are policies that affect the *rewards and costs of farming*. These include Soviet policies that set the procurement price for a bushel of wheat produced on a state farm and the post-Soviet subsidies to private farmers. Both sets of policies had a direct effect on the costs and benefits of farming. The second policy area comprises campaigns and reforms that affect *land use*; these include measures to encourage intensive versus extensive land-use patterns, or cultivation versus fallowing. The third set of policies, focusing on external trade, consists of measures that either encourage or hamper the *flow of resources and ideas* between the international arena and Russian rural producers.

Solutions have evolved and agricultural reforms have looked very different over the years as policies in these three areas have oscillated along various axes:

Should more or fewer rewards be extended to farmers? Should policies aim at expanding cultivation or facilitating intensification? Should international exchange be more open, or should it be subject to more restrictions? Regardless of shifting policy positions, governments relied on a chosen set of actors, favoring their practices and technologies. The privileged actors were thought to be the most economically efficient and politically appropriate agents of change. Collective farms and tractors were Stalin's chosen social and material technologies, and oligarchic agroholdings and high-yield seeds are Putin's. Technopolitical regimes feature precisely these kinds of arrangements: they are dominated by the technologies and skills favored and supported by political elites, planners, and policy makers in pursuit of a set of political goals. At each point, other actors were considered economically backward or politically suspect and possible threats to the state's paternalistic project. The chosen actors sometimes thrived and delivered, but often they failed to realize the elusive goals of Soviet and Russian agrarian high modernism. These successes and failures drove change in technopolitical regimes in agriculture. The desired outcomes were highly contingent and ultimately unpredictable, depending on how policies interacted with local actors, the biophysical realities of farming, and other aspects of the context in which grand schemes were actually implemented. In general terms, technopolitical regimes in agriculture succeed if the material technologies, nature, and social actors perform as expected and as designed. They fail when the social organization and material technologies are too costly to sustain in the long run, or if they are too vulnerable to environmental changes and social pressures. When they fail, they sometimes fail spectacularly, as was true of Khrushchev's Virgin Lands campaign or Yeltsin's privatization. They also sometimes just flounder and muddle through until some new technology or social or material fix promises new success. But even the failed campaigns and policies, for all their problems, profoundly transformed Russia's countryside.[12]

Success is always a moving target, and there are often no definitive matrixes or measures that determine whether a particular technopolitical regime in agriculture failed or succeeded. Whether or not the Soviet Union's planned economy realized the promise of plenty was in fact one of the big questions of the twentieth century that both Russian and American observers pored over and debated.[13] On the one hand, agricultural output grew with every five-year plan. Bread became more abundant, cheaper, and tastier, and Soviet citizens ate more of it than the subjects of imperial Russia. Urban consumers generally had access to low-cost food: in François-Xavier Nérard's assessment, "extreme scarcity gave way to relative abundance."[14] Soviet planners also realized that, in the long run, bread alone was not enough to fulfill the promise of plenty.

What was plenty, precisely? Although not subject to electoral constraints, the Soviet state was not autonomous and paid attention to evolving tastes and ideas about the good life. Successive governments made concerted efforts to address shortages and satisfy consumers. The state mastered the provision of adequate calories, but flavors and nuance often came from home-produced items, such as pickled vegetables and gathered mushrooms and berries. The meals on Russian tables, in other words, continuously evolved as a result of successive reforms and campaigns as well as their successes and failures and the social and political responses.

The emphasis in this chapter is on the Russian government's efforts in wresting more from soils that are thin in some places and fertile in others.[15] Change in the Russian food system was also contingent on the international context of these efforts. Agricultural markets have long been global, though to different degrees over the years, and global overproduction, booms, and busts mattered for Soviet agriculture even during the more autarkic years. The Russian state's policies were always reflections of ideas and resources available in the international realm. The availability and types of expertise, technologies, and money—and the international supply and demand of food commodities—each influenced the options that Soviet and post-Soviet leaders had at their disposal. Since the thirties, and even during the height of the Cold War, Soviet party officials and agronomists have traveled to the US and Western Europe, and conversely Westerners visited the Soviet Union and offered assessments and advice. Various types of technologies were imported, either as blueprints or as machines. In the postwar period, global food commodity markets were flush with grain exported by the surplus economies of North America (and by the mid-eighties, the same was true for chicken meat), tempting Brezhnev and Gorbachev to rely on these resources to solve the problem of shortages. Finally, since the early years of the 2000s, unprecedented financial flows and foreign technologies have come within reach and have been embraced as the key pillar of the reform programs of the Putin years. None of these international resources determined policies, but their changing availability nevertheless was central in shaping the tools and resources that Russian governments had at their disposal. Technopolitical regimes in agriculture shifted in response to homegrown successes and failures as well as rapidly evolving international agricultural technologies.

Socialist Planning and the Provisioning of Soviet Citizens

Peter Holquist writes that during World War I, "agriculture was central to the Russian economy (it was by far the largest sector), to Russian society (more subjects were engaged in agriculture than in any other pursuit), and to Russian political life (the peasant and land questions were burning issues of the day)."[16] When the imperial government ran out of grain to feed troops and urban residents in 1917, the ensuing unrest unsettled the established order, and the October Revolution overturned it for good a few short months later.[17] Peace, land, and bread were core demands of the Russian poor, many of whom were hungry. The Bolshevik government inherited the problem of catastrophic food shortages from imperial authorities. In the years and decades that followed, agriculture played a critical, and in many ways a first-order role in the ambitious social and economic transformation of the Bolshevik government: as a matter of immediate survival, agriculture had to provide food for the Soviet army, and in the medium-to-long term, agriculture had to be modernized to free up labor for factories. Grain exports would provide capital for technology imports, drivers of Russian industrialization since the nineteenth century.[18] After the revolution, the People's Commissariat of Agriculture (the Narkomzem) was keenly aware that agricultural production and modernization were vital for the new Soviet economy. The commissariat's agronomists and agricultural geneticists sought to employ scientific practices and new technology to make these changes happen. They wanted to "bring light" to the village—by applying modern science and agronomy, changing inherited practices, and putting an end to ancient inefficiencies and cultural backwardness.[19]

They soon realized that nothing about rural modernization and peasant mobilization was spontaneous and inevitable, and that the "peaceful partnership between city and countryside" was largely wishful thinking.[20] Peasants in turn mistrusted and resisted the communist party's efforts. Resistance was at least in part a result of the party's policy, which in essence "gave nothing and demanded everything from the peasants," as Bukharin already observed in 1925.[21] The political questions of the day revolved around how peasants were to be enlisted: should they be coerced or rewarded for the essential work of growing grain? Soviet-era rural reforms materialized as a series of campaigns imposed from above, with directives implemented via the channels of the party and the planning bureaucracy. If plans and campaigns failed to reach their stated objective, Soviet observers tended to blame the peasants' "backward" mentalities and practices and "flawed" political affiliations. In the West, observers generally blamed the failures on the socialist structure of public ownership and planned production. Zhores Medvedev, a dissident commentator on Soviet agriculture, argued that "poor agricultural performance was linked to bad management."[22] Alec Nove reasons that Soviet-era policy initiatives failed because collective farm managers had to appease party officials, writing up reports and doing Moscow's bidding, which was often at odds with good stewardship of the farms' land, plants, and animals.[23] Jenny Leigh Smith locates the main resistance to the state's policy initiatives in nature itself: "The Soviet state overlooked its primary adversary, which was natural. . . . In terms of success or failure of state-sponsored intervention on farms, nature mattered more" than peasants' "backward" mentalities.[24]

Regardless of where the emphasis is placed on this question, the deep distrust between planners and actual rural workers was profound and lasting.[25] This disconnect, and its absurd outcomes, is satirized in the writer Fazil Iskander's fictional account of the travails of a collective farm in Abkhazia that was singled out by planners as a breeding site for a novel farm animal, the so-called Goatibex, which would be superior in every way to conventional sheep or goats. While the predicament of kolkhozniki caught between plan targets and the limits of something as practical as sheep genetics was obvious enough to Iskander and his audience, political change came only during the Gorbachev era. Indeed, it was not until the final years of perestroika that Soviet leaders finally trusted collective farms enough to allow them to lease land and to make decisions regarding production and how to respond to local environments. Peasant opposition, mutual mistrust, the cumbersome and politically motivated planning process, and nature's resistance to utopian schemes are all critically important for understanding the performance of Soviet farms. The account here tracks the chronology of *price-related, land-related,* and *trade-related* policies and campaigns, showing how successive technopolitical regimes responded to earlier failures in these three areas. Each campaign to solve the grain problem was hampered by some of these causes at different junctures, and future policies responded to these failures by championing new actors, new material technologies, and new knowledge.

What Is the Value of Grain?
Prices and Subsidies for Farm Products

In agriculture, as in other sectors of the planned economy, procurement prices were a central governance tool of the Soviet regime. They reflected the political priorities of the party and the planning bureaucracy, often far more so than the cost of production. Indeed, throughout the years of central planning, the relationship between price and cost was one of ongoing and vexing debates for planners and politicians. In the early decades of the Soviet Union, the extraction of grain from the countryside was addressed using a combination of two methods, each favored by different factions of the party apparat and implemented at different times. One faction favored the use of coercion, while the other wanted to foster improvements in farming methods through rewards and higher prices.²⁶ Narkomzem, or the Ministry of Agriculture, wanted to supply tools and seeds, start land reorganization, and implement education programs to encourage peasants to produce more. The Food Supply Commissariat, meanwhile, prioritized the needs of the war economy and favored forced grain seizures and confiscation to produce quick results. During the Civil War, emergencies and the urgent needs of the Red Army trumped the gradual and educational approach. The situation on the ground during these years was also a great deal more chaotic than either Narkomzem or the Supply Commissariat's plans envisaged. Forced grain seizures were the norm, and violence, famines, and disease plagued the countryside. All of this greatly strained relations between the Bolshevik government and the countryside.²⁷

After the Civil War, the state of Russian agriculture was nothing short of disastrous—Russian peasants produced very little grain compared to the prerevolutionary period. Grain harvests in 1921 were less than half of what they had been in 1913.²⁸ Fields lay fallow, transport and communications networks were destroyed, and hunger was widespread. In the early 1920s, nearly a third of the Russian population was affected by famine, and at least three million died from hunger.²⁹ During the NEP, communist attempts at the "mass reorganization of peasant farming" turned away from wartime coercion, and Bukharin and others managed to steer the party away from forced and excessive requisitions. Agrarian specialists were given the mandate to use "peaceful methods in transforming the countryside," with a "focus on 'enlightening' farmers via persuasion about the most efficient modes of farming."³⁰ Alexander Chayanov, a scholar with an international reputation by that time, was one of the specialists employed by Narkomzem in the 1920s to enlist peasants to help build a "brighter future for rural Russia" in which the countryside was "technically sophisticated, highly productive and socialist," with "an agrarian economy that would surpass those of the Western countries."³¹ New farming methods and technologies were central to how this was to be achieved. Agronomists were sent to the countryside to convert peasants to the value of innovations such as crop rotation and multi-field farming, and to promote switching to industrial crops (including flax, sugar beets, and tobacco). Collective farms, sovkhozy and kolkhozy, were created as the organizational basis for modern farming. Sovkhozy were formed on the basis of imperial-era large landed estates. They were owned by the state and managed directly by a branch of the Ministry of Agriculture. Kolkhozy were technically owned by rural worker collectives and meant to function as cooperatives, but in reality they were controlled by regional party hierarchies.³² The sovkhoz directly exchanged its products with the state in return for inputs, while the kolkhoz "sold" output, in accordance with an obligatory delivery/sale contract (*plan zakupok*) between the kolkhoz and the buying and storage parties for each subsector (*zagotoviteli*), which were in turn determined by the "general agricultural plan" (*orgkhozplan*) worked out by the Ministry of Agriculture.

This version of rural modernization ran into troubles. From the farmer's perspective, there were several problems with the programs imposed from above. Procurement prices continued to be so low that they hardly served as incentives. Farmgate prices reflected Stalin's dual aims of maximizing resource extraction and ensuring political control over peasants. "Stalin the Industrializer" continued to keep grain prices low, placing a heavy tax on agriculture.[33] While prices for agricultural goods were depressed, prices of industrial goods increased rapidly, creating a "scissor crisis," in which the price graphs for the two types of goods resembled the two blades of a scissor.[34] Moreover, most Russian farms were still small, and fearing that state agents would seize any grain, farmers opted to produce just as much as they needed to survive. Producing more could in fact increase the risk of being targeted as kulaks and considered political enemies of the socialist project. The switch away from traditional three-field farming methods toward multi-crop rotations required resources—machinery, advice, and seeds—that many farms simply did not have. It also decreased the availability of common land used for grazing.[35] As peasants saw few advantages in joining collectives, by the late 1920s, only 4 percent of them had done so.[36] Much to the consternation of Bolshevik party elites, the total volume of marketed grain continued to fall throughout the twenties, even during years with relatively good harvests. Rapid urbanization and an insufficient grain supply necessitated bread rationing in towns at several points during the decade. Peasants were blamed for these problems. Party elites accused them of hiding grain and consuming livestock.[37] They were deemed culturally backward, ignorant, inert, and steeped in religion and tradition.[38] Labeled kulaks and class enemies, they were forced to hand over any grain as "surplus" crops for very low compensation, or none at all.[39]

Faced with resistance from below on nearly all fronts of the modernization agenda, Soviet political elites and Narkomzem bureaucrats were torn about how to proceed. Agronomists considered forced requisitioning and low prices as counterproductive, detrimental not only to rural development but also to efforts to bring the peasantry into the Bolshevik fold.[40] They argued that higher procurement prices would allow farmers to buy machinery. Yet a Marxist interpretation of rural change viewed this kind of private capital accumulation with suspicion. Within the party, the balance shifted from the advocates of NEP and a gradual approach to rural development to those who argued for "stricter" policies to oppose rural enemies of the Bolshevik cause. Throughout the twenties, the authorities repeatedly reverted back to the coercive policies that had been the norm during the Civil War. The agrarian specialists were increasingly bypassed. Because most of them were not communist party members, they were vulnerable to being labeled bourgeois traitors. Chayanov and his colleagues at Narkomzem were accused of being ringleaders of a kulak party in July 1927. They were removed from their positions in show trials and purges in 1928 and 1929.[41]

In November 1929, Stalin declared that only a rapid acceleration of the fight against peasants as class enemies would solve the grain problem. In a departure from the gradualist approach associated with Narkomzem and its discredited specialists, forced collectivization was to move peasants from small, "backward" family farms to large, "advanced" collectives. In an unprecedented campaign of terror, arrests, and deportation, collectivization was achieved within a few short years. Anyone who opposed or resisted collectivization was very likely to be identified as a kulak. Peasants singled out as belonging to this class were typically executed in the village. Otherwise, they were treated so badly en route to exile or upon arrival that survival was all but impossible, or they starved during the famine that followed collectivization. Peasant resistance took many forms, though ultimately villagers had very little power to oppose party officials' brutal drive to collectivize.[42] By 1933, nearly all Soviet peasants belonged to collectives. Collectivization was meant to address the problem of peasant resistance, thereby solving the problem of food shortages. Instead, it led to widespread misery, famine, and death, as many millions of peasants across the Soviet Union starved, with Ukraine, the North Caucasus, and Kazakhstan hit hardest. Whole villages suspected of harboring kulaks were deported from the southern regions of the Soviet Union to Siberia and Kazakhstan.[43] In Ukraine, collectivization and the famine came to be known as the Holodomor, a term built from the Ukrainian words for hunger and dying. Millions of peasants were exiled or executed during the violence that accompanied the "spontaneous" movement to collectivize.

Stalin's efforts to impose his will upon the countryside persisted well after collectivization. Production quotas escalated for all the main agricultural crops—grain, meat, milk, and industrial raw materials such as cotton. Among its many long-term repercussions, forced collectivization allowed for the state procurement apparat to extract grain at the lowest possible prices. In the thirties and forties, price policies were also accompanied by more overt forms of political control and coercion. Kolkhoz workers, whose precarious position was compounded by forced confiscations of products and livestock from subsistence plots, continued to be viewed with suspicion.[44] Party officials were charged with routine and daily checks on farms, ensuring plan fulfillment and correct political behavior. The agricultural machine depots, known as the Machine

Tractor Stations (MTS), were the unlikely institutional tools of political control. MTS provided tractors, but, along with them, they dispensed "political-economic guidance." From 1929 to 1934, each MTS had a political department charged with monitoring and eliminating subversive peasants.[45] More generally, a system of internal passports and residence permits, the *propiska*, was established in 1932 to regulate rural outmigration. Kolkhozniki were denied access to these documents for decades. Although the system had gaps allowing some degree of mobility for those who knew how to exploit them, it worked as an effective tool of state control over rural populations.[46]

Despite the costs, the Stalin-era combination of political control and ruthless extraction managed over time to realize one important policy goal. Though hampered by the trauma of collectivization and disrupted by World War II, the reorganization of rural production led to a gradual increase in farm output throughout the 1930s and then again after the war. One of the areas of increased production was pork, which was industrialized in the 1930s and grew significantly after the war. Stalin and Anastas Mikoyan also placed great emphasis on making available a set of affordable luxuries for mass consumption. They encouraged the industrial production of champagne and chocolates (hallmarks of upper-class prosperity in imperial Russia) and canned corn and ketchup, foreign novelties and innovations.[47] These policies mostly benefited urban consumers in the larger cities. Kolkhozniki continued to be underpaid for the grain they produced, earning little for their work on the land well into the 1950s.[48] Though Stalin's overt war on peasants had ended, there were few signs of the "peaceful partnership between city and countryside" that Bukharin had imagined.

After World War II, communist rural planning shifted slowly and incompletely from coercion to a system of rewards. Food commodity prices remained a tool of control, but more consideration was given to how they would impact farmers. Nikita Khrushchev ascended to the party leadership after years at the head of the Ukrainian Soviet Socialist Republic. He was intimately familiar with the realities on the ground and Stalinist agrarian reforms that had been particularly disastrous for Ukraine. A loyal and exemplary Stalinist who shared responsibility for enforcing collectivization and postwar repression, he was also known to privately disapprove of their brutality and disastrous consequences. After Stalin's death, then, Khrushchev heralded a new era of communism by returning to promises of "the good life" that were in many ways about consumption. But he also concluded that only modern farming methods and a radically new approach would be able to solve the grain problem, even as he acknowledged that the ideals of Stalinist agricultural high modernism had not been realized and that the conditions facing rural residents were nothing short of desperate.[49] Production was insufficient, livestock herds were too small, productivity indicators were low, and investments in farm equipment were inadequate.[50] Rural residents went hungry and earned next to nothing for hard labor. Stalin-era policies came to be seen as too draconian, too reliant on labor-intensive production methods, and altogether insufficient to transform the countryside.[51]

Under Khrushchev, Soviet agricultural policies placed a higher value on rural production and material rewards for agricultural labor. New measures included guaranteed wages for kolkhozniki, price incentives to grow more, and various bonuses for exceeding plan targets or raising specific crops.[52] Collective farm workers became wage earners, and procurement prices for farm output were raised several times in the 1950s and 1960s. Before 1953, it had been forbidden to discuss procurement prices; under Khrushchev, low procurement prices were singled out as the core problem hampering production, and in an initial set of reforms in 1954, procurement prices for the main cereal crops and for meat were raised by about a factor of five.[53] Further price increases followed: while a kolkhoz had received 8.4 rubles for a metric ton of grain in 1952, it received 83 rubles in 1962. The procurement price for potatoes rose from 5.3 rubles to 49 rubles, and the price of sunflower seeds went from 19.2 to 181 rubles during the same period.[54] Price increases and other reforms of the complex procurement systems were meant to take into account costs and inputs that were needed for different crops. Further, peasants were also allowed to apply for internal passports for the first time, although the state still controlled the movement of populations. These changes were quite fundamental, altering rural life and production. But while farmgate prices increased, they still remained only imperfectly tethered to the costs of inputs. Farms were on the receiving end of a complex array of subsidy payments and in-kind contributions for farm inputs, such as fertilizer, feed, and machinery. A mismatch between plan targets and the availability of inputs scuttled production, and shortages continued to be a problem. Labor-saving technologies, which were in many ways a prerequisite for efficient field crop production, were often in particularly short supply. Kolkhozy needed large workforces, and it was common practice to bring in students and workers from nearby towns to help during potato, corn, and cotton harvests.[55] After more than a dozen years of price reforms, it became clear in the mid-sixties that material rewards alone did not solve the problems of Soviet farms. Khrushchev's pensive stance captured in an iconic image taken on a farm in 1964 may well be a reflection of the mixed results of his ambitious rural reforms (see figure 1.1.).

Under Brezhnev, agricultural inputs came into focus as a critical factor of success. Farms received a wide array of subsidized inputs—machines, fertilizer,

Figure 1.1 First Secretary of the Communist Party Nikita Khrushchev visits fields of the Moskovsky State Farm, Kazakh SSR, 1964. Valentin Sobolev/TASS.

fuel, and lubricants—to enable them to ramp up production. Agrochemicals, especially fertilizers, became available in huge quantities at low cost due to a Brezhnev-era campaign to "chemicalize" agriculture.[56] Farms with labor shortages received free labor through the dispatch of military personnel. Agricultural policies also included the construction of very large livestock farms and processing facilities, as well as drainage and irrigation systems.[57] US irrigation systems and center pivot technologies were imported and replicated in attempts to deal with persistent droughts in some areas of the Soviet Union. Investment in agronomy research and plant and animal breeding was also elevated and recognized as an important contributor to increasing yields. Funds flowed to agricultural universities in each of the Union Republics and to branch institutes dispersed across the country.[58] These expenditures were essentially subsidies for infrastructure and knowledge inputs for state farms, meant to lower costs and increase rewards for collective farms. Some of these policies brought successes: fish and pork production increased, for example. In other subsectors, successes were accompanied by waste and failures. Though fertilizer supplies increased, a shortage of bags, means of transport, storage, and spreading machinery prevented the most useful application of the nutrients. Moreover, nutrient needs varied greatly across regions, and planners had few, if any, information on the types and quantities of fertilizer needed on each farm or field.[59] By the end of the Brezhnev era, fertilizer application levels were extremely high, while yields still remained below those of capitalist food systems.

Despite and because of persistent problems, the flow of resources from the state to the collective farm sector continued to grow. During Brezhnev's time in office, over a quarter of the state's total budget was poured into agriculture.[60] One of the principles of state funding puzzling to Western observers was that weaker farms consistently received more funding than strong farms. The rationale was to keep farms in marginal areas afloat. At the same time, planners were unwilling to pass on these costs to consumers. In 1962, Soviet authorities had been confronted with food riots in the town of Novocherkassk, which they suppressed by force.[61] In the decades that followed, authorities learned that consumer prices were indeed sensitive—and retail food prices remained at the level of the mid-sixties. This meant that the costs of subsidizing agriculture and processing were mounting. Public subsidies for meat production, for example, increased from 2.8 to 22.6 billion rubles between 1965 and 1989.[62] The increasing subsidization of the sector was only possible because the Soviet government's foreign currency earnings also increased during this same period, through the sale of oil at a time when global commodity prices were high. And as we will see, hydrocarbon earnings were exchanged for feed for growing numbers of Soviet livestock herds.

Land Use Policies: Who Can Grow What, and Where?

A second type of policy that Soviet planners used to influence agricultural production concerned the control of land and land use. The Soviet state's main concern was to consolidate and modernize collective farms; successive policy schemes focused on how to expand production and improve methods used by large-scale farms. Throughout the Soviet period, the state was hostile toward the second important type of rural land use—small-scale household farms, or LPKh. Since imperial times, rural households had been allowed to farm garden plots (*usad'by*) to grow vegetables for family use.[63] The Soviet government's policy toward these plots was torn between an ideological aversion to private, inefficient, and "backward" land use and an increasing realization that this form of production acted as an important supplier of food. Only after many decades of hostility did Soviet planners grudgingly acknowledge LPKh for the critical source of food it had always been, not only for rural residents but for the Soviet population as a whole.

Russian reformers had long debated the merits of collective versus private individual farming. In late imperial Russia, collective ownership and use of farmland were the norm after the emancipation of serfs in 1861. At the beginning of the twentieth century, Pyotr Stolypin introduced an enormously important legal change by allowing the enclosure of common land and private ownership of farmland, a reform that was meant to increase agricultural productivity. The implementation of Stolypin's 1906 decree was far more protracted than reformers envisaged in part because communal authorities denied private claims on property.[64] Only a decade later, the events that unfolded before and after the socialist revolution charted a different path for land use in Russia. In the months leading up to the October Revolution, peasants took advantage of the collapse of authority and seized lands from noble estates and the church in what came to be called the "black repartition." The Decree on Land (Dekret o zemle), passed on October 25, 1917, was one of the Bolshevik regime's first legal acts. It ex post facto legalized these massive land seizures and brought about sweeping institutional changes. The decree further abolished all private land ownership and forbade land sales and rental arrangements. All land was confiscated from former owners without compensation.[65] Land was to be controlled by "the people." These legal changes were radical on paper. At the same time, the central government had very little real control of actual land use. Without authoritative administrative bodies who could exert control and compliance, realities on the ground were governed by the local communal structures that made decisions about farming methods and production before Stolypin's reforms. Most Russian farms at that time were small, and cultivation decisions were made by rural communes in highly localized agreements.[66] This pattern of land use continued during the first few years of the NEP period: although land was de jure publicly owned, de facto land was largely used by rural communes and farms for their own subsistence.

Collectivization was the world's largest top-down reorganization of land use in the twentieth century. Stalin violently and decisively handed control of land to collective farms, via planning bureaucracies and party organs. By 1937, the government had forcibly collectivized the vast majority, 93 percent, of agricultural land. For the remainder of the century, Russian rural workers had neither ownership nor usage rights of the land they farmed. Collectivization was also the founding moment of a system that combined rural resource extraction with political control. With the creation of collective and state farms, virtually all decisions related to land use (what was sown, harvested, and sold—as well as to whom and at what price) were taken from the peasants and handed to party officials and the planning bureaucracy. Although collective farm members were allocated into various distinct work units, each officially in charge of a specialized subsector and permitted the use of farm equipment, their responsibilities were largely confined to implementing changing directives that emanated from political authorities. Decisions about farming became political questions about rural modernization made by elites and economic planners. One set of land use directives, for example, mandated the abandonment of pre-Soviet communal strip-farming in favor of larger, consolidated fields that could be ploughed more easily with new machinery. This directive was just as much about taking away decisions from former communal authorities as it was about crop growing.[67] Land use practices changed dramatically as a result of "tractorization"—a shorthand for the increasing use of all manner of farm machinery. The MTS provided kolkhozniki with access to more machines, horses, tools, and repair services than ever before. At the same time, having access to more tractors and machines did not always mean that they could be effectively used: collective farm workers often had little say over when and how to operate equipment. One of the most salient problems of the MTS was a mismatch between the supply of machinery, determined by party officials, and on-farm demand for them, shaped by weather, soil conditions, and crop maturity.[68]

Whatever normalcy had returned to the Russian countryside after collectivization, the devastation wrought by World War II destroyed most of it.[69] The Red Army destroyed crops, farms, and machinery in Western Russia and Ukraine as a defensive measure against the encroaching German troops. As the agents of the state were attending to the urgent demands of the war, farms reverted back to subsistence production, a practice ignored by the state since it could ill afford to discourage any form of food production. By the late forties, farms were more independent and less organized than they had been before the war. After the war, the Ministry of Agriculture was tasked with not only reconstructing the physical infrastructure for farming but also rebuilding the chains of command and the authority to direct the work of state farms from the center. Party officials reverted back to a more restrictive position on private cultivation and punished the illegal and informal marketing of produce grown on household plots. The late Stalin period was thus once again marked by repressive state control and the overzealous grain requisitions that caused famines in Ukraine and Kazakhstan in 1946 and 1947. Grain harvests in the early fifties were sufficient at best.[70]

When Nikita Khrushchev heralded a new approach to the grain problem and the modernization of the Russian countryside in 1954, two of his most ambitious programs were related to land use—the attempt to bring corn to the Soviet Union, and the Virgin Lands campaign. Khrushchev had high hopes for both as remedies for and departures from the coercive policies of the Stalin years. Khrushchev's fascination with corn as a "miracle crop" was born from a visit to Iowa in 1954, from which he returned with a conviction that corn was the technology that would bring prosperity to the Soviet Union: "The United States is riding a race horse, which is corn, and we must catch them on the same racehorse."[71] Khrushchev's bet led to a rapid increase in corn growing in the traditional grain-growing regions of the Soviet Union.[72] Khrushchev's crusade also rested on a vast expansion of arable land. In a 1954 memorandum to the Central Committee titled "Ways of Solving the Grain Problem," he proposed the exploitation of at least 13 million hectares of uncultivated and fallow "Virgin Lands" in Kazakhstan, eastern Siberia, and the Volga basin.[73] Appealing to the Komsomol (the Communist Youth League), he urged Soviet youth to move to these areas to plant wheat and corn. Planners spared no resources—people, tractors, and ploughs would have to move to these areas. Local party elites subdued Kazakh resistance to settling and working on newly established collective farms.[74] Khrushchev's reforms also meant giving the kolkhozy more autonomy to plan their own production and herd sizes, though they remained responsible for meeting procurement quotas set by the planning bureaucracy and party. One of his reforms pertained to the shared use of machinery administered by the MTS. Khrushchev realized that the split authority over machines between MTS and farms was hurting farmers and jeopardizing harvests. In what was considered a political gamble at the time, he abolished the MTS, selling their equipment to the kolkhozy to allow famers more control over machines and tools. This left the kolkhozy with the responsibility to maintain farm machinery, an expensive and challenging burden. Mechanics with the skills to repair tractors had to be retained with generous wages, and machine parts were in short supply.[75]

The corn crusade and the Virgin Lands campaign were initially successful. Between 1953 and 1956, the total sown acreage increased by more than a fifth, or 35.9 million acres.[76] The medium and long-term record of Khrushchev's agricultural reforms is more complicated. Grain and corn harvests during the Khrushchev era were volatile. In some years, harvests were disappointing, and many of his reforms were deeply unpopular. Kolkhozy were faced with intense pressure to implement plans that fulfilled output targets in the short term but disrupted established crop rotation patterns and led to soil erosion in the long term. Alec Nove notes that "the party machine in rural areas was used to imposing a cropping pattern and delivery obligations that had little to do with local conditions or the realities of the given situation."[77] The critics of Khrushchev's campaigns claimed that the reforms failed. These voices grew over time and contributed to his fall from power in 1964. At the same time, the Soviet Union brought in record harvests in 1966, 1967, and 1968—harvests that followed Khrushchev's ouster but still owed much to his campaigns. In fact, the CIA noted with some alarm in 1968 that "for the third year in a row the USSR has harvested an excellent grain crop, which will permit it to meet current domestic needs, to fulfill current export commitments, and to add to the sizable grain stocks."[78] The long-term track record of the corn and Virgin Land's campaign were ultimately problematic. Corn, seeded across the Soviet Union in soils and climates that were not well suited for growing the miracle crop, did not perform well over time.[79] Similar troubles affected wheat cultivation in Central Asian territories: overly ambitious plantings in soil that was not fit for spring wheat led to soil erosion within a few short planting seasons.

Khrushchev's reforms entailed large-scale surges in inputs in terms of labor, equipment, and animal feed that had many important consequences. They transformed many rural areas, as could be clearly seen on the Kazakh steppe and in the town of Tselinograd, forever transformed by Khrushchev's ambitious developmental plan.[80] While Stalin had encountered reluctant peasants, the kind of trouble that Khrushchev's plans ran into were different. It seemed to become apparent to some party elites and planners that their ability to marshal natural resources had limits. Rural populations could be ruled with terror and fear, but some biophysical realties could not. Limits imposed by soil conditions and climate revealed that nature had a kind of agency and could perhaps resist more forcefully than reluctant peasants had been able to.[81] The Brezhnev government's response was to double down on its attempts to harness natural resources. Now the focus shifted from expanding arable land to altering soil conditions and climate. Erosion and dust storms led planners to devise new irrigation schemes rather than walk away from intensive cultivation of crops. From the late sixties through the eighties, thousands of acres of crops in Central Asia were irrigated, initially mostly in the Uzbek SSR but later also in the Kyrgyz, Turkmen, and Kazakh Soviet Socialist Republics. As almost all the ground water in this region drains into the Aral Sea basin, the expansion of cotton, a notoriously thirsty crop, had disastrous environmental consequences. Although the rising salinity and declining water levels were increasingly apparent to local residents, it took party officials another decade to acknowledge this. A 1987 Central Committee Resolution reported on rapidly declining water levels and collapsing fisheries in rivers and the Aral Sea, flagging them as problems needing urgent attention.[82]

The Soviet government's intense efforts at modernizing collective farming were mirrored in its hostility toward small subsistence plots in the LPKh sector. In the Stalin era, kolkhoz and sovkhoz workers were initially permitted to maintain these plots only because they could not survive without this source of food. At the same time, stringent quantitative restrictions limited acreage and the number of cows and pigs. Even if the land use in the subsistence sector kept citizens alive, especially during the years of the Civil War and World War II, political elites always viewed subsistence farming as part of the problem of rural backwardness rather than as a solution to food shortages. "Economically it is backward, ideologically it is alien, politically it is suspect and morally it stands in the way of the creation of the new Socialist Man": this was Karl-Eugen Wädekin's assessment of Soviet authorities' attitudes toward subsistence production.[83] It was seen as something of an atavistic remainder of archaic farming practices—a social formation that was bound to disappear once collective farming realized its full potential. Some observers thought of it as a manifestation of the backward psychology of rural dwellers. Habituated into the routines of small-scale, labor-intensive production and bound by their labor intensity, they were unable to embrace mechanized, modern farming methods. In the Khrushchev era, this attitude prevailed. Official observers had become increasingly frustrated with the stubborn persistence of small-scale production, "a social evil" that had gone on too long already.[84] With no natural "end in sight," Khrushchev made aggressive moves to restrict activity on private plots, arguing that this would increase activity in the socialized sector.[85] This crackdown was damaging to the country's food supply and exceedingly unpopular.[86]

In the early 1970s, more than four decades after collectivization, Soviet authorities finally adopted a more pragmatic stance toward private plots.[87] Accelerating urbanization was forcing the regime to acknowledge that small-scale household production was an indispensable source of food, and one of Brezhnev's first policy changes was to reverse Khrushchev's restrictions on subsistence plots. The government now allowed larger plots to be farmed privately and permitted irrigation and holding livestock, without actively encouraging these activities or supporting them with resources. Animal proteins were a particular concern for Brezhnev, who recognized that a growing share of meat, milk, and eggs originated on household farms. Gorbachev continued the policy of turning to personal plots to bolster food supply, though he also realized that they were very labor-intensive and could not ultimately solve the problem of Soviet agriculture. In 1983, roughly half of the Soviet population, or 160 million residents, tended private plots.[88] Some of the products of rural production were allowed to be sold at so-called kolkhoz markets set up in cities. (The *kolkhoznyi rynok* was not unlike the farmers markets that have grown in popularity in the US over the last thirty years.) Largely incompatible with the ideology of state planning, these kinds of markets were restricted in many ways. Farmers were required to personally sell the products, which had to be classified as "surplus" by collective farm managers. Markets did not offer storage facilities, so farmers could only take along whatever they could carry in one trip. These restrictions made selling at kolkhoz markets time-consuming and onerous to discourage farmers from participating in them: selling at these markets was often only viable if public transport routes were available and if the farmers and rural residents were able to buy scarce consumer items at the markets in urban areas to resell in their villages.[89] Kolkhoz markets flourished despite these restrictions and challenges, providing some of the flexibility to sell and buy fresh products that the planned economy lacked. Especially in southern regions, with rich soils and suitable growing conditions, these markets played an important role in provisioning households. Wädekin observed that while in 1961 only about 7 percent of produce was sold in kolkhoz markets across the Soviet Union, in Kiev it was 14 percent; in other in smaller southern towns, such as Rostov, Saratov, Kharkov, and Dnepropetrovsk, it was about 20 percent; in L'vov it was 37 percent; and in Odessa it was 43 percent.[90] Prices at these markets were higher, but consumers realized that the quality of the produce was also superior as kolkhozniki carefully selected the best products for private sales. With Gorbachev's economic reforms, restrictions on kolkhoz markets were lifted and they became an increasingly important outlet for private production.

In sum, land use policies—the rules governing who can own land and who can grow what (and how and where)—were the focus of Soviet-era rural campaigns with the most lasting impact. Had Stalin not evicted and killed peasants, the post-Soviet corporatization of Russian farmland would likely have progressed quite differently and would certainly have been much slower. Had Khrushchev not expanded production, and had Brezhnev not irrigated Central Asia, Kazakh top soil and the Aral Sea might still be around. What all these campaigns had in common was that they made sweeping decisions about diverse landscapes and maintained few, if any, mechanisms for feedback about how top-down policies affected local contexts. Not until 1989, when an initiative by Gorbachev about land leases was approved by the Party Plenum, did any significant authority devolve to the kolkhozy. The new law permitted individuals to lease land and assets from collective farms for up to fifty years; individuals would pay a fixed rent to the collective farm while being able to grow what was considered profitable and being allowed to keep whatever profit was achieved over and above this rent payment. This would, Gorbachev argued in 1989, make the farmers "masters of the land"—thus in significant ways handing back control of land to rural residents. Only a year later, Yeltsin became chairman of the Russian Supreme Soviet and in many ways competed with Gorbachev on agricultural policies by promising to make much more sweeping changes to land rights and land use provisions.[91]

External Trade

The Russian food system takes part in global markets and the global food regime. The main hinges of global integration are imports and exports of food commodities—mostly grains in the Russian case. Ideas and technologies are also important; their exchange has been at times encouraged and at other times prohibited. Changing policies have led to the ebb and flow of exports and imports of not only grain but also tractors, processing technologies, and agricultural experts traveling to and from the Soviet Union—each contributing to change in the Russian food system.

Late imperial Russia was the breadbasket for increasingly industrialized Western European countries. Large quantities of wheat—mostly grown in Ukraine, the North Caucasus, and the Volga Basin—were sold to Germany, Britain, and the Netherlands.[92] Sergey Witte fostered a global trade regime in which Russia exported grain in exchange for agricultural machinery and other industrial technologies and goods from Western Europe. In the second half of the nineteenth century, Russian grains made up between a quarter and a third of globally traded wheat, much of it feeding British industrial workers.[93] Since the eighteenth century, Russia had also exported seeds for agricultural production. One Russian export of that period deserves mention because it forever changed North America's agriculture—a wheat variety known as Turkey Wheat. Russian Mennonites brought small amounts of seeds of this variety to North America, and it thrived on the prairies of the US and Canada.[94] By 1900, USDA agronomists led ambitious expeditions to Russia, Ukraine, and Central Asia to bring back durum wheat varieties that they introduced in Kansas, Nebraska, and parts of Montana and Colorado.[95] During World War I, Russia was the largest exporter of sugar beet seed to the allied forces. These seed exports may in fact be Russia's most underappreciated successful technological export. But many other agricultural inputs were imported. Throughout the first tumultuous decades of Soviet history, Soviet and American farmers were keenly interested in each other's experience of industrializing agriculture and exchanged expertise. Thousands of American technical experts went to the Soviet Union as advisers on industrial farming.[96] Interrupted by World War II, this kind of agricultural diplomacy and exchange picked up again in the mid-fifties, after Khrushchev personally invited the farmers of Iowa to come visit Soviet corn and hog farms in 1955.[97]

Knowledge, machines, and seeds were important, but the rise and fall of Russia's bulk grain export transformed Russia's countryside even more. The turmoil of World War I, the revolution, and the Civil War marked a dramatic turning point; grain exports dwindled after 1917 and didn't recover until more than a century later.[98] The architects of NEP tried to rebuild the prerevolutionary system of exchanging grain for machines. Their attempts were thwarted in large part by an "uncooperative world economy." Though autarky is often described as a deliberate strategy, Oscar Sanchez-Sibony has argued that it was as much a result of an international economic order wrecked by the economic turmoil of the twenties and later the Great Depression, which left former trade partners unable to buy Russian grain and unable to invest in foreign industrial ventures.[99] The state of the global economy and Stalin's turn from Leninist internationalism to "socialism in one country" led to the shift to autarky. In the following decades of Stalin's rule, the Soviet economy industrialized rapidly, but largely—though not entirely—in isolation from the global economy.[100]

The Soviet Union's trade relations changed during and after World War II with the establishment of ties to Eastern European satellites. ComEcon was created in 1949, initially perceived to facilitate transnational planning. The organization's main task was ultimately the negotiation of trade arrangements among socialist planned economies; under its auspices, the Soviet Union imported growing quantities of meat from Hungary and Romania, for example. Global trade in bulk commodities was limited in the fifties, but the Soviet Union sent aid to a growing number of countries, such as India, Egypt, and Cambodia.[101] After 1960, the Soviet Union also imported large quantities of sugar from Cuba, at prices that were called "extraordinarily favorable" to Cubans. By buying well above the world sugar price and with aid, the Soviet Union's aim was to demonstrate the advantages of an affiliation with the Soviet-led trade bloc.[102] Trade patterns that favored client states or political allies were not at all uncommon at that time. In years with good harvests in the late 1960s, the Soviet Union also exported several million metric tons of grain to Czechoslovakia, East Germany, Poland, and Cuba—and in some years (1967/68) also to North Korea, North Vietnam, the UAR, and Algeria.[103] International trade in agricultural products was nevertheless quite limited overall in the fifties and early sixties, as countries protected their markets with a myriad of trade barriers and turned to suppliers in former colonies or to political allies for commodities not grown at home.

Soviet aid and credits financed knowledge exchange, allowing Egyptian scientists to study in Moscow and dispatching Czech experts to build textile factories in Cambodia.[104] Changes in Soviet domestic policies on agriculture-related knowledge exchange and technology imports came in the mid-fifties, as Khrushchev set his eyes on the ambitious goal of revolutionizing Soviet farming by growing corn. Among the most important agricultural technologies in midcentury America were livestock and crop genetics, which had led to the widespread use of high-efficiency broilers (chickens bred specifically for meat production) and double-cross hybrid corn seeds. Since the 1960s, the Soviet Union imported many other agro-technologies from abroad, including food processing technologies, such as extruders and evaporators, and feed additives. These technology imports from the US to the Soviet Union profoundly changed crop farming and livestock breeding.

Few trade policy turns were as consequential for the Soviet and global food system as Leonid Brezhnev's decision to import large quantities of American grain in 1972.[105] Riots in Poland over food prices during the Christmas holidays in 1970 contributed to the general secretary's conviction that the Soviet Union needed to boost meat production to satisfy the appetites of an increasingly urban population for proteins. Collective farms of the Brezhnev era were thus desperately in need of grain for animal feed, which in turn led planners to set ambitious grain production targets in the five-year plan for 1971–75.[106] Poor weather conditions and a series of lackluster harvests thwarted these plans; domestic grain production fell well short of plan targets in the early seventies.[107] In 1972, Brezhnev charted a radically new path, giving his approval, for the first time, to a large increase of the amount of imported grains, dairy products, and vegetable oils to make up for domestic production shortfalls. Most of the grain was to be procured from the US in an agreement that came to be known in the US as the "Great Grain Robbery." In early July of that year, the US agreed to sell $750 million dollars of grain to the Soviet Union, a deal spread over three years and secured with a loan guaranteed by the US Credit Commodity Corporation. The US officials involved in the negotiations were uncertain as to whether and how the agreement would come to fruition; many did not expect the Soviet Union to fulfill its side of the commitment. Yet just a few months later, the Soviet Union purchased 19 million metric tons of grain from the US, boosting the price of grain in the US (from $1.65 per bushel to $5) and on global markets.[108]

In the midst of Cold War tensions, both the US and the Soviet government had initially tried to keep the grain deal a secret. Yet the deal was so large that the surging demand for wheat caused instability in global grain markets, making it all but impossible to conceal. When details of the agreement with the Soviet government reached the American public, it drew considerable protest. Many objected to a deal that benefited the Soviet side and offered overly favorable loan terms, and some voiced suspicions of insider dealing by USDA agency employees and fears of price increases of food commodities. US Secretary of Agriculture Earl Butz worked hard to portray the deal as a great coup for US agriculture. He emphasized its benefits for American farmers and reassured consumers that enough grain would be available for domestic consumption.[109] The political context of the deal, the US public's concern, and rising global food prices overshadowed future US-Soviet trade negotiations. In 1975, US trade negotiations attempted to create predictability for domestic and global markets by requiring the Soviet Union to purchase between 6 and 8 million tons of wheat or corn for five years. It also reserved the right to reduce the amount sold to the Soviet Union should the American harvest drop below a certain threshold; commitments to Poland and Japan that were already in place would be honored first. In return, the US committed to purchasing 200,000 barrels of crude oil from the Soviet Union. This second grain deal caused much less controversy than the first mainly because US farmers were able to adjust planting in advance.[110]

The US-Soviet grain deal appeared initially as a perfect match between an economy with chronic shortages and another with constant surpluses. The Soviet Union needed grain and silage to feed livestock, and the US needed a grain export destination to sustain domestic farmgate prices. The Soviet need for livestock feed grew continuously throughout the seventies.[111] By the mid-1970s, meat consumption had reached levels comparable to Western Europe and the US.[112] Dairy products, too, had become dietary staples, contributing to the need for both dairy imports and feed grains. Yet Soviet-American grain trade was subject to the seesaw in political relations between the two Cold War superpowers. Responding to the Soviet invasion of Afghanistan, US president Jimmy Carter imposed a trade embargo in 1980.[113] The Reagan administration, in turn, sought to reestablish the grain trade with export subsidies for grains destined for Russia—Soviet grain purchases were essentially lucrative for US farmers. Overall, between 1972 and 1984, more than 132 million metric tons of wheat and corn had been shipped from the US to the USSR.[114] Map 1.1 shows food imports to the Soviet Union in the late 1980s and where they originate.

While the Soviet Union's dependence on imported food increased during this period, the country was also producing large amounts of grain, industrial crops, meat, and other food commodities and continued to export some of it to political allies such as Cambodia, Vietnam, and India. In response to Carter's embargo, Soviet policy makers increasingly shifted imports from the US to Eastern Europe and started to purchase more food from Western Europe, Australia, New Zealand, Brazil, and Argentina. Overall, the Soviet Union became far more integrated into global food commodity markets in the seventies and eighties than ever before. When the Soviet planned economy began to unravel and collapsed in 1991, Russia had already established trade ties with grain merchants, food importers, and commodity exporters around the world.

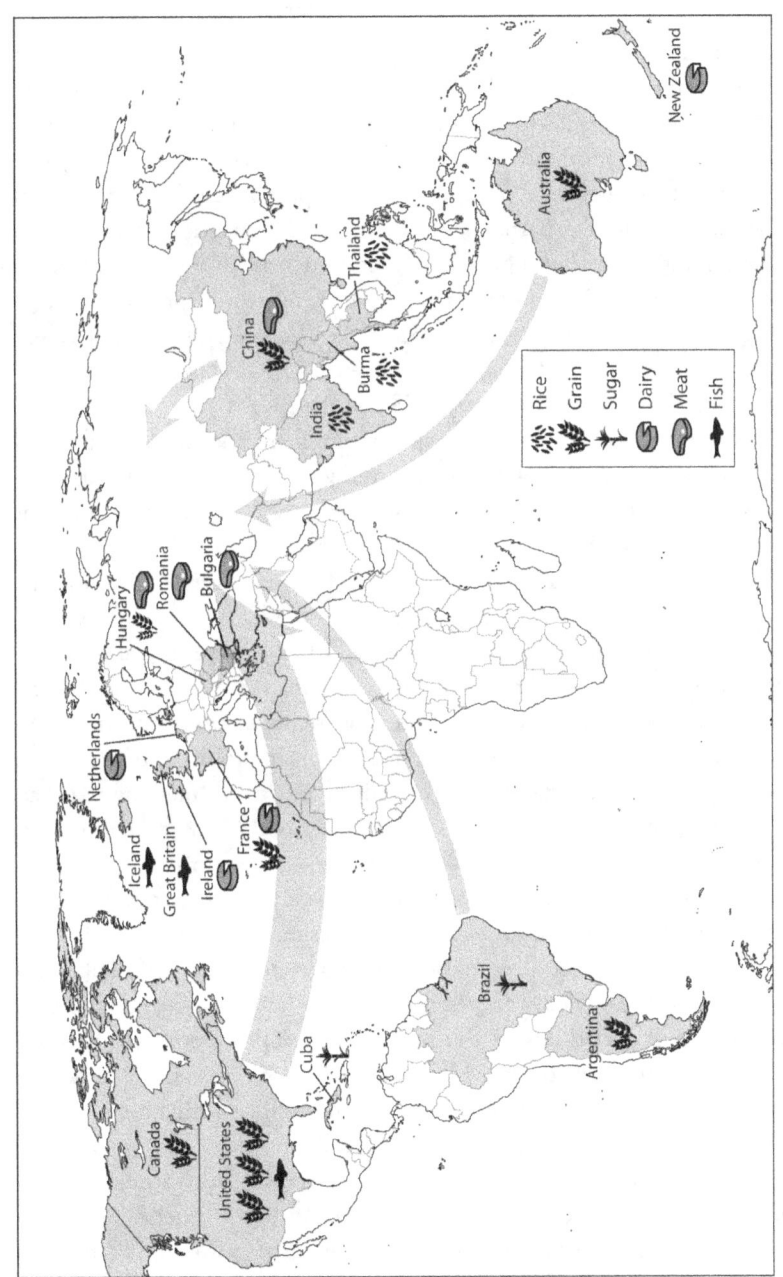

Map 1.1 Food imports to the Soviet Union, late 1980s, based on data from Goskomstat.

Post-Soviet Food System Governance
Yeltsin's Radical Land Reforms

The turbulent years of 1991 and 1992 were marked by the threat of hunger and widespread food shortages. Residents in large industrial cities—Moscow, Nizhny Novgorod, Chelyabinsk, Volgograd, Moscow, and Tula, for example—were most affected, as they had the least access to food produced on subsistence plots. Many cities introduced food stamps to ration supplies. This happened across Russia, from Belgorod to Barnaul, including in southern cities and towns that had been traditionally well supplied with food, such as Rostov-on-Don, Krasnodar, and Stavropol. What worried citizens even more were prices: little food was available, and prices for staples skyrocketed each month. "Everything is very expensive!" noted one contemporary observer.[115] On several occasions Russia received significant food aid from the US and the EU.[116]

This crisis was both a legacy of Soviet-era problems and the result of rapid liberalization spearheaded by Yeltsin's team of young reformers. Yeltsin's rural reforms drastically accelerated the cautious steps toward farm autonomy that Gorbachev had enacted. With a presidential decree passed in December 1991, Yeltsin allowed rural workers to withdraw land from collective farms for private use. For the first time since 1917, the state allowed private ownership of farmland. Russia's rural citizens were expected to take ownership and make a living from growing and selling crops and running farms as businesses.[117] The combination of individual ownership and usage rights was unprecedented and, on paper at least, quite radical. Aside from ushering in private land ownership, the reforms allowed for the breakup of collective farms, something that had still been quite unthinkable in the Gorbachev period.[118] The scale of reforms was extremely ambitious: 40 million former collective farmworkers became landowners, and 130 million hectares of farmland was privatized practically overnight.[119] The reforms rested on hopes that food shortages would be solved by Russian farmworkers finally free to choose to grow what was most suitable and profitable. Privately owned family farms would have incentives to update production methods once they were free from Soviet-era procurement quotas and prices. As prudent stewards of the land who would be properly rewarded by private gain, it was assumed that farmers would opt for farming methods and technologies that would increase yields and production.

In retrospect, the idea that Russia's newly privatized farms would succeed in this way appears far-fetched. The late eighties and early nineties were years when the challenges for family farms elsewhere, outside Russia, had become plainly obvious. US small farmers were experiencing a crisis brought about by the consolidation of farming. The Russian context was one in which the state rapidly withdrew from the countryside—while the retrenchment of state guarantees in the US and Europe was far more gradual. In Russia, then, the ownership changes on paper did not usher in the rise of yeoman farming that reforms had promised. Many observers noted that only very few farmworkers, though owners "on paper," opted out of collectives to farm privately: "land reform [of the 1990s] was 'largely cosmetic,' involving little more than changing the name plate of the farm."[120] Even in 2001, observers pointed to the failure of these reforms: "[collective farms,] awkwardly renamed joint stock companies (JSCs), continue to be the dominant agricultural producers. Now they are largely owned by their employees. Their profitability is decreasing. Their efficiency is low and falling. . . . They produce half of the country's agricultural output, they own more than 80 percent of agricultural land, and they refuse to disappear."[121] Stephen Wegren pointed out that the social and economic requirements for the vision of small-scale private Russian farming to be realized were nothing short of momentous. Rural workers would have needed to do more than change how they farmed. They would also have had to change how they related to their neighbors, the former collective, the state, and a range of other actors.[122] None of these changes were automatic, and they did not in fact materialize within a few short years. For most of the nineties, collective farm privatization was a reform in name only. By the end of the decade, the majority of collective farms were bankrupt and insolvent. Yeltsin's reforms impoverished millions of rural Russians, hardly what they had intended to do.[123] Former collective farm workers either stayed on as underpaid or unpaid employees or left for cities.

There were many mutually reinforcing obstacles to the marketization of rural economies. Initially, de facto restrictions on land transfers hindered private farming—land rights could not be bought and sold. There were a few exceptions—land that was sold back to local authorities or inherited could be transferred—and restrictions eased somewhat over time. By 1993, former collective farm workers could sell their shares to other rural workers who formerly belonged to a collective farm. At the same time, limitations on land transfers curtailed the development of land markets well into the twenty-first century. Such limits on land transfers were an "illiberal" feature of land reforms that Wegren identified as a central institutional deficiency of Yeltsin's reforms, and he considers the limitations an important part of the explanation for why these reforms failed to achieve their stated objectives.[124] A further reason for the gap between reform objectives and realities on the ground were collective farm managers. Jessica Allina-Pisano and Andrew Barnes point out that managers were often reluctant to allow members of the collective to remove their plots from collective land resources and resisted reforms.[125] The increasing costs of inputs constituted perhaps the most crushing problem for all Russian farms at the time. The disparity between the cost of agricultural inputs and the market prices for outputs has been known in Russia since early revolutionary times as the "price scissor" problem.[126] Throughout the nineties, this issue became ever more salient as the cost of fuel, seeds, fertilizer, and many other vital farm inputs increased rapidly as the state withdrew its subsidies for them.[127] And while the costs of farming increased, farmers had very little, if any, access to loans to buy inputs and equipment. As these difficulties were compounding, it was nearly impossible for former collective farm workers to make a living on the land they formally owned. Many rural residents responded to this crisis by selling their privatization vouchers for cash, "real money," at a low value.[128] Leo Granberg and Ann-Mari Sätre show that while this was in one respect a response to need, it also stemmed from rural residents' skepticism that their shares and land titles might be of value in the future.

In short, few rural citizens were able or eager to become independent farmers, and privatization did not forestall the gradual disintegration of Soviet-era rural infrastructure. Rural reforms under Yeltsin had been intended to address rural inefficiency, yet combined with a domestic policy agenda that strongly favored rapid marketization and liberalization, Russian farms were vastly underfunded and outmatched by foreign competition. Russian agriculture plunged into crisis, marked by a tremendous collapse in output, decultivation of arable land, and rural outmigration. From 1991 to 2000, output dropped by nearly two-fifths, and livestock production was cut in half.[129] Even though privatization created historically important changes in the legal and political context, it also allowed infrastructure and machines to crumble. The relationships of Soviet-era state farming and the procurement system came undone. Some elements of the state procurement system were maintained for a few years. Bread, once again, was deemed particularly sensitive, and the state retained a monopoly on bread production through the mid-1990s. Overall, however, the state withdrew from production and from supporting rural communities, leaving behind uncultivated land and rural residents at a loss about how to make a living. Social services that had been provided by former collective farms were transferred to village or municipal authorities, though without the requisite financial resources to maintain them.[130] Alexander Vorbrugg shows that the loss of material infrastructure and social support that had underpinned rural livelihoods during Soviet times occurred slowly but was profoundly disruptive.[131]

The decline of livestock herds and shortages of meat products were noted by Russian authorities and citizens as among the most painful elements of these trends. The regime's ability to put meat on the table had been a point of pride and an achievement of the Soviet system, an axis along which it measured its success and failure vis-à-vis capitalism. After 1991, livestock production and holdings shrank year after year, as feed grains and other inputs became unavailable or too expensive. In 2000, cattle and hog inventories were recorded at less than half their 1988 levels, and sheep and goat inventories were at about one-third the level for 1988.[132] This decline meant that consumption fell too, but it also made Russia an attractive market for meat imports. The import of meat products soared in the 1990s, with US chickens—inexpensive and abundant—leading the way. Average annual poultry imports more than quadrupled in the twenty years from 1991 to 2010, from 0.2 million metric tons to over 1 million metric tons per year.[133] More generally, both the quantity and range of imported agricultural and food commodities widened as the first post-Soviet decade progressed. International markets for such commodities had become highly competitive over the preceding decades.[134] When Russia opened its borders to these markets in the early nineties, plenty of multinational agrifood companies were more than ready to satisfy consumers' demand for imported foods of all kinds, from chicken wings to ready-made meals.

Putin's Food Security Agenda

Under Vladimir Putin, "food problems" (*prodovol'stvennye problemy*) were once again elevated as a central concern of the state. The sad state of Russian livestock herds reappeared as a political issue: "we are particularly concerned about the situation in livestock production," noted Alexey Gordeev, minister of agriculture in 2007.[135] Like Soviet leaders in generations past, Putin saw the need to address both the production and consumption sides of these problems.[136] Over the first two decades of his presidency, the Russian government developed a full-fledged rural recovery program, known as the food security or food sovereignty agenda. Agricultural policies during these years aligned with a broader shift toward economic nationalism and the strengthening of state capitalism, which were tied up with Putin's political project of strengthening the state and its control of natural resources. A cornucopia of evolving policy interventions have served the goal of reviving domestic agriculture: trade restrictions, a variety of subsidies and subsidized credits, local content rules, simplified and lower tax regimes, and newly created state-owned banks and other enterprises, outlined in more detail below. The first program for rural recovery, adopted in 2000, was known as the Basic Directions of Agrifood Policy.[137] Initially hamstrung by a tight budget, as oil prices rose and tax collection improved in the middle of the first decade of the new millennium, state support for domestic agriculture strengthened. By around 2005, several programs had been established under the umbrella of the National Priority Project: Development of the Agro-food Complex (2005). Between 2005 and 2010, total state support for agriculture more than tripled in nominal rubles, rising by 135 percent in real rubles.[138] Sustained public support and trade protection have brought more meat to Russian tables and helped boost grain exports. By 2010, wheat—Russia's most important crop, grown on 22 percent of arable land—had once again become one of Russia's most important export commodities.[139] Figure 1.2 shows an export terminal for Russian grain in Rostov in 2012.

The Russian government's most high-profile policy initiative was the National Food Security Doctrine, first published as a draft in 2008 and adopted in 2010.[140] As noted earlier in this chapter, in contemporary Russia, food security is largely seen as a question to be addressed at the level of the national economy. Food insecurity is not primarily seen as a problem affecting individuals (the more common interpretation of this term) but as a threat emanating from politically motivated foreign actors cutting off the sale of food commodities to Russia. In this interpretation, food security is a sovereignty problem, and the two terms are in fact often conflated. The centerpiece of the Food Security Doctrine was a set of precise and ambitious self-sufficiency targets for staples of the Russian diet.[141] These goals were to be realized through support to producers in targeted subsectors. The doctrine was in many ways a response to the failure of Boris Yeltsin's reforms. Yeltsin had intended to reshape rural property relations and modernize agriculture, but reforms of the nineties did not actually center on food provision. Like Soviet leaders before him, Yeltsin sought to

Figure 1.2 Russian grain loaded for export, Rostov-on-Don, August 2012. Valery Matytsin/TASS.

respond to the failures of Gorbachev's reforms, which he perceived as too slow and too timid. At the same time, Yeltsin was deeply influenced by the international economic policy consensus at the time that considered the state to be the source of inefficiencies, and market forces the solution. The ideational core of the reforms in the 1990s was market liberalization; the "food problem" should be left to the markets, not the state. Vladimir Putin, in turn, responded to the problems of the newly privatized but utterly failing collective farms he inherited from the Yeltsin year. He rejected the Yeltsin-era embrace of "market fundamentalism" that had, in his eyes, undermined the legitimacy of the state and greatly weakened Russia internationally. Putin-era rural recovery plans were food policies as much as they were agricultural policies.

The Food Security Doctrine had both domestic and foreign policy goals, each reflecting past experiences and current opportunities. On the domestic side of the equation, price stability for basic staple foods was one of the main aims. This was a direct response to hyperinflation, output collapse, and skyrocketing prices of staple foods in the nineties, which had led to widespread hardship that had undermined Yeltsin's legitimacy. Food security was about guaranteeing that citizens had access to a minimum of affordable staples, and this was to be achieved via the state-supported expansion of domestically produced food and occasional price ceilings on retail prices. The Putin government repeatedly adopted measures to control retail prices for basic "socially important" food commodities, such as wheat, sugar, and oils; this happened in 2010, a drought year, and in 2021, an election year, for example. Food retail prices were controlled through a freeze agreed upon by the Russian Federal Tariff Service, the industry association, and the country's major retail chains. "We will not allow any surges in grain or food prices," declared Aleksey Gordeev in response to less-than-expected wheat yields in 2012, for example.[142] The government also went back to a Soviet-era practice of setting "rational norms of consumption" (*ratsional'naya norma potrebleniia*) that were then translated into production targets. For meat, the Food Security Doctrine set the norm at a relatively high seventy-five kilograms per person per year.[143]

At the same time, food security and food sovereignty were also elements of Russian foreign policy that were explicitly coordinated with the country's national security policy. Russia had inherited its dependence on foreign food imports from the Soviet Union, but the crisis of the nineties broadened and deepened the range of food imports. When Putin became president, he essentially declared this kind of deep market integration in food commodities a threat to Russian sovereignty. A sharp increase in global food commodity prices across the world between 2005 and 2008 also contributed to rising concerns.[144] Putin's agriculture policies held out a greater degree of food commodity autarky as a desirable policy goal—a sharp break indeed from free trade and the globalization of food commodity markets that dominated the Yeltsin agenda. Russia still imported food, but the Food Security Doctrine defined self-sufficiency targets for the basic staples of the Russian diet. For example, Russia was to supply itself with 95 percent of the required grain and potatoes; 95 percent of milk and dairy products; 85 percent of salt, meat, and meat products; and 80 percent of sugar, vegetable oil, and fish products. These were political goals, providing metrics to measure success in attaining food security. When Russian wheat exports not only recovered but also gained global market shares after 2010, Russia went further and started to promote the possibility of influencing global affairs via global grain prices—that is, to use grain exports as a foreign policy tool. Gordeev boasted that Russia has become a "major agrarian power" in 2008.[145] Government officials even floated the idea of a global wheat cartel modeled on OPEC. This vision was never realized as it relied on close cooperation with Ukraine.[146] In less zero-sum terms, Russian commentators framed Russia's wheat bonanza as a contribution to feeding a growing world population. More concretely, the relations between Russia and a number of countries that are major importers of Russian grain—Turkey, Syria, Egypt, Nigeria, Bangladesh, and Pakistan—strengthened. Map 1.2. shows the main export destinations for Russian wheat, illustrating the truly global reach of the country's most important field crop.

While firmly rooted and embedded in domestic realities, the food sovereignty agenda was also a response to the increasing availability of foreign and domestic capital for rural investment. Although many factors contributed to the failures of Yeltsin's land privatization, in retrospect, one of the most important differences between the nineties and the new millennium was the scarcity of capital in the former period and its availability in the latter.[147] For a number of reasons addressed in detail in the next chapter, domestic oligarchs and international investors took an interest in Russian farmland starting in the early twenty-first century. The Putin government in turn realized that Russia's arable land was an attractive investment opportunity for global and domestic investors and actively sought to enlist them for his political goals. Note an interesting paradox here: the food security agenda was essentially an economic nationalist agenda, aimed at reducing dependence on foreign food. Yet the Putin government was not at all hesitant to rely on both domestic and foreign capital to achieve this goal (although the share of foreign capital declined after 2014). Various policy tools and an evolving series of programs fostered the growth of a new type of private actor in the Russian countryside, the large corporate agricultural operators known as agroholdings. Putin referred to these policies as "market *instruments*," deployed to "*react* to international markets."[148] Much

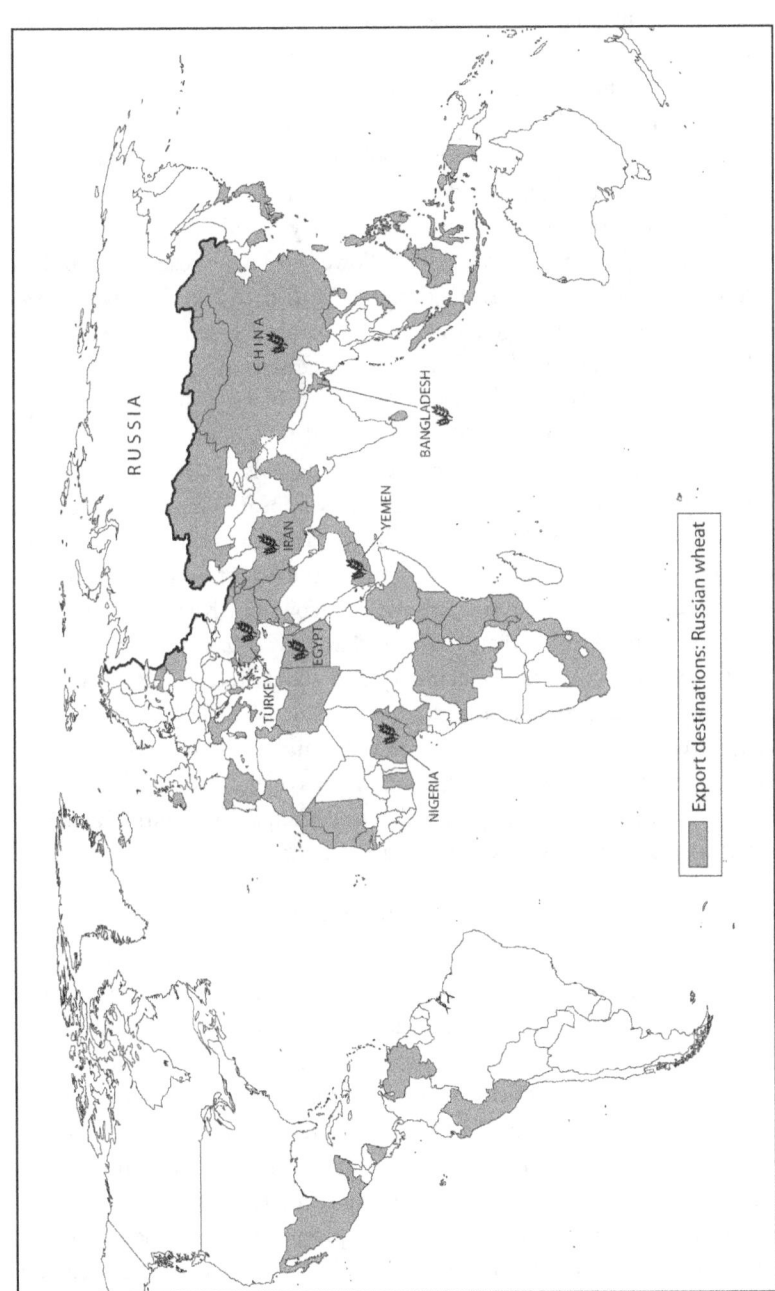

Map 1.2 Export destinations: Russian wheat, 2019, based on data from Chatham House Resource Trade.

to the frustration of Western observers who wanted to see a commitment to market mechanisms, markets were seen as a means, not an end in themselves.

As had been true during the Soviet era, now three types of agricultural policies were key. The first type comprised subsidies, or policies related to the costs and rewards of farming. The second type consisted of policies related to land use, and the third was made up of trade policies. While rural reforms initially paid lip service to and afforded a degree of rhetorical support for small-scale farming, by 2010, Putin's economic team had largely abandoned Yeltsin's notion of supporting small farms. In part, this followed from the reality that only a few kolkhozniki had pursued private farming. More than that, however, it was a reflection of a belief that large farms were better able to achieve the political goals they set out to accomplish. Putin and successive agricultural ministers, Alexey Gordeev and Alexander Tkachov, were firmly convinced that "large farms were necessary to provide food security of the country."[149] As we will see, Putin's agenda entailed a very particular relationship between the state and agroholdings. One company will repeatedly appear as an example of this special relationship—EkoNiva. The company was founded in 1994 by Stefan Dürr, a German entrepreneur who had gone to the Soviet Union as a student and became an intern on Soviet farms in Moscow and Kursk. Dürr stayed in Russia and founded EkoNiva as a farm that grew organic buckwheat and imported Western agricultural machinery and seeds. Today, EkoNiva is the country's largest milk producer and is known as Russia's Milk Empire. A large, vertically integrated dairy producer, with dairy and crop farms across European Russia and Siberia, in 2020 the company was operating production facilities in Voronezh, Kursk, Leningrad, Moscow, Kaluga, Orenburg, Tatarstan, Bashkortostan, Tyumen, Novosibirsk, and Altai.

Subsidies and Cheap Loans

Agriculture Minister Gordeev and Vladimir Putin were well aware that agriculture in the twenty-first century was capital and technology intensive, and they stressed on several occasions that the scarcity of these two resources was the main problem farmers faced in the 1990s. Various types of subsidies to foster rural production thus became the centerpiece of Putin-era agricultural reforms. In the early twenty-first century, subsidies were administered as simple area payments—any farmer who grew crops on a certain amount of acreage was entitled to a nominal per-hectare payment. The state also purchased grain to guarantee a minimum price, shield producers from price volatility, and improve the logistics of the wheat trade.[150] Tax breaks or moratoriums for specific subsectors were also important subsidies for certain targeted sectors. Cherkizovo, for example, noted in its 2015 annual report that it enjoyed a "favorable regulatory environment" and that the company had been exempt from income taxes for nearly a decade.[151] Finally, both regional and federal authorities also invested in agricultural infrastructure, such as irrigation and drainage, as well as in soil monitoring and agronomy research for particular regions.[152]

Subsidized credits were by far the most effective and enduring policy tool used by the government to support technological change in agriculture. In a country with high commercial interest rates, subsidized credit was one of the most important incentives for producers to take on large loans to expand production. The government created Rossel'khozbank, later also known as RusAg, by presidential decree in 2000 to administer subsidized credits. Initially the bank was weakly capitalized, and its lending portfolio was limited. Over the years, it became the most significant lender and insurance provider for several agricultural subsectors. In its first years of operation, loans were mostly directed to farmers in Chechnya as part of the government's attempt to channel funds to the war-torn region. Throughout the decade, the bank received growing capital infusions. By 2010, it had become one of Russia's largest banks in terms of capitalization and had built up a national retail network. The bank also started offering a series of insurance instruments for agriculture that had been difficult to obtain in Russia. By 2018, RusAg extended trillions of rubles of subsidized loans and was the government's main financial institution for the implementation of agricultural support programs.[153] In addition to creating and endowing RusAg, the Putin administration also substantially increased funds for Rosagrosnab and Rosagrolizing—two state-owned entities that lease agricultural machinery to rural producers at subsidized rates.[154]

One of the interesting aspects of Putin-era agricultural subsidies is that, although generous, they were highly targeted, limited in duration, and meant to be used as policy tools to foster particular subsectors. Poultry and pork producers were early beneficiaries. They relied on extensive government support to update facilities and benefited from state-funded breeding programs, to name just the most important examples. Another set of short-term programs sought to smooth out market volatility, such as spikes in feed prices.[155] State support for pork producers was particularly strong. The National Priority Project: Development of the Agro-food Complex supported the (re)construction of 750 pork production facilities in the five years after its adoption. Between 2006 and 2011, the equivalent of $8 billion of state funding supported the upgrading of pig-rearing facilities, according to the Russian Union of Swine Breeders. The state also financed the import of large numbers of purebred piglets from Europe on a few occasions. In 2014, the pork industry received further targeted support payments under a new program, Pork Production Development. These programs all contributed to the adaptation of Russian pig farms to the technological standards prevalent in the US and Western Europe, and rapid expansion of overall production volumes in just a few short years.[156] As the poultry and pork sectors recovered from the collapse of the nineties and became profitable, subsidies shifted to other sectors and subsectors. For example, the state directed funding to research and development aimed at building up livestock genetic resources. State support also shifted to beef and dairy operations, where public and private investments tend to require longer time periods to yield returns. Several other sectors received subsidies—for example, sugar beet and sugar beet mills were targeted in a 2013 policy program that earmarked budget funds to support the "development of the sugar complex of the Russian Federation."[157]

Many Russian agroholdings credit the state's generous subsidies as instrumental for their growth. Miratorg, Russia's largest pork producer, boasted in 2013 that it became a "leading meat market operator" after "[an] investment of 24 billion rubles was supported at the top government level: *Vnesheconombank* provided loan financing for over 20 billion rubles and the loan agreement was signed personally by Vladimir Putin."[158] EkoNiva acknowledges that it benefited greatly from subsidized credits to rapidly expand its dairy facilities and crop farms and equip them with the most technologically advanced milking parlors. In recent years, SberBank and RusAg financed the construction of several new EkoNiva complexes in the Liskinsky, Bobrovsky, and Buturlinovsky districts of Voronezh.[159] Adrian Shairer, an EkoNiva manager, summarized the availability and importance of subsidies as follows: "The Russian government currently grants three types of subsidies to companies in raw milk production: investment grants, soft loans and operating subsidies. Investment grants and soft loans play the most important role for the EkoNiva Group. If these subsidies were no longer paid or were significantly reduced, the growth of the [EkoNiva] Group would cease or continue at a much slower pace."[160]

Unlike Soviet-era subsidies that allocated funds to both strong and weak collective farms to make up for unfavorable climate and remote locations, post-Soviet policies strengthened only the largest actors in each sector. Although subsidies were not explicitly restricted to large corporations, they were structured in a way that benefited them most of all. Subsidized loans in particular favored those enterprises with collateral and ambitious plans to expand production facilities, picking and making "winners" in Russian agriculture. Subsistence producers, small farms, and former collectives in peripheral areas were unable to borrow from banks and could not take advantage of subsidized credits. In the eyes of the state, these farms lacked a future. This dynamic was particularly obvious in the livestock sector, where state support disproportionally favored large, modern livestock operations.[161] A further casualty of the state's favoring of large farms were the kolkhoz markets, roadside stands, and small vendors. These retail outlets of small-scale agriculture in public spaces had been a common sight in the nineties—selling potatoes, kvass, and homemade pastries, for example. In campaigns to crack down on racketeering networks and uphold food safety standards, municipal governments became much more restrictive about small, informal food markets and closed them during Putin's second term in office.[162]

Land Use

Land use patterns during the Putin years were radically transformed by the purchase of vast stretches of Russia's most fertile land by agroholdings, in what Andrew Barnes has called a "radical transformation of asset control in agriculture."[163] This shift, and the consequent consolidation of land ownership by agroholding companies, was facilitated and made possible through political protection and financial support by the federal and regional governments.

The Yeltsin-era architects of privatization had anticipated that it would lead to the breakup of collective farms and decentralization of land ownership. Yet, much like rural production elsewhere in the world, Russian farms became larger, not smaller. Rather than breaking up Soviet-era land assets, agroholdings consolidated land ownership in larger, private farm enterprises. What is important here is that this shift in land ownership followed decades of top-down rural modernization. In other words, Putin was able to hand Russian farmland to agroholdings because Yeltsin had privatized land a decade earlier, and because Stalin had consolidated it into large farms in the 1930. Though land transfers are difficult to track as there is no official data available on them, by all accounts, a handful of new agricultural holding companies controls extremely large farms. A Russian expert estimated in 2014 that around forty companies control landholdings of more than 100,000 hectares each.[164] Rusagro, one of the largest agroholdings, stated in 2014 that its land bank consisted of 460,000 hectares in Russia's Central Black Earth region, which is known for its soil rich in organic matter. By 2018, its land bank had grown to over 670,000, which includes 85,000 hectares in the Far Eastern region of Primorye.[165] Gazprom reportedly holds more than 500,000 hectares of land via an agricultural subsidiary.[166] By 2020, five agroholdings controlled over 500,000 hectares of farmland. Since a Soviet-era kolkhoz tended to farm around 6,000 hectares, the largest agroholdings control and work farmland that is around 80 times larger than a typical Soviet-era collective farm.[167] By 2020 Russia's corporate farms have accumulated truly large landholdings, as table 1.1 indicates.

Note that land consolidation was a geographically uneven outcome. Corporate land holdings are concentrated in Russia's most fertile regions with the

Table 1.1 Russia's five largest landowners and land holdings, 2020

Company	Land holdings	Main commodities
Miratorg	1,047,000 ha	pork, chicken, beef
Prodimex and Agrokultura*	865,000 ha	Prodimex: sugar beets, sugar and grains Agrokultura: wheat, barley, soybeans, sunflower, corn
Agrokomplex	653,000 ha	meat, dairy, vegetable, fruit, rice, sugar, egg, oil
Rusagro	643,000 ha	sugar beets, sugar, pork, oilseeds, veg. oil/fat
EkoNiva	599,000 ha	dairy, seeds, feed grain

*Prodimex and Agrokultura are separate companies but are controlled by the same majority owner.
Sources: Based on information published in *Agroinvestor* and company communications.

highest agricultural yields: they dominate landholding in the Central Black Soil and Volga regions and in the southern provinces.[168] Agricultural production in the Russian Far East has recovered over the last decade or so, initially as a result of Chinese rural migrants who set up small farms and greenhouses. Encouraged by both the Chinese and Russian governments, these small-scale investments were followed by larger capital investments in the first decade of the 2000s and over the years expanded hectares under cultivation, focusing on grains and soy.[169] In the Far East, land acquisitions by private companies were encouraged by a land lease act through which the Russian government sought to encourage companies to move east. In other parts of Russia, agroholdings accumulated land holdings largely through land purchases and long-term leases from the former collective sectors. There have also been reports of illegal appropriations of land shares without the consent of former collective farm members. Many of these cases seem to concern land for oligarchs' private residences in the regions around Moscow.[170]

Uneven trajectories of agricultural development were also in part the result of regional governance. Some governors focused on agricultural development as an important sector of regional economies and matched federal support with regional funds and support programs. This was the case in Belgorod, Voronezh, and Bryansk, for example. Bryansk and Belgorod are the home bases for several of Russia's largest agroholdings. Voronezh is one of Russia's largest sugar beet producers and a productive dairy region. Yevgeny Savchenko, the governor of Belgorod oblast, and his agricultural policies are credited for what is known in the region as the "Belgorod Miracle"—the region's rural recovery;

Savchenko is also known to push agroholdings to provide social services for local communities.[171] Alexey Gordeev, minister of agriculture from 1999 to 2009 and governor of Voronezh oblast from 2009 to 2017, was deeply involved, interested, and personally invested in agricultural development, and dairy farming in particular. Agroholdings in Voronezh benefited in multiple ways from regional support programs, infrastructure updates, and Gordeev's ability to channel federal funds to his region.[172] EkoNiva is thriving in Voronezh, in no small measure helped by a supportive regional administration.

Trade and International Integration

On the one hand, Russia made an overall commitment to free trade in agricultural commodities during the first decade of the 2000s and was aligning trade policies on the whole with the requirements of an anticipated WTO accession. On the other hand, the Putin government also frequently used targeted trade policies as tools to achieve the goals of the food sovereignty agenda. In the early years of the decade, a series of temporary trade quotas were imposed on politically sensitive commodities. Import quotas on American poultry in 2003 followed outrage over the import of large quantities of low-cost chicken parts from the US. These meat products came to be widely known as "Bush-legs" and were officially rejected for having been treated with chlorine. Chickens were at the center of Russian-US trade disputes for years to come, with the two countries engaging in protracted negotiations on quotas, which were routinely lowered on a temporary basis, only to be reimposed again after a few years. Similarly, temporary import restrictions on raw sugar and pork were quite common. Sugar imports were limited through a system of tariffs and quotas that varied annually, adjusted to the volume of sugar beets harvested in Russia and international sugar prices. To prevent imported sugar from underbidding domestically produced sugar, tariffs would be increased when international sugar prices were low and domestic production was high.[173]

The government also occasionally imposed export taxes and even a temporary export ban on grains to ensure sufficient domestic grain stocks and stable prices. The most important case was an export embargo that lasted from August to December 2010, when a historic drought dramatically diminished the harvest and threatened to send food and feed prices soaring. This ban was one of the most contested policy interventions—and an interesting case to illustrate just how important stable domestic prices were for the Putin administration.[174] Although boosting grain exports was important for the Putin government, it was subordinated to the domestic objectives of the food sovereignty agenda. None of these trade restrictions lasted longer than a few months, however. Russia joined the WTO in 2012, and trade restrictions and quotas for meat imports were reduced. Almost immediately, Russian producers were faced with declining prices. Over the two years that followed, the government continued the practices of imposing temporary bans on specific products with reference to sanitation and food safety concerns. In 2014 the Russian government banned the import of live pigs as well as pork and pork products from the EU due to concerns about African swine fever virus.[175]

A more sweeping change in trade regimes came after Russia's annexation of the Crimean Peninsula in March 2014. The US, the EU, and a number of other countries imposed economic sanctions on Russia, targeting Russian companies and individuals, banning visas, freezing assets, and restricting trade of certain Russian financial products and technologies. On August 7, 2014, Russia retaliated with an embargo on agricultural products from the US, Canada, the EU, Norway, and Australia. The embargo banned a long list of food products, including beef, pork, poultry, fish and other seafood, fluid milk, vegetables, fruits, nuts, and various processed foods like sausages and dairy products. Baby food, live animals, seeds, and a number of specialized ingredients for food and animal feed (e.g., minerals and vitamins integral to livestock feed) were excluded from the ban.[176] The fact that agriculture was at the heart of countersanctions confirms that Russia's dependence on imported food was a central concern of the Putin government—that is, the food security agenda was not just another empty rhetorical commitment with goals that were overly ambitious and difficult to realize. Not that rhetoric and public displays of power did not also play a role. The political salience of food security was on display on a few occasions in 2015, when Russia's veterinary authorities (Rosselkhoznadzor) publicly destroyed hundreds of tons of illegally imported Western food.[177] These were highly symbolic policing moves, widely broadcast in Russian and international media. When the embargo was first introduced, it was not clear how it would affect domestic consumption and production. Politicians and economic nationalists argued that it would boost domestic agricultural capacity as domestic production would be substituted for imports. Others doubted the ability of Russian producers to compete with imports from non-affected countries—such as Belarus, Moldova, Brazil, and New Zealand—and argued that the embargo would primarily result in a geographical shift of imports from Europe and the US to these countries.

The ban on products from the US and Western Europe and the food security agenda in general had very real and significant effects on the Russian economy, as the next chapters will detail. This was also made explicit in the political decision to uphold the food embargo after its initial term had expired. Prime Minister Dmitry Medvedev announced in May 2016 that Russia would uphold the embargo until at least the end of 2017, and this decision has been renewed annually since then. The continuation is certainly a response to Western sanctions still in place, and it is likely also intended to further hurt European producers, who have experienced the strongest impacts from the embargo.[178] It was clearly also influenced by domestic political and economic goals. Medvedev in fact referred to the benefits of the embargo to Russian producers when committing to an extension of the food ban in 2017, arguing that it would be helpful to give them a longer time horizon to recoup investments.[179]

Politics and Change in Russian Agriculture

How can we sum up the politics of agriculture under Putin? Over the past twenty years, the Russian government has strategically used agricultural policies as tools to realize the political goal of strengthening domestic producers. In advanced industrial economies, the political economy of agriculture tends to single out institutional structures or lobbies as drivers of generous support measures. Given their enormous landholdings, Russia's corporate farmers have also been called "the Land Barons" and likened to the Latin American Latifundias. Though similar in size, Russian agroholdings' historical role and political position are not comparable to that of corporate lobbies in the US or powerful landowners in Latin America. The politics of agriculture in the Putin years saw a remarkable change in the nature of private actors. When Putin initiated the first set of policies to support rural producers, it can hardly be said that he was influenced by agroholdings or other rural interests. At that point, collective farms were still the largest landowners and rural producers, but they were struggling to survive and were not organized to influence policy in any way. Early accounts of post-Soviet rural reforms had predicted the emergence of a farm manager lobby or an agrarian party that would shape outcomes.[180] Russia did indeed see the creation of an agrarian party, but its influence was negligible, and it failed to reach the 5 percent threshold to make it into the Duma after 1995.[181] Russia's oligarchs were widely considered to be the most powerful actors influencing economic policy, but at least in the nineties, they were scarcely interested in owning and operating farms and poultry plants. Early post-Soviet elites inherited the Soviet-era urban bias, and rural Russia was considered the epitome of "unreformable" backwardness for much of the 1990s. It was thus not the case that corporate or capital interests brought about the recent transformation as preexisting, stable, and organized forces.

That said, agricultural interests have formed over the last twenty years in a policy context that was deliberately designed to strengthen agroholdings. A closer look at timing is critical here. Many of the agroholdings that benefited from the transformation in the early 2000s were not yet formed, or they were focused on food imports. With a few exceptions (mostly food processing companies that had an interest in securing the supply chain), agroholdings emerged *after* 2000.[182] What is more, it took another few years for these economic actors to grow and a few more years for them to organize and form industry associations—that is, to become political actors. A few industry associations were formed in the early 2000s. By 2010, especially in negotiations leading up to Russia's WTO accession, these agricultural actors became vocal political actors. The Russian Grain Union (Rossiiskii Zernovoi Soyuz), the Union of National Dairy Producers (Soiuzmoloko), and the National Union of Swine Breeders (Natsional'nyi Soiuz svinovodov) are all industry associations that have been critical of Putin's reforms and trade policy; they were created in 1994, 2008, and 2009, respectively.[183] Various agroholdings played a well-documented role in the policy to continue the food ban after 2014. EkoNiva's Stefan Dürr, for example, was a vocal supporter of the ban.[184] That said, even though private interests are at stake and played a role, the food sovereignty agenda largely emanated from Russia's federal and regional authorities.

The Putin government's attempts to enlist private actors for its goals is the central element of the political logic of Russian agriculture. Agroholdings benefited from generous public support in the form of subsidies, tax breaks, and trade measures. They are now Russia's largest landowners and have repaid the government by contributing to its political project of strengthening domestic food production and reducing food imports. In turn, agroholdings are under pressure to demonstrate that they in fact contribute to meeting the government's political goals. EkoNiva, like many other agroholdings, very explicitly aligned its expansion with political goals in corporate communications, as the next chapter will document in more detail.[185] For this enlisting logic to work, agroholdings and political leaders at the regional and federal levels cultivated mutually beneficial relationships and informal arrangements, characteristic of Russian state capitalism more broadly. Stefan Dürr has very close connections with federal and regional authorities. In 2017, EkoNiva bought two agricultural companies that belong to politically connected elites: from Nikita Gordeev, Alexey Gordeev's son, he purchased the agricultural holding company OkaAgro with its land assets, and from Yuri Luzhkov, the former mayor of Moscow, the company Moskovo-Medynskovo AP. Finally, Dürr also received several prizes and honors for his contributions to the development of agriculture in Russia and became a Russian citizen in 2014, by a decree personally signed by Putin.[186]

What these close personal connections and the abundant state support make clear is that Putin's reforms are not unlike many Soviet-era reforms. Enlisting a particular group of actors—agroholdings, this time—constituted Putin's attempt to solve the twenty-first-century version of the grain problem. In the face of crisis, Stalin had resorted to sheer violence to force peasants to succumb to his agenda, while Putin is trying the carrot-and-stick approach to enlist oligarchic conglomerates. The carrot, notably, was private ownership of vast stretches of land that Stalin had consolidated in the 1930s. The stick was the threats to property rights that are a characteristic of Russia's post-Soviet economy. So far, this approach has worked in the twenty-first century. What the future of the state-agroholding relationship holds is not yet clear. Political control is notoriously centralized in the presidency in Putin's Russia. Yet agroholdings have potentially amassed leverage vis-à-vis the state through the ownership of vast stretches of arable land, the capacity to produce and export grains and meat, and control over technologies that are necessary to realize the state's domestic and foreign goals.

Both Soviet and post-Soviet governments pursued the political goal of providing plenty for citizens. Achieving this goal, and being recognized for having achieved it, legitimized the authority of the communist party and later President Putin's rule. Citizens are both political subjects and discerning consumers of food who can judge whether or not policies have filled their plates. No wonder, then, that the success and failure of agricultural policies were critical for the paternalistic regimes of the Soviet and post-Soviet region as well as for foreign observers in the US and in the Global South. During the Cold War, the Soviet Union needed to demonstrate the legitimacy of the socialist path to modernity and the viability of a planned economy. In the post-Soviet period, the question turned to the legitimacy of global markets as the ultimate organizing principle of economic activity. Putin departed from the path charted by Yeltsin and turned to deploying a variety of state-directed policy tools, relying on private actors but also subordinating markets and market forces whenever this seemed to be a more direct or promising path to achieving political goals. Whether Putin's state-capitalist agricultural policies succeed or fail, in the short and long run, will affect Russian history and will thus matter for Russian citizens and the global food system.

2

Production

The heart of thirty thousand tractors beats day and night, advertising their powerful beat to the Kuban steppe, mountains and valleys.
—*Ogonek*, 1930

Without exaggeration, we can note that agriculture is undergoing a technological renaissance today.
—D. Iu. Katalevskii and A. Iu. Ivanov, 2018

Agricultural Production: Social Organization and Material Technologies

In 2017, the Russian company Cherkizovo launched a new pig farm in the Lipetsk region, increasing its pork production by over 350,000 head a year. Cherkizovo, already the country's second-largest meat producer, ended up with a pig herd of more than 2 million head by the end of that year.[1] Meanwhile, in March of that same year, 1,327 pigs belonging to small household farms in Irkutsk oblast were slaughtered within three days.[2] This event was precipitated by the death of a pig infected with African Swine Fever (ASF), a lethal disease that rapidly spreads and swiftly kills affected animals. The Irkutsk pigs lived within a five-kilometer zone around the animal that tested positive for Asfivirus, the virus that causes ASF; they were culled as a precautionary measure to prevent the spread of the disease. The expansion of pig herds by vertically integrated agroholdings, and the simultaneous blow to livestock holdings on household farms, is characteristic of the changes that took place in Russia's agrifood system in the first two decades of the twenty-first century. During that period, the domestication of animals in large-scale, technology-intensive, and highly efficient confinement facilities run by private, vertically integrated agricultural companies increased dramatically. Meanwhile, livestock holdings that relied on manual labor and human care on a small, backyard scale dwindled. This was an important change in how pigs are reared, and thus how the pork that reaches Russian tables is produced. It is only the most recent change in how Russian farmers have raised animals and grown crops.

This chapter documents the evolution of *who* farms and raises livestock and *how* they have done so over the last century. We will see that far-reaching, even radical changes in production methods, such as the one described above, are not singular. In 1930, nearly eighty years before the ASF scare, a mass slaughter of animals set the stage for the twentieth century's most consequential transformations of agricultural production. Within a few short months, Russian peasants slaughtered hundreds of thousands of domestic animals on which their very livelihoods depended. These dramatic events happened on the eve of collectivization, as peasants anticipated the knock on their door by the state's agents. Collectivization entailed the pooling of larger livestock—cows, pigs, and sheep—in newly created state-controlled facilities. Rather than turn over their animals, rural families opted to kill and consume them, as this was one of the few ways available to them to resist the state's efforts to take possession of their most valuable assets.[3] Stalin's brutal collectivization deeply traumatized the rural residents, as the previous chapter discussed. It also decimated Soviet livestock herds for a generation: animal holdings on Soviet farms declined from 70.5 million head in 1928 to 38.4 million in 1933, a dramatic fall that affected daily life in both the countryside and cities for decades to come.[4]

How food is produced and *who* produces it—what we could call modes of production and domestication—are central aspects of any food system. This chapter traces the arc of change in production and domestication since 1917. The focus here is on the technology part of Russian agro-technopolitics and also on the social organization of production. These two aspects of agriculture are inextricably linked. Social organization refers to de jure ownership and de facto control of land and rural production—whether the land is owned and farmed by small private landholders, by collective farms, or by agricultural corporations. Major shifts in ownership, from private to collective and back to private, have ushered in consequential changes in technologies that these actors use to grow, harvest, and process proteins, grains, and other food commodities. In no small measure, Stalin collectivized Russian farms to mechanize farming. The tractors that the *Ogonek* author in the chapter's first epigraph hears on the Kuban steppe were fueled, operated, and maintained by collective farm workers. After 1991, Yeltsin reprivatized farms, and Putin handed control of large tracts of Russia's most fertile farmland, including much of Russia's chernozem, to oligarchic agrifood conglomerates, the agroholdings. The "technological renaissance" that the authors of the second quote are concerned with was financed and realized by these agroholdings. In the years between 1930 and 2018, each successive modernization entailed radical reorganizations of the *who* and the *how* of farming.

Despite recurring efforts to modernize agriculture, two distinct modes of production existed side-by-side in Russian agriculture throughout the twentieth century: large-scale industrial and small-scale subsistence farming. Large-scale collective farms were the backbone of industrial agriculture starting in the 1930s. Yet for the remainder of the century, between a quarter and a third of all foodstuffs originated on LPKh farms—the private "subsidiary" or subsistence farms. Subsistence plots shaped the work, byt, and diets of virtually all Soviet residents, and by the end of the twentieth century, nearly every family was in some way or another engaged in or at least connected to somebody growing food. The prevalence of LPKh is an aspect of Soviet agriculture that is overlooked by accounts of the totalizing nature of collective agriculture: though often brutal and universalizing by design, in reality the state's reach did not extend to every field and table, largely because of the failure and shortcomings of planned agriculture. The material technologies and social organization of both types of farms profoundly shaped what was scarce and what was abundant. Although Soviet authorities were hostile toward LPKh, the two forms of production complemented each other and coexisted in a symbiotic relationship throughout the twentieth century.

A second aspect of the changing modes of production that receives special attention in this chapter relates to the global connections of Russian agriculture. Global integration of Russian farming was on the one hand related to bulk commodities, mostly grain. Russia was both an exporter and importer of grains and other commodities. Volumes of each fluctuated depending on local and global harvests and domestic demand. Global integration was always also about knowledge, technology, and skills and about "catching up" with Western farming methods. Russia's rural reforms had the goal of wresting more food from Russia's abundant land: more grains with which to bake bread and feed livestock, more meat with which to improve the protein content of diets, and more sugar with which to sweeten them. These reforms were efforts to update existing farming methods and technologies that were often seen as backward and inefficient compared to those of Western Europe and the US. As the global frontier of technological innovation moved relentlessly, each reform was an attempt to bring cutting-edge technologies to Russian fields and food processing plants. The results never amounted to the simple replication of blueprints invented in the West or the simple application of foreign technologies. They were a combination of domestically forged solutions using imported and adapted foreign technology. Foreign farming technologies met Russian soil, climates, and collective farms, and together they helped set the table.

Importantly, state-sponsored technologies, whether based on foreign or local ones, coexisted all along with the small-scale, labor-intensive private farms in the LPKh sector that relied on local skills and knowledge rather than Western technologies. This chapter shows that the particular forms of this coexistence between large-scale and subsistence agriculture aligned with the evolving agro-technological frontier and modes of global integration. Table 2.1 summarizes the historical evolution of these axes of production. One of the insights we gain from tracing this arc of change throughout the twentieth century is that the Putin years mark a watershed moment, likely as significant and irreversible as Stalin's collectivization in the 1930s. Important and unprecedented changes, marked with a double line in the table, occurred along nearly all the axes of production and global integration. The legal and institutional changes of the Yeltsin years were important precursors for the most recent transformations of rural production, and the nineties brought a dramatic decline in standards of living, but the most consequential changes in terms of rural production followed in the 2000s.

Successes, Failures, and Their Consequences

Changes in the *who* and *how* of production were largely a result of successes and failures of dominant technopolitical regimes. When modernization attempts were successful, new initiatives expanded and deepened the new modes of production and technologies. Soviet-era collective farms, though often criticized for lagging behind capitalist farms in terms of grain yields, did indeed succeed in fulfilling two of the main purposes set out by Lenin and Stalin in the early decades of Soviet rule: they produced increasing volumes of grain and raised enough livestock to adequately feed the Red Army and a growing urban population. Yet Soviet-era technopolitical regimes in agriculture of course did not always succeed. Soviet-era collective farms often struggled to meet plan targets. After World War II, they generally produced enough calories overall but didn't quite manage to produce enough of the foods that Soviet citizens wanted to eat and thought would make them happy. Reliance on LPKh farms was largely a result of the failure of the collective, state-controlled sector. Successes and failures are usually interpreted as victories and losses in the struggle to catch up to or compete with the West. They were, however, just as important for the domestic social, political, and economic consequences they entailed. They affected diets and, in feedback loops that saw policy makers trying to address shortcomings, reshaped future reforms and rural realities. Although long lines and empty shelves in the eighties pointed to mounting problems of collectivized agriculture, they also increasingly signaled that planners were unable to keep their promise of plenty and were thereby contributing to the unraveling of the planned economy and the collapse of the Soviet Union in 1991. Boris Yeltsin's liberalization allowed Russia's rural residents to own land privately for the first time since the 1930s. This step was meant to be a profound transformation of both the social and technological organization of farming. Yet Yeltsin-era legal and political reforms proved to be insufficient to change

Table 2.1 Timeline of changing production technologies and global integration

Timeline:	Stalin		Khrushchev	Brezhnev		Gorbachev	Yeltsin	Putin		
	1930s	1940s	1950s	1960s	1970s	1980s	1990s	2000s	2010s	2020
Social organization of production *(who?)*	collective farms = dominant form of production since 1930 *(privatized, but intact in the 1990s)*							rise of agroholdings		
Subsistence agriculture *(who and how?)*			symbiotic relationship between subsistence and industrial agriculture					subsistence production declines		
Technological frontier *(how?)*			tractors & combines, food processing techs.			ag. chemicals		ag. biotech		
Global integration			technologies imported as blueprints				capital and material technologies from abroad			
	largely autarchic					increasing import dependence		import substitution; grain exports surge		

economic practices on the ground. The technologies, social organization, and global connections of farms only started changing when domestic and international capital investors took an interest in Russian farmland.

These new corporate farms relied on highly capital-intensive forms of farming, and their rise to prominence in the early 2000s had far-reaching consequences. At least five aspects of this most recent change in Russia's agrifood system deserve mention. First, agroholdings have become the most important new landowners. Encouraged by rising prices of land assets and political support, agroholdings sought and gained control of vast stretches of Russia's most fertile farmland. Second, agroholdings have invested in cutting-edge farm and processing technologies, which have made possible sizable increases in production of many of Russia's staple commodities—wheat, sugar beets, and livestock, most notably. The increase in grain production has made Russia the leading global exporter of grain. Agroholdings are thus the main actors in Russia's integration into the global food system—they use technology from across the world, are financed by global sources of capital, and in turn produce grain that is marketed over a hundred countries in all of the world's major regions. Third, in the regions where they operate, agroholdings have redefined rural social relations, unraveling the symbiotic, eighty-year bond between collective and rural subsistence farms. New private owners do not rely on a large labor force in the countryside, as collective farms did. Instead, they prefer to hire highly trained agronomists and seasonal labor at harvest time. Fourth, agroholdings are reshaping Russian diets. And fifth, agroholdings have brought about a shift in how farmers relate to nature. As chapter 1 has already addressed the first aspect, this chapter turns to the second and third, and later chapters address the fourth and fifth points. It bears noting at the outset that despite the broad trends in the development of corporate farms, the recent transformation was quite uneven. Many northern and remote Siberian farms and villagers continued to struggle, receiving little or no investments. Some farms were abandoned, villagers left, and the taiga or forests reclaimed former agricultural land. On other farms, diminishing groups of workers remained, farming at a loss, with outdated machines and under increasingly precarious conditions.

Agricultural Technology and Patterns of Global Integration

The political nature of innovation and technological change in planned economies has long drawn the attention of historians. Economic historians document the ways in which Soviet political priorities shaped the adoption of technologies in the planned economy. Domestic technological innovation was discouraged and lackluster in the Soviet Union, some argued, because no private gain rewarded and incentivized the hard work and genius that it springs from. To the degree that innovation did happen, it remained highly insulated from applied industrial sectors and largely ineffective in bringing about change. The classical formulation of this argument is Joseph Berliner's claim that the planned economy "gave maximal encouragement to decision makers that favor established products and processes, and to discriminate against innovation . . . 'as the devil shies away from incense.'"[5] Alec Nove attributed the avoidance of new designs by Soviet manufacturers to the fear of disruptions and temporary plan underfulfillments, which were generally bad for careers.[6] Loren Graham similarly concluded that "the fatal flaw of the Soviet economy was its inability to create creativity and innovation."[7] While Berliner blamed the lack of incentives from commercial gain for this problem, Graham argued that the dominance of the communist party suffocated the brilliant ideas of Russian scientists outside research labs. One of the case studies that Loren Graham relied on to make this point is Russian genetics and agricultural science. In the 1920s, once world-renowned Russian geneticists were arrested and sent to labor camps, casualties in a struggle with Trofim Lysenko, a scholar favored by Stalin. In Graham's reading, the history of Russian genetics is both a tragedy and a telling example of how the promise of Russian science failed and was then followed by a reliance on Western technologies.[8] Countering this canonical narrative, other historians have documented that in some industries and in other instances, innovation was domestic and effective. Richard Allen, for instance, pointed to Soviet experimentation and innovation in the cement industry, which happened across Russia and "at the plant site" rather than just in research institutes.[9]

Most scholars agree, however, that the Soviet Union did rely on technologies, skills, and knowledge imported and copied from the capitalist West. The appeal of Western, and especially American, agricultural and food processing technologies was indeed powerful for planners concerned with Russia's agricultural backwardness. Throughout the Soviet period, planners sought to copy the most promising tools: tractors and combine harvesters, irrigation systems, and food processing technologies, to name but a few. Despite political hostility and tension between the US and Russia, a great deal of exchange between Soviet and American experts facilitated the transfer of technologies and knowledge throughout the twentieth century. Yet, as appealing as Western technologies appeared, they all were (and had to be) adapted to the political, social, and climatic conditions of farming on the Eurasian steppe. Other Soviet agricultural and food processing technologies and skills were essentially local. This was true for both large-scale collective farms and food processing facilities, as well as for LPKh and home processing. Household production, by its very nature, is based on profoundly local knowledge and domestic technologies, passed down in families over generations. Keeping in mind the importance of subsistence agriculture sheds new light on the still-standard assessment that Russian agriculture is heavily reliant on Western technologies.

The point here is not to adjudicate the weight of either foreign or domestic innovation, nor is it to refute the theses advanced by Berliner and Graham. The history of technological change in Russian agriculture outlined below suggests that although West-to-East flows dominate, technologies and ideas, especially those related to seed technologies and wheat farming, traveled from Russia to the US as well. Throughout the period under discussion, agriculture and food processing technologies were both imported from the West and forged domestically. Both the Soviet and post-Soviet states were deeply involved in fostering technological change. The main argument about technology that emerges from this chapter is that a changing technological frontier connected Russia to the world economy in different ways as these technologies changed over time. In the twenty-first century, new material technologies and knowledge were brought to Russian farms by agroholdings. These technologies, supported and subsidized by the Putin government, were catalysts for tremendous change. They reduced the need for manual labor on farms and hence for human bodies in villages; they changed the relationship between large and small farms; they were the basis for the integration of Russian agricultural production into the global food system; and finally, they changed the relationship between producers, consumers, and their surrounding environment. These are precisely the political, social, and economic consequences of changing agro-technopolitical regimes that this book traces.

SOVIET AGRICULTURAL PRODUCTION

Soviet-Era Collective Farms

Starting in spring 1917, Russian peasants seized control of noble estates and church land in anticipation of the revolutionary changes that transformed Russia later that year. When the Bolshevik government took power, the sweeping Decree on Land ratified these actions through the nationalization of land that transferred ownership rights to the state and use rights to peasants.[10] Realizing Lenin's promise of land for all thus merely affirmed changes on the ground that had already taken place. In stark contrast, the other half of the socialist promise, bread for all, turned out to be a far more protracted challenge.[11] The state's attempts to control the production, collection, and distribution of grain and bread faced numerous obstacles during the tumultuous first postrevolutionary decade. During the Civil War, the state resorted to forced requisitions to extract grain and other food crops from peasants. The New Economic Policy (NEP) tried to replace violence with monetary incentives. Such incentives, however, largely failed to have the desired effect because peasants had little reason to hand over grain to state procurement officers. The young country experienced a series of devastating famines and chronic food shortages, and almost all Russians struggled to feed themselves during this time. Although land was nationalized and ownership was formally "public," rural production remained firmly within the purview of rural households and communes, who decided autonomously what to grow and whom to sell to. The disruption of rural production brought about by World War I, the Bolshevik Revolution, the nationalization of land, the Civil War, and the onset of NEP meant that Russia's peasants overall grew far less grain.[12] For much of the 1920s, the Bolshevik government sent agents to the countryside to coax or force peasants to grow more grain with new methods, but these efforts mostly failed to enlist peasants for the cause of rural modernization. More often than not, peasant farmers opted either to produce for subsistence only or to sell what they grew on black markets, where higher prices rewarded those taking the risk of evading state agents.

If there was one event in the twentieth century that most radically and lastingly changed how food was produced in Russia, it was Stalin's forced collectivization. Collectivization was the founding moment of a system of production that combined resource extraction with political control of peasants. It created state farms (sovkhozy) and collective farms (kolkhozy), and the resulting social organization of farming remained in place throughout the twentieth century. Sovkhozy were formed from large landed estates, while kolkhozy resulted from the aggregation of smaller plots of land that had previously been privately or commonly owned. The drive to collectivize farms effectively expropriated the Russian peasantry, and millions of skilled farmers died or were forced to migrate. Invaluable inputs and skills were lost, seeds were not sown, and harvests were not reaped. The slaughter of livestock ahead of collectivization was also devastating. In the Central Black Earth region, 25 percent of cattle, 53 percent of pigs, 55 percent of sheep, and 40 percent of chickens were slaughtered in the first three months of 1930 alone.[13] Even the animals that survived were in jeopardy as new collective farms still lacked the facilities to appropriately care for them all. After collectivization was complete, the Soviet Union's livestock herd was diminished by half.[14] The remaining peasant population was traumatized, and rural recovery was slow and painful. Despite their catastrophic beginnings, collective farms became the organizational form that dominated economic, social, and political life in the Soviet countryside. The new social organization of the collective farm transferred control of agriculture to the state and the planning bureaucracy. Party officials set priorities, and bureaucrats devised plans to realize them. Decisions on what to plant, where, when, and how were made elsewhere. At the same time, collective farms had very little or no control over tools, machines, and other inputs, and throughout the Soviet period, collective farms struggled to fulfill the many demands placed on them. Naum Jasny called kolkhozy the "Achilles Heel of the Soviet regime."[15]

Nevertheless, collective farms produced most of the country's grains, sugar beets, and oilseeds as well as much of the fish, meat, milk, and eggs that fueled Soviet modernization, industrialization, and urbanization. They played an enormously important role in placing food on Soviet tables, even while shortages of some goods and low yields overall were a vexing source of concern for successive Soviet governments. Collective farms grew many types of food and industrial crops and raised livestock for meat, dairy, eggs, and wool. Across the very large and extremely diverse geographical expanse of the Soviet Union's territory, the types of crops and animals varied considerably. The Chernozem was the Soviet Union's most fertile region for field crops, especially wheat and other grains. There were more apple orchards in the Ukrainian SSR than anywhere else in the region. Central Asia's lowland deserts were ideal for extensive grazing. Soviet fish farms thrived in the Black and Caspian seas.[16] Murmansk and other regions in the Far North were the home of Soviet-era reindeer collective farms. Map 2.1 shows the main agricultural commodities across the Soviet Union.[17] Overall, the most important commodities that Soviet-era collective farms produced were always grains. Milled into flour and baked into bread, or grown as livestock feed and turned into meat, grains were destined for the cafeterias and kitchens of the Soviet Union's growing industrial workforce. The most common cereal crops were wheat, rye, oats, barley, and buckwheat. Wheat varieties became the Soviet Union's most common field crops, with winter wheat planted mostly in European Russia and the south, and spring wheat in Siberia, Central Asia, and the Far East.[18] Rye declined in the postwar decades to make room for wheat, while barley's position remained stable, and relatively high in Russia compared to the US, as it was the main animal feed and was also used for brewing beer.[19] Corn, millet, and rice were also grown, but in far lower quantities than the other grains. Despite Khrushchev's efforts, corn never thrived in the Soviet Union as it did in the US. Sugar beets, sunflower seeds, cotton, and flax were among the main industrial crops grown on Soviet collective farms. Livestock collective farms raised animals for pork, beef, veal, lamb, goat, and even reindeer meat.[20] Eggs and wool were also produced on a large scale.[21] In the decades after World War II, the Soviet fishing industry caught ever-larger quantities of fish, primarily in open ocean fishing grounds but also on collective fish farms.

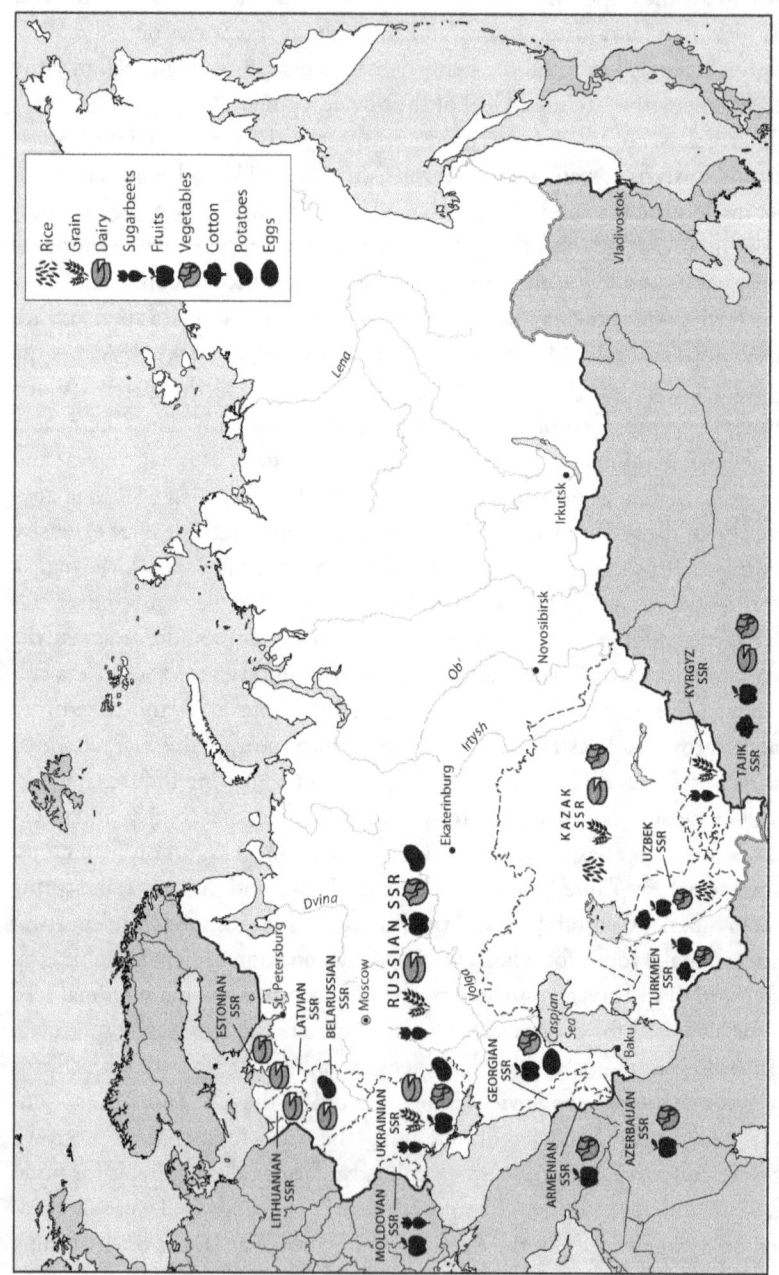

Map 2.1 Agricultural production in Soviet Republics, 1980s, based on data by Gosudarstvennyi komitet SSSR po statistike.

Soviet rural producers had strong but varied attachments to the land, and the struggles first to collectivize and then to manage farming and peasant life proceeded in different ways across the country. Yet rural production everywhere was profoundly shaped by central directives. After collectivization, authorities were intent on controlling collective farms and on keeping rural workers, their families, and livestock *in place*. They achieved this through various mechanisms, some brutal, and others bureaucratic, as chapter 1 introduced. Although the Soviet Union urbanized over the course of the twentieth century, as did Western Europe, a higher proportion of Soviet citizens remained in the countryside than in countries of the capitalist West.[22] Depending on how the rural labor force is calculated, about 24 percent of the labor force participated in agricultural labor in 1974; in the US, the rural labor force had already dropped below 5 percent at that time. Jenny Leigh Smith's history of Soviet livestock rearing shows that collective farms employed far more human caretakers of animals than we see in livestock operations of capitalist countries.[23] In fact, for decades, Soviet peasants were not allowed to obtain internal passports and residency permits to migrate to cities with better living conditions (although the propiska system was not as watertight as authorities intended it to be).[24] Employing rural populations was thus a central task of Soviet farming (see figure 2.1).

The technological frontier on Russian farms changed continuously and significantly but remained labor intensive throughout the twentieth century. The

Figure 2.1 Collective farm workers during harvest, 1944. TASS.

mechanization of farms that followed collectivization was the first major shift in Soviet-era farming. The mass destruction of livestock, and of horses in particular, had left the new collective farms with far too little horse power to fulfill the ambitious procurement targets.[25] In 1928, Russian peasants owned 33 million horses. By the end of 1932, new collective farms housed only 12 million horses.[26] The Stalin-era campaign to accelerate rural production was thus premised first and foremost on bringing tractors to the countryside. Mechanization in the thirties and forties was meant to replace the work of horses with that of tractors, trucks, and combines. The state's main tool to do this was the Machine Tractor Stations (MTS), centralized equipment depots built to supply farms with tractors, trucks, ploughs, horses, and expertise.[27] A network of such stations was created in the early thirties and grew rapidly in the years that followed. By the end of the decade, the MTS network claimed to service 94 percent of all collective farms. MTS were meant to pool capital-intensive machinery and allow their use by several farms. In reality, pooling was less than smooth, as many observers have pointed out, and horses continued to play a role in the Soviet village for many years to come, especially outside the Chernozem. Nevertheless, the number of farm machines involved in Soviet farming increased dramatically in those years: tractors increased from 18,000 in 1928 to 684,000 in 1940. The number of grain combines increased from 2,000 to 182,000, and the number of trucks from 700 to 228,000 during the same twelve years.[28] By 1940, collective farms were "mechanized," at least officially, and had access to the trucks, tractors, and combines needed for transport, ploughing, and harvesting.

Throughout the early decades of Soviet rural reforms, farms adopted technologies that were already well established in Western capitalist countries.[29] Deborah Fitzgerald documents how this technology transfer was made possible and went along with a great deal of exchange between American agro-technical experts and their Soviet counterparts. American agronomists and company representatives from Ford, General Electric, and Caterpillar were sent to share advances in cutting-edge farm machinery and to help "Americanize" collective farms, but they also came back with new ideas about large-scale farming, especially of wheat—Russia's most productive crop.[30] Soviet planners were deeply enamored with Henry Ford and Fredrick Taylor's innovation in factory management, and Henry Ford in turn took great interest in Soviet industrialization. The Soviet Union purchased twenty-five thousand Fordson tractors, and Ford helped found the Soviet Union's first tractor factory outside Leningrad in the mid-twenties.[31] In 1929, a delegation of Soviet agriculturalists visited the Campbell Farming Cooperation in Montana. Late adoption of foreign technologies was nothing new for Russian farms and industry, and as in earlier instances, twentieth-century technologies performed differently in Eurasian soil. For example, the iron plough (*plug*) replaced the wooden one (*sokha*) in Russia in the late nineteenth century, well after English farms had made this shift. The adoption of the plug greatly reduced labor input and therefore increased imperial Russia's wheat production. Yet it also relied on the use of more draft animals and therefore larger quantities of feed throughout the year—no small challenge in Russia, given the country's long and cold winters.[32] In a similar fashion, mechanization and the increasing use of agricultural machinery in the twentieth century solved some problems but created others. The combine harvesters modeled on Western agricultural machinery, for example, allowed for significantly higher wheat yields. They were less helpful for other grains. In the postwar decades, wheat increasingly replaced winter rye, a traditional Russian crop used for rye bread, even though rye had excellent nutritional qualities and was widely considered an ideal crop for Russia's climate. A much taller and stronger crop than wheat, rye was traditionally harvested either with hand-held scythes or horse-powered mowers. The combines designed to harvest wheat flattened rye; hence, as harvesters became more common, rye gave way to wheat.[33] New technologies changed not only how crops were raised but also which crops were favored.

World War II interrupted technological change in the countryside as the state's attention had turned to more urgent threats. Postwar reconstruction had to make up for lost years and repair and restock farm machinery that had been neglected or destroyed during the war. In the long run, the mechanization of farming in the Stalin era was deemed a success. When Nikita Khrushchev sought to address the problems related to arbitrary production quotas and rural coercion, he looked to expand the use of technologies and introduce new methods and tools that had revolutionized farming in capitalist countries. Khrushchev set his eyes on planting and reaping more field crops than ever, even more than the US, the Soviet Union's Cold War rival, by further intensifying cultivation and expanding the area under cultivation, largely by tilling the vast steppe of northern Kazakhstan and Siberia with a growing fleet of agricultural machinery.[34] This expansion would not have been possible without the forced settling and collectivization of Central Asian nomadic societies in the twenties and thirties. In a profound and traumatic shift in the social organization of domestication in this region, hundreds of new collective farms were created.[35] Khrushchev's reforms pushed Stalin's modernization forward with a huge influx of agricultural machinery. By the mid-fifties, 50,000 tractors, 6,000 trucks, and a host of other machinery had been supplied to Central Asian Republics.[36] The iconic imagery of the time shows rows of tractors and harvesters at work on the flat arid steppe. The sheer size of the land newly tilled and cultivated was astonishing. By the early sixties, the Virgin Lands Campaign expanded the Soviet Union's arable land by 32 million acres, an area roughly the size of Canada's arable land at that time. Soviet collective farms initially harvested a great deal more wheat during these years: wheat production increased from 42.6 million hectares in 1952 to 66.6 million by 1965.[37] This increase in production was an indicator of success, at least for some time. Corn production, famously, increased as well: from 4.4 million hectares to 5.9 million during the same period. This was the main thrust and the material manifestation of Khrushchev's intention to create a Soviet corn belt to mirror the American Midwest.

Khrushchev also wanted to imitate American levels of meat production. In 1953, Soviet livestock herds had barely recovered from the twin catastrophes of collectivization and World War II, and that meant little meat was available for Soviet tables. In an attempt to increase state production and procurement of meat, Khrushchev initiated a series of measures that restricted private livestock holdings. "Private animals" were deemed to divert too much grain from collective livestock farms. Although they did contribute to the protein content of Russian diets, they did not register in official statistics on Soviet livestock herds and could not be counted as achievements of the planned economy. In 1958, Khrushchev issued orders to restrict how much fodder could be given to LPKh farms. Animals from backyards were seized and handed over to collective farms to bolster headcounts of collective herds. The immediate result of this policy was the following: collective animal operations grew, but the number of animals preemptively slaughtered by incensed peasants also increased—repeating the pattern of peasant-state interaction during collectivization. Collective farms also ended up with more animals than fodder. Due to chronic feed shortages, many animals starved or fell ill. The year 1963 was one of meagre grain harvests, and planners were left scrambling to find even a minimum of feed to keep animals alive. Collective farms were forced to reduce livestock holdings again, reversing the apparent gains in headcounts of only a few years earlier.[38]

Production on collective farms thus continued to be shaped decisively by political priorities and the successes and failures of the technologies employed to realize them. Over time, it became clear that some goals were attainable and indeed profoundly changed practices and crops in this period. Others were too ambitious and unrealistic, did not resolve old problems, or generated new ones. Khrushchev's achievements in grain output were partly, or even mostly, reversed by the mid-seventies. The tilling of fragile steppe ecosystems had disastrous environmental consequences as soils eroded quickly. By 1975, the area under cultivation with corn contracted to 2.6 million hectares, from

5.9 million in 1965.[39] The area dedicated to wheat production also shrank: by 1985, it was grown on only 50.2 million hectares, though wheat yields on the most suitable soils improved in the 1970s. Soviet-era collective farms struggled with a number of problems that reflected the more general coordination issues characteristic of the Soviet planned economy. Chief among them were inconsistencies between production plans and supply plans: it was common that aggregate output targets did not match plans for labor, wages, and other inputs. While collective farm output targets specified the amount of wheat and potatoes to be grown, kolkhozniki often did not receive enough seeds to meet the targets, lacked fuel or spare parts for machinery, or perhaps had no bags to store the grain upon harvest. As the economy grew and became more complex in the postwar decades, these problems became more serious.[40]

Fresh fruits and vegetables are a case in point as they are a vital and desired element of any diet but are also fragile and perishable. Potatoes, for example, challenged the logistics of the planned economy. Tubers were relatively heavy and thus costly to transport. They were also harvested late in the fall, leaving very little time for transport before winter frosts spoiled the crops. The state procurement system had few temperature-controlled storage facilities and railcars, making it difficult to transport potatoes to stores without spoilage. (Most of the potatoes shipped by rail were destined for vodka factories, where it didn't matter that they had been frozen along the way.) Cabbage, the least fragile and fussy vegetable, made up most of the vegetables planted in the collective sector. Unlike more delicate crops, cabbage could handle frosts and rough handling en route to consumers, who largely turned it into soup or sauerkraut.[41] Soviet planners also had trouble adjusting to fluctuations in the harvested quantities of highly perishable fruits and vegetables. While shortages are an obvious and well-known problem, an abundant harvest could sometimes present just as much of a conundrum for planners. Orchards and vineyards illustrate both sides of the challenge of an unpredictable harvest: in some years, a bad grape or fruit harvest created challenges for downstream industries, while in other years, producers did not know what to do with an oversupply of nature's bounty. Fresh fruits, in fact, were always in relatively short supply in stores, even in years of bumper harvests. For example, in the mid-sixties, during two years of overabundant plum and apple yields, kolkhozniki in the Western Ukrainian village of Khmil'nyk dried the fruits to preserve their value, but still much of the harvest went to waste. They received letters from as far away as Altai asking for the fruit, but they found that procurement officials were not interested in transporting it. By themselves, Ukrainian kolkhozniki had no way to move them to other parts of the Soviet Union. Similarly, in Gomel, a region in Belarus, thousands of pounds of apples, melons, pumpkins, and cabbages were fed to farm animals although in the same province stores had none of these fruits and vegetables to sell.[42] Abundant harvests are a challenge for all agricultural systems. In market economies they drive down prices, and in planned economies they expose the weaknesses of a system badly equipped to deal with fluctuations. Not only was transport a challenge, plans in downstream industries could not be easily adjusted. In one sense, fruit's fragility and variability is a kind of natural resistance to planners' intentions of shipping them across a large country. Similarly, an overabundant harvest effectively resists planning that tries to calculate quantities for industrial production.

Soviet planners came up with and borrowed new technological solutions to old problems in the sixties and seventies. The problem of perishability had to be solved with technologies that could arrest the biophysical cycles of decay.[43] New production systems and technologies were introduced to catch more fish and raise more pork. For example, new technologies made it easier to refine sugar from beets and provide more and better sugar to the Soviet food processing industry. Soviet planners had been trying to increase pork production since the thirties but had repeatedly failed because of wartime disruptions and the lack of treatments for sick and undernourished animals. After World War II, new hog farming methods led to a dramatic increase of pork production. Jenny Leigh Smith shows that central to the success of the postwar pork industry was the creation of a new cohort of skilled animal tenders, the *svinarki*—rural women who were trained and in charge of animal care. The svinarki not only supervised feeding and nursed runty piglets; they recorded detailed information on diets, growth, and disease, invaluable knowledge for pig breeders.[44] In the late 1960s and 1970s, the Soviet Union also invested heavily in updating its fleet of trawlers and sea-bound processing plants, contributing to steady and healthy growth in the fishing industry.[45] Herring was the most commonly caught fish until the 1970s, when cod caught up. Pickled herring and frozen cod were widely available as a result. Salmon, tuna, and sturgeon catches also increased in the seventies, but these fish were still much scarcer than cod and herring. Fishing was one of the untold success stories of Soviet-era food production. The state managed to increase catches, making frozen or canned fish the most readily available proteins in the Soviet Union. The expansion of fishing also involved the construction of canning factories and fish farms, even if most fish was wild-caught in open waters. Finally, the fish industry thrived without the large state subsidies that flowed to the livestock sector.[46] Figure 2.2 shows work on a canning floor of a fish collective farm.

While pork and fish production succeeded in notable ways, centrally planned agriculture had a hard time solving other problems. Fruits were not the only perishable items that created difficulties for planners. Fresh fluid milk presented

Figure 2.2 Sprats and workers at the S. Kirov Fish Collective Farm, Estonian SSR, 1972. Yuri Belinsky/TASS.

its own problems in getting to the consumer. Refrigeration technology remained relatively expensive and scarce, and although refrigerated warehouses became more common, refrigerated trucks and railcars did not.[47] Soviet food processing technology also has a history of successes and challenges that is distinct from, though inherently related to, those of collective farms. In general, food processing received far less attention and far fewer resources overall compared to either farms or heavy industry. Considered a branch of light industry, it ranked fairly low in the hierarchy of the Soviet planned economy. Nevertheless, Soviet planners at times formulated quite ambitious plans for certain high-prestige projects of the food processing industry. In the early postrevolutionary years, for example, Leningrad bakeries pioneered a new model for bread production—a bread processing line that proceeded in a circular spiral in a multistory, purpose-built factory. Ingredients were hauled to the top floor, and the bread took shape as it was processed and moved downward, until perfect loaves, ready to be shipped to bakeries, popped out on the ground floor.[48] Jukka Gronow documents that under Stalin, certain affordable luxuries such as champagne and chocolates were considered essential. This meant that planners and bureaucrats supported producers of these goods with funds and political attention.

Some foreign observers argued that the Soviet processing industry had compelling reasons to avoid new methods and novel products; they disrupt existing plans and falter in the face of input shortages.[49] At the same time, it did not escape Soviet planners that consumers desired novel and high-quality food items. The need to make available new and appealing food items provided the impetus for a number of Soviet-era processing innovations and adaptations of Western technologies. Many of the Soviet Union's processing accomplishments were spearheaded by Anastas Mikoyan—a Leninist revolutionary and minister of foreign trade under Stalin. On trips to the US in the 1930s, Mikoyan's excitement was kindled by hamburgers, sandwiches, ketchup, cornflakes, and ice cream, as well as processing innovations that he tried to bring to the Soviet Union.[50] By the seventies, Soviet planners were also willing to allow iconic Western processed foods for domestic consumption. In a 1972 deal between the Soviet government and PepsiCo, Pepsi was allowed to bottle and market its trademark sugary soda in the Soviet Union starting in 1974, in exchange for distributing Stolichnaya Vodka in the US market.[51] Successful food processing technologies of earlier decades included canning and freezing, which helped preserve fresh products at low cost and send them along their sometimes long and windy ways through the procurement system. Other food processing technologies were the products of indigenous ingenuity. This was the case for Soviet champagne, an industry built on a 1928 invention of a

Soviet chemistry graduate, who had devised a way to ferment sparkling wine in large tanks instead of in individual bottles, significantly reducing costs.[52] Despite these efforts to improve the availability of processed food with foreign and domestic technologies, the gap between what Soviet stores stocked and the appetites of an urbanizing population widened over time. On the one hand, this was the result of shortages of goods in high demand that became more acute over time. By the late Soviet decades, urban citizens were eating more varied proteins and carbohydrates, while taking low prices for all food items for granted. But they also wanted more high-quality food, both processed and fresh, and were unhappy about the flaws of, say, overly starchy macaroni and other noodles. Even the expectations of bread quality had risen, and many consumers found fault with baked products.[53]

Leonid Brezhnev, like Khrushchev before him, tried to increase the availability of meat as a way to satisfy the appetites of urban consumers. He paid bonuses to farms that increased livestock herds as demanded by plan targets. While meat production did indeed increase, growing livestock herds again threatened to outpace the ability of collective farms to produce feed grains and other vital components of livestock diets.[54] Brezhnev ordered a shift in production from grains to forage crops and increased the use of fertilizer to deal with this problem. The "chemicalization" of agriculture under Brezhnev led to vastly expanded deliveries of mineral fertilizers to collective farms, from 2 million tons in 1965 to 82 million tons in 1980.[55] While more grains and fodder were produced as a result of Brezhnev's intensification of production, collective farms still did not produce enough animal feed and grains. To make up for the gap, the Soviet Union came to increasingly rely on imported grain and livestock feed, exchanging hydrocarbon revenues for grain. Soviet grain purchases accounted for about 20 percent of all world grain during the seventies.[56] The larger story about Brezhnev-era agro-technopolitics is that the inability of collective farms to grow enough feed grains decisively shaped the pattern of the Soviet economy's global integration.

Brezhnev-era rural policies had noticeable effects on urban diets and were also meant to improve rural life and infrastructure. Rural residents were better connected through new roads and received new schools and cultural centers. At the same time, work on the kolkhoz and everyday realities in the countryside continued to be hard, and many rural citizens sought ways to leave their villages. After Stalin-era population controls were loosened, many Russians left their villages. The pace of outmigration from rural areas picked up in the late seventies and eighties, especially from the least fertile regions of Russia. Gorbachev's perestroika barely reached villages, and rural citizens took advantage of new opportunities in cities.[57] By the end of the Soviet period, outmigration had decimated many villages, leaving behind impoverished and mostly elderly people. The Soviet rural population shrank by 30 percent between 1959 and 1989. An average village in the less fertile northern and central regions lost close to half of its population.[58] The 1989 census also reveals a stunning fact about just how small the tiny remnants became: 20 percent of Russian villages were inhabited by fewer than 10 people, and many rural dwellings were single-person households.[59] Accelerating rural-urban migration meant that collective farms were rapidly losing their most critical resource—labor.[60] This then set the stage for the collapse of Russian agriculture in the early nineties, documented below.

Soviet-Era Private Farming and Subsistence Plots

No account of Soviet agriculture is complete without attention to subsistence production—the informal food economy. Household plots played an important role in feeding Soviet citizens; they contributed to keeping peasants in the countryside and on collective farms. Food produced on state farms was supplemented by the flexible, decentralized, low-technology and labor-intensive mode of production in the LPKh sector. Collective farm workers were allowed to farm small areas adjacent to rural dwellings or in plots (ogorody), and urban residents had access to shared gardens or dacha plots (see figure 2.3 for an urban garden plot in Petropavlovsk-Kamchatsky). LPKh farms were especially vital lifelines during the Stalin years, when peasants were barely paid for giving up most of their harvest to the state procurement agents. Before the introduction of a compulsory minimum wage in the sixties, kolkhozniki were paid only once during harvest times. For the first decades after collectivization, rural Russians kept plots as a means of survival. Products from LPKh plots also made it to cities via family connections and black markets. Though planners rejected small-scale production and trade as ideologically alien, they had been accepted as a necessary and temporary "social evil."[61] During World War II, the Soviet army encouraged military units to set up their own gardens to improve food supplies for troops stationed at army bases. While at the front, the army encouraged soldiers to forage for food and turn to rural private plots for additional provisions.[62]

Farming on personal plots was labor intensive and done with little capital. This labor was performed by extended rural families, especially by women, the elderly, and the young. One of the many overlooked aspects of private subsistence farming is that labor was largely female. According to Karl-Eugen Wädekin, 90 percent of the labor force on subsistence farms consisted of women and older members of a household.[63] In other words, Soviet women kept everyone fed and cared for the animals that supplied fresh meat, dairy, fruits, and vegetables. Backyard farms and dacha plots were capital scarce because the state was uninterested in providing tools or expending resources of any kind on this sector. Even elementary farm implements, like shovels and scythes, were said to be of poor quality and hard to obtain.[64] For better or worse, subsistence production was subjected to none of the state-sponsored modernization, mechanization, fertilizer application, and prescribed changes in crop rotation. Livestock grazed on communal pastures and were fed hay from marginal soils or grain and turnips diverted from collective farms rather than composite feeds. Cows were milked by hand, not in mechanized milking parlors, and slaughtered in backyards, not in dedicated facilities. Subsistence plots were tiny compared to collective farms, typically around 0.2–0.5 hectares. Limits on the size of private plots changed over time and varied across regions. In the 1950s, their size was reduced to 0.03–0.05 hectares, although this change was later denounced as "excessive implementation of official policy" and gradually reversed. Retired army cadres received larger allotments.[65] Though only about 3 percent of arable land was worked in this way, much of the potatoes, meat, milk, and eggs—as well as vegetables, fruits, and honey—came from these farms and fed a large share of Soviet citizens.

Figure 2.3 Backyard plot, Petropavlovsk-Kamchatskii, Kamchatka, October 2007. Photo by E. Jay Rehm.

This kind of farming could be thought of as a form of resistance to the state's attempts to control agriculture and the food supply, a kind of social response to failures of the Soviet-era centrally planned food system, the dominant agrotechnopolitical regime. Yet, while the two modes of farming—collective and private farming—differed in many ways, they were also mutually dependent and interacted in multiple ways. Many, if not most, of household farms' inputs were obtained via the collective sector, through either formal or informal channels. Workers were often paid in kind rather than in cash wages for work on collective farms—this is how private farms obtained grain and hay for animal feed, as well as young animals. One of the ways in which Khrushchev cracked down on private farms was via a ban on fodder for privately owned livestock, which made it virtually impossible to (legally) feed a backyard cow. Kolkhozniki also bartered for (or sometimes stole) goods and services. Workers would borrow tools, state farm veterinarians would lend a hand when cattle were sick, horses would be borrowed from the collective sector for the harvest and transport of private crops, and tractor drivers would moonlight on private plots. Indeed, the line between what belonged to the collective farm and what was available for private use was often a blurry one. Subsistence farming relied on a whole range of infrastructure—water, roads, and electricity—that were all secured via the collective farm.[66]

Collective farms also relied on LPKh for their survival. Subsistence farming quite literally sustained the labor of collective farms; without these plots, peasants would have starved or left as soon as they could safely do so.[67] In the fifties and sixties, collective farms often relied on the household sector to rear animals and help meet plan targets for meat. Until 1958, private plots were subject to compulsory procurements and had to regularly give up calves and piglets to state farms. By the 1960s, some households entered a semiformal system of contracts with collective farms, by which the households were ordered to fatten young animals for the collective farm in return for allocations of feed.[68] The relationship between collective and subsistence farms changed and varied over time but remained a symbiotic one shaped by the exigencies of the planned economy.[69] While some observers described Soviet collective farms as black holes that sucked up a growing stream of resources, clearly some of these resources were put to excellent use on private plots.

LPKh's share of total production waxed and waned over the years. Just how much food originated in backyard farms also varied greatly for different products and regions. A rough and relatively conservative estimate is that between a quarter and a third of all food produced in the Soviet Union stemmed from these small-scale personal plots. For some foods, the share was much larger: the majority of potatoes and most goat meat, milk, and cheese, for example, were the products of private farming. Generally, the more perishable and fragile a product, the more likely it was to be produced privately. Vegetables, berries and other fruits mostly originated on subsistence farms or were gathered in the wild. Hunting and fishing added proteins to diets. Backyard livestock holdings were an important part of household production as stores in rural areas only rarely supplied meat, milk, butter, or eggs. In Stalin's Russia, backyard goats were common and outnumbered pigs. Feed was scarce, and goats are able to survive on almost anything. Starting in the late fifties, the number of goats declined as families found enough scraps to feed pigs, sheep, and sometimes even cows.[70] Small livestock, such as rabbits and hens, were also common. In the 1960s, roughly half of all domestic animals were raised in rural and suburban backyards.[71] Strict rules limited the number of cows, pigs, and sheep that could be tended. Under Khrushchev, each household was allowed "one cow with a calf up to one year of age, one heifer or bull up to two years of age, one sow with pigs up to three months of age, or two hogs that are being fattened, up to ten sheep and goats (combined), beehives, poultry and honey."[72] Notably, the state did not place restrictions on the number of rabbits and the size of chicken flocks as these smaller animals consumed less feed and did not compete with collective herds for scarce grain.

Subsistence production varied greatly across regions. The more marginal an area, the more likely its residents were to survive by the fruits of their labor on private plots. In the central and northwestern regions, household farms were on average less prevalent as these regions were better provisioned by the planned economy. Subsistence farming was more common in the south—the Chernozem and the Caucasus, regions with soils and climates most conducive for farming—as well as in the more distant regions, such as Siberia and the Far East, where the state-directed provisions petered out.[73] Somewhere around a quarter of all meat—often more, sometimes less—stemmed from animals raised

Table 2.2 Share of Soviet food production from household farms

	1950	*1965*	*1985*
Potatoes	61%	44%	60%
Vegetables	24%	12%	29%
Meat	47%	17%	28%
Eggs	74%	37%	28%
Wool	16%	14%	26%

Sources: Karl-Eugen Wädekin, *Privatproduzenten in der sowjetischen Landwirtschaft* (1967), 96; Stefan Hedlund, *Private Agriculture in the Soviet Union* (1989), 28.

by households. Wädekin shows that overall household farms accounted for a significant share of output (see table 2.2).

Subsistence farming was important not only for villagers but also for city residents. A large share of potatoes and other vegetables consumed by urbanites were planted on dacha plots. Wädekin estimates that 31 percent of all potatoes, 18 percent of vegetables, 20 percent of milk, 37 percent of eggs, and 14 percent of meat consumed by urban residents stemmed from these types of farms in the 1960s.[74] Despite rapid urbanization in the postwar decades, many Soviet citizens thus engaged in small-scale farming. An observation made by Wädekin in 1964 about the village Kulebaki is telling here (the village was located in Gorki province, in the country's industrial heartland):

> This small city has 50,000 inhabitants, and there are 7,500 individual houses with adjacent plots of 6–8 are [600–800 square meters], 1,400 cows, several thousand pigs, several thousand sheep, over ten thousand chickens and geese, 37,000 fruit trees (before the war there were more, but they were chopped down, new ones were planted after the war). . . . As we see, not only do several thousand metal workers live in this city, there are also over seven thousand people who own and work plots, which produce not only vegetables and fruit, but also livestock.[75]

Finally, in addition to private production, other forms of "subsidiary production" (podsobnoe khoziaistvo) provided food. Especially in the late Soviet period, enterprises were encouraged to maintain their own gardens and farms to supply cafeterias with high-quality and fresh food. The army and navy, too, increased funds for dedicated farms to feed officers and soldiers alike.[76] Although these were considered "subsidiary" agriculture, these farms were maintained by dedicated army and factory staff and in fact were often quite large.

Agricultural Production in Post-Soviet Russia

In 1991, the Russian Federation inherited the technologies and social organization of rural production that had been in place for decades. For all its flaws, this way of organizing food production had underpinned the Soviet Union's war efforts and adequately fed the Soviet Union's roughly 280 million citizens in cities and villages. Yet it was the failures, inefficiencies, and shortcomings of collective farms that dominated the reform plans of the 1980s and 1990s. We saw in the previous chapter that Gorbachev's rural reforms tried to give collective farms more autonomy and that Yeltsin's reforms envisioned kolkhozniki taking over their shares of former collective land. Both reformers, however, neglected the vital role of small-scale backyard farms, even as these forms of agriculture once again served as vital insurance against hunger in the late eighties and nineties.

The underlying rationale of Yeltsin's rural reforms was that privatization would allow farmers to use land as a productive asset, thereby creating the conditions for a new class of private farmers to flourish. Reformers expected that former kolkhozniki, finally freed from top-down directives devised in faraway planning and party offices, would choose technologies that fit well with local contexts. It soon became clear to rural residents and almost everyone else that freedom to choose and the ability to choose were two altogether different things. According to one Russian observer, there were virtually no "financially sound enterprises or organizations capable of large capital investments and of the modernization of agricultural production."[77] For a decade, collective farms remained de facto intact as kolkhozniki declined to farm their shares independently. These farms, still collectively operated but de jure privately owned, remained by far the largest landowners throughout the nineties.[78] At the same time, they were battered by the storms unleashed by market liberalization, and agricultural output dwindled. Liberalization created several problems for rural producers. Perhaps most urgent was the rapid increase in the cost of farming as inputs became more expensive while farm earnings rose at a much slower rate, creating the second scissor crisis in Russia's twentieth-century history. While the price of fuel increased by more than nine times between 1993 and 2003, the price of wheat only doubled over this period.[79] At the same time, farmers had exceedingly few opportunities to get loans. As Jessica Allina-Pisano notes succinctly, "farming land required . . . capital, and villagers had few ways to get it."[80] Investment in rural production decreased from 39 billion in 1990 to 2 billion in 2000.[81] The vast majority of Russian collective farms were essentially bankrupt by the end of the decade. As the planned economy collapsed, distribution networks for inputs deteriorated. This meant that essential tools and supplies were not only too expensive but also nearly impossible to acquire in the countryside.

Russian agricultural production declined precipitously throughout the nineties. The difficulty of obtaining animal feed meant that meat production on collective farms shrank year after year. Cattle and hog inventories in 2000 were at less than half their 1988 levels, and sheep and goat inventories over the same time period dropped to about one-third of their previous levels.[82] The rural sociologists Grigory Ioffe, Tatyana Nefedova, and Ilya Zaslavsky wondered whether the decline they observed among poultry farms during the 1990s heralded the end of the Russian peasantry: "out of 166 large poultry farms, only 29 are working at full capacity; 119 farms require modernization, and 30 percent of all poultry producers are on the verge of bankruptcy."[83] An ethnography of Kazakh farming notes the many terms used to characterize the first decade of the post-Soviet agrarian transition, and all of them apply equally to the Russian context: *zastoi* (stagnation), *razrukha* (devastation), *upadok* (decline), *bardak* (chaos), *razval* (breakdown), *raspad* (disintegration), *razbombili* (destroyed), and *razderbanili* (torn apart).[84] Meanwhile, foreign imports became widely available in cities as a burgeoning army of importers brought goods from abroad to Russian markets, stores, and restaurants. Meat was imported from the US and Brazil. Most of the sugar that Russians consumed in the nineties was also largely imported.

All Russian farms suffered, but their decline was geographically uneven, and those in the least fertile regions were dealt the heaviest blow. In northern rural regions, villages were often completely abandoned, and arable land was reforested or reclaimed by grassland (figure 2.4 shows an abandoned greenhouse of a former kolkhoz).[85] In some cases, a small handful of villagers held on against all odds, growing their own food and seeking jobs in forestry or public service that earned them at least some cash incomes. A much-reduced dairy farm in the Republic of Sakha, for example, was still milking a few hundred cows in the early 2000s, but after years of mounting troubles with failing equipment and fewer and fewer resources to buy enough hay to feed cows through the winter, it closed in 2007.[86] The collapse of the state procurement system and the economic crisis left Russians in peripheral regions with extremely limited access

Figure 2.4 Abandoned greenhouse of a former kolkhoz, Village of Krasnoye, Grachyovsk district, Stavropol Krai, 2014. Photo by Natalia Mamonova.

to affordable food. Money was also generally scarce in the countryside. Ioffe, Nefedova, and Zaslavsky recount that many villagers had "no exposure to monetary exchange."[87] Subsistence plots once again became vital and ubiquitous lifelines. In some villages, hardly any food from outside was available, and residents became largely self-sufficient, but with dwindling support and inputs from the collective farms.[88] Subsistence farming was as labor intensive and decentralized as it had always been, with local climates and the availability of inputs shaping what was produced and where. Across Russia, no food was more important for securing minimal survival than the potato, and almost all potatoes were grown by households.[89] In some regions, villagers built elaborate greenhouses to extend the growing season for vegetables. Hunting returned as a survival strategy that had been common until the 1950s. In the Kola peninsula and Chukotka, some urbanites relied on reindeer meat to survive, resorting to a kind of hunter-gatherer existence.[90] The gathering of wild foods, especially berries and mushrooms, had remained an important part of Russian foodways in almost all regions.[91] In the nineties, though, homegrown potatoes and food that was hunted or gathered had to replace nonexistent or inadequate incomes: a teacher's salary, for example, was worth little in real terms and only paid sporadically.

The Rise of Agroholdings: Connections Gained and Lost

The devaluation of the ruble following the 1998 financial crisis, along with sharply rising prices of imported foods, was initially disruptive. The aftermath of the ruble devaluation shifted the terms of competition between domestic and foreign goods, ultimately triggering recovery among domestic food processors in the years after 1998.[92] The recovery of Russian agriculture began when food processors looked to source ingredients domestically and therefore invested in rural production, especially in Russia's most fertile regions. The revival of rural production sped up over the first twenty years of the twenty-first century, helped by several political and economic dynamics. The most important feature of the Putin-era recovery was the rise of a new kind of actor in the Russian food system, the corporate agroholdings that channeled capital to agriculture and the processing sector. Starting in 2005, billions of rubles were invested in these sectors each year, as table 2.3 documents. This newfound interest by Russian oligarchs and foreign capital investors in Russian agriculture took many by surprise. After all, Russian oligarchs had been rushing capital *out* of Russia, preferring Manhattan and London real estate as investment vehicles. The wave of investments was made possible by domestic political shifts and by a number of unrelated trends in global capital markets. European and US ethanol policies and growing middle classes in China and India had put pressure on global arable land. Arable land became a more valuable asset as food commodity prices appreciated, triggering what has been called the Land Rush.[93] The 2008 financial crisis was followed by capital flight from mortgage-backed securities, further strengthening the interest of global investors in agricultural assets. The capital influx to Russian agriculture was thus part of a global trend. In Russia, fixed capital investments in agriculture and food processing have continued to grow throughout the Putin years. Not only did investments not slow significantly during the economic recession that followed 2008; they were also not affected by the Western sanctions that started in 2014. In fact, 2016 was a record year as Putin's food import ban spurred rather than slowed production, as we will see below.

Capital investments were undertaken by a new type of rural actor—corporate farms and processing firms, known initially as "new agricultural operators" (NAOs) and more recently as agroholdings. They are large corporate farm enterprises with a focus either on grain production or on vertically integrated animal production. Agroholdings brought about a radical transformation of material technologies in the Russian food system. New technologies and methods of farming led to higher yields and more output. The privileged position of agroholdings in the political and economic context of Putin's Russia meant that they had a profound effect on the Russian countryside, reconfiguring the relationships Russian agricultural production had with villagers and with the

Table 2.3 Fixed capital investments in Russian agriculture and food processing, 1994–2016 (bln RR/year)

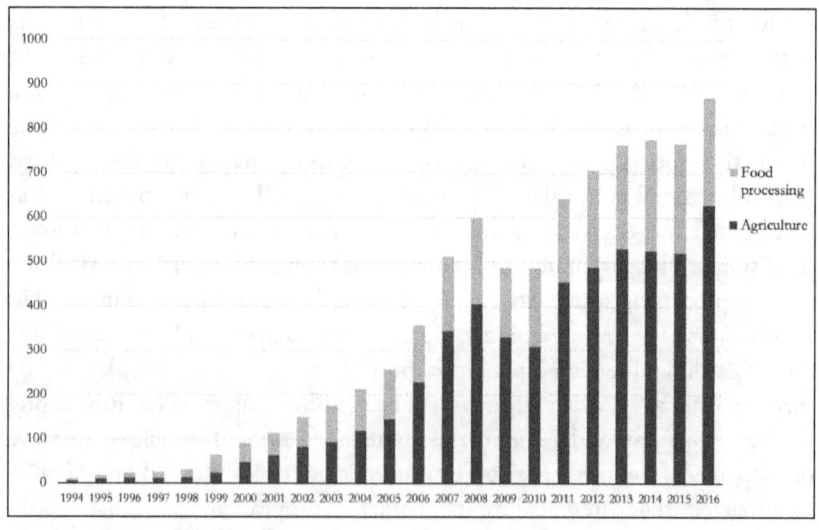

Source: Federal'naia sluzhba gosudarstvennoi statisiki / Goskomstat.

world. On the one hand, the agrifood sector became an important site for Russia's integration into global markets. New connections were created in multiple ways: through *capital investments* from across the world, and through *technology and knowledge imports* supplied by Western and transnational companies. A third set of global connections was created through the *export* of Russian food products, especially grains. Finally, the post-Soviet period also brought foreign seasonal *labor* to Russian farms, mostly from Central Asia but also from Turkey, Korea, and China. On the other hand, old ties were lost and destroyed, notably the Soviet-era subsistence production that had been intricately linked to the collective farm sector. When corporate farms first arrived in rural Russia, new owners and managers were often asked by rural residents and regional authorities to "look after" the local populations, much in the same way that collective farms had done in the past.[94] It is widely acknowledged that agroholdings ended up having a different relationship to subsistence farming—one observer contrasted their "market-driven" orientation with the "social" orientation of the sovkhozy and kolkhozy.[95] Though many corporate farms engage in charity, have corporate social responsibility (CSR) programs, and employ some village labor, they were unwilling to continue the tight and symbiotic relationship with subsistence farmers of the Soviet era.

Russian food processors recovered relatively early from the shock of privatization and started expanding in the late nineties. Wimm-Bill-Dann, Russia's largest dairy and drinks producer, expanded production in Russia by importing the technologies and adopting the marketing strategies of Western processing giants at that time. Western processors, like Danone, for example, as well as the largest Western fast-food chains had moved to Russia already in the late nineties. By the early 2000s, oligarchic conglomerates from other sectors of the Russian economy started buying and investing in processing plants.[96] These Russian and Western food processors needed high-quality inputs and were an early and strong source of demand for Russian agricultural products. In large part, agroholdings formed to meet this demand. Some are affiliated with Russian parent companies in the cash-rich finance, energy, and metals sectors. Others focus on agriculture alone. Some of them are publicly traded, while others are not. Some of the most successful agroholdings are owned by Russian entrepreneurs and oligarchs, and others have significant foreign ownership stakes. While Russia's new "Land Barons" are domestic oligarchs, Oane Visser and Max Spoor have shown that the origin of capital investments in Russian agroholdings in the first decades of the 2000s was in fact remarkably global. Investors in Russian agricultural assets include sovereign wealth funds from the Gulf States (Bahrain, UAE, and Saudi Arabia), Libya, South Korea, and China and various institutional investors (pension funds, hedge funds, private equity funds) from the United States, Canada, Israel, and Europe (Denmark, Germany, Luxembourg, Sweden, and Switzerland).[97] Some of the capital investment in Russian agriculture has been "repatriated"—that is, Russian capital that had fled abroad during the 1990s was reinvested in Russian companies. Chinese private entrepreneurs and state-owned companies were particularly interested in the Russian Far East. The motivations of investors in Russian agricultural assets have varied. Some have pursued these investments as part of a strategy of spreading short-term risks; others invested in Russian agriculture as part of long-term strategies of investing in food and biofuel production across the world.[98] While capital was global for the first fifteen years of Russia's rural recovery, since 2014, some Western investors became more hesitant about remaining in Russia. Two large foreign-owned companies that had been listed on European stock exchanges, Black Earth Farming and Agrokultura, were taken over by Russian investors.[99]

In primary production, agroholdings tend to cluster in one of two categories: vertically integrated livestock producers, or crop producers with a focus on grains, sugar beets, or vegetable oils. Prodimex (founded in 1992) and Rusagro (founded in 1995) are examples of agroholdings that have focused on sugar beets and grains. Both were sugar importers before they started growing sugar beets, and both operate mills and refineries domestically. Prodimex invested in several Soviet-era sugar mills in the late nineties. Rusagro also acquired a sugar plant in the Belgorod region around the same time. Sugar beets and sugar production remain Prodimex's core business, but the company also produced thousands of tons of wheat, barley, sunflower seeds, corn, and soy. By 2019, it owned sixteen sugar refineries, producing nearly 1.5 million tons of sugar from more than 10 million tons of sugar beets. It is today Russia's largest sugar producer and sugar supplier to Coca-Cola and Pepsi. In 2001, the company owned a mere 60 hectares of land; in 2020, it was Russia's second largest landowner, owning 865,000 hectares of land. Rusagro, much like Prodimex, moved from importing sugar to refining sugar in the late 1990s. In 2004, Rusagro expanded to vegetable oils, and in 2008 it built a pig facility. It has expanded its meat production since then, adding more facilities in more regions across Russia. Rusagro is Russia's largest producer of margarine, its second largest producer of mayonnaise and vegetable oils, and its third largest sugar producer. It now owns farmland in the Urals in the Russian Far East, where it grows corn and soy for export to China.[100] Prodimex is majority owned by Igor Khudokormov, a Russian oligarch who became a citizen of Malta. Rusagro is majority owned by Vadim Moskovich, also a Russian oligarch, who represents the agricultural region Belgorod in the Federation Council. In 2020, Rusagro was Russia's largest landowner, with a land bank of approximately 643,000 hectares.

A second type of agroholding in Russia consists of vertically integrated meat companies, with meat broadly defined to include poultry and dairy farms. Miratorg and Cherkizovo, Russia's two largest meat producers, each grew rapidly in the early 2000s by building large pork and poultry facilities. In 2020, Miratorg was Russia's largest pork producer and the country's second-largest poultry producer. Cherkizovo was the second-largest pork producer and the third-largest poultry producer. Cherkizovo started as a meat processor in the 1970s and survived the 1990s by making sausages. Miratorg was founded in 1995 as a company that imported dried milk powder from the Netherlands.[101] Cherkizovo became a crop producer in the late 1990s, and both companies invested heavily in meat processing and packing in the early 2000s. Miratorg began adding beef and sheep in 2015, and Cherkizovo opened a turkey facility in 2017. Both companies produce their own feed; Cherkizovo produces wheat, corn, peas, and soy.[102] Cherkizovo owns 9 feed plants and 12 grain elevators, and as of 2020 it owned nearly 300,000 hectares of farmland in Russia's Chernozem. In 2020, Miratorg was Russia's largest landowner, having accumulated more than a million hectares of farmland in many regions—including in Bryansk, Belgorod, Kursk, Smolensk, Kaluga, Kaliningrad, Tula, and Orel. At that time, the company also owned feed mills in Bryansk and Belgorod. Miratorg's overall slaughter volume was 521,000 tons (slaughter weight), or on average 520 head of pork per hour. Both companies are fully vertically integrated—Miratorg's slogan is "from field to counter" (*ot polia do prilavka*). Miratorg and Cherkizovo are well-known brand names in the Russian market, and both sell to other former Soviet Republics and increasingly in Asia as well. Miratorg has retail stores across Russia, and its product range includes hundreds of finished products and dozens of convenience and ready-made meals, as well as a wide range of slaughter by-products, such as bones, bone meal, rendered fat, blood plasma, and gall.[103] Miratorg has also long supplied the meat for McDonald's, Burger King, TGI Friday's, Pizza Hut, and Carl's Jr. as well as for several high-end hotel and restaurant chains, including the Hilton, Radisson, and Marriott. Miratorg is majority owned by the brothers Victor and Aleksandr Linnik. Cherkizovo is majority owned by Igor Babaev. Maps 2.2 and 2.3 show the activities of Russia's largest agroholdings in the south and west and in Siberia and the Far East. Agroholdings are most active in Russia's Chernozem region. Though they operate and own land across many regions across Russia, they are largely absent in some parts of the country, especially in the north.[104]

The universe of post-Soviet agroholdings also includes state-owned corporations. One of the most important state-owned actors in agriculture is the United Grain Company (UGC, Ob"edinennaia zernovaia kompaniia), a behemoth that controls a great deal of strategic assets in the wheat sector. UGC

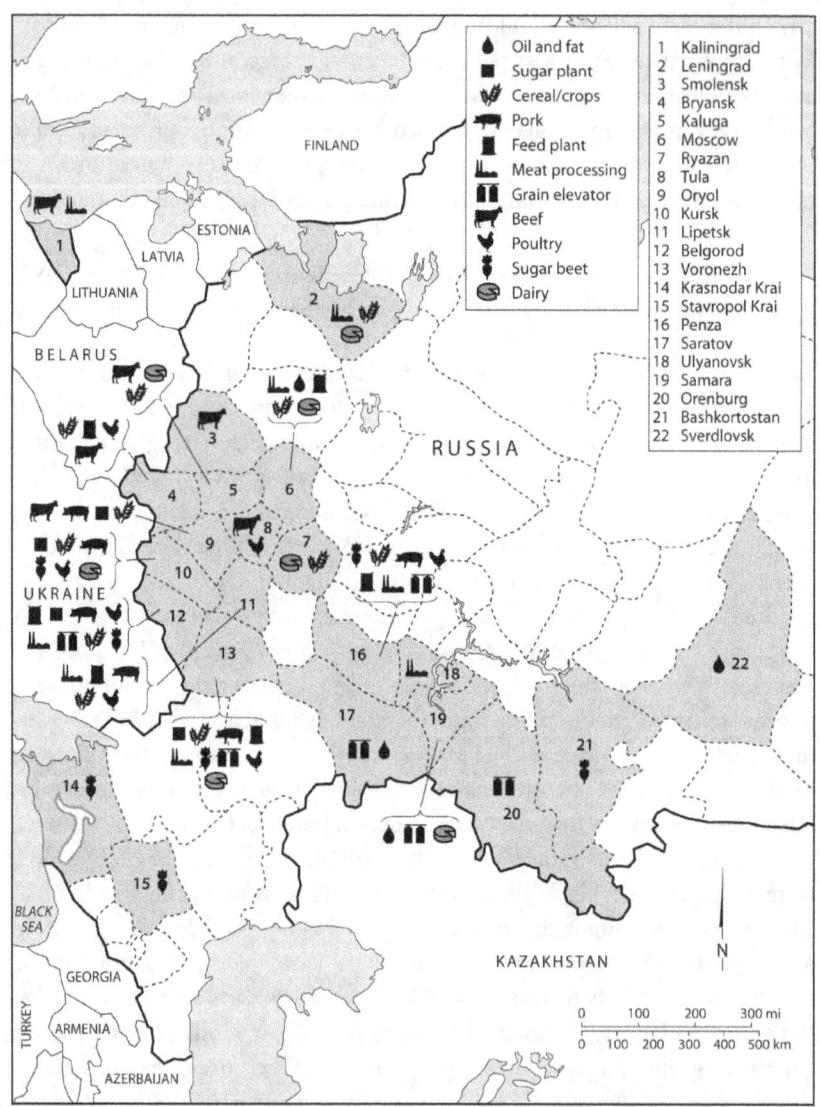

Map 2.2 Agroholding activity: south and west, 2019, based on data from agroholdings' annual reports.

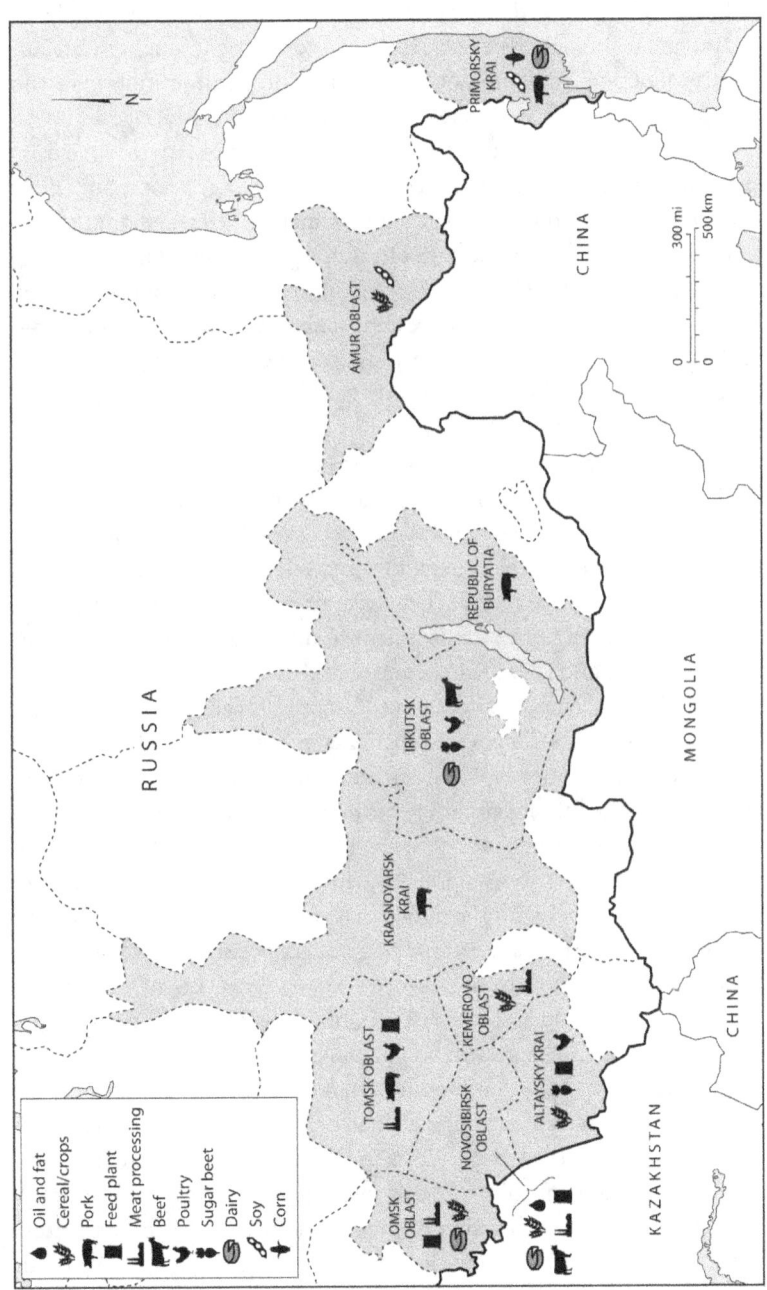

Map 2.3 Agroholding activity: Siberia and Far East, 2019, based on data from agroholdings' annual reports.

was created in 2008 as a state-owned grain company with the initial purpose of responding to problems with state grain purchasing and infrastructure development programs. In the early 2000s, the Putin government sought to encourage grain production by buying grain from producers, promising high and stable prices. Several grain traders realized the potential for arbitrage and speculation with grain harvests and tried to buy grain ahead of harvest time from growers. Grain purchasing programs continued in the early 2000s, but with a record harvest in 2008, concerns over their cost, inefficiencies, and disorganization mounted. Responding to these problems, the government transferred huge government-owned wheat stocks, storage elevators, grain transport infrastructure, and port facilities to a newly created, state-owned trading company—UGC. (Note that these are highly strategic assets in the grain sector because they allow the trader to wait out low-price periods.) Yet only a year later, in 2010, a presidential decree stipulated that 50 percent-minus-one-share of UGC should be sold to private investors, and by 2012, the government proceeded to sell a large stake in UGC.[105] This process created a new powerful private company with consolidated ownership of critical infrastructure. These steps were widely criticized by foreign observers, though they made sense as part of the Russian government's food security agenda. The government managed to enlist UGC for its goals of attracting private investment to update grain storage and port infrastructure while also centralizing control of these strategic assets.[106]

Whether oligarchic or shareholder controlled, private agroholdings have consistently demonstrated a willingness to align themselves with dominant political priorities. Many companies explicitly mention in corporate communications that they share the political goals of the Putin government. The United Grain Company says that the company's strategy is to "expand the infrastructure of the grain market in order to strengthen the international position of Russian grain." Cherkizovo shares with the public that the company's leadership "realized the need for import substitution."[107] A stronger position for Russian grain producers and import substitution are well-known elements of the government's agenda in the grain and meat sectors, respectively. The Summa Group, the winning bidder in the reprivatization of UGC, mentions that the expansion of infrastructure for agricultural production in the Russian Far East is at the core of its business strategy; not coincidentally, this has also been a goal of the Putin government over the last decade or so.[108] Exima, a swine breeding firm, states its participation in political goals even more directly: "the company actively takes part in the realization of the government's plan for agriculture until 2020."[109] Images of corporate executives shaking hands with Vladimir Vladimirovich are frequently published on corporate websites and in reports and the media to suggest this alignment of political goals and private interests.

Miratorg's corporate values are particularly useful to show how the company signals a synergy of corporate and government goals, with technology at the center of both. In a communication with shareholders, the company states that "all our work is driven by our strongly held core corporate values," which include the following:

> (i) The effective integration of the interests of national governmental policy with the interests of our company, and those of end-user consumers.
> (ii) Using modern technology and innovation to achieve our manufacturing goals.
> (iii) Adherence to Russian and international standards in all aspects of the vertical integration structure of our group of companies.[110]

These core values could be interpreted as sending the following signals to the government and shareholders, the two important constituents for the company: we are good corporate citizens because we contribute to realizing political goals (see the reference to "national governmental policy"); and at the same time, we make products that Russian consumers will love. The statement of values cites "modern technology" as key to achieving these goals, along with a commitment to "international standards" as a way to attain global competitiveness.

Technological Change

The rise of agroholdings had enormous consequences for every aspect of Russia's food system. The capital that these companies brought to the Russian agrifood system was by and large invested in two types of assets: land and technology. Land investments resulted in the historically large and rapid shift in land ownership detailed in the previous chapter. Capital investments in agricultural machinery and factories brought about far-reaching change to how crops were raised and how food was produced in Russia. The magnitude of technological change led the group of Skolkovo economists quoted at the beginning of the chapter to argue that "agriculture is undergoing a technological renaissance."[111] Another observer proclaimed in 2014 that Russia was "now dramatically ahead of America in terms of industrial farming technology," inferring this from the sheer volume of capital invested in new technologies in the sector. Before the 2000s, investment in farming technologies materialized only very slowly and selectively, or not at all. Farm technology inherited from the Soviet collective farms was ailing, but new machinery was often unaffordable for the newly privatized collective farms. Repairs of Soviet-era tractors had been a challenge in the best of times, but with the collapse of the planned economy, the number of stranded machines multiplied. A 1994 report noted that 20 percent of trucks, 16 percent of tractors, 15 percent of ploughs, and 14 percent of seeders were in serious states of disrepair, and the share of useless machinery increased as the decade progressed.[112] The supply of new agricultural machinery to Russian farms had nearly stopped, though some foreign manufacturers started selling to Russia as early as 1992. Claas, one of the world's largest manufacturers of farm machinery, discovered a market for used German combine harvesters in Russia and gradually increased the company's exports to Russia throughout the decade. John Deere followed a similar strategy. As agricultural production started to recover, importers of Western European and US farm machinery opened representations in Russia in anticipation of a technological shift. Still, by the early 2000s, there was a shortage of agricultural machinery in Russia. According to Ioffe, Nefedova, and Zaslavsky, new agricultural operators were often forced to rent fleets of combines from Turkey during harvest time, complete with Central Asian seasonal work teams.[113]

As agricultural production recovered, the business for agro-technologies thrived in Russia. Profit-oriented agroholdings grew by acquiring thousands of hectares of land and by adopting modes of production that maximized output and yields. The range of technologies they deployed included diverse and sophisticated methods that reflected the technological frontier of capital-intensive farming in the capitalist West. Every subsector of farming, from field to dairy to slaughterhouse, as well as different processing facilities, relies on a wide range of technological solutions. Field crops rely on tractors and trucks, balers and rakes; livestock operations rely on feeding and waste disposal systems; dairies rely on milking parlors; processing plants use conveyors, refrigeration, and other specialized processing equipment. Table 2.4 is a partial list of some of the technologies that Russian producers and processors invested in between 2000 and 2020. "Precision agriculture," for example, refers to tractors, sprayers, harvesters, and other machinery equipped with and directed by information systems that use GPS data to precisely target the application of inputs. Agrochemicals (e.g., fertilizer, herbicides, pesticides, and seed treatments) and agricultural biotech are two other important agricultural technologies. Over the first two decades of the twenty-first century, Russian agriculture greatly expanded the use of agrochemicals. Some of them are produced in Russia, but the presence of the world's agro-chemistry giants—such as Dow, DuPont, Bayer (which acquired another giant, Monsanto, in 2016), and Syngenta—increased in Russia during this time.[114] The overall use of mineral fertilizer by Russian agricultural producers more than doubled between 1999 and 2018, from 1.1 million to 2.5 million tons. For grains, sugar beets, and potatoes, the application of agrochemicals as measured in kilograms per hectare nearly quadrupled

Table 2.4 Partial list of imported agrifood technologies, 2010s

Machinery and infrastructure related to field crops	Tractors, trucks, balers, rakes, and drills
	Combine harvesters, other dedicated harvesters (e.g., for forage, beet, potatoes)
	Grain elevators and other storage systems
	Irrigation systems and greenhouses
Production systems and processing technology	Pig, broiler, beef and dairy complexes with feeding systems and waste disposal systems; milking parlors and bottling facilities for dairy
	Breeding facilities for pork, hatcheries for broiler
	Slaughtering facilities, meat and poultry processing plants, rendering plants
	Refrigeration equipment
	Packaging equipment
	Feed mills, oilseed processing, sugar beet processing and sugar mills
Agrochemicals and livestock drugs	Fertilizers and soil conditioners
	Pesticides, insecticides, fungicides, and herbicides
	Seed treatments
	Livestock drugs such as antibiotics, antifungals, antiparasitics, and growth promoters
	Feed additives
Agricultural biotech	Pig, poultry, dairy, and other livestock genetics
	Seeds for grain and other field crops
IT	Precision agriculture; data driven soil, hydration, input management systems
	Accounting systems

Source: Based on data from agroholdings' annual reports and industry reports.

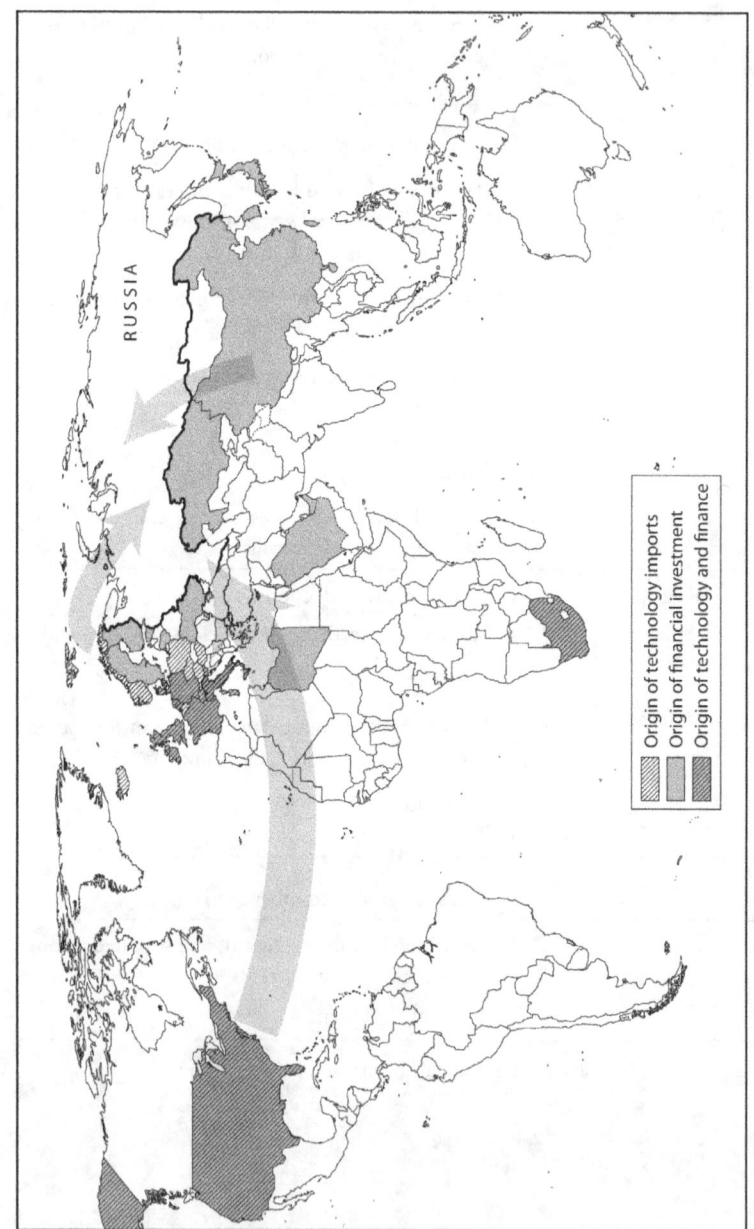

Map 2.4 Origins of technology and financial investment in Russian agriculture, 2010s, based on data from Visser and Spoor (2011) for finance, agroholdings' annual reports, and industry reports for technology.

in this period. Sugar beets, one of Russia's main industrial crops, are among the most fertilizer-dependent plants of Russia's new agriculture.

For the first ten years of the rural recovery, the vast majority of the technology in new agroholdings originated abroad. Map 2.4 shows the global origin of technology and financial investment in Russian agriculture.[115] The demand for agricultural machinery by the rapidly growing agroholdings was strong, and they were excellent customers for Western and transnational companies. Imported technologies were typically accompanied by training programs in which the supplier would send technical experts to train Russian personnel, and by long-term service contracts that created lasting connections between supplier and client. Many foreign companies initiated joint ventures with Russian partners to foster these new relationships. These kinds of connections between Russian agroholdings and foreign companies form an important part of Russia's integration into the global economy. Many foreign companies strengthened their "Russia connections" over the years and started operating in Russia. In 2005, Claas built an assembly plant for combines in Krasnodar to respond to rising demand for agricultural machinery and to supply "Russian" tractors to agroholdings.[116] Operating in Russia to supply the domestic market was important beyond agricultural machinery. Mondi, a transnational producer of food packaging products, followed a similar trajectory—from initially exporting products to Russia to acquiring two packaging producers in Russia in 2016, Uralplastic and Lebedyan.[117] Packaging is especially important in the meat, fish, and dairy sectors, as these industries work with highly perishable raw materials. By 2019, Mondi was supplying the growing packaging needs of the Russian meat giants.[118] We saw earlier in the chapter that perishable and fragile foods were a particular problem for the Soviet planned economy. As we will see in the next chapters, twenty-first-century packaging made new types of products available to Russian consumers, but it also created a new kind of waste.

A further interesting aspect of machinery imports relates to the legal requirements that are "built into" these material technologies. When Russian producers imported agricultural technologies from Europe, for instance, they introduced not only equipment but also the EU food safety and regulatory standards that these machines are built in accordance with. At Cargill's Russia facilities, the equipment duplicates standards operative at other Cargill plants across the world, resulting in the Russian food industry's movement toward what a Cargill representative called "quiet standards."[119] Such standards in turn help Russian companies reach global markets. In the livestock sector, for example, this matters for the future of meat exports, where the discrepancy between Soviet-era food safety standards (known as GOST, which stands for *gosudarstvennyi standart*) and Western standards (known as HACCP, hazard analysis and critical control points) currently remains as a barrier between the former East and West. It is well known that a shift to HACCP systems is costly and inaccessible to producers that have limited resources to undertake the investments that the HACCP system calls for.[120] The "built in" HACCP compatibility of machinery imported by Russian agroholdings creates the basis for future connections to export markets. Though the meat sector still largely produces for Russia's domestic market, a few agroholdings have started to export chicken and pork, mostly to China. The high-tech production systems that companies like Miratorg, Cherkizovo, and Rusagro have built have created excess capacity, as a result of which the companies are actively seeking to expand exports to other countries.[121]

Agroholding cadres have placed technology at the center of their operations primarily for economic reasons, to secure market shares and returns for owners and investors. In many ways, however, investments in technology were also a way for agroholdings to align corporate and political goals, and to uphold their share of the political bargain with the Putin administration. Especially after 2008, agroholdings, much like consumers, were encouraged to source inputs domestically, or to "buy Russian." Chris Lander has documented that Russian authorities encouraged Cargill to rely on domestic grain for most of the animal feed it produces in Russia.[122] The Russian government urged all agroholdings to purchase domestic machinery rather than the newest John Deere or Claas combines. Though agroholdings generally seek to comply with government directives, they are also ultimately fiercely competitive with each other and with global producers and have generally opted for foreign machinery that reduces costs or improves efficiency. The share of domestic versus foreign technology has varied for different types of inputs. The Russian agricultural machine industry gained market shares over the last decade: the Russian government reported in 2019 that 60 percent of agricultural machinery originates in Russia. In other sectors, Russian agriculture has remained overwhelmingly dependent on foreign technology.[123]

Agroholdings have been intensely concerned with adopting the most up-to-date machinery, equipment, and production systems. In addition to these material technologies, the knowledge component of twenty-first-century agriculture is an increasingly important part of agricultural practices. Agricultural research institutes suffered during the nineties, and Soviet knowledge was lost when researchers retired without replacement. In the first decade of the boom years, neither the government nor the agroholdings supported the knowledge aspect of technological change or accorded it the same respect as they did material technologies.[124] Domestic capacity in the knowledge-intensive subsector has been lagging as Russian agroholdings have either relied on imported knowledge or deemphasized the knowledge element of technological change and disregard practices and ideas considered foreign.[125] Trends in agro-biotech in Russia illustrate some of these challenges. As agroholdings built new livestock facilities and capital-intensive crop production, they realized that the genetic material used in agricultural production—seeds and parent stock—are critical inputs. Seeds and animal breeding are knowledge- and research-intensive sectors; however, crop and livestock genetics are industries dominated by a few transnational companies that supply farms across the world.[126] Russian pork, poultry, cattle, and dairy operations largely used international animal breeds—first from imported parent stock and later from domestically raised parent stock. Russian crop farmers have similarly relied on foreign seeds. Corn, soy, and sunflower seed are mostly imported as Western seed companies offer high-yield seeds that are not available in Russia. Even seeds for barley, a traditional Russian grain, are mostly imported. Russian breweries have been requesting barley with high malt content, which can only be grown from seeds imported from Germany. Vertically integrated livestock producers largely grow their own feed for dairy and cattle. This has meant seeking out seed mixes that optimize the protein content of the feed mix produced from the grasses and pulses on their pastures. Wheat production is an exception to this kind of import dependence: it draws on Russian seeds—that is, genetic material that is based on domestic research and plant breeding. Imported seeds and parental livestock lines are in high demand in Russia. With each imported seed or animal, Russian producers also import the knowledge and scientific research that produced them. This kind of import dependence on foreign genetic resources has caused alarm inside the Putin government, and over the last decade, Russian research institutes have developed Russian paternal lines for pork and broilers.

Productivity, Production, and Increased Exports

Russia's corporate agroholdings have invested in fertile farmland and in the most cutting-edge farm technology. Though corporate farming has struggled in some places, overall, productivity and total output surged in the handful of sectors that agroholdings focused on. Wheat yields, production, and exports have all increased since the turn of the millennium.[127] In some ways, the recovery of grain production in recent years represents a reversal of the decline in the eighties and nineties: Russia is now harvesting as much grain as it did in the late 1970s. In 2017, Russia harvested its largest-ever grain crop—between 128 and 135 million metric tons (MMT) of grain, depending on the estimate—exceeding the record harvest of 127 MMT of grain in 1978.[128] What is particularly remarkable about the 2017 harvest is that it was grown on a much smaller area of cultivated land: "In 2017, Russian farmers used half the acreage as in 1978 and got double the yields," noted the USDA.[129] Specifically, the acreage under cultivation with wheat was 27.3 million hectares in 2017, up from the nadir of 1998, when only 19 million hectares were sown.[130] Average wheat yields in 2017 were around 3 metric tons per hectare (MT/ha).[131] Yields vary every year, of course, depending on the growing conditions, but 3MT/ha is more than twice the per-hectare harvest of 1998 (the worst harvest of the nineties), when yields of 1.36 MT/ha were recorded. See table 2.5 for yield trends over the past thirty years. Yields and productivity increased in a number of other crops as well—especially other grains and sugar beets. The production of sugar has followed a similar trend: in the late 1960s and 1970s, the Soviet Union produced around 9 million tons annually, nearly a third of the world's sugar. Sugar production bottomed out in 2000, when Russia only produced 1.5 million tons, just 1.2 percent of world production. In 2017, Russia harvested more than 6 million tons of sugar beets.[132]

The recovery of grain and sugar beet production was important in its own right, but it also mattered for the livestock sector, which relied on grain as feed, and for food processing, which relied on refined sugar as an input. The demand for feed grains by companies such as Cherkizovo, Miratorg, and EkoNiva was in fact partly responsible for the surge in domestic grain production. Meat production in Russia, like that of wheat, has also recovered to levels last seen in the 1970s.[133] Unlike in the Brezhnev period, domestic grain producers can keep up with the feed needs of the livestock sector. Under Putin, dependence on grain, meat, and sugar imports declined, while in the 1970s and 1980s it had steadily increased. The most important consequence of the rise of large meat conglomerates, however, is that agroholdings rely on very different technologies of production and on different swine breeds, feeds, and confinement facilities.[134]

Table 2.5 Yield gains, Russian wheat, 1992–2019 (MT/ha)

Source: FAO.

The growing volume of Russian grain thus met the nutritional needs of ever-larger herds of pigs, cattle, and dairy cows. Russian grain is now also sold to over 110 countries all over the world, with Egypt, Turkey, Nigeria, and Bangladesh as the largest recipients in 2019 (map 1.2). Populous countries in Africa and Asia are thus the second main destination for Russian grain. With these exports, Russia has reclaimed its prerevolutionary role as the world's breadbasket. It now exports more grain than the Soviet Union ever did and has become the largest wheat exporter of the global economy. Exports are made possible primarily by plentiful harvests of agroholdings and by investments in export infrastructure, such as ports and storage facilities, heavily supported by the state. Grain traders such as Cargill and the United Grain Company have played an essential role in connecting growers with world markets. Table 2.6 shows export patterns for Russian wheat.

Agroholdings as Employers and Rural Corporate Citizens

As connections to global actors formed, the relationship between agroholdings and rural residents changed. Soviet-era collective farms had two main ties with rural residents: first, as employers, and second, as sources of inputs for subsistence farming. Both kinds of ties weakened greatly in the 1990s, though collective farms continued to fulfill critical social functions for some years.[135] In the early 2000s, many of these ties were undone: old collectives in marginal areas were increasingly unable to maintain social functions, and in thriving

Table 2.6 Russian wheat exports, 1993–2019 (MMT)

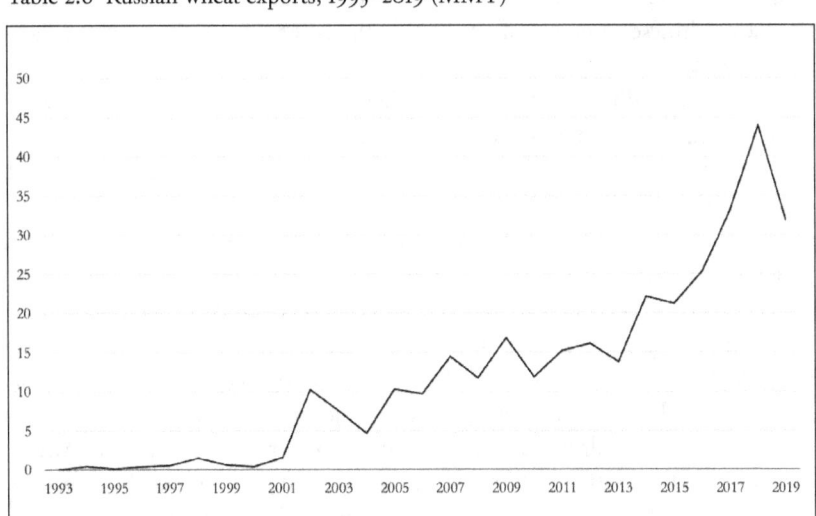

Source: FAO.

agricultural regions, agroholdings were increasingly unwilling to do so.[136] At the beginning of the rise of agroholdings, many villagers had already been devastated by outmigration. By around 2006, about a third of Russia's rural settlements had either disappeared or were disappearing.[137] The rise of agroholdings did nothing to reverse this trend or help ailing villages in the less fertile and remote regions. In the Chernozem and the northern and southern Caucasus—that is, in the regions with growing agroholding activity—population density had not suffered as much. Even in these regions, however, only select locations and some villagers benefited. While some agroholdings make a point of investing in local workers and emphasizing their value to the company, others try to avoid Russian rural workers. Whether justified or not, agroholdings representatives accepted the mantra that villagers were prone to drinking and were not to be relied on, arguing that "good people" were difficult to find.[138]

Avoiding the employment of villagers was made possible by the shift to technology-intensive modes of production; in other words, the farming by agroholdings was far less labor intensive than Soviet-era collective farms had been. As agroholdings used more technology, they needed more highly skilled employees whom they trained through corporate training programs or partnerships with local agricultural universities. Some agroholdings argue that they can afford to "ignore" local Russian populations since they rely on high-tech machinery and skilled workers hired at different times in the production cycle.[139] They also employ seasonal labor during harvest time, but even seasonal labor is often supplied by migrants rather than villagers, most often from the North Caucasus and Central Asia, but also from Belarus and Ukraine. In the Russian Far East, Chinese migrants often provide the labor needed on both Russian- and Chinese-owned farms.[140]

Some agroholdings emphasize that they do hire local workers and try to remain on good terms with rural residents. EkoNiva's thriving dairy empire, for instance, has created jobs in Voronezh oblast. Overall, though, the trend over the past twenty years has clearly been toward fewer workers and more machines: agricultural employment has decreased in precisely the same time period that investment in agriculture has increased (table 2.7 shows the declining share of the agricultural labor force). Instead of providing employment, many agroholdings have corporate social responsibility programs, supplying funds to maintain schools and restore churches, for instance.[141] Cherkizovo, Rusagro, and EkoNiva all run charitable projects and support local orphanages, schools, and cultural or sports organizations in each of the cities where they operate. Oane Visser and Natalia Mamonova report on one of the reasons to support local communities supplied by an agroholding representative: "If you help the local population, they also help ensure that theft and sabotage on

Table 2.7 Employment in agriculture and food processing, 1998–2017

Source: Federal'naia sluzhba gosudarstvennoi statisiki / Goskomstat.

your territory stay at a minimum. If you do not participate in social issues, then people have less of an incentive to protect your interests."[142]

The dwindling flow of resources from former collective farms to subsistence producers was a further important change in the Russian countryside. Large farms no longer served as the funnels of resources that they had been in Soviet times. Without the cross-subsidies from collective farms, backyard farming became more difficult and costly. The strategy that subsistence producers adopted in response to the dwindling resources ranged from innovation to resignation. The most entrepreneurial took advantage of demand to turn subsistence production into a business: they scaled up production and built on existing ties to consumers to expand the informal distribution network.[143] Though feeding a few chickens remained within the range of possibility for small-scale producers, rearing larger livestock like cows, sheep, and horses became costly. Families might have kept a cow, for instance, as long as a retired aunt or grandmother was still able to take care of it, but once she was too old for the hard work of daily milking, the families tended to give up this kind of asset. There is regional variation in animal husbandry practices: even as household production of chicken is declining overall, in the south, where feed grains remain more available, raising chickens continues to be a common practice.[144] In regions where animals need substantial grain-based feed to survive the winter, the decline of family livestock holdings was particularly swift.

Overall, many families that had practiced subsistence farming for generations were giving it up as family members moved to cities, had more demanding jobs, or just preferred to buy goods in stores once they became more accessible and more affordable with the economic recovery of the first two decades of the Putin presidency. Since about 2005, subsistence production has been in a steady and in some sectors steep decline, especially if measured relative to production in large-scale facilities. Poultry and pork inventories at large agricultural establishments have been increasing, with the largest producers growing the fastest, while inventories of private households are dwindling. In 2000, households raised 58 percent of Russia's poultry, according to Rosstat.[145] By 2013, that number had declined to 33 percent. The Russian Union of Poultry Producers estimates this number at less than 10 percent.[146] With pork, the decline is even more marked: from 70 percent in 2005 to about 13 percent in 2018 (see table 2.8).[147]

Several mechanisms contributed to the shrinking role of household production. One of the reasons why Russians no longer grow food themselves has to do with the increasing availability of affordable products in stores. Many Russians also think of the decline of subsistence farming as a generational and culture change: younger generations of Russians have neither the time nor the skills for the labor-intensive work of growing food and rearing animals. The state has also contributed directly to the decline of subsistence farming, in both cities and the countryside, through a number of phytosanitary campaigns that decimated the livestock holdings of subsistence farmers, in particular pork and poultry. Government agencies considered this kind of livestock holding outdated and unsafe as well as a threat to the "profitability and

Table 2.8 Pork output from household farms, 2000–2018

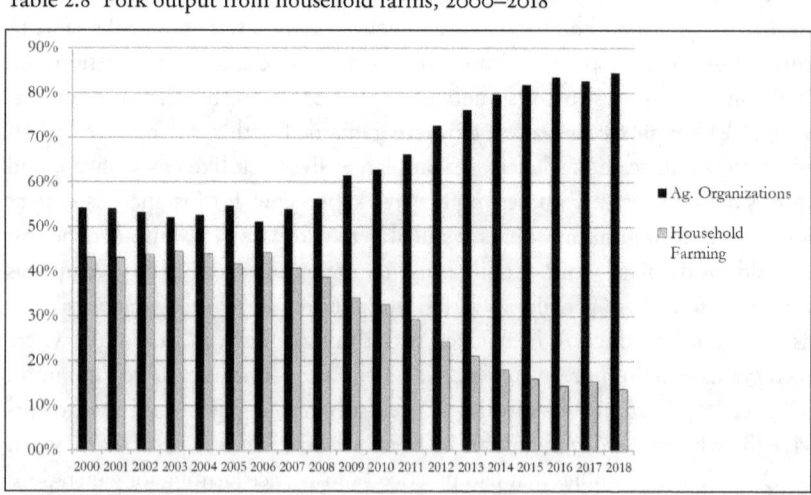

Source: Federal'naia sluzhba gosudarstvennoi statisiki / Goskomstat.

investment attractiveness" of the modern pork industry.[148] They argued that household farms had inadequate food safety standards and were breeding grounds for African swine fever and avian flu. Small farmers themselves rejected this reasoning and saw it as an excuse to sideline competition by subsistence farms.[149] The episode mentioned at the outset of the chapter was just one of several similar events that have occurred with some regularity since about 2009. In the five years between 2009 and 2014, a period of intense growth for livestock agroholdings, the Russian veterinary watchdog Rosselkhoznadzor culled tens of thousands of pigs held on household farms.[150] Given that subsistence producers tended to rear only a handful of swine, these campaigns affected a large number of families. The fate of Russian subsistence farming is noteworthy because it has traditionally been important; dissolution thus represents a major transition in Russia's food system. Remember also that in the 1920s, Russian agrarian intellectuals debated the viability of small-scale farming, and Alexander Chayanov lost his life over his argument in favor of it. Finally, there are today many critics of industrial farming in the capitalist West that emphasize the benefits of small-scale, decentralized production as a remedy for the environmental shortcomings of large farms.

Since 2014, some forms of small-scale production have again strengthened.[151] Oane Visser, Natalia Mamonova, Max Spoor, and Alexander Nikulin note that household farms do continue to supply some food for Russian tables. Still employing "largely traditional methods" and practicing "environmentally friendly agriculture," they still produce essentially without support from the state.[152] Self-provisioning has historically been the most important reason for subsistence farming, and part of the demand for local food since 2015 stems from weaknesses in the Russian economy. But demand has also started to emanate from affluent urban consumers. This niche for artisanal production has encouraged some families to look to farming as a way to make a living. Reflecting the local food movement in the West, small-scale famers emphasize their connectedness to local soils in communication with consumers, employing narratives that describe values and justify the higher cost of their products. Many rural villagers still view this new kind of small-scale production as using old-fashioned and inefficient "grandfather's methods" (*dedushkiny metody*).[153] Yet urban consumers in many cities are increasingly interested in artisanal and local products. Sales and communication with discerning consumers are facilitated via social networks (virtual and traditional) linking small-scale producers to affluent urbanites. Lavka Lavka plays this role for producers supplying Moscow's market, but alternative food networks exist in other cities as well. Lavka Lavka is a store, restaurant, and cooperative that promotes farm-to-table supply chains that bring farm products from Russia's regions to the metropolis.

Lavka Lavka sells dairy products from a Ryazan farm, run by Nina Kozlova, who dates her family recipes to the imperial era, for example; and fish from the catch of Ruslan Sheltenko, a Black Sea fisherman from Kerch.[154] Residents of the city of Irkutsk, much smaller and less affluent than Moscow, can also buy locally produced craft food products from Sergei Perevoznikov, for example, a farmer and advocate of local food. Smaller-scale and informal networks also exist in many villages where urbanites have dachas and directly purchase from local farmers.

Effects of the Food Embargo

The food embargo imposed in 2015 also decisively shaped the *how* and the *who* of Russian agriculture. As intended by the embargo's architects, imports of a range of food and food-related products did indeed fall quite substantially in 2015 and 2016.[155] Though the embargo affected a range of foodstuffs, the fate of meat and dairy has been the most politically salient and economically relevant. In the first few years of the embargo, imports of milk and dairy to Russia fell considerably.[156] In 2014, Russia had imported 1.15 million tons of meat. In 2015, more than a year after the embargo had been in place, Russia imported 860,000 metric tons of meat and meat products, a reduction of nearly 300,000 tons.[157] Pork imports declined from 515,000 metric tons to 200,000 between 2014 and 2016.[158] Beef imports did not initially decrease as much as poultry and pork and made up the largest share of Russian meat imports in the first few years of the embargo.[159] The key question that this decline in imports has raised is whether or not the embargo created new opportunities for Russian producers and whether declining imports were matched by rising domestic production. The answer has several components. First, the effects on producers varied across subsectors. Poultry and pork producers were able to fill the supermarket shelves that were emptied by the embargo. Domestic production of beef, fluid milk, and other dairy products did not increase in the first years of the embargo. A second important observation is that even though production increased overall, consumption declined during the same period of time—unsurprisingly, since food became more expensive. Finally, though Russian agricultural production has thrived, many agricultural inputs are still imported, including soy beans for high-protein feed and many types of agro-technologies.

Pork and poultry are often hailed as the success stories of Russian agriculture.[160] Miratorg and Cherkizovo both reported significant sales increases of around 20 percent for 2015.[161] According to the Russian Poultry Union, domestic poultry production in 2015 reached 4.5 million metric tons, which was 319,000 tons more than in 2014, and rose to 4.7 MMT in 2016.[162] Pork production reached 2.6 MMT in 2015, a 4.2 percent year-on-year increase.[163] The pork and poultry industries had grown so much that they also increased exports during these years. Russian pork exports increased from 500 tons in the first quarter of 2015 to 3,700 tons in the first quarter of 2016, mainly to Ukraine and Belarus.[164] Domestic dairy, beef, and fish producers, by contrast, were initially not able to increase their output to make up for declining imports. The size of Russia's industrial fish catch has persisted at around 4.3 million tons of fish annually in 2015 and 2016, the first two years of the embargo.[165] Russian domestic milk production also remained stable at around 30 million tons during those years.[166] Instead of boosting domestic production, the ban on Western imports led to a geographical shift in imports. Embargoed Lithuanian milk and dairy products were substituted with imports from Belarus. (Belarus was in fact the main winner of the Russian food embargo; it has supplied most of Russia's fluid milk, butter, and cheese.)[167] Fish from Norway was replaced by fish from the Faroe Islands. Beef from the US and Europe was replaced by beef from Brazil and Paraguay. Domestic cheese production has benefited somewhat from the embargo, though a shortage of milk fat created new challenges. Cheese producers switched from importing milk fat from the US and Europe to importing the cheaper palm oil from East Asia.[168] According to Rosselkhoznadzor, more than two-thirds of Russian cheese in 2016 contained palm oil, surely an an unintended effect of the food ban. This is only one very small part of the bigger picture of the ban's effects, but it illustrates how Putin's agro-technopolitics are characterized by a particular kind of global economic integration and types of foods.[169]

Over the next few years, the import ban also created the conditions that fostered long-term investments in the beef and dairy sectors. Before the onset of the ban, the Russian dairy sector had been troubled by lack of investment, by the volatility of milk prices, and by cheap Belarusian, Lithuanian, and American milk and dairy competing for the Russian market. Investments in the beef and dairy sectors take longer to mature, and before the food ban, these and other factors impeded investments in the sector.[170] Ownership and production in the Russian dairy sector had been far more fragmented and less concentrated than in the meat sector, with many small producers barely breaking even. Unlike the poultry and pork sectors, where large vertically integrated actors took advantage of highly subsidized credits, small milk producers were less able to benefit from state support programs. With a lack of domestic capacity and declining imports, raw milk prices increased more than 40 percent in 2015 and 2016.[171] The import protection of the continued food ban and higher prices ended up being strong incentives that helped a small handful of domestic dairy companies. EkoNiva had already been growing in the first decade of the 2000s, and it continued to invest heavily in all areas of operation after 2015. In 2017 alone, the company launched three new dairy plants, in Voronezh, Kaluga, and Tyumen oblast, increasing its milk production from 600 to 800 tons per day. EkoNiva constructed several state-of-the-art grain elevators in Voronezh, Kursk, and Orenburg. As of 2019, the company milked over 67,000 dairy cows and produced more than 1,600 tons of raw milk per day across Russia.[172] EkoNiva operated dairy and crop farms across Russia—in Voronezh, Kursk, Leningrad, Moscow, Kaluga, Orenburg, Tatarstan, Bashkortostan, Tyumen and Novosibirsk, and Altai. It has accumulated thousands of hectares of farmland and employed around 9,000 workers, sponsoring a range of corporate social responsibility programs in many regions, supporting churches, kindergartens, and sports events.[173] The company's rise to become Russia's undisputed dairy empire is a remarkable corporate success story; it also owes much to a political environment that has fostered its growth with a panoply of support measures.

Technologies, New Vulnerabilities, and Unintended Consequences

The default reaction to most rural problems by successive Soviet governments was to look to new technologies in much the same way that American administrations and the USDA have done. Stalin mechanized farms and radically changed rural life. Brezhnev increased the use of fertilizer and hastened the construction of new processing plants. Putin sought changes through new genetic material and technologies to improve livestock production. Over the course of the long twentieth century—from the earliest days of the Revolution to the Putin era—myriad new technologies, each with its own history, sites of innovation, and local adaptation, were introduced to Russia's food system. On the one hand, many of these industrial technologies were imported from capitalist food systems, and a great deal of exchange between Soviet and American experts facilitated technology transfers throughout the twentieth century. On the other hand, all technological fixes were profoundly shaped by the political, social, and climatic conditions of farming on Eurasia's black earth and the steppe. Technologies are usually seen as machines or processes that work according to immutable laws of physics, organic chemistry, or biology. Yet technologies always function in the environment and political context in which they are implemented, and within these particular contexts, the technologies sometimes succeed and sometimes fail but very often have unintended consequences. Khrushchev's Virgin Lands campaign depleted soils within a few years. The harvest of 1963 was particularly bad and seemed to serve as a stark symbol of failure, contributing to Khrushchev's fall from power the following year. Farm technologies adopted by agroholdings in the 2000s, by contrast, have spurred production and have so far helped buttress Putin's claims that his political, economic, and social order has strengthened Russia.

A remarkable aspect of Soviet farming was that small-scale farms were relatively untouched by modernization attempts. Despite decades of hostility by Soviet authorities, subsistence production continued to exist as a labor-intensive and informal food provisioning system that coexisted with large-scale industrial farms. Backyard farms used a whole different set of technologies and knowledge, such as seed saving and home processing—often passed down in families over generations. Over the past decade, the production methods of agroholdings, focused on scale and efficiency, have increasingly sidelined small-scale backyard production, even as potatoes are still grown by friends and families. The shifting balance between small and large—from symbiotic coexistence to nearly undisputed dominance by agroholdings—has far-reaching consequences. First, the rise of agroholdings has shaped Russia's integration into global food commodity markets, contributing to the country's shift from one of the world's largest importers of grain to one of its largest grain exporters. Second, the apparent success of the agroholdings and the technologies they employ afford legitimacy to Putin's political and economic projects. Third, the balance between large and small shapes what is produced and hence Russian diets and the patterns of "who eats what," traced in the next chapter. Finally, technological change hinges on and profoundly affects agriculture's reliance on the natural environment, the subject of the final chapter.

3

Consumption; or, Perestroika of the Quotidian

The morning was quite cold. We began [the day] with tea and white bread. . . . We ate well: boiled liver, noodles with lamb, semolina porridge with milk.
  —Sergei Grammatin, teacher, 1951

The rich are not like us. They don't have to stand in line for rotten sausage.
  —Erkin Zholdasov, Uzbek artist, 1983

Bring me fucking Dover Sole and bring it now!
  —Russian oligarch, late 1990s

CHANGING DIETS AND PERESTROIKA BYTA

Food consumption is part of Russian citizens' quotidian experience, or byt. Bolshevik revolutionaries wanted not only to transform politics and the economy but to cast new men and women through the transformation of everyday lives—what Lenin called the transformation of byt (*perestroika byta*). Soviet planners and bureaucrats devised detailed plans to transform urban spaces, factories, and homes to achieve the revolution of the everyday. In the post-Soviet period, markets have transformed everyday lives no less profoundly than the Bolshevik revolution once did.[1] Changing foodways—a restructuring of what foods are consumed by whom—offer a unique perspective for understanding the perestroika byta of Soviet and post-Soviet Russia. During the Soviet period, government officials deliberated "rational norms of consumption" and cafeteria menus. Yet the foods that were actually available and groups of citizens who had access to them changed greatly over the course of the twentieth century. Bread serves as the most basic marker for understanding food's role in Soviet and post-Soviet byt. In diaries throughout both periods, citizens commented on its presence or absence, its quality and its price. For example, in the late 1930s, in the context of food shortages, a major cause for concern was the deterioration of black bread, perhaps the most reliable staple:

In Moscow, food products are insufficiently available. . . . Even the quality of black bread is deteriorating.[2] (V. V. Ivanovich, Moscow resident, biochemist, January 25, 1938)

After World War II, white bread was a marker of a satisfying diet, appearing together with other fine foods, friends, family, and a chess game in the diary of a teacher quoted in the first chapter epigraph.[3] Similarly, in 1960, bread is mentioned in the same sentence with sweet treats, and sufficient quantities of both are noted with relief:

They gave us plenty of bread and sweets.[4] (B. I. Vronsky, geologist on a field excursion, March 5, 1960)

In the 1980s, white bread was used to win wars and make friends abroad:

Via the army the Afghans became accustomed to our fluffy white bread. At the beginning they asked modestly for a few loaves. . . . We gave them dozens of hot loaves as presents, which they accepted with pleasure.[5] (I. M. Lapshin, Soviet army commander in Afghanistan, August 25, 1988)

In the 1990s, the price of bread caused concern and outrage:

The survival minimum in January in Moscow is 1619 rubles. For food alone 800 [are required], in previous years [it was] 330–350 rubles. A loaf of white bread is 2 rubles and 63 kopeks.[6] (V. A. Bessonov, historian of Moscow, January 4, 1992)

The stores are stocked with diverse and plentiful foodstuffs. But prices are outrageous! Compared to 1989 and 1990, they have increased 30 times. From 2 to 11 rubles for a loaf of black bread.[7] (L. A. Osterman, biochemist and author, June 2, 1992)

These diary entries establish that citizens were concerned about whether bread was available in sufficient quantities, whether they personally and others had access to it, and whether it was of good quality and affordable. Bread, of course, was only the beginning of the story, as socialism and post-socialism both promised abundance and cheerfulness, not just mere survival. Many other food items—including meat and sweet treats—were important features of Soviet and post-Soviet everyday experience. Meals are deeply personal and therefore offer a window on byt, but they are also profoundly shaped by technopolitical regimes in agriculture. We eat what tastes good but also what is available to us, what we can afford, and what we are told we should desire. Desires are in turn shaped by social and political norms about what foods are valuable, healthful, and appropriate for citizens and workers. Availability, access, and allure are complex social facts that are shaped by the political goals and agro-technologies outlined in previous chapters. The discussion below highlights the *availability* of food items, *access* to particular foods by different groups, and the *allure* of certain foods to consumers and government officials. Taken together, these three determinants of food consumption create evolving maps of what is abundant and what is scarce, who has access and who does not. Availability, access, and allure all changed dramatically over the course of the twentieth and twenty-first centuries as Soviet and post-Soviet technopolitical regimes evolved.

Availability, the most material of the three determinants of consumption, is the one most directly tied to the technopolitics of food. For example, the postwar period saw a general increase in animal fat and proteins and a decline in starches—a broad trend that mirrors industrializing countries across the world.[8] A technopolitical lens provides many more detailed and granular insights, such as these: The construction of industrial bakeries in the early Soviet decades brought more bread to urban stores, and workers' diets improved. The expansion of the Soviet fleet of fishing trawlers under Brezhnev made canned fish the most readily available protein. State support of sugar mills by the Putin government turned sweets from occasional treats to ubiquitous ingredients of new processed foods. These dietary manifestations of agro-technopolitics are sometimes intended and sometimes accidental. The displacement of rye (and black bread) by wheat (and white bread) was an unintended outcome of the introduction of modern combines that could be used only to harvest the shorter, sturdy wheat, not the long, willowy stalks of the rye plant. Whether intended or unintended, politics and technology crucially shaped what Soviet and Russian citizens consumed. Susan Reid makes the case that consumption was political in Khrushchev's Russia: a "highly paternalistic . . . regime and its specialist agents intervened even in such seemingly mundane and intimate matters as . . . dress, housekeeping, taste, and consumption."[9] Highlighting the politics and culture of consumption, Reid distances consumption from the economic realm. Seeing consumption through a technopolitical lens allows us to grasp that consumption and byt are in fact closely linked to both the political and the economic order.

A closer look at the history of Russian food consumption over the twentieth and twenty-first centuries reveals general availability and patterns of access and privilege. Access to food was shaped by political and economic stratification, and unequal access was a marker of both Soviet and post-Soviet inequalities. Maps of "who eats what," not just of general availability, show how the planned economy and markets reshaped byt for different groups of citizens and thus offer a new way to understand the contours of Russia's old and new inequality. Despite rejecting bourgeois decadence and material luxuries, Bolshevik party elites enjoyed the best food that could be had at any one time. Opulent and sometimes foreign meals typically included caviar, schnitzel, elaborate baked goods, and wines from the Caucasus, for example.[10] Bolshevik leaders also worried about precisely which consumer goods and foods would keep the socialist revolution's promise to provide the good life for all. Champagne had been a universally recognized marker of upper-class living, and making it available for mass consumption became an important political goal of the 1930s. The general availability of "affordable luxuries" and a growing range of high-quality food items was a political goal, but at least initially a largely aspirational one. Access to desirable foods varied widely, and throughout the early decades of the Soviet Union, many citizens suffered from hunger. Similar disparities are characteristic of the post-Soviet period. Post-Soviet oligarchs could eat rare foreign treats, such as Dover sole and sushi.[11] Meanwhile, pensioners had a very meagre range of choices and limited access to staples.

Finally, this chapter also tracks the value attached to different kinds of meals. Allure refers to the symbolic nature of particular foods—what is valued and desired—shaped by the political context but also in opposition to dominant political norms. Diets and food preferences are tricky to capture precisely because of the diversity of human experience. Russia is a large, multiethnic country with highly varied natural resources. Most Russians regularly eat thin pancakes called *bliny*, but Tatars eat more *pilaf* and lamb than Karelians, who rely on fish as a dietary staple. *Kumys*, fermented mare's milk, was considered healthful and tasty in some Soviet regions but not in others. Regardless of cultural differences, the Bolshevik revolutionaries and the Putin government alike sought to universalize "rational" norms of consumption. Other than quality and provenance, which have dominated concerns about appropriate diets in Russia as elsewhere, what precisely were the aspects of food consumption that governments sought to universalize, and how did citizens respond to them? Soviet and post-Soviet political elites and planners were particularly interested in four categories of food items: (i) industrially processed foods, (ii) meat, (iii) home-cooked meals versus food prepared at public eating facilities, and (iv) domestic foods versus foreign goods. Processed food served as a stand-in for the successful adoption of scientific methods and the modernization of Soviet diets. Eating out, similarly, was considered more efficient, hygienic, and healthy. Meat mattered to Soviet and Russian elites as a marker of political success. And shifting values around domestic versus foreign foods reflected the fact that Russian elites famously oscillated in their valuation of ideas and items originating in "the West," torn between thinking of Russia as belonging to or standing apart from Europe. Sometimes Western foods were thought of as the most modern; at other times Russian foods were thought to be superior. Russia's agro-technopolitics at different times promoted these four categories of diets as elements of the good and healthy life. These four elements and their availability—industrially produced foods, meat, institutionally prepared meals, and foreign versus Russian ingredients—will structure the discussion below, though with the caveat that they privilege a view of urban consumption. We will see a great deal of continuity but also gradual change and a radical shift when moving from the Soviet era to the post-Soviet period.

In the broadest terms, the map of food consumption evolved in the following ways from Soviet to post-Soviet Russia. In the Soviet era, kasha and vegetables were the staple of everyday diets. Shortages limited the availability of foods. Queues and informal work-arounds to acquire supplies required a great deal of "planning, ingenuity and scheming" by Soviet citizens, especially Soviet women.[12] The shortage economy, with its implications for how a family procured food, was thus a hallmark of Soviet byt. Expanded choice and access to a large array of foods were privileges reserved for a small stratum of political elites. At the same time, even as Soviet citizens often had few choices about what to cook and eat, some types of food were usually abundant and universally accessible. In the years after World War II, kasha, cabbage or pea soup, bread, boiled potatoes, salted herring, and vodka—along with occasional sweet treats—were usually available to all at little cost. The Soviet food system was industrialized, and Russians ate processed food, but apart from a few exceptions, the planned economy did not prioritize food processing innovations. Soviet foods tended to be less elaborately processed and less conveniently packaged than their Western counterparts. Ironically and importantly, it was precisely the shortcomings of the planned system that led to a diet made up of a large share of entirely unprocessed food items that originated on household farms. As noted in earlier chapters, homegrown and home-processed foods were a central aspect of most Russians' diets. The taste, appearance, and makeup of food on Soviet tables thus differed from food items consumed by citizens in capitalist technopolitical regimes.

Post-Soviet abundance and well-stocked grocery stores were perceived with relief compared to the scarcity of earlier eras. Initially, Western products were imported, but many of these imports were barely within reach for the majority of regular citizens, who either could not afford them or could only occasionally splurge on them. After around 2000, Russian food consumption changed significantly: more affordable food became available to most Russians, and urban citizens' diets increasingly began to resemble those of citizens of the advanced capitalist West. Many Russians began eating breakfast cereals, hot dogs, home-delivered pizza, and chicken nuggets. Abundance and choice are the result of the rise of private agroholdings, the inflow of capital, and political support for domestic agriculture, as discussed in earlier chapters. The technopolitics of agriculture in Putin's Russia has thus made affordable, high-quality, domestically produced options more available, but it has also produced a culture that values processed and convenient options over alternatives. Unlike in the Soviet era, the most accessible and affordable foods are also often convenience foods that are high in sugar, highly processed, and heavily marketed. However, as has also occurred in the advanced capitalist West, an alternative food sector carved out a niche for locally grown and minimally processed foods. By the Putin period, a cultural shift in food values led to more demand for domestically produced and native (*nashi*—"our") foods that was reflected on menus in high-end and fast-food restaurants alike.

At the same time, access became even more unequal as patterns of privilege changed. In the post-Soviet period, provenance, quality, and cost have become more urgent concerns. There are now more choices in stores, but choice is still not a simple category. Choice and access are now contingent on household incomes, not on political privilege.[13] Income inequality and income fluctuations are just as much the result of post-Soviet economic policies as the abundance of domestically produced poultry products. Homemade and locally produced foods are available to two groups in Russia today: moneyed urban elites, and those who can commit time and resources to obtaining food from small farms and household gardens. In sum, policies, technologies, and culture together shaped the availability, access, and allure of different meals and foods in the Soviet and post-Soviet periods. The agro-technopolitics of the future will determine whether Russian consumers can fall back on homegrown staples during the crises of the twenty-first century as they did in the twentieth century.

Availability

The *Book of Tasty and Healthy Food* (*Kniga o vkusnoi i zdorovoi pishche*) was the Soviet Union's officially endorsed cookbook. Published for the first time in 1939 with a foreword by Anastas Mikoyan, Stalin's minister of foreign trade, the book was meant to demonstrate to Soviet citizens the contours of an adequate and rewarding diet. While initially largely aspirational, its recipes nevertheless modeled the changing foods and diets that political elites identified as the fulfillment of the socialist promise. The four categories outlined above each appear in the book's first edition and in the revised editions issued during the postwar period, including vegetarian and meat dishes, and with processed and "industrial" foods appearing alongside recipes using fresh ingredients. It also afforded glimpses at new culinary trends from abroad that were interspersed with the recipes for meals considered typically Russian. Finally, it served as a guide for meal preparation in private kitchens but also included recipes for the stalwarts of canteens and cafés. Overall, the book was guided by planners' aspirations as much as by reality, featuring dishes with ingredients that were not readily available. How did these aspirations translate into the food on Soviet plates?

Soviet Processed and Fresh Foods

Though processed food's history in Russia is distinct from its American trajectory, the two stories are closely intertwined. Anastas Mikoyan traveled to the US in 1936 to survey American food processing innovations.[14] He encountered sandwiches, ketchup, and cornflakes, but he was most impressed with hockey-puck-shaped meat patties and thought these convenient and tasty food items should be available to Soviet workers. About eighty years later, processed foods such as potato chips, cookies, and soda epitomize all that food system critics think has gone wrong in underregulated capitalist food systems.[15] They are among the cheapest and most readily available foods in just about every food system, but they are also high in calories and low in nutrients, and they are widely recognized to be among the main factors contributing to the global obesity epidemic.[16] From the vantage point of 2020, industrially processed foods are fascinating because they are both beloved and reviled in equal measure by discerning consumers in Russia and the West. Even if the food-conscious urban intelligentsia publicly professes its hate for processed foods, the addiction to single-serve flavored yogurt and power bars runs deep. A vast share of food dollars in advanced industrialized countries is spent on products that have been processed in one form or another. Convenient packaging, easy preparation, and long shelf life are almost universally taken for granted. A few vocal critics aside, most consumers in the West are ardently in love with processed food. By 2020, most Russian consumers have come to embrace things like breakfast cereal and frozen pizza, opting out when possible from the more tedious and less exciting option of preparing every meal from scratch.

Long before Twinkies became known as "junk food" in the US, the engineering of food items to produce a highly specific flavor, texture, and decay resistance was enthusiastically embraced in both the US and the Soviet Union. At the beginning of the twentieth century, political and economic elites in both countries were excited by the idea of pairing science with food processing to bring about a better life for citizens. In the 1920s, the Bolshevik government wanted to harness science to guide its dietary advice to Soviet citizens, just as science was to replace tradition and religion in other spheres of the revolutionary transformation. Right from the beginning, however, there were many uncertainties and competing philosophies about how to transform diets. Whether new socialist citizens would have to renounce chocolate, meat, and caviar as useless bourgeois habits, or whether they should actually eat them in abundance, was an important debate at the time.[17] A vocal group of food futurists wanted to do away with food as it was known and replace traditional meals with synthetic food and food surrogates that had optimal nutritional value. Others advocated for vegetarian diets.[18] Though science and economic planning were to remake the Soviet food system, the creation of a vast state procurement system to feed a large and urbanizing society was an ambitious goal. Utopian discussions about ideal diets took a backseat to more pragmatic considerations of how to feed people in the twenties and thirties, decades marked by food rationing and hunger. Most Soviet citizens at the time survived on the basic staples of black rye bread, potatoes, cabbage, and some tea and vodka.[19] During World War II, the government prioritized the diets of soldiers at the front; adequate provisions for civilians were at best a secondary concern. Unlike US troops, who were provisioned with dry and canned (i.e., processed) foods, Soviet troops had field kitchens that sourced food locally and prepared meals at the front. Brandon Schechter documents a typical meal of a Red Army soldier during World War II as listed below; note that white bread was reserved for higher-ranking army personnel.

Typical Red Army Meal (Western Front, 1943)

Bread, white bread for commanders and pilots, black for other ranks and positions

Soup or stew, with either cabbage, potatoes or carrots.

With some meat for commanders, sometimes with meat for other ranks.

Tea, with either cookies for commanders, chocolate for pilots, or tobacco for other ranks.

Vodka.[20]

In peacetime, urban consumers were the primary beneficiaries of state procurement and the distribution system designed to feed industrial workers. Starting in the 1930s, some select mass-produced luxury items became available: white bread, sausages, cheese, canned fish and vegetables, chocolates, and even champagne and liquors. These delicacies were meant to reward citizens for their contributions to the socialist project and prove that socialism was indeed desirable.[21] After the war, Khrushchev's renewed focus on consumption and byt was reflected in improved food provisions. At least in cities, dietary staples were available at a low cost to most citizens. Although some commodities were scarce, others were abundantly available. Salted herring (*sel'd'*) with potatoes or beets, onions, and vodka is an example of a popular dinner for party elites and workers alike, and one for which all ingredients were usually available.[22] In the postwar decades, meat consumption in the Soviet Union increased steadily, as did the consumption of sugar and vegetable oils. The latter two were increasingly consumed as ingredients in processed food items. The state allocated sugar beets to mills and processing plants and requisitioned imported cane sugar for the food industry, often leaving little sugar for retail stores and individual consumers. When sugar was actually available in stores, it was one of the commodities that consumers liked to buy in bulk and hoard, contributing further to its uneven availability.[23]

The sweet side of the Soviet diet included chocolates, ice cream, soda, and fizzy lemonade from vending machines that dispensed drinks into shared glasses. Cotton candy was sold at zoos and fairs.[24] Jukka Gronow documents how chocolates and sparkling white wine became treats for the masses in the 1930s. Jenny Leigh Smith traces how ice cream cones and sandwiches became well loved and widely available during the postwar period. Both ice cream and chocolate were singled out in the 1930s by Anastas Mikoyan as treats that should become available to all Soviet citizens.[25] Clearly everyone loved them; hence, they were designated an affordable luxury to prove the point that ordinary socialist citizens could eat desserts that had previously been reserved for aristocrats. Soviet champagne also became available at low cost and in large quantities, providing ordinary citizens with a bright, sparkling alcoholic beverage for celebrating life events and socialist holidays.[26] For ice cream to become part of Soviet citizens' recreational joys in all major urban areas, several technological hurdles had to be overcome. This didn't happen until the 1950s, when technological advances made it possible to deliver and sell ice cream from dedicated pushcarts for immediate consumption. Ice cream vendors sold either unwrapped cones—as shown in figure 3.1—or brightly colored, individually wrapped bars, the most iconic of which were Eskimo bars. Other widely available sweets in the postwar years were cookies (*pechen'e*) and candy (*konfety*); cakes and other treats with chocolate and sometimes marzipan were made in dedicated confectionary plants. The "Kiev cake," invented in 1956 by two workers at the Karl Marx confectionary factory in Kiev, became a legendary luxury dessert throughout the Soviet Union.

The Soviet Union thus produced industrially processed food, but as food processing continued to be classified as "light industry," it never quite made it to the top of state planners' priority lists. This meant that many foods were

Figure 3.1 Ice cream vendor, Leningrad, July 26, 1978. Oleg Porokhovnikov/TASS.

sold in an unprocessed or minimally processed state. Chickens were usually sold whole, complete with giblets, heads, and feet. Most meat was sold with bones. Fish was sold frozen and whole.[27] The most common form processed packaging took was cans: for example, peas and squid in cans were Soviet staples. Pasta with canned fish was a fairly typical Russian family meal.[28] The care Stalin and Mikoyan devoted to the packaging of caviar and champagne as highly symbolic luxury goods was not given to most other foods. Packaging was usually either nonexistent or scant. Plastic was too expensive and rarely used. Most products were wrapped in simple, sometimes flimsy materials such as thin paper or light cardboard. Frozen meat dumplings, or pelmeni, were sold in cardboard boxes that sometimes stuck to the dumplings. Many products arrived in stores in bulk, and consumers often had to bring their own containers to transport the unpacked or lightly packaged items home.[29] The sale of fresh fluid milk was logistically challenging for reasons related to packaging and refrigeration, so most of the milk sold in the Soviet Union was either condensed or dehydrated; alternatively, citizens could buy cream and a variety of fermented milk products (*kislomolochnye produkty*).[30] Since processors did not compete with each other, they spent minimal resources on branding. If food was wrapped or packaged, the packaging indicated in simple lettering the contents, weight, and price.

The quality of some processed food products was good, but for others, it was inconsistent and at times poor. Soviet citizens joked, for example, that pasta (*makarony*) was rough and thick because it was made by the same production lines that had produced gun cartridges.[31] Others thought that Soviet noodles were "white, fragile and starchy" and lost their shape when boiled.[32] Pelmeni often stuck not only to their packaging but also to each other in a clump that didn't come apart during cooking. Quality issues arose in part from the fact that simple packaging did not prevent spoilage. Glitches in the procurement system also contributed to quality problems. Supply problems existed everywhere in the planned economy, but with perishable food items, delays or the lack of inputs were particularly problematic. Refrigeration proved a particular challenge for the state-run provisioning system. It was impossible to sell ice cream to stores, for example, as long as reliable freezers and refrigerated transportation were rare.[33] A further aspect of Soviet food processing was that only a limited variety of processed foods was available. A handful of types of breads, sausages, cheeses, sodas, and candies were sold in stores, but Soviet consumers did not have a choice between the virtually unlimited brand extensions and minor modifications that capitalist food systems produced. Limited brand variety and minimal processing made for a much simpler array of processed goods. Often, the novelties of Soviet food processing had more to do with what was available abundantly and less to do with what consumers demanded. Soviet cookbooks attest to the fact that this in turn required consumers to work out how to use these novelties of Soviet food provisioning. Creativity and thoughtfulness were part of this process: women were encouraged to consult recipes for how to prepare canned squid, for example, or to look up vegetarian meals when meat was unavailable.[34]

Though the Soviet food system had its sweet spots and some forms of simple goodness were abundant, shortages were pervasive and became crippling by the 1980s. Eggs, for example, were for much of the Soviet period and in most parts of the country only intermittently available in stores. During World War II, they disappeared altogether, though they became more readily available in the Brezhnev years. In the late Soviet period, the number of goods that were in short supply multiplied. Shortages became an urgent and often miserable everyday reality: store shelves were sometimes almost bare, with the exception of some items—canned eggplant and herring, for example—that everyone already had plenty of at home. Individuals and families expended a great deal of time and ingenuity in securing desired and at times even basic food items, often through informal channels. Procuring a meal was always, as Sarah Moir describes it, a sort of "group effort"—as it often relied on time and favors from several family members and friends to procure one ingredient or the other.[35] Consumption patterns were decisively influenced by what was available. Often families would eat one type of food for days or weeks because that was all the stores had to offer. Caroline Humphrey observes that "the range of products was so limited as to enforce an involuntary homogeneity on all consumption."[36] In 1989, shortages became even more severe, and in the winter of 1990/91, many cities introduced food rationing.[37]

As noted already, most potatoes and vegetables—cabbage, beets, turnips, carrots, onions, and various "greens" (*zelen'*)—along with fruits, such as apples, pears, cherries, and melons—originated from ogorody and dacha plots. Zelen' include various fresh herbs, such as dill, parsley, and chives, that add valuable vitamins for Russian diets. Meat, milk, and eggs also often originated on LPKh plots. These foods were foundational to the Russian diet throughout the Soviet and post-Soviet periods. In contrast to the industrially processed foods produced at the direction of Soviet planners, they were either entirely unprocessed and consumed fresh or they were home processed. Fermented dairy products, such as sour cream and tvorog, were prepared in large buckets and preserved and passed on in jars. The category of well-loved, home-processed foods with ingredients that originated in the household sector also includes pickles, preserves, honey, dried fruits, herbs, and teas. Berries, nuts, mushrooms, and herbs gathered in the wild were eaten fresh, pickled, or dried by households. Fermented cabbage (*kvashenaia kapusta*) was another staple of home processing, as was homemade aubergine paste. Fermentation and pickling were ubiquitous practices. Enameled buckets with weighted lids could be found on virtually every balcony of an urban apartment building and in the kitchens of rural households. These home-processed foods were largely consumed by family members or bartered among neighbors and friends. Some were sold in the informal economy. Urban consumers without access to garden plots could buy these products from pensioners at roadsides and at simple stands at outdoor markets (figure 3.2 shows berries at an urban outdoor market). These goods were often available at train stations or metro underpasses as rural residents used public transport to reach cities and supply the urban demand for homemade pickles and preserves.

With the liberalization of small commerce under Gorbachev and later the economic collapse in the nineties, roadside stands and public markets that

Figure 3.2 Fresh berries, outdoor market, Petropavlovsk-Kamchatskii, Kamchatka, October 2007. Photo by E. Jay Rehm.

sold preserves, dairy products, and kvass from home kitchens became an important feature of urban life. In addition to pickled and preserved fruits and vegetables, various baked goods such as *pirozhki, chebureki,* and *khachapuri* were Soviet and early post-Soviet street food.[38] We saw in chapter 2 that overall subsistence production has dwindled under Putin, and the future of subsistence farming in Russia is uncertain. Perhaps it will be important that Russian households have a recent history of relying extensively on homegrown products and that at least older Russians have a direct relationship to this kind of food. For many families, the experience and knowledge of subsistence farming are only one generation removed.

The Marketization and Ubiquity of Highly Processed Food

Today's nostalgia for Soviet food often evokes an era of sweet and simple pleasures. The end of the socialist food provisioning system and the onset of economic liberalization dramatically reengineered tastes; even "sweetness" itself changed, thanks to new sources of sugar. Pepsi-Cola, available in Russia since the mid-1970s, was the first harbinger of industrially processed foods from the capitalist world.³⁹ Coke and candy bars—especially Mars, Snickers, and Cadbury chocolates—followed in the late 1980s. Considered small luxuries whose desirability was tied to their novelty value and bright packaging, they were often sold by traders in small kiosks near train and metro stations.⁴⁰ These products brought a new type of sweetness to Russian diets. Russian sugar was largely sourced from beets, which produce a somewhat different sweetness than sugar cane and corn syrup, the main ingredients of imported candy. More radical differences in processed food items were brought about by the arrival of fast-food restaurants in the nineties. McDonald's had opened its first restaurant in Moscow in January 1990, and many other fast-food chains followed, bringing with them a particular kind of highly processed food.

During the nineties, processed goods imported from all over the world were increasingly present in Russian stores. They included pizza, flavored yogurt in single-serve containers, juice in tetra packs, imported pasta, sausages, candy, and soda, along with many other novelties. They arrived in Russian stores in bright and fancy packaging, ready to eat and safe from spoilage for months. This kind of packaging was the Western answer to the problem of perishability that had eluded the Soviet planned economy a few decades earlier. In capitalist food systems, branding, packaging, and marketing have long been a central element of product development, as they often make or break a product. Russian products with a very different history suddenly had to compete with these flashy marvels with long shelf lives in the country's new supermarkets.

Parallel to these changes in grocery stores, local and largely unprocessed foods originating in private gardens and local forests continued to play an absolutely vital role in the diets of many Russians during this time. In the turmoil of the early years of post-Soviet marketization, virtually every family supplemented its diet with fresh and homegrown products, and many Russian households survived on them. During this time of extreme need and uncertainty, these goods assumed a relevance beyond their nutritional value. Homegrown potatoes, Nancy Ries argues, came to signify an ability to survive any crisis, even thrive against the odds that fate might deliver.⁴¹

Beginning in the early 2000s, the availability of home-processed and homegrown food declined significantly, especially when compared to the peak relevance of these goods in the difficult nineties. As the previous chapter outlined, affordable, attractive, and domestically produced foods became increasingly available to Russian consumers during the first two terms of the Putin presidency. Juice, candy, and new dairy products were the first products to make this transition from foreign import to affordable, domestic, mass-produced goods. Chips, breakfast cereals, and a vast array of prepared and frozen meals followed close behind. The attributes that had been characteristic of imported foods—they were highly processed, cleverly packaged, carefully branded and marketed, resistant to spoilage, and easy to prepare—also became features of Russian-made products. Today's pelmeni are packaged in plastic bags and contain ingredients that prevent them from clumping together. Processed foods are also available in a variety of flavors, sizes, and packaging, uniquely engineered to appeal to the Russian consumer. Finally, they are sweet and sweetened in new ways. While sweet treats had been part of Soviet diets, they had only been available in far smaller quantities. The new ubiquity of processed goods such as bottled soda and juices or flavored, sweetened yogurt dramatically sweetened post-Soviet diets. These products were now produced in domestic facilities and from Russian ingredients, using the very same processing technologies and branding strategies used by global food giants. The marketization of the Russian food system thus largely blurred the distinction between Western and Russian products. It became impossible to say whether frozen pelmeni in a Russian food store should be considered "Russian"; indeed, the distinction appeared to be as political as it was material.

Meat

Industrially processed foods are central to contemporary, capitalist food systems. They are also their least healthy products. Meat is another central component of diets that has come under increasing scrutiny, though debates about whether or not humans should rely on animal proteins have a much longer history, in Russia as elsewhere. Lev Tolstoy made an eloquent and resonant ethical plea for meatless diets in 1891 that gave rise to a Russian tradition of vegetarianism.[42] Successive Soviet and post-Soviet governments veered in the opposite direction. Since the 1930s, more meat on the table was an explicit and important political goal because it was seen as a way to make good on the party's promise of the good life. This priority is not uniquely Russian, of course—it maps onto consumption trends in other industrializing societies, where citizens consume more meat, poultry, and fish as they grow more affluent and urban. Though meat remained a political priority, the quantity and types of meat that were actually consumed changed significantly throughout the twentieth and twenty-first centuries—largely as a consequence of the successes and failures of technopolitical regimes in agriculture.

In the Civil War and NEP years, meat was in very short supply, and collectivization damaged livestock herds for a decade. High-level Bolshevik revolutionaries occasionally dined on fine cuts of meat if they were available, but for everyone else, meat was a rarity. Portions of meat and fish in Soviet cookbooks of the 1920s were half the size found in prerevolutionary cookbooks.[43] In the 1930s, the absence of meat is a subject that appears frequently in diary entries, such as the following by K. F. Ismailov, a Komsomol organizer, on July 2, 1933: "My meals today were weak and nauseating. We have been out of dried pork for two days. And we no longer have [fresh] meat."[44] During World War II, herds on collective farms and at processing facilities were destroyed by invading German troops and meat, dairy, and eggs were all tightly rationed.[45] Limited availability, lines, and rising prices were preeminent civilian concerns, as noted by F. N. Parshinskii, a pensioner in Arkhangelsk. According to a diary entry dated November 4, 1941, "Today there was a long line for cabbage at the produce vendor, out to the street: the whole world rushed to the market. Prices suddenly rose, within two days. Cabbage was 6r. instead of 3r. Beef was 50r. instead of 30r."[46] In the 1950s, meat slowly became more available. This was much appreciated by those who could get access, as S. D. Grammatin, a teacher, noted on December 10, 1951: "I was in a good mood. I was able to buy 3 kilo of pork on the way to the post office. As well as those little chicken legs for the Christmas holidays."[47] Pork and beef were the most commonly consumed meats in the Soviet Union. Pork was usually consumed in the form of sausages, or alternatively as *salo* (cured slabs of pork fat) or ham in cans. All three products were salty and fatty, requiring vodka to wash them down.[48] Canned pork, known as *tushonka*, was initially imported from the US during World War II. "Salty, fatty, and slightly grey-toned" canned ham was included in Red Army soldiers' rations and remained available in Soviet stores for years after the war.[49] Other forms of meat that were available on a somewhat regular basis were pelmeni and staples at institutional kitchens such as meat patties or chops, meatballs, and meat-stuffed cabbage rolls (*kotleti*, *bitochki*, and *golubtsy*). Many of these dishes used various added ingredients (grains, rice, or cabbage) to make small amounts of meat stretch to feed large groups of diners.[50] In stores, meat was usually sold unprocessed and whole as tough cuts that required long cooking times. Soups and stews were the main forms in which Russians generally consumed meat. Cattle and chicken varieties in the Soviet Union were almost all "dual-purpose" breeds that were raised not for tenderness, but for milk or egg production before slaughter.[51] Those with backyard farms who were able to feed their livestock could provision their families with meat, but this meant that it was available infrequently and in bulk, whenever an animal was slaughtered. Since there were few ways to preserve meat, families slaughtered animals on special occasions—such as holidays, weddings, and funerals—and distributed the meat among family members and friends.

Overall, meat and fish consumption more than doubled between 1950 and the 1980s, from about 26 kilograms of meat per person per year to more than 50 kilograms per person per year. Milk consumption increased by 80 percent over the three postwar decades, while wheat and potato consumption decreased by 20 percent.[52] By the mid-1970s, Soviet citizens' average meat consumption approached the diets of their Nordic and East European neighbors—between 50 and 70 kilograms per person per year. Meat consumption in Finland and Poland, for example, was quite similar to that of a Soviet citizen in the 1970s. See table 3.1 for meat consumption levels in the Soviet Union and Russia. German and French consumption at that time was somewhat higher (70–80 kilograms), while American meat consumption was always greater than all of Europe's—more than 100 kilograms per person per year since 1970.[53] Despite increasing consumption in the USSR overall, meat was quite unevenly distributed. In Estonia, for example, meat consumption was on average 50 kilograms per person per year in 1970, while it was 31 kilograms per person per year in Uzbekistan.[54] In virtually all cities, though, demand outstripped supply via formal channels. Supply, and therefore consumption, was also quite unpredictable. Sometimes there was no meat available at all in the local stores; then it would mysteriously reappear and people would stand in line to procure some, as noted by L. A. Levitskii, a literary critic, on September 14, 1978: "No meat is to be found in Smolensk. If they 'throw some out there,' which does not happen every day, long lines appear at stores."[55] Over the decades, planners tried to come up with pragmatic solutions and alternative proteins for Russian dinner tables. Canned squid and saltwater fish were not traditionally part of the Russian diet but were suggested substitutes for chicken and beef.[56] More generally, fish, especially frozen, was the most readily available animal protein.

Table 3.1 Meat consumption, Soviet Union and Russia, 1950–2015

Year	Meat consumption Soviet Union / Russian Federation (kg/person/year)
1950	26
1970	48 (63 urban; 45 rural)
1980	58–70
1985	70
1990	75
1995	55
2000	45
2005	55
2010	69
2015	73

Sources: Zhores Medvedev, *Soviet Agriculture* (1987); Federal'naia sluzhba gosudarstvennoi statisiki.

Just as the choicest cuts of chicken and beef were largely unavailable, tender varieties of fish such as sole were similarly far less readily available than larger fish that were mostly suitable for fish soup or fish sticks. While in the seventies and for some years in the early eighties more meat than ever was consumed, severe shortages returned in the late eighties, leaving some Soviet citizens wondering, ironically, if they remembered how meat tasted.[57] In the late Soviet period, complaints about queues to procure meat were ubiquitous: "I waited in line for two hours to buy pork!" notes T. Iu. Korob'ina on January 17, 1991.[58] For much of the nineties, most meat was a high-priced luxury.[59] Imports were too expensive, consumers worried about provenance and quality, and hardly any Russian meat was available.

After around 2005, meat consumption was transformed again in important ways. Not only did it increase overall, but the origin and type of meat changed as well, with pork and poultry in particular becoming increasingly available and affordable. In the decade between 2005 and 2015, Russian pork consumption nearly doubled.[60] Putin-era technopolitics not only made meat more readily available but also increased the range of chicken and pork products consumers could buy. Meat was now increasingly sold fresh as well as in highly processed, conveniently packaged form. In fact, most of the meat offerings in Russia, around two-thirds, was sold in processed form.[61] The abundance of processed meat was evident in any super market as well as in the following excerpt from the 2018 product catalog of the Miratorg meat processing plant.[62]

From Miratorg's Product Catalog (2017)

Classic chicken nuggets
Crispy chicken nuggets
Cheesy chicken nuggets
Ham-stuffed chicken nuggets
Cheese- and mushroom-stuffed chicken nuggets
Potato-coated chicken strips
Crispy rosemary chicken strips with cheese
Chicken strips with corn chips and paprika coating
Spicy pepper-coated chicken strips

Dining In versus Eating Out

Foods prepared at home versus in an institutional kitchen differ significantly in quality, texture, and taste. Public and private cooking and eating are always in some way linked to *what* was consumed and the labor involved in food preparation. In other words, the locale of cooking and food preparation matter because they have a great deal to do with the kind of meal being prepared and who is preparing it. Of course, institutional and commercial kitchens vary widely, and no two home kitchens are alike. At the same time, institutional and commercial kitchens share a few key attributes: food is prepared by employed labor, in larger quantities, for many more diners, and for purchase. Food preparation in institutional kitchens follows a set of deliberate principles shaped by planners, policy makers, and later post-Soviet firms. Home kitchens share a different set of attributes: labor is usually unpaid, quantities are smaller, and most diners live at the same address. Home cooking is influenced by cookbooks, magazines, and TV shows, as well as the changing nature of food retail stores, but the space in which it occurs is far less regulated and less supervised than public eating establishments.

Soviet-Era Canteens (*Stolovye*) and Restaurants

From the earliest days of the revolution, the Soviet government had a decidedly negative view of private kitchens and fought to diminish their importance in citizens' everyday life. Public initiatives tried to shift food preparation and consumption from the home to communal kitchens, food service enterprises, and cafeterias. The Bolshevik government considered communal dining halls and public catering preferable to private kitchens for many reasons: the public dining options would be (in theory) more efficient and sanitary as well as less wasteful. They would assure the provision of healthy and nutritious food to the masses, making sure Soviet citizens were fed in the most economical and "scientific" way.[63] They were also meant to be meeting places where workers, students, and bureaucrats could absorb the collectivist spirit and learn about good nutrition as they consumed daily meals.[64] Canteens, or stolovye, would increase worker productivity and serve as public "hearths" that could produce and nourish socialist citizens and generally "accelerate the tempo of socialist construction."[65] Private kitchens and home-cooked food were deemed inferior: cooking in private kitchens was seen as "a lot of fuss with dirty pots and pans" that "deform[s] women's bodies and souls."[66] Public eateries and professional meal preparation at institutional kitchens would liberate women from the yoke of cooking for the bourgeois family unit.

Restaurants, cafés, and stolovye in factories and other institutions were the three types of public eateries that prepared and served food to Soviet citizens. Stolovye, where workers, teachers, and students ate several meals per day, were the most important public eating site for most urban citizens. Initially, the promise of a system to provide public catering (*obshepit'*) was largely incongruent with the realities, especially during times of crisis. In the early years of communal dining, complaints arose over the poor quality of ingredients and the lack of kitchen equipment and dishes, not to mention the flies, dirt, and untrained staff. During times of shortages and war, customers were often served thin gruel and watery soups that were, by some accounts, "barely edible." This fare could include, according to one description, "soup with herring head or rotten sour cabbage and for the main course moldy millet gruel or a piece of old herring."[67] Soviet restaurants and cafeterias did sometimes receive more supplies than retail stores, although they received the same types of items. Not surprisingly, some cafeterias were better supplied than others, and some were well loved, while others were not. Overall, though, collective dining establishments were part of urban infrastructure in the Soviet Union and much of Eastern Europe as well, feeding millions of citizens during much of their lives. As food supplies improved in the postwar decades, cafeterias served meals that presented a selection of dishes, such as salads, soups, a main course, and a dessert that added up to a "complete" or "complex" meal (*kompleksnyi obed*). Cabbage soup, salads with mayonnaise, and buckwheat were staples at cafeterias, and tvorog pancakes (*syrniki*) or pirozhki were also common. Drinks made from fruits (such as *kompot* and *kisel'*) and kefir were served in glasses. These meals and the experience of cafeteria eating became central features of Soviet byt, even if they did not fully displace private kitchens or home-cooked meals.

Typical Menu in a Well-Supplied Thaw-Era Stolovaia
Soup, such as *shchi* or borscht
Zakuski (starters), such as *vinegret* (beet and diced vegetable salad) or *forshmak*
 (pâté made from cooked and minced meat or fish)
Main course, such as stew, pelmeni, or buckwheat with meat or fish
Additional course, such as kisel,' kefir, or kompot
Dessert, such as cookies or sweet pirozhki with tea

The more upscale restaurants tended to receive choice products and were able to serve more elaborate and higher-quality dishes. Especially better cuts of meat—steaks, schnitzels, and escallops—were available at restaurants but not in stores. Unlike eating in the stolovye, which were usually quite functional and a bit drab, restaurant dining was more about the atmosphere and spending time with friends and family than it was about the food. In the 1930s, Moscow's most famous restaurants, the Metropol', the Natsional, and the Praga, featured interiors decorated with chandeliers and had butlers on staff.[68] Restaurants were expensive, and visits were rare for almost all Russian citizens, although they were meant to be accessible on special occasions. Planners had to strike a delicate balance between, on the one hand, democratic accessibility and, on the other, demonstrating prosperity and aspiration to higher levels of well-being through dishes and interiors that would formerly be associated with upper-class living.⁶⁹ Over the decades, the décor at restaurants and at smaller and more casual cafés reflected what planners decided to highlight as distinctive and valuable features of Soviet culture. As Soviet achievements in space travel in the fifties and sixties came to define many aspects of cultural production, cafés across the Soviet Union were decorated with themes inspired by cosmology and space (see the interior of the Kosmos Café in figure 3.3). Public eating was thus never only about refueling workers with the necessary starches and proteins.

Meanwhile, kitchens and home cooking did not disappear. They remained important aspects of everyday Soviet lives. Kitchens were the "central square" of communal apartments, where everyday life happened and residents shared joys and sorrows.⁷⁰ Figure 3.4 from the mid-1990s shows a communal kitchen as a space where pots hang next to drying socks amid various other artifacts of byt. Shared kitchens were also spaces of contention where the frictions of communal living materialized as conflicts erupted over shared space, cooking times, and standards of cleanliness. In the Khrushchev era, when many Soviet families moved from communal apartments to separate apartments, kitchens remained important social and political sites. In part, the centrality of the kitchen was related to Cold War politics of consumption. The US chose to define the terms of the competition with the Soviet Union with a fully automated "miracle kitchen" that was installed at the American National Exhibition that opened in Moscow in the summer of 1959. This is where the famous kitchen debate between Khrushchev and Nixon took place that singled out the American kitchen as the ultimate fulfillment of the promise of capitalism. Susan Reid notes that the official Soviet response was initially dismissive— "the fully mechanized kitchen, being in the domestic and traditionally feminine domain, did not count as a display of advanced technology"—and tried to highlight achievements in shared public infrastructure, canteens, and cafés.⁷¹ Given that retail stores in the Soviet Union did not feature the same abundance of products as American supermarkets, the odds were stacked against the Soviet kitchen. But the kitchen competition was not easily called off. Soviet women (despite the official rhetoric, gender roles in the home barely budged) weren't willing to entirely give up meal preparation. Perhaps less impressed with communal dining than party officials, they continued to place great importance on home cooking. In response, Soviet planners tried to improve kitchens and make time-saving appliances more widely accessible.⁷² Soviet women's journals continued to publish columns with titles such as "What to Cook?" typically featuring tips on family meals, entertaining, and preserving.⁷³ By the late Soviet period, the kitchen had become even more important as a sanctuary of privacy, where the most interesting and heated discussions of all matters of private and public life could be discussed.

Figure 3.3 Kosmos Café, Moscow, July 1966. Nikolai Akimov/TASS.

Figure 3.4 Kitchen in a communal apartment, St. Petersburg, 1997. Photo by Ilya Utekhin for the Communal living archive, Colgate University.

The Growth of Fast-Food Chains

Both home cooking and eating out changed dramatically in the post-Soviet period. In the 1990s, enterprises and public-sector institutions still operated stolovye and cafés, and some of them continued to serve the food they always had. By the 2000s, new firms and privatized companies were shedding "non-core" assets and services, and cafeterias often fell into this category. Cafeterias attached to public-sector organizations remained a feature of public life, but they too have had to fight for funding and compete against other restaurants. Starting in the 1990s, American fast-food restaurants moved to Russia and offered a whole new range of options for where and what to eat. Though some food items at Soviet-era stolovye had been prepared off-premises, they did not resemble the high-tech feats of food engineering that are the hallmark of what is served at Western fast-food restaurants. McDonald's opened its first restaurant in 1990 at a prime Moscow location and was swiftly followed by other chains—Kentucky Fried Chicken, Sbarro, Baskin-Robbins, and later Pret a Manger and Pain Quotidian.[74] Public dining was now being shaped by the intentionally designed and carefully themed experiences in which fast-food chains specialize. International fast-food and restaurant chains became ubiquitous as the major European and US chains moved to get in on Russians' fast-growing appetite for eating out.[75] A number of Russian restaurants and café chains—Elki Palki, Teremok, Shokoladnitsa, and Kroshka Kartoshka—competed with global brands, with interiors and menus that were meant to draw on Russian tastes and traditions. The Russian Pitstsa Fabrika now competes with Domino's, Pizza Hut, and Papa John's. Various ethnic restaurants opened as well, relying on Russified versions of Central Asian, Japanese, and Chinese food to compete with Western chains. In the 2000s, as incomes rose, these kinds of restaurants multiplied, and Russians began eating out more. Middle-income and affluent urban consumers have been eating at restaurants styled as Soviet-era stolovye or cafeterias, Irish pubs, or French bistros, along with anything else that fast-food marketing has thought of. The number of fast-food franchises and coffeehouses, and the annual turnover at these establishments, doubled in the decade after 2004.[76] Initially, these restaurants were mostly present in cities in European Russia. Since 2010, these and other fast-food places have increasingly moved beyond the Urals to smaller cities in Siberia and the Far East.[77] By 2015, there were 6,500 food-service franchises operating in Russia, feeding millions of Russians. Five US-based fast-food chains dominate 60 percent of the Russian fast-food franchise: McDonald's, Subway, Burger King, Baskin-Robbins, Cinnabon, and Starbucks.[78]

Most urban residents now eat at a fast-food restaurant at least several times a month.[79] Their growing popularity has served as the engine for the consumption of maximally processed food and chicken products. The food served at Russian restaurants is essentially global fast food—from shchi, syrniki, and shashlik to sushi, bliny, burgers, and baguette sandwiches. Chicken meat is the most common item on fast-food menus as it is the cheapest meat and can be sold most profitably. The menu of a Russian McDonald's restaurant differs only slightly from its American counterpart; other than the sour-cherry pirozhki for dessert and a few other items, most of the meals are identical. Baskin-Robbins sells a few different flavors in Russia—VDNKh (named after the Exhibit of the People's Economic Achievements), Forest Nut (*lesnoi oreshek*), and a flavor called "Russian Premium" in place of Miami Vice sorbet—but the establishments are otherwise nearly indistinguishable from those in America. Rocky Road/Roki Roud ice cream is apparently appealing to both Russian and US customers. Although the type of food that is served varies and each restaurant carefully caters to a particular set of tastes, aspiring to capture a segment of urban Russians' food budgets, fast-food restaurants adhere to strict protocols about how food is prepared. Recipes are based on proprietary formulas, and each ingredient must meet a number of criteria that are defined by corporate actors. The rise of Russian fast-food restaurants at once transformed diets and consumption, acting as a feedback loop that stimulated the changes in production detailed in chapter 2. The burgeoning fast-food and franchise sectors initially imported a large share of their ingredients—fats and sugars among them. Most hot dogs sold at popular roadside stands in the late 1990s and early 2000s were imported from Denmark. McDonald's relied on Cargill to import almost all its ingredients. Contractually bound to highly specialized and proprietary recipes, fast-food chains did not make the switch to Russian ingredients until they were forced to do so by a changing political climate. Today, the cooking oil for every serving of McDonald's french fries and the egg liquid for fast-food breakfast sandwiches are Russian.[80]

Finally, at the same time that fast-food restaurants were becoming ubiquitous, a series of cooking shows pushed back against the trend of eating out. Russian kitchens are still valued as sanctuaries, and in the post-Soviet period they have served as a refuge from new kinds of upheavals associated with market economies. Russian grocery stores have also changed in significant ways. Competing with the rise of fast food has meant stocking highly processed, ready-to-eat meals. One well-known line of processed food is called Edim Doma, which means Let's Eat at Home. Ironically, the same name is used for a brand of prepared foods sold at supermarkets, a TV show about home cooking, and is also the proposed name of a new Russian fast-food chain.[81] Similarly paradoxical is Miratorg's "a-la-home-made chicken wings," one item in the company's vast lineup of processed chicken products.[82]

Imported versus Domestic Food, Global Integration versus Russian Foodways

Some consumers in Russia and elsewhere care deeply about not only the quality of food but also its source. Assessments of value and the origins of foods are of course linked, but at least for Russia, the two have not always had a stable relationship. Foreign foods have at times been considered the most desirable kind, and at other times they have been seen as less healthy, valuable, or tasty than domestic alternatives.[83] It is worth noting that the value of Russianness is rising precisely at a time when Western fast-food chains and processed foods are becoming ubiquitous. The simultaneous globalization of food, the debate about how far food should travel between farm and table, and the revaluation of local food indeed constitute a global trend.

One of the ways to gauge the evolution of consumption, then, is to trace the origin of food products. For many decades, most food consumed in Soviet Russia originated from other socialist republics, and imported food was not a large part of Russian diets. "For the most part, the Soviet Union [managed] to feed itself," notes Stephen Wegren.[84] Throughout the Soviet period, a small number of imported luxury foods were available in special stores, available only for elites (discussed below). The changing political context of Soviet external trade shaped the availability of particular food items. In 1950s, the Soviet Union developed trade ties with communist and nonaligned countries and imported select foods from these new partners. The recipe for Kiev cake in the 1952 edition of the *Book of Tasty and Healthy Food* called for cashews instead of locally available hazel or walnuts, for example. This extravagant adaptation was included in the book because cashews had become more readily available in the Soviet Union due to rising trade with newly independent India. Cashews were traded in return for Soviet development assistance and therefore made their way into Soviet-era cakes. Over the decades, as other global consumers discovered the joys of Indian cashews, the global market price of the nut increased. This meant that the nutty ingredient in Kiev cake was replaced, first by domestically available hazelnuts and later, in the seventies, by peanuts, which were relatively cheap and available from the US after 1972.[85] In the seventies, the Soviet Union produced more and more sugar and oilseed, but it also increasingly imported these products to satisfy the growing demand for sweet and processed foods.[86]

Russia's integration into global markets after 1991 led to larger quantities and varieties of food imported from all over the world to Russia. Initially, nonperishable foods such as candy bars and Italian salami were more readily available. By the mid-nineties, skinny and crunchy cucumbers arrived from Holland and glossy apples from Argentina. Camembert arrived from France and became revered as a delicious novelty; Soviet agro-technopolitics had not provided a precedent for the creamy raw-milk cheese. Imported beef was cheaper than Russian beef as highly efficient and large Brazilian and US farms had far lower production costs than Russian meat producers. Chicken legs were a notorious item in this regard. More generally, the food situation of the early nineties was truly perplexing for many Russians. On the one hand, there were all kinds of new goods available from across the world. At the same time, the fresh products that had been part of the Soviet-era food system disappeared. The cucumbers, tomatoes, apples, melons, grapes, and stone fruit that had been brought to Russian urban centers from rural areas in Russia, Ukraine, the Caucasus, and Central Asia simply no longer made these journeys. Established supply chains were disrupted, and farms in rural Russia and these other post-Soviet countries had a hard time surviving. The overall consumption of fruits and vegetables by Russian citizens dwindled: the average per-capita consumption of vegetables, for instance, fell from 85 kilograms per year in 1990 to 71 kilograms in 1994.[87] Shuttle traders imported large quantities of consumer goods, including popular foreign food products, through informal import businesses that employed millions of Russians.[88] During the worst years of Russia's economic crisis, imported food was accompanied by food aid from the US and Western Europe.

The balance of imported to domestic products changed after the 1998 devaluation of the ruble, which made domestically produced food cheaper and imports more expensive.[89] By 2014, the ban on food imports from Western countries meant that imported foods declined as a share of consumption. A whole series of imported products from the US and Europe were no longer available: beef from the US, salmon from Norway, cheese from France, milk from Lithuania, and apples from Poland. The shift in the origin—and along with it the nature of products—affected the most expensive food items and mass-market products alike. Russians began to eat Belarusian or Russian cheese rather than Lithuanian *džiukas* or Italian parmesan. More domestic chicken and pork were consumed due to the embargo, and Belarusian butter and cheese from New Zealand took the place of Lithuanian and Irish dairy products. Brazilian beef replaced steaks from Texas, though beef also became more expensive and consumption dropped.[90]

Unequal Access

So far we have seen that the types of foods that were available to Russian consumers, especially urbanites, changed over the years. The history of food consumption in Russia is shaped, first and foremost, by availability and absence, abundance and scarcity. At all times, though, access has varied greatly across the country and for different groups of citizens. Bolshevik party elites and the upper echelons of the nomenklatura enjoyed the most prized food items. In the 1930s, a newly emerging Soviet middle class, which included administrative cadres, industrial specialists, and workers rewarded for special services, gained new access to privileged food items.[91] At the same time, a large part of the Soviet population still lived at the mercy of good or bad harvests, with little access to proteins or luxury items like white bread.[92] Throughout the decades of the Soviet experiment, the special rewards became available to a growing number of citizens, though shortages always meant that mass access was patchy and unpredictable. By the Brezhnev years, Russian diets had "normalized" and included a greater number of readily available staples.[93] The nineties brought more turmoil, but the Putin years restabilized and broadened overall food supplies. A Russian citizen in 2020 was far less likely to be hungry than a Soviet citizen in 1920, or 1990, for that matter. The post-Soviet period brought new abundance, first of imported, then increasingly of domestic food products, though new abundance has not meant more choices for everyone. Soviet-era shortages did not preclude choice entirely, and by the same token, it is wrong to think of post-Soviet abundance as having been accessible to all. Patterns of privilege have shifted in important ways between the Soviet and post-Soviet periods. How access was granted and barred has also changed: the shortages of the planned economy largely curtailed choice for average citizens while having less impact on party elites. Contemporary market mechanisms make prices the limiting feature, thus elevating income and material wealth as the most powerful enabling forces of status consumption.

Soviet-Era Inequality of Access

Throughout the Soviet period, access to a range of staples—bread and herring, for example—was relatively equal and retail prices for all basic food items were low and predictable.[94] A loaf of white bread (*baton*) cost 20–22 kopecks, and a loaf of "black" bread (*bukhanka*, traditionally made from rye flour) cost 16–18 kopecks for most of the seventies and eighties. Meat cost 1.80 rubles per kilogram, and sausage about 2.50, a kilogram of butter cost 3.40 rubles, and a can of sweetened condensed milk was 55 kopecks.[95] All stores sold the same products at the same prices, although products at kolkhoz markets were sold at significantly higher prices.

Soviet-era access to food items was stratified by official hierarchies and social networks rather than by prices. A complex array of political, economic, and spatial positions, networks, and resources provided access to some groups and not to others. Not surprisingly, Soviet elites had far better access to sought-after food items, especially meat and luxury items, than regular citizens. For one thing, high-ranking party members could shop at special stores and eat at the best-supplied restaurants. Even during the direst shortages, black markets and underground restaurants allowed groups with the right connections to enjoy Russian and imported delicacies.[96] The Soviet-era procurement system also had an extremely steep geographical gradient. Jukka Gronow provides fascinating data from 1933, a year of hunger in the countryside, to illustrate the inequality of access: "Moscow and Leningrad, with 3–4 percent of the total population . . . , received about half the available margarine and meat; one third of all fish products, wines and spirits; a quarter of all flour and grains; one fifth of butter, sugar, tea and salt centrally distributed to all the cities and towns of the USSR." During times of crisis, rationing was meant to ensure equal access. But even then, rations were given according to one's position on certain "lists." Workers of the high-priority industrial enterprises received higher rations than workers of small enterprises or in light industry. Kolkhozniki were not allocated any rations.[97]

Throughout the Soviet period, all cities were ranked in a multitiered system: Moscow and Leningrad were in the first tier. Moscow was the epicenter of politics and privilege; it was densely populated by party functionaries, civil servants, and factory workers in prestigious industries, all of whom enjoyed the best access to the most delicious foods. Industrial centers and other "strategically important areas" constituted the second tier. Cities with important mining, metallurgical, and large electric power plants received this kind of priority status. Included in this tier were cities in the north and Far East, which were often better provisioned than third- and fourth-tier cities elsewhere in the Soviet Union.[98] Regional capitals were in the third tier and received more meat provisions than provincial cities. All other towns and villages were provisioned via the principle of "whatever is left," which meant that residents in these areas de facto only infrequently actually received meat and dairy products from state-run stores. Factories and their stolovye were also provisioned according to this geographical hierarchy—with some receiving more meat and others far less—but they were also subject to another tier system, depending on the importance of the branch of the economy they served. The factories deemed important for heavy industry and militarization received better provisions and were allowed to run their own farms. These farms could supply pork, eggs, milk, and rabbits to the factory canteens, thereby providing valuable proteins to workers and sometimes even their families.

A further level of stratification happened within every workplace, institution, and factory: cadres and some higher-ranking workers had better access to goods than rank-and-file workers.[99] Workplace hierarchies mattered also because the higher-ranked members could travel to Moscow and Leningrad for business trips (*komandirovka*) and were thus able to bring back foods unavailable in poorly provisioned cities. Through these various channels, well-situated professional elites ate better. At festive and important occasions, meals for Soviet nomenklatura elites consisted of elaborate appetizers and several courses—featuring delicacies such as caviar, sturgeon, trout, salmon, veal, or game such as venison, for example. Chocolates, cognac, fruits, or nuts—served with tea—were the desserts of choice. An underground restaurant in the 1920s served filleted fish and roast goose with onions and apples.[100] The following menu, served to Richard Nixon on the occasion of his visit in 1973, illustrates what political elites at the time considered suitable for an important guest:[101]

Menu on the Occasion of Visit by Richard Nixon, 1973 (excerpt)
Caviar and butter
Seafood assortment: crab, oysters, balyk, Atlantic salmon, prawns
Woodland game birds: partridge, pheasant, grouse, quail
Fresh cucumbers and tomatoes, as well as lightly pickled cucumbers
Borscht with pampushka (garlic-topped bread roll)
Sturgeon solyanka soup
Starry sturgeon with champignon mushrooms
Russian-style meat and potato stew cooked and served in pots
Strawberry mousse
Coffee, tea, fruit, biscuits

Other than nomenklatura elites, Soviet citizens were, in Caroline Humphrey's words, largely "on the receiving end of a state-planned system of distribution."[102] Sometimes this meant deep deprivation and hunger.[103] Soviet rural citizens always had the least access to the goods of the formal food distribution channels that tended to peter out before they reached villages. Although the postwar decades were generally marked by growing prosperity, rural residents had far less access to meat and other special items, such as sugar. The absence of meat in the stores in a Ukrainian village, for example, was noted in a diary entry by a visiting poet, Mikhail Ia. Grobman, on July 12, 1969: "At the mouth of the Dniper.... We walked around Kherson. It's a pleasant, charming old town. The stores are empty and sausages were nowhere to be found."[104] While rural residents had the least access to the products of the public production and procurement systems, they had more access to food grown on household plots. A further aspect of the geography of access and distribution was shaped by climate: citizens in northwestern regions consumed more meat, dairy, and processed food. Residents of Central Asia, meanwhile, consumed fewer processed items such as canned and frozen proteins than any other Soviet citizens.[105] Fruit and vegetable consumption was higher in the south, particularly in the Caucasus.[106] Siberia and the Far East had relatively little access to fresh produce, meat, and fluid milk.[107]

Soviet-era stores also reflected unequal access. Regular stores for the general public organized access to their goods by means of long lines. Shopkeepers were gatekeepers of access. Unlike post-Soviet and Western grocery stores that provide shoppers open access to products, Soviet-era stores kept their products on shelves behind the vendors or in glass-encased counters. Customers often needed to queue several times to obtain goods: first to order, then to pay, and finally again to hand the receipt to a clerk in return for the purchased products.[108] Some goods were available regularly, and others infrequently: among the prized but rarely available luxury goods available in stores were elaborate boxed cakes, such as the Kiev cake.[109]

Throughout the Soviet period, special retail stores provided access to select social and political groups. In the 1930s, such stores served party elites; army, navy, and secret police officers; and the high cadres of the railway and heavy industry.[110] In the postwar period, a network of stores called Beriozka sold sought-after consumer and food products that were not available elsewhere. They provided access to washing machines, TVs, tape recorders, imported clothing, and other desirable consumer goods, including food items to those with access. Cognac and whiskey were usually stocked, along with specialty cured meats. Beriozka stores required "foreign currency certificates," only available to foreigners and citizens who had interactions with foreign economies.[111] Included in this group were diplomats, foreign news correspondents, military personnel, and development consultants who worked abroad, along with artists and writers who performed and published abroad. Access to these stores widened over the post-Soviet years, but they remained officially closed to the public as a whole. Unlike prices at regular stores, the items at Beriozka were relatively expensive and remained out of reach for most citizens.[112]

Although access was largely defined by political and economic status, consumers were not left entirely without agency. Families and individuals pursued various strategies to obtain access to the best products that were available within their radius of obtainable goods. Hoarding was one obvious strategy: with prices low, consumers bought whatever they could, whenever they could. Bulk purchases made sense for goods that were irregularly supplied and could easily be stored. Sugar was almost always in short supply and rapidly sold out when it was available. It was easily put aside for future consumption, trade with friends and family, or for home-distilleries. Another kind of agency was the reliance on connections and networks to obtain food items. The foreign currency certificates needed to pay for goods at the Beriozka stores were widely bartered and exchanged in this way. Holidays were a particularly good time to mobilize connections to procure ingredients for popular holiday meals, such as the famous salad Olivier or aspics. As in most societies, holidays in Russia revolve around special dishes, and pies, various salads rich in mayonnaise, desserts, and liquors were staples of New Year's celebrations. To obtain ingredients for these meals—mayonnaise, for example—Soviet women scanned store shelves and networked with friends, colleagues, and shopkeepers weeks (if not months) ahead of time to secure the necessary ingredients for festive meals. Residents in undersupplied provincial cities used public transport to larger nearby industrial cities to purchase ingredients for special meals.

Though navigating stores and informal networking were forms of agency, they were generally perceived as exhausting pursuits. Russian women in particular often devoted a great deal of time and thought to navigating their limited options, standing in lines, and procuring items that were in short supply. The most valued and desirable food items had to be earned with social capital, patience, and persistence: "'real goods' must be procured with difficulty," noted Humphrey.[113] While goods were scarce, for many Soviet citizens, time was less so. Unlike post-Soviet and Western capitalism, the Soviet system generally did not require self-sacrificial devotion to work and careers. This allowed workers to spend more time and energy on obtaining food—by either queuing or working household plots. As shortages become more acute in the nineties, these informal procurement strategies became more frustrating and exhausting.

Marketization and Changing Access

Market liberalization brought with it a new abundance of goods, but also a whole new experience of skyrocketing costs for basic staples. In the early and mid-1990s, access to newly available food items was severely limited by high prices. Even prices of staples rose rapidly as the state-run procurement system was dismantled and the era of controlled prices was followed by hyperinflation. Food price inflation was in fact an entirely new phenomenon—and the unaffordability of many basic foodstuffs was astonishing and maddening for most Russian consumers. Any given food item—a package of buckwheat kasha, a carton of sour cream, a pound of meat, a package of tea—that had cost a few rubles or kopecks now cost hundreds of rubles. Meanwhile, families and pensioners had very little cash with which to buy food as wages and pensions remained low or were in arrears. Food insecurity became a serious problem, and poverty increased from 12 percent to 46 percent between 1992 and

1998.[114] The vast number of new types of products were either very expensive or inaccessible. Danone single-serve flavored yogurts were sold in the company's flagship store on Moscow's most exclusive streets, but their price was only within reach of regular Muscovites' budgets after they had been discounted near the end of their shelf life.[115]

Even basic staples that had been regular parts of diets became less accessible: Russians drank less milk in 1992 than they did in the early 1960s.[116] The price for bread increased from 2 rubles to 150 rubles during the first few years of the market transition, though bread remained one of the few items for which the state retained a monopoly. Bread was in fact often the only item that households could afford. All households spent a growing share of their incomes on food—around 50 percent in the late nineties. The elderly, single parents, and families with several children had the least access to adequate diets, and in urban areas many members of these groups ate at soup kitchens. Stephen Wegren observes an inverse relation between family size and food consumption: the larger the family, the less per-capita consumption.[117] The meals of regular Russian consumers at that time were basic and often insufficient. A 1993 survey classified 70 percent of households as hungry.[118] Especially elderly pensioners were hungry during the worst years of the crisis of the 1990s, and meals remained meagre during the initial years of the 2000s.

Typical Menu of a Pensioner in the 1990s and early 2000s
Kasha or potatoes with butter or with sour cream or herring, on a good day.
Or: borscht or schchi, sometimes with meat, on a good day.
Tea, with homemade preserves or a candy, on a good day.

The geography of access for some regions was the inverse of what it had been in the Soviet Union: remote northern regions like Chukotka had enjoyed privileged supply status as frontier regions in the Soviet era. Once this status was lost, the remoteness drove up the cost of provisions, and hunger and malnutrition became more severe. Peripheral spaces included rural areas in general, which suffered a similar fate. In the late 1990s, two-thirds of rural residents in rural areas were poor or very poor.[119] Rural residents had better access to the products of household plots, which provided nutritional safety nets and an income opportunity for families with somewhat more human and capital resources. Higher-income rural producers could rent land from neighbors and produce more food, some of which they sold and bartered for other goods. The poorest rural residents on average had one cow and one pig, while the better-off families in rural areas had several head of livestock (5.82 cows and 5.12 pigs, on average).[120]

For Russia's new middle class, access improved gradually as the decade progressed; on average, at least, Russian caloric intake recovered by the year 2000. While the poorer families and pensioners still struggled to put food on the table and ate less meat, a growing segment of the Russian population was able to buy higher-quality and reasonably priced food after 2005. Even pensioners could afford meat occasionally (see figure 3.5).

The products on Russian plates changed too. Chicken became the most affordable and widely consumed meat. Berries, for example, became available in processed foods and as flash-frozen items for ready consumption. Some families still pick fresh berries in local forests, but many others are happy to eat them in processed form. Prodded by fast-food chains' marketing campaigns and with new daily work-life realities, many citizens became more inclined to eat out. The most affordable chain restaurants, known in Russia as the most "democratic" (*demokratichnyi*), were particularly popular. This change in access to food and options for eating out had a significant impact on Russian byt in the 2000s. As noted in the introduction, Masha Gessen has argued that Russia's new upper middle class was so pleased with its new consumption choices and the possibility of enjoying delicious meals in pleasant surroundings

Figure 3.5 Pensioner's meal, Anna Ivanovna's kitchen, Vladivostok, October 2007. Photo by the author.

that it has chosen to overlook the shortcomings of Putin's regime, at least for a time.[121]

Affluent post-Soviet elites initially had virtually unlimited access to a vast array of products and restaurants. Given that post-Soviet access is limited largely by cost, post-Soviet oligarchs, along with their families and entourages, were feasting and consumed whatever they considered the most desirable and alluring foods. As access was unlimited, allure and desire became more important. Elites were well positioned to add fresh fruits and vegetables to their diets, along with expensive cuts of meat and imported delicacies such as oysters, prosciutto, or the Dover sole mentioned in the chapter's third epigraph. For most of the nineties and early 2000s, tastes began to assimilate an array of Western foods, though some of these were no longer available after 2014. In sum, patterns of access came to resemble those of mature capitalist societies, where consumption choices correlate with income inequalities.

Food's Allure and Consumer Desire

Byt and foodways are shaped by availability and access but also by desires and tastes. Consumption is not just the outcome of economic structures: it is deeply imbricated in the political and cultural construction of value around what is tasty, healthful, and appropriate. Another way to think about the link between social constructions of food and status is that good meals were valued as symbols of a good life. It is a well-known Russian truth that daily meals and social status are inherently linked. Soviet-era values of appropriate meals often borrowed from the markers of upper-class living in late-imperial Russia, although there was never just one version of what should be valued. In Lev Tolstoy's *Anna Karenina*, Stiva Oblonsky and Konstantin Levin disagreed about what a good meal is. Oblonsky ordered oysters, turbot in a thick sauce, roast beef, a capon, fruit kompot, and parmesan cheese. He also asked for a bottle of Chablis and another of champagne—though he insisted on calling the latter by its Russian name, *shampanskoe*. Levin meanwhile preferred buckwheat kasha and cabbage soup, simple and traditionally Russian foods, but joined Oblonsky in savoring a lavish meal.[122] Oblonsky and Levin both belonged to Russia's upper class, but they made markedly different choices. In the scene, Tolstoy contrasts the allure of opulent, foreign pleasures with the value of simple Russian food. In more general terms, consumption is shaped not only by availability and access but also by the fickle desires of humans who eat not only for sustenance, but to mark their identity and status. Technopolitics is thus not only a logistical question of making food available and accessible; it also involves vexing questions about how the state should try to shape or respond to what is valued and desired by consumers. Though Russian values have changed dramatically over time, there is striking continuity in two sets of debates over the following questions: Should dishes be simple or elaborate? And should Russian dishes be valued more than foreign and especially Western foods?

Early Soviet elites agreed that diets were a critical component of new socialist citizens and workers; they disagreed about what precisely those diets should entail. One of the questions turned on the value of eating meat. Following Tolstoy and others who denounced carnivorous eating as a Western and capitalist habit, early socialist utopian dietary thinking in the 1920s eschewed meat. This perspective contended with other theories that associated vegetarianism with religious values, thus deemed outdated and in need of replacement with scientifically determined diets. By the 1930s, multivalent dietary debates became muted, and meat was very much back on the table as a reward for workers' contributions to building socialism. Stalin and Mikoyan steered Soviet culture away from asceticism and self-sacrifice and toward an embrace of hedonism and individual rewards as acceptable socialist values. These rewards were to materialize, at least occasionally, on Russian tables, and workers were allowed to consume chocolate and champagne.[123] Thus in the Stalin era, the *Book of Tasty and Healthy Food* featured meat and other elaborate dishes, and the USSR Pavilion at the 1939 World Fair included a select array of luxury items on the dinner menu, including filet mignon and lobster, along with Russian specialties such as delicate pancakes with apricot sauce.[124] These were certainly dishes that were fit for international elites. Yet everyday decadence was a utopian dream rather than a reality in the prewar decades. Though few households had access to all the ingredients for feasts conjured in the official cookbook or on display at the World Fair, they were nevertheless portrayed as within reach of Soviet citizens and as appropriate for celebratory occasions. They were assertions of what the diet for the socialist good life should look like, and as such made a lasting impression on successive Soviet citizens and bureaucrats.

Over the postwar decades the aspirational meals that had been promised during the Stalin era shaped consumers' expectations of a broader array of choices and more desirable options. There was a general consensus that more meat, high-quality dairy products, and an assortment of appealing processed goods, including some luxuries and sweets, should make up part of byt. These expectations then informed political debates and mattered greatly as goals for future planning and policies. Adrienne Jacobs documents that planners and party bureaucrats began to worry in the 1960s that perhaps science had been privileged too much, promoting foods that were healthy but a bit boring and lacking in popular appeal. One prominent voice in this debate was iconoclast and dissident historian Vil'iam V. Pokhlebkin, who wrote a series of books and columns that presented the history of Russian cuisine as a cultural artifact that had to be revalued and recentered in the science-dominated Soviet-era dietary discourse.[125] The call for more authentic Russian cuisine proved to be appealing to consumers, and planners became concerned about how to distill an authentically Russian diet while also providing a variety of culinary options to consumers. This was ultimately an impossible quest that gave rise to a whole new set of questions, such as whether vodka was invented by the Poles or Russians and whether borscht was really Ukrainian and not Russian.[126] By the sixties, a cautious embrace of culinary traditions from the non-Russian socialist republics had also led to the adoption of a range of dishes and flavors adopted from non-Russian regions as appropriate meals for Soviet citizens. There had long been a small number of Georgian restaurants in Moscow, and Georgian wines were a beverage of choice for Soviet elites. In the 1960s, a popular book of Georgian cuisine with recipes for many dishes, including multiple versions of the famous soup kharcho, made these dishes available to regular citizens.[127] Other non-Russian foods also began appearing on tables without any help from the state. Some Korean specialties, such as kimchi, shredded spicy carrots, and pickled seaweed (known in Russia as *morskaia kapusta*), became increasingly popular during the sixties.[128]

As more information about the West became available through movies and music in the late sixties and seventies, Western consumer goods became valued and desired. Though initially they remained largely out of reach for most Russians, they were in some ways appealing precisely because of their scarcity. They were convenient, neat, modern, and attractive, as well as sweet and salty in a whole new way. When select processed foods became available in the 1980s, they too became symbols of Western consumer culture. Svetlana Barsukova notes that in the context of the late Soviet shortage economy, "foreign consumer goods became symbols of quality, beauty, and fashion," and the "taste of overseas delicacies was both wonderful and unusual."[129] Western food items were initially distributed through informal channels, tempting and appealing precisely because they were so different and rare. A Snickers bar, a McDonald's hamburger, or a Coke were all "symbol[s] of a better life," part of the unattainable and imaginary West.[130]

The cult of Western goods continued to thrive in the early nineties, even as more and more such items became available. As Western products flooded stores, they initially benefited from their allure from the late Soviet period. Yet they did not end up shaping preferences for good and for everyone. While some Russians embraced these imports, others were wary or even suspicious. Western goods were suspected of containing more chemicals and of being less nourishing. It is thus perhaps not a coincidence that precisely at a time when Western foods became ubiquitous, there was also a backlash against what was called *snikerizatsiia*—the uncritical adoption of Western consumer goods. In the context of this backlash, Russian foods became valued as more healthful and natural. Melissa Caldwell argues that these dietary and consumption choices were a way to demonstrate belonging to an imagined, national collective. Russian products were explicitly valued as "nash" and juxtaposed with Western foods that were foreign (*ne nash* / not ours).[131] Barsukova again astutely observes that by "buying products with a Soviet name, the consumer effectively makes symbolic contact with a past shorn of unhappy memories."[132] "Narodny Produkt" was a label of origin designating domestically produced goods and was introduced by a Russian producers association to raise awareness among consumers and encourage them to buy Russian products. Some affluent urbanites have sought out homegrown food and home-processed jam, pickles, and dairy products. Debates about revaluing and recombining food-related symbols recognized as authentic shaped post-Soviet food culture during the Putin era. A work by the Blue Noses Art Collective from the early 2000s, titled *Kitchen Suprematism*, shows this cultural process at work in an arrangement of black bread and sausage in a pattern that mimics Kazimir Malevich's Suprematist constructions.

The explicit revaluation of all things Russian and native intensified after 2014. On state-dominated media, coverage of the ban on Western food was accompanied with images of public authorities destroying so-called enemy food that had been brought to Russia illegally. This was a public spectacle that conveyed to Russians and the West alike that Russia was done with its dependence on Western imports. It showed the food ban as an act of Russian resistance against Western forces seeking to humiliate Russia. Buying Russian goods was portrayed as a way to profess patriotism.[133] More subtly, the message was also directed to the decadent West that Russia no longer needed foreign luxuries. In this political climate, affluent Russian elites—many of whom wanted to demonstrate their loyalty to Putin's political projects—rediscovered the allure of home-processed, artisanal, local, "meaningful" food. High-end restaurants in Moscow seized the moment and followed the trend of favoring traditional Russian and local food.[134] They serve *riashenka*, *shchi*, and *okroshka*, for example, and desserts proudly feature the hardy *smorodina* (gooseberries or red or black currants) that have long thrived in household gardens. Beets, cabbage, bliny with caviar, and sturgeon are now valued for their local provenance and for their idiosyncratic paths to the tables of urban elites.[135] The chefs of Moscow and Petersburg restaurants have emerged as high priests seeking to define what precisely counts as authentically Russian food in the early twenty-first century.

They source unique local specialties from across Russia and establish connections between guests and farmers, who are featured in the menus. Lavka Lavka, introduced in chapter 2, shares information about the family farms that supply food with urban consumers: every farmer has a story, and the implication is that every meal is richer and more valuable because of it. Some high-end chefs dare to push the boundaries between foreign and domestic by pairing everyday food items with rare and expensive items. For example, the "Russian Evolution" menu of White Rabbit features salo, oysters, and black bread.

Excerpt from the "Russian Evolution" Menu at the White Rabbit (Moscow, 2018)
Salo (cured pork fat)
Oysters
Ryazhenka (fermented dairy product)
Scallops
Sea urchin caviar
Cabbage pie
Shashlik
Black Bread

Of course, not all Russians have been converts to the new food nationalism. Keith Livers points to how the contemporary postmodern Russian writer Vladimir Sorokin satirizes the Putin-era resurgence of nationalism and "a brave new world in which restaurant menus and fancy dishes fall under the purview of the authorities."[136] Sorokin's skepticism underscores the flawed premise or even absurdity of any authoritative pronouncements about which products are authentically Russian in the face of complex early twenty-first-century global food systems. Nevertheless, as any human food consumption decision involves processes of attaching value to things, it is not surprising that consumers consider and deploy the markers that saturate culture and politics in Putin's Russia. Melissa Caldwell shows that many Russians have turned to foods from dachas, rural gardens, and nearby forests not only and not primarily because of their nutritional value but because they consider them tastier, more healthful, "ecologically clean," and deeply satisfying.[137] Though jam and frozen berries are readily available in stores, the different kinds of berries that are hand-picked and then home-preserved are far more evocative of the joys of summer than their processed (non)equivalents—and therefore recognized as more valuable.[138] Even as growing food remains labor intensive and, in many ways, has become relatively costly, it is deeply rewarding for many, and finding informal supply channels for home production of food is not only not a deterrent; it adds to the allure and symbolic value of native berries and mushrooms.

Ironically, during the first two terms of the Putin presidency, the roadside stands and open markets that supplied urban areas with food grown at dachas and ogorody were largely swept off city streets. Especially in Moscow, but also in many other cities, municipal authorities cracked down on what they saw as unregulated and disorderly commerce. This meant that Central Asian traders and elderly pensioners selling berry preserves disappeared from central squares and metro underpasses in major cities. Meanwhile, the value of authentic and homegrown food continued to be debated on TV shows and in magazines and social media.[139] What precisely should be considered authentically Russian and Soviet culture and cuisine? What are the most and least healthful foods? Vodka, for example, was again caught up in debates about its origins, though now subject to an entirely capitalist struggle as different vodka companies claimed to have the only "original" vodka recipe.[140]

Paradoxically, the search for authentically Russian dishes and original Soviet recipes was both a rejection of Western, capitalist foodways and a replication of it. Emphasis on the value of local food and the involvement of farmers' stories borrows from the thoroughly global locavore movement that originated in the West and has converted elites in many other advanced capitalist countries.

At the same time, the technopolitics of the 2010s made available Russian processed replicas of these foods to fulfill the need to consume domestic products. Producers and advertisers recognized, reproduced, and capitalized on the emerging patriotism and did much to (re)produce the binary distinction between what is "native" ("ours") and what is not. Product names invoke Russianness or Soviet-era values, or claim that they are based on inherited Russian recipes. The branding of Russian processed foods has often mobilized nostalgia for Soviet-era brands and longing for trusted foods of a happy (Soviet) childhood. Examples include Alyonka chocolate, Druzhba cheese, and Buratino fizzy lemonade. Today Russian consumers can again buy Tushonka, the ham in a can, packaged and branded with Soviet-era designs.[141] Riding the wave of patriotism and nostalgia has enabled agroholdings to boost mass preferences for convenient and processed foods, all while borrowing from notions of healthfulness, simplicity, and natural foods of earlier times.[142]

The valuation of Russian authenticity is also clearly visible in fast-food menus. They often feature a seasonal lent menu (*postnoe meniu*), for example, in a nod to a traditional Russian food practice. The Russian fast-food chain Teremok claims that it serves "traditional" Russian dishes. At first glance, the Teremok menu (see below) is similar to what could have been served at a Soviet cafeteria. Yet it also reflects twenty-first-century ideas of the good life. For one thing, the range of choices is enormous and includes twenty-seven savory and nine sweet bliny to choose from (though likely not every restaurant has each of these available at all times). Choices include fusion items, such as the Blin Burger, the Caesar Blin, and the Russian Caesar Salad, internationally branded products (Kinder Chocolate eggs), and low-calorie options. Many items are highly processed, and all of them are based on proprietary, corporate recipes. In Putin's Russia, these are also among the most "democratic" foods available in public eateries.

> *Excerpts from a Typical Menu of Teremok, a Russian Fast-Food Outlet (various locations, including Moscow, Tomsk, Krasnoyarsk, Vladivostok, 2018)*
> Soup, such as borscht, *lapsha*, or okroshka
> Bliny: savory and sweet (fillings for the bliny include Russian classics, such as mushrooms and cream). Bliny with Caesar salad filling are also available.
> Pelmeni and salads, such as vinegret or *oliv'e* (salad Olivier), but also "Russian Caesar salad"
> Syrniki, sweet bliny, and Kinder Chocolate egg[143]

In sum, Russian diets and byt in the twentieth and twenty-first centuries were shaped through the availability of food, through the values that consumers attached to meals, and through the access that different groups had to ingredients. Increasing availability and access to a broad range of desirable foods was a goal of both the Soviet and post-Soviet agro-technopolitical regimes. They each failed and succeeded in idiosyncratic ways. One of the key aspects of the perestroika of the quotidian from the Soviet to the post-Soviet era was this: during the twentieth century, access to the most valued, scarce, and tasty treats was made possible by social connections and by politically informed preferential treatment. The nineties were still a time of very few choices for most Russians as consumers were struggling to find acceptable and affordable things to eat. Cost and price thus mattered in a way they never had before. Under Putin, food scarcity gave way to relative abundance. By 2014, on the eve of the annexation of Crimea, more Russians had access to affordable, industrially processed, and domestically produced foods and meats. Yet still a relatively large share of household incomes was being spent on food (compared to what US consumers were spending), and many Russian families needed to worry about fluctuating prices and food price inflation. Unequal access still persists. As the Russian economy is now more exposed than ever to fluctuating global prices for oil and to other economic shocks, a new kind of vulnerability of consumption has been created and is an important characteristic of post-Soviet byt.

4

Nature

There are no universal [wheat] varieties which can be sown in all the climatic zones from the Baltic to the Black Sea—and such an approach is abiological.
   —Fyodor Kirichenko, Soviet geneticist, 1920

[Libra] is a true type of a unique parent sow adapted to the conditions of industrial livestock farming. . . . In the selection of F1 pigs the emphasis was on characteristics that ensure the constant increase in the efficiency of production.
   —Znamensk Genetic Selection Center, on the Libra/Svinka F1 parent stock pig, 2020

Agriculture in situ; or, the Human-Nature Nexus in Russian Agriculture

Agriculture happens in particular places and environments, with their characteristic soils, rainfall patterns, hours of sunlight, and lengths of winter. The territories of the Soviet Union and post-Soviet Russia were and continue to be large, with extremely varied growing conditions from the Baltic to the Black Sea and from Vilnius to Vladivostok. The Soviet grain belt stretched across so many climatic zones that total harvest failures were less likely there than in other countries. Yet most of Russia's crop land is situated quite far north, further north than the arable land in the US and most of Western Europe. Average growing seasons—that is, the consistently frost-free periods each year—are short, even in central and southern Russia.[1] Many Soviet and Russian agricultural regions are distant from sources of moisture, and droughts have been a persistent problem. During the twentieth century, Soviet farmers had to contend with major droughts at least twenty-seven times: according to the records, the country experienced too little rain, on average, every fourth year.[2] Rainfalls and temperatures were also quite volatile, resulting in large annual fluctuations of yields. Russian crops and farm animals had to contend with dry, cold, and unpredictable conditions.

There is little doubt that climate and soil played an enormously important role in interfering with Soviet and post-Soviet plans to wrest more grain from soils.[3] Since the late imperial era, authorities, planners, and scientists have sought to understand these conditions and to find ways of overcoming perceived disadvantages and harnessing opportunities. Counting on science as the motor of progress, they built research institutes to learn from nature and to bring this learning to the task of making nature pliable and useful to human efforts to thrive and achieve political goals. Insights and experiments by agronomists studying plant and animal genetics were enlisted to help the Bolshevik government solve the "grain problem" introduced in chapter 1. At the same time, successive rural modernization attempts profoundly affected the natural environment in which agriculture took place. The steppe grasslands of Central Russia, Ukraine, and Kazakhstan are one of the world's largest ecological systems to ever be transformed by the expansions of field-crop farming in the nineteenth and twentieth centuries.[4] One of the reasons, perhaps the main reason, why technopolitical regimes in agriculture warrant attention is that they connect human societies to nature. Agrarian-based societies have cleared woodlands, drained wetlands, and plowed grasslands for thousands of years in many regions of the world. Industrial agriculture has been a powerful force of change that has touched on virtually all aspects of human interaction with the natural environment over the past three hundred years.[5] And at an even more basic level, grains are grasses, potatoes are tubers, and pork and poultry are animals, even if the plants and animals we eat have evolved in the long processes of coevolution, domestication, and artificial selection orchestrated and institutionalized by humans.[6] Few human endeavors have transformed human-nature relations more significantly than agriculture in general, and industrial agriculture in particular, in the form in which both capitalist and socialist governments embraced it in the twentieth century.

This chapter tries to gain an understanding of the human-nature nexus at the heart of agriculture and food systems by taking a closer look at seed and livestock breeding strategies. Nature is almost impossible to define, and in this chapter alone, it refers to all of the following: the landscapes, climates, soils, plants, animals, fungi, bacteria, and viruses that comply or interfere with, and are involved in, human schemes. Seeds and animal genetic material are just a tiny aspect of the complex symbiosis that humans and nature are embroiled in through agriculture. Plants that grow from seeds and domesticated animals are themselves sustained by many other organisms and materials. Yet they provide a useful and interesting lens on this symbiosis because they are profoundly manipulated by humans but are still part of the natural environment of human agriculture. Courtney Fullilove explicitly treats seeds not as products of nature but as "deep-time technologies, domesticated some 10,000–12,000 years ago and improved by successive generations of farmers."[7] This conceptual move of distancing seeds from the natural world, locating them instead in the technological and human world of domestication, opens the door to Fullilove's account of how they were embedded in the relations she explores between production and exchange in nineteenth-century US and global agriculture. This chapter heeds Langdon Winner's call to "attend more closely to *technical objects themselves*" in the process of trying to discern how nature is mobilized in political projects. In our case, seeds and animal breeds were mobilized by Soviet and Russian agro-technopolitical regimes.[8] Unlike Fullilove's account, this narrative does not draw a sharp boundary between human technologies and the realm of nature; instead, it tracks breeding strategies pursued by scientists and institutions to find out how planners, bureaucrats, and scientists thought about the relationship between human technologies and nature. What traits of crops and animals did they value, and how did these values change? How did breeding strategies in turn transform plants and seeds? Answers to these questions will give us some purchase for describing how the characteristics of the human-nature nexus involved in agriculture changed over time.

The two most fundamental rationales for plant and animal breeding are economic gains and ecological resistance. Yield gains are the axiomatic economic rationale for breeding strategies: more efficient cultivation of plants and animals leads to more food, feed, and meat—more carbohydrates and proteins—per unit of input. By seeking higher-yielding varieties, artificial selection aims to make plants more "useful" to humans in this one particular way. At the same time, plant and animal breeding is also about the creation of new varieties that are adapted to soils and climates and that are pest resistant. We could think of any modification of plant or livestock genetic material as a provisional experiment that hinges on the success of a symbiotic relationship between humans and nature in a particular environment. As long as plants and animals are situated in a unique natural context, and as long as their thriving is contingent on their adaptation to this context, there are no universally "best" breeds or species. When Russian plant breeders made decisions between high-yielding varieties and local adaption, they had to navigate a path between a universalizing human project that tries to control environmental context of agriculture and one that respects the inherent diversity of arable land in a vast empire. Early Soviet plant and animal breeding emphasized and valued local adaptation. In the 1920s, Fyodor Kirichenko, a geneticist in charge of the renowned Plant and Breeding Genetic Institute in Odessa, expressed this idea, quoted in this chapter's first epigraph.

A critical aspect of the shift from Soviet to post-Soviet plant and animal breeding is the changing emphasis on local context. In the Soviet era, plants and animals were bred specifically for particular regions. The notion of crop cultivation as an inherently site-specific endeavor was at the core of the theory of the evolution of domesticated plants by Nikolai I. Vavilov, arguably Russia's most famous geneticist. Site-specific conditions were responsible for the genetic diversity of wild and domesticated varieties of wheat, barley, rye, lentils, beans, flax, and cotton across the world. Vavilov's ambitious expeditions to Afghanistan, Pakistan, Palestine, Syria, Ethiopia, and many other places were undertaken to collect the unique and valuable reservoirs of genetic material contained within the seeds of these plants. Of course, scientists and planners were concerned all along about cultivating plants across larger areas with uneven conditions. They also focused on yields and the general usefulness of seeds and animal breeds for human consumption. Given that Soviet technopolitics emphasized bread for all, the "bread-making" quality of wheat was also a priority. But they were acutely aware that their efforts could only thrive if seeds and animals were carefully inserted into the climates, soils, and other conditions of the natural environment where growing would take place. What is more, plant breeders took into account that the actual conditions on collective farms across the many and diverse regions of the Soviet Union were significantly less ideal than those on experimental stations and model farms. Ignoring the specificities of local conditions would ultimately be counterproductive for the attainment of economic gains. Soviet plant and livestock breeding efforts thus were always a balance between local adaptation and universal, economic concerns. There were more or less successful varieties that grew on larger or smaller territories, but Soviet plant and animal breeders understood that seed or animal breeds would only thrive if they close paid attention to the particular environment where cultivation would take place. Breeding was about contingent modifications rather than the quest for a universally useful technology.

In the post-Soviet period, the technological frontier of plant and animal genetics for agricultural use shifted quite dramatically. With the influx of private capital and new technology, the mode of breeding shifted toward a reliance on seeds defined primarily by economic criteria and on high-performance animals that maximized meat and milks yields. A majority of crop seeds that are used in contemporary Russian agriculture were developed abroad, by agro-biotech firms that have developed and refined them for global markets. Hundreds of seed varieties for all crops are used in Russian agriculture; each is developed for a range of soil and climatic conditions, but most of them are imported and only a few of them are developed in Russia for Russian soil. This chapter examines wheat and pork as two divergent model mechanisms to show how Russia's agro-technopolitical regime transformed with the rise of agro-holdings and capital-intensive agriculture. For the parent stock of pork production, the genetic material of the animals was first largely imported and later engineered and assembled from internationally vetted blueprints that were only tenuously (if at all) connected to Russia's natural, social, and political geography. The wheat sector, by contrast, largely uses Russian seeds for all the major winter and spring wheat varieties and thus relies on locally developed and adapted genetic material. Over the last few years, efforts have been afoot to create a particular Russian version of the imported high-performance crops and animals. The main emphasis of the efforts to strengthen Russian crop and animal genetics is on singling out varieties that maximize economic efficiency. The Russian pig variety Libra was "a unique parent sow adapted to the conditions of industrial livestock farming," according to the scientists who developed her. Libra was to solve two problems that the Russian livestock sector inherited from the Yeltsin period: it would allow the Russian pork industry to both operate efficiently and replace imported parent stock with domestic pork genetics. In this technopolitical regime, and with varieties such as the Libra, pork producers are successful and competitive if they can modify and control the environment in which plants and animals are raised. This dynamic is particularly obvious in livestock production: purpose-built confinement operations have allowed agroholdings to use animal breeds that maximize economic efficiency. This form of meat production quite literally locks out the natural environment, obviating the need for animal breeds that are adapted to local contexts. Wheat, by contrast, is a field crop that remains far more exposed to soil and weather conditions and evolving pathogens in situ.

The Third Paradigm

What do we make of these trends in livestock and crop genetics and their implications for the larger question of how the Soviet and post-Soviet technopolitical regimes changed the relationship between human and nonhuman actors in agriculture? Given that the Bolshevik government's urge to transform the social, political, and economic order from the very start involved the natural environment, environmental historians have called for attention to the nonhuman and nonliving elements of the natural world. In Andy Bruno's words, they are actors in their own right and "participants in the dramas of Soviet history."[9] The natural environment is a prevaricating force, preventing the realization of utopian schemes. Jenny Leigh Smith tells the story of how Stalin- and Khrushchev-era pork producers grappled with cold weather and insufficient animal feed. She emphasizes that these harsh and hostile conditions contributed to low yields on Soviet farms, more so than peasants' backward practices or badly organized farms: "Humans mattered in the Soviet rural landscape. . . . However, in terms of success and failure of state-sponsored interventions on farms in the Soviet Union, nature mattered more."[10] Andy Bruno and Bathsheba Demuth document the long and fraught efforts by Bolshevik agents to domesticate and collectivize reindeer herds on the Komi Peninsula and along the Bering Strait.[11] Reindeer grazing, migration, and reproduction patterns and epizootics all eluded attempts to bring scientific methods of livestock holding to the northern and far eastern reaches of the Soviet empire. Reindeer survive Arctic winters by foraging on lichen, a critical resource for nomadic herders.[12] Neither a plant nor an animal, lichen are organisms composed of a symbiosis of fungi and algae species that sustained traditional reindeer herds through long winter months. Reindeer in turn have kept alive humans in these climates. Party officials and planners seeking to industrialize reindeer herding not only failed to understand the essential role that lichen played for reindeer herds; the workings of the entire complex web of sustaining relationships in the Arctic largely escaped their grasp.

What the complexity of these webs teaches us is that the ways in which nature is involved in the story of Russian domestication defy simple explanations. Indeed, the environmental history of the Soviet modernization project has drawn attention to varied notions of how humans relate to nature. Stephen Brain argues that Stalin-era Promethean plans to force nature to comply to human designs were opposed by a group of technocrats "who acknowledged local variation and experimental results."[13] The Promethean hubris of attempting to redesign nature was accompanied by a humbler approach to natural processes that sought understanding and coexistence. Andy Bruno also observes two distinct understandings of coexistence with nature that were prevalent throughout the Soviet period—one hostile, the other holistic. In the first view, nature and humans were in an antagonistic relationship in which human designs continuously struggled to overcome resistance from an inert and harsh natural environment. In the second view, a harmonious, mutually enriching symbiosis between humans and nature was possible. Both views conceptualized nature as a "treasure chest" containing the riches of the earth that humans could unlock to better themselves.[14] A key difference between these two conceptions of the human-nature nexus is that the first subordinates nature to human desires and Promethean schemes. It puts the needs of industrious workers and demanding consumers above those of plants, animals, and soils, positing nature as a stubborn set of forces that can be tamed and exploited for the benefits of high-modernist progress. The second view suggests that human-nature encounters need not be zero-sum games. Human gains do not result in losses for the environment as long as prudent stewardship and conservation are used as guides for the development of sustaining long-term relationships.[15] Bruno's work explores the Soviet Arctic, where much of the interaction with nature centers on the exploitation of natural resources for industry. He concludes that Soviet and post-Soviet planners often evoked a harmonious notion of the human-nature nexus to obscure the urgent and "genuine contradictions between the imperatives of industry and the needs of nature protection."[16] Nature is in this account relatively vulnerable to the unrelenting drive for economic extraction.

The will to harness nature for the creation of a better world for humans defines the Promethean paradigm. The harmonious paradigm is premised on the assumption of a mutually beneficial relationship between nature and humans allowing for the thriving of both. The history of Russian agriculture, and of seed and livestock genetics, suggests a third paradigm—that of interdependent vulnerability. James Scott urged us to think of the vulnerabilities stemming from novel infections and malnutrition that humans encountered during the gradual shift to sedentary agriculture.[17] Pathogens and nutritional deficiencies were indeed salient problems for party bureaucrats, planners, scientists, and (more recently) agroholdings. Not only humans were vulnerable, though. The plants and animals involved in Soviet and post-Soviet agriculture were just as exposed to damage as they were mobilized for human schemes, as illustrated in the accounts of the Irkutsk pigs and the replacement of rye with wheat detailed in earlier chapters. Soviet and post-Soviet plant breeders' efforts reveal an understanding that humans, agricultural crops, and domestic animals are vulnerable precisely because of their symbiotic dependence on each other. This third paradigm, that of interdependent vulnerability, understands that nature is modified and altered by human schemes (as the Promethean paradigm does), and it grasps the interdependence of humans and nature (as the harmonious paradigm does), but at its core it recognizes the fragility of webs of mutual sustenance, such as the one involving reindeer, lichen, fungi, algae, and humans in Russia's Far North. In the case of wheat, the interdependent vulnerabilities have to do with wheat varieties, soil nutrients, the use of synthetic fertilizer, the tastes of consumers, and diseases such as *puccinia triticina*, the fungus that causes wheat leaf rust. Each of these human and nonhuman components has its own life cycle, path, and logic of survival but is also dependent on the others. Wheat breeding efforts are ultimately about understanding and manipulating these covulnerabilities. In this third paradigm, humans do not stand apart from nature; they are inextricably part of it. The human-nature nexus is composed of ties that are part of a larger whole within the environment that sustains them. Giving and taking, tending and harvesting, adding and subtracting, sheltering and slaughtering are interactions among humans, animals, and plants within the same ecological system, even though they tend to empower humans through the technopolitics described in earlier chapters. There is thus no need to arbitrate whether or not seeds are part nature, or part of the human realm of domestication and technological improvements.

Soviet and Russian plant and animal breeding was shaped by all three paradigms of human-nature interactions—by human desire to modify nature, by understandings of mutual thriving, and by interdependent vulnerability. The two ideals—that of altering nature for human betterment and that of mutual thriving—were fundamentally important for plant breeding: when new animals and crop varieties resist droughts and pests, they yield strong harvests that help feed citizens. Nikolai Vavilov was convinced that genetics and plant breeding would help the Soviet socialist project succeed.[18] We also see fragility, though: even the most successful plant varieties and animal breeds were susceptible to unanticipated or new environmental pressures. The Krymka wheat variety, for example, had been grown for hundreds of years in Ukraine and southern Russia until it was replaced by new varieties in the postwar period. Imported hybrid corn seeds, considered true miracles of human plant engineering by the global plant breeding community in the sixties and seventies, did not thrive in many regions of the Soviet Union and ended up being vulnerable to pathogenic agents and harsh climates. Producers, breeders, and officials were faced with two options for dealing with the fragility of seeds and breeds: either they could try to modify local *contexts* to help the successful varieties and breeds maximize economic efficiency, or they could further modify and diversify *varieties and breeds* to broaden their adaptation to local contexts. Soviet livestock and crop breeders, agronomists, and officials chose both paths: even as they worked hard to control conditions, the imperfections of the planned economy never quite allowed for the high degree of control that the first path requires. Contemporary Russian livestock breeding, by contrast, has largely veered toward the first option: more capital-intensive livestock agriculture has allowed for tighter regimes of control and imports of high-efficiency breeds. This choice has had compounding and reinforcing consequences: the more production came to rely on a narrow group of varieties and breeds, the more it depended on keeping out any unruly forces belonging to local contexts with elaborate systems of high-input agriculture and confinement rearing. This is the Promethean paradigm at work, in which humans attempt to alter nature, and in this case, to exert control and extract resources. At the same time, new vulnerabilities were impossible to ignore as viruses slipped through the barriers of even the most effective confinement facilities. Notably, contemporary Russian wheat breeders continued to follow the first path. The wheat scientific community has been more aware of local adaptation, and of the mutual dependence of seed varieties, local soil conditions, and agricultural success. To the extent that bureaucrats, planners, and scientists are concerned with how seeds and animals would fare on local Russian land, they constructed and operated within the assumptions of the third paradigm.

Beyond Yields

Before the discussion on plant and livestock breeding, a note on yields is in order. Yields have long been the most important index and measure for the success of rural modernization and agricultural reforms. Yields are measures of productivity—the quantity of proteins and carbohydrates that can be extracted from one hectare of soil, the amount of meat that can be harvested from one animal, the number of eggs a hen can lay, or the number of metric tons of milk a dairy cow can produce. Agricultural technologies were almost universally geared toward increasing yields. During the Cold War, these measures were part of the competitive matrix that both Soviet and Western policymakers used to assess the merits of capitalist versus socialist agriculture. Wheat yields, for example, were consistently lower in the Soviet Union than in the US (see table 4.1; contemporary wheat yields are given in chapter 3). Soviet planners worried about the yield gap, and the climatic conditions of Soviet agriculture were considered one of the main culprits. In livestock agriculture, climate and soil were responsible for low feed-conversion rates for swine and low milk-per-cow indicators. The Soviet Union grew far less corn (a high-energy crop) than the US, and far lower quantities of soybeans and alfalfa (high-protein feeds). Soviet livestock feed was thus generally lower in protein and energy. Soviet planners were acutely aware of these limitations and used various technologies to address them—through livestock breeding programs or the reliance on corn as livestock feed.

Though yields have always been and remain an important consideration for all actors involved in agriculture, they are ultimately a metric that is most useful in a productionist approach to agriculture. Debates about yields have largely focused on the quantities of resources that can be extracted for human

Table 4.1 Wheat yields, Soviet Union and the US, 1961–1991

Wheat yields; hg/ha		
	USSR	US
1961	9920	16070
1971	14497	22829
1981	12947	23229
1991	15693	23038

Source: FAO.

use, but as a concept, yields are not only not helpful to grasp mutual vulnerabilities but have hindered a better understanding of the workings of the third paradigm. There is by now plenty of evidence that the constant push for higher yields and for a technological and competitive edge on global commodity markets has caused cascades of unintended consequences, risks, and vulnerabilities that render both nature and humans vulnerable. Earlier chapters outlined some of these unintended consequences—for example, the reduction of Central Asia's water table through irrigation systems that transformed the Aral Sea basin from a once thriving ecosystem to one of the world's largest environmental disasters.[19] This chapter will turn to new vulnerabilities and corollaries of crop and livestock breeding practices. We could think of nature's agency in both cases as resistance to human schemes to extract more resources. Humans have technology on their side, while nature has the awesome power of organic and ecological systems that humans have barely begun to understand, let alone replicate. Though this paradigm of agency and resistance is revealing, it obscures interdependent fragilities and covulnerabilities. In the minds of planners, scientists, and inventors, technologies are perfect blueprints. Their fallibility is often only revealed once interventions in poorly understood environmental contexts have misfired. The important point here is that new technologies do not just affect yields and the quantity of resources extracted from the natural realm for the human realm. As technopolitical regimes, they create new vulnerabilities for animals, crops, and humans alike. James Scott reminds us that not only do humans share many diseases with poultry, pigs, sheep, goats, rats, and mice, but the list of such diseases keeps growing.[20] This ultimately also means that we can no longer afford to rely on yields as the main conceptual device for understanding the human-nature nexus that agriculture entails.

Plant Breeding in Soviet and Post-Soviet Russia

For millennia, humans have been breeding plants and animals; the result is a unique and evolving symbiosis between humans and domesticated crops and livestock.[21] Nikolai Vavilov thought of domestication and crop breeding as "evolution at the hand of man." Geneticists today refer to it as "artificial" selection, opposing it to natural selection precisely because of the outsized role humans play in the intergenerational selection of particular phenotypes and genetic profiles. The selected traits, however, have changed over time and varied widely across societies. In the twenty-first century, breeding strategies and the continuous adaptation of agricultural seeds and livestock are increasingly seen as important elements of the response to climate change.[22]

Most studies on the political economy of genetic modification stress the power of global giants, such Monsanto and Syngenta, in defining plant breeding in accordance with their needs to generate corporate profits.[23] Yet a number of histories also link breeding practices with particular political projects and cultural values. Tiago Saraiva shows how pork breeders in fascist Germany valued the production of lard as a way to reduce dependence on imported vegetable oils, thus contributing to the Nazi party's efforts to strengthen autarky.[24] Joseph Anderson documents how hog breeding in postwar American agriculture shifted from valuing lard and fatty tissue to favoring a hog type that produced lean meat to mimic and compete with increasingly popular chicken on American plates.[25] Thus fascism and liberal market capitalism shaped breeding efforts. The Soviet track record of genetics is largely overidentified with the political project of Stalin and Trofim Lysenko. In the post-Soviet period, Western observers have mostly focused on Russia's ban on GMO crops. Neither of these perspectives on Soviet and Russian agro-genetic technologies is adequate: they neglect the fact that in both periods, governments, scientists, and plant breeders crafted a strong set of institutions and a growing body of knowledge that have produced a great diversity of crop and animal varieties in the twentieth and twenty-first centuries.

Lysenko's rise absolutely deserves attention as an astonishing case of how scientific research thrived because it served political ends. It was Nikolai I. Vavilov's work, however, that defined Soviet agro-genetic research in the long run. Born in Moscow in 1887, Vavilov graduated from what was then called the Moscow Agricultural University and became the center of gravity for a group of brilliant Russian geneticists and intrepid collectors of plant species. They gained international recognition for their insights into evolutionary biology and put Russia on the map of the global and thriving scientific plant-breeding community that emerged at the turn of the century.[26] After the revolution, Vavilov tried to enlist his scientific research for the goals of the socialist project. In the 1920s and 1930s, he directed the Soviet Academy of Agricultural Sciences, one of the most important actors in the drive to deploy science to help modernize rural Russia. Plant breeding was to serve the needs of the revolution through the development of varieties that would improve yields while preserving their hardiness in particular local climates. Vavilov was both a researcher and adventurer and led several ambitious expeditions across the world to collect thousands of plant species between 1916 and 1933, traveling to Iran, Afghanistan, China, Cuba, and Mexico. The resulting collection was stored in a seed vault in what is now known as the N. I. Vavilov Institute of Plant Genetic Resources (VIR) in St. Petersburg. Expeditions, collections, and hybridization strategies were based on Vavilov's theory that for each of the most useful agricultural crops—wheat, rice, potatoes, and so forth—scientists could find the most varieties in the regions where these crops had originated, the cradles of artificial selection. With varieties collected from around the world, Vavilov set up experimental breeding programs throughout the Soviet Union to test new hybrids in various domestic habitats.

Vavilov's research was increasingly at odds with the views of Trofim Lysenko, who gained political clout in the second half of the 1930s, taking over leadership of the All-Union Agricultural Academy in 1938. Lysenko rejected the role of genetic mutations in evolution and proposed instead that seeds, plants, and animals changed as living organisms, and that acquired traits were passed on to future generations through inheritance. His theory of *iarovisatsiia*—or "vernalization"—sought to improve the quality of seeds and livestock through exposure to cold climates and became the dominant paradigm for scientific and breeding efforts largely because of Stalin's support for Lysenko. Nikolai Vavilov became a victim of Stalin's purges; arrested in 1940 for opposing Lysenko, he died in prison in 1943. Many other geneticists who had conducted pioneering work in plant genetics shared his tragic fate—those who did not manage to emigrate in time were imprisoned, exiled, or executed.[27] Lysenko remained the most influential figure in Soviet genetics until the 1960s, and his dominance resulted in a nearly three-decade-long interruption of the Soviet Union's genetic research and a de facto divorce with international plant breeding community. Lysenko prevailed because vernalization offered a technological solution to plant breeding that was more politically useful to Stalin than Vavilov's plant genetics and collection. Vavilov's approach required time and patience as each hybrid variety was tested during one growing season, resulting in incremental progress in reaching overarching goals. Vernalization, meanwhile, promised quick success. Loren Graham and Jenny Leigh Smith point out that the idea of genetic stock improving in challenging environments, essentially what vernalization promised, was uniquely appealing in a country where climate and soil quality clearly posed huge challenges to the modernization of agriculture. Smith makes the point that a theory that "maize plants and young calves might somehow learn to tolerate a frosty Siberian spring" made sense to Soviet planners who wanted to improve cereal yields and livestock production.[28] Even though Lysenkoism and its effects on Soviet agriculture have been widely condemned, she argues that Lysenko's paradigm nevertheless offered Soviet agriculture a way to work with what they could control—human labor, livestock management, and plant breeding stations—to deal with what they could not control—climate and soil conditions.[29]

Though the politics of plant and animal genetics alternated between favoring genetic-hereditary approaches and those that emphasized acclimatization, Soviet agronomists and geneticists continued breeding programs throughout the Soviet period and were always keenly aware of the link between typical yields of crops and fitness of animal breeds, along with central characteristics such as pest and drought resistance. The search to foster plant varieties that promised higher yields, while also retaining local breeds adapted to local climatic conditions, was a central concern of Soviet agronomy and breeders. One of the most important technologies of midcentury agriculture was livestock and crop genetics that revolutionized farming first in the US and later across the world. Starting in 1955, Lysenko orthodoxy was challenged in important ways by Nikita Khrushchev. After Khrushchev's visit to the US, he deliberately endorsed and supported the research of high-yielding hybrid seeds as a tool to realize the promises of corn. He arranged for the purchase of double-cross hybrid corn seeds as well as for the import of technologies needed to produce them in the Soviet Union. The government also invested in domestic capacity and planned for two thousand collective farms to use new hybrid seeds for corn production. This endorsement of hybrid seed technology was an important turning point in the technopolitics of Thaw-era Soviet agriculture. Khrushchev thereby opposed Lysenko's orthodoxy and challenged his hold on Soviet agricultural research institutes. And even though these seed technologies faced an uphill battle for success in the Soviet research environment and in the planned economy, Aaron Hale-Dorrell notes that "the Soviet Union's hybrid seed program achieved significant success despite difficulties and delays."[30]

Wheat Breeding

Wheat was the most important cereal crop in the Soviet Union, and wheat research and breeding were exceptionally well developed. Russian peasants had cultivated wheat for centuries and introduced varieties from European Russia across the empire, extending into Central Asia in the mid-nineteenth century. Central Asia had its own history of wheat cultivation that went back to the seventh century BC, giving rise to many native landraces. Across the territory of the Russian empire, wheat landraces were exceptionally heterogeneous—Russian settlers spread the cultivation of wheat while continuously crossing it with local varieties and selecting for stress resistance in different parts of the vast and climatically diverse empire. German Mennonites brought some of these varieties to the US and Canada in the 1870s, including Turkey Red Wheat, the parent variety of most wheat varieties grown on the US Central Plains. In Russia, Turkey Red Wheat was known as Krymka for its origin on the Crimean Peninsula.[31] Many successful Canadian wheat varieties are also related to a Russian variety called Ladoga and brought to North America from Russia in the 1880s. A fledgling group of agricultural scientists and imperial ministries recognized the value of these landraces and sought to study them more systematically. The first Russian school of agronomy and the first wheat breeding station were established in Moscow in 1898, with the explicit aim to develop modern agronomy based on crop breeding experiments. Experimental stations with the same aims were set up in Saratov and Samara in 1910 and 1912, respectively. When the Bolshevik government took over, they thus inherited a cadre of experts, well-developed institutions, and a rich and growing body of research on crop genetics.[32] Soviet agronomy built on the imperial network of research and breeding stations and built new ones in the 1920s. It relied on the research conducted by scientists in previous decades and used many of the highly heterogeneous wheat landraces that were commonly used across the Russian empire, rejecting the idea of "universal" wheat varieties. Under the direction of Vavilov, Soviet breeders developed cultivars derived from inherited Russian landraces, crossing them with varieties collected from across the world. The Poltovka, Beloturka, Rusak, and Khivinka were varieties long used by peasants in the Russian southeast that were all crossed and developed at Soviet research stations for decades. They were used to cultivate millions of hectares of wheat in the Soviet Union well into the postwar period.

The Soviet wheat breeding networks ran more than forty agricultural research institutes and stations across the country, each developing several new and more hardy varieties every year. The main criteria of Soviet breeding were yield potential; ability to withstand the cold, drought, and pests; and bread quality. Given the climatic differences across the Soviet Union, the kind of tolerance that wheat cultivars needed differed across regions: rust is a problem everywhere, and weather hardiness was crucial for all Soviet wheat varieties. In some regions, seeds were bred for early frost tolerance; in others, winter hardiness meant tolerance to ice cover or waterlogging. Wheat breeders further considered that wheat diseases, such as leaf rust, mildew, and root diseases, affected cultivation differently in different climatic zones. Wheat strains were developed for drought tolerance at different stages of the plant's growing cycle because the timing and likelihood of droughts varied across Russia. Interestingly, breeding programs also had two different yield-related objectives. The first was to breed intensive varieties that yielded highly in the context of high-input farming and advanced technologies used at scientific breeding stations. The second was to develop what were called "semi-intensive" varieties for less technologically ambitious, more ordinary farming practices. Researchers took into account that "real" farming practices on collective farms involved less fertilizer, later sowing dates, and many other contingencies, and they adapted their research strategies accordingly. This two-pronged approach was essentially an acknowledgment by scientists and breeders that trials on research sites were not a particularly realistic environment for simulating yields on average farms. It was also well known that collective farm workers sometimes preferred tall wheat varieties because tall wheat stalks worked better for cattle bedding.[33] Finally, Soviet plant breeding programs considered the bread-making qualities of wheat an important goal of artificial selection. Wheat types were selected to meet thresholds for protein and gluten content as well as for their alveographic properties. The latter is a measure of how properties of the wheat kernel and flour affect dough quality during industrial baking and bread-making. Genetic research and breeding resulted in a large range of wheat varieties that were used on collective farms; by the late 1980s, the majority of the Soviet Union's wheat cultivation consisted of 144 winter and 130 spring wheat varieties.[34] In the decades after World War II, the large-scale breeding efforts and ongoing development of new strains by various research institutes led to a rapid turnover.[35] A few leading varieties were particularly popular: six winter and ten spring wheat types were cultivated on about half of all acreage during the 1980s. The Soviet Union's leading winter wheat was the Mironovskaya-808, which was grown on 3.16 million hectares in 1988 (see figure 4.1). The leading spring wheat, the Saratovskaya-29, was grown on 9.87 million hectares. Though these were the reliable champions often used by collective farms, the breeding stations of the Soviet Union created and released many new varieties, many of which were widely adopted and used successfully in situ.

The Soviet wheat breeding efforts were conducted through a network of strong but geographically distributed research institutes and experimental stations. One of the country's leading breeding stations was the Agricultural Research Institute of the Non-Chernozem Zone, located on the outskirts of Moscow (now called Federal'nyi issledovatel'skii tsentr "Nemchinovka"), also known as the Nemchinovka. Its most well-known innovations were the Inna and the Moskovskaya-35, both of which were strong varieties that spread widely across European Russia. The Agricultural Research Institute of the Southeast (now called the Nauchno-issledovatel'skii institut sel'skogo khoziaistva Iugo-Vostoka), located in Saratov, was the country's leading institution in spring wheat breeding.[36] This institute's most famous breeding achievements were spring wheat types that drew on the genetic material of durum landraces, developed in the forties and fifties. The Sarrubra and the Sarrosa were based on the Beloturka landrace, and both were in turn progenitors of the Saratovskaya-29, the Saratov Institute's most successful variety, released in 1950 and grown on millions of hectares since then. These strains all rely on crosses of local germplasm and have unique drought-resistant qualities. Saratovskaya-29 was so successful that it replaced some regionally established varieties in other parts of the

Figure 4.1 Mironovskaya winter wheat and bread baked from this variety, July 30, 1984. TASS, Remeslo Research Institute of Selection and Seed Production.

Soviet Union, such as the Milturum-553, developed by the Siberian Agricultural Research Institute in Omsk and commonly used for wheat cultivation in Siberia in the 1940s–1960s.[37]

A notable aspect of Soviet wheat breeding is that the different breeding stations and research institutes were competing with each other. They developed different breeding methods, followed different strategies, and relied on germplasm from various parts of the world to achieve the most outstanding results, which were publicized and compared in various journals and at conventions and competitions. The Samara Agricultural Research Institute, located in Bezenchuk (now known as the Samarskii nauchno-issledovatel'skii institut sel'skogo khoziaistva im. N. M. Tulaikova), was known for a strategy that drew on a particularly wide range of germplasm from across the world to develop new hybrids. A variety developed by the Krasnodar Agricultural Research Institute focused on high-yield and wide geographic adaptability. This institute developed Novoukrainka-83 in the late 1930s and the Aurora and Kavkaz varieties in the 1970s, each relying on germplasm from Western Europe and distinguished by high levels of leaf rust resistance. The Krasnoufimsk Breeding Station in Ekaterinburg developed a variety of crosses involving Scandinavian (particularly Swedish) varieties that are well adapted to the Ural region's late planting, cold summers, and early frosts. The Siberian Agricultural Research Institute in Omsk relied on varieties from Norway and the US. In the late 1970s, Soviet researchers began experimenting with CIMMYT germplasm, which were responsible for the "Green Revolution" in Latin America and Asia, although they proved to be less attractive to breeders and growers in Russia than they were to their counterparts in other regions of the world. Soviet wheat breeding methods were thus varied and characterized more by competition between units than by centralization. A final fascinating fact of Soviet wheat cultivation and wheat genetic material relates to the heterogeneity of cultivars. Wheat varieties were recognized and registered by a regulatory body, the All-Union State Commission for Varieties and Testing (which later became the Gossortkommissiia). Unlike similar agencies in Western European countries, the Soviet Commission that certified crop varieties did not require complete homogeneity of new strains. Indeed, many Soviet wheat breeders valued a degree of within-variety heterogeneity as proving more stable yields and wider adaptability in varying environmental conditions. The widely cultivated Mironovskaya-808, for example, is known to be relatively heterogeneous. Indeed, this heterogeneity was thought to be one of the reasons the Mironovskaya-808 provided stable yields across large and diverse areas under cultivation.[38]

After the collapse of the Soviet Union, the network of agricultural research institutes and breeding stations was starved of funding, triggering an existential crisis. The US donated large quantities of plant seeds (mainly corn and pea seeds) as part of a larger food aid program for Russia and seed began to be imported.[39] Russian seed research institutes, meanwhile, were required to transition to a financial model in which they were funded by seed sales to make up for rapidly diminishing funds from federal and regional budgets.[40] This was a significant transformation for the storied and well-regarded plant breeding centers, many of which date back to imperial Russia and thrived in the Soviet Union. Yet, over the decade that followed, many of these institutions managed to adapt and now sell seeds derived from newly developed and legacy varieties from the late Soviet period. The Nemchinovka, for example, continues to sell two varieties of Moskovskaya wheat (Moskovskaya 39 and 40), a winter wheat that had been a specialty of the institute for decades.[41] Research institutes continue to develop new varieties, but they also started functioning as seed retailers in the early 2000s, selling seeds to commercial farms across Russia. The most active institutes sold seeds for a range of different crops, but many specialized in a particular crop. Their focus and strength depended on their history and geographical location. Many concentrated on either winter or spring wheat, and some provided other seed grains or vegetable seeds. The Krasnodar NIISK (Krasnodarskii nauchno-issledovatel'skii institut sel'skogo khoziaistva im. P. P. Luk'ianenko), for example, specialized in winter wheat seeds, offering no fewer than fifty-one varieties of winter wheat for commercial farmers. The Samara NIISK, one of Russia's oldest seed breeding centers, specialized in spring wheat, and the Siberian NIIRS (Sibirskii nauchno-issledovatel'skii institut rastenievodstva i selektsii) also offers a large range of Russian traditional field crops other than wheat, such as triticale, oats, and barley. Table 4.2 provides a summary of the seed varieties developed and sold by Russia's most established plant breeding institutes for the main field crops in 2020. Note that they offer far fewer vegetable seeds and no sugar beets seeds. These are the five most active institutes; there are at least fourteen institutes of this kind that commercially develop and sell field crop seeds.

The breeding aims of the post-Soviet wheat breeding institutes were in many ways quite similar to Soviet-era strategies: in addition to economically relevant criteria such as yields and uniformity of crops, resistance to old and new environmental risks remained important. Erratic rainfall patterns have historically been a problem for wheat production in Russia, and drought resistance remains a key breeding aim. Contemporary wheat breeders also recognize that with climate change, droughts are likely to occur more often. Soviet researchers were well aware of the problem of pathogen mutations: pathogen-resistant wheat strains sometimes lost this advantageous trait when pathogens evolved. Wheat, barley, and rye have all long been susceptible to leaf rust and other

Table 4.2 Seed varieties for main Russian grain crops developed and sold by Russian seed breeding institutes, 2020

Institute	Nemchinovka	Samara NIISKH	Krasnodar NIISKH	Siberian NIIRS	Altai NIISKH
Year established	*1931*	*1903*	*1914*	*1926*	*1950*
Winter Wheat	Y (8)	Y (7)	Y (51)	Y (5)	Y (3)
Spring Wheat	Y (8)	Y (21)	Y (2)	Y (20)	Y (20)
Triticale	Y (6)	Y (1)	Y (11)	Y (2)	N
Rye, oats, barely	Y (3)	Y (2)	N	Y (13)	Y (2)
Vegetables, incl. potatoes	N	Y (3)	N	Y	Y
Legumes, incl. soy & alfalfa	N	Y	N	Y	Y
Oilseeds	N	N	N	N	Y

Y = Yes (number of commercial seed varieties in brackets). N = No.
Source: Based on information provided by the plant breeding institutes.

fungal diseases, but the future occurrence and mutation of each of these pathogens are largely unpredictable with changing global climate patterns. Contemporary Russian plant breeders and scientists are increasingly trying to take into account how climate change affects pathogen mutation and crop resistance.[42]

Given these new challenges, the expertise and institutional capacity of the wheat and crop-breeding community are perceived to be crucial. The Russian government has tried to retain and strengthen Soviet-era institutions. The outcome of these efforts varies: in the wheat sector, Russian researchers and seed developers have managed to develop seeds that are widely used; in other field crops, Russian seeds were displaced by imported varieties. The strength of Russian wheat varieties is reflected in the share of Russian varieties approved by the Gossortkommissia, a federal agency that registers and provides copyright protection for all plant and animal varieties in use in Russian agriculture. The Gossortkommissia publishes a roster of thousands of approved varieties along with information about patent holders, each identified with a name and address. In the wheat sector, more than seven hundred varieties are listed as approved and only about 3 percent of them are patents that belong to foreign entities (see table 4.3). Locally adapted genetic material continues to be valued, used, and developed in wheat and a few other field crop seeds (buckwheat, barley, oats, and millet). While Russian wheat has globalized as a product, as chapter 2 outlined, the genetic material of wheat seeds remains rooted in the seed breeding strategies pursued for decades by Soviet wheat breeding institutions and their successors.

Table 4.3 Russian and foreign patent holders for seed varieties registered with Gossortkommissiia, 2020

Crop	Total patents	Russian patent holders	% RU
Sea buckthorn (Hippophae rhamnoides)	90	90	100
Durum wheat (Triticum durum)	77	75	97
Soft spring wheat (Triticum aestivum)	427	402	94
Potato (Solanum tuberosum)	1030	802	78
Sunflower (Helianthus annuus)	843	398	47
Sugar beet (Beta vulgaris)	375	156	42
Corn (Zea mays)	1166	453	39
Winter rape (Brassica napus)	114	16	14

Source: Based on information provided by Gossortkommissiia.

Seeds are imported for other field and industrial crops, such as sugar beets, potatoes, canola, soy, and corn.[43] This is particularly interesting in the case of sugar beet production. In 2020, Russia was the world's largest sugar beet producer, but the country imports most seeds for sugar beet production from one of a few global suppliers, such as DLF Seeds, based in Denmark. Like wheat, the sugar beet is considered native, or "ours," because beets have a long and successful history of growing in Russian soil. In the mid-nineteenth century, when industrial sugar extraction reached imperial Russia, Russian growers relied on imported seeds from Germany and France, where the large-scale production and sugar extraction industries had developed a few decades earlier. These imported seeds were expensive, and late imperial-era scientists set up selection and experimental stations starting in the 1890s. On the eve of World War I, 42 research stations tested and developed sugar beet varieties across European Russia, most of them belonging to a network of sugar beet breeders set up by the All-Russian Society of Sugar Factory Owners.[44] The Russian sugar beet seed industry thrived, and during the war, Russia was by far the most important exporter of sugar beet seeds to the Allied forces.

The Soviet history of sugar beet breeding in many ways mirrors that of wheat, though the paths of the two crops diverge after 1991. The revolution thoroughly disrupted sugar beet breeding and sugar beet production, but they were rebuilt and restructured in the 1920s. With the rise of Lysenkoism in the 1930s, genetic research on sugar beets that had generated successful varieties became politically untenable and was abandoned as scientists were arrested and purged.⁴⁵ Over the decades, and despite this interruption, Soviet beet seed breeding recovered and was an institutionally strong and scientifically rigorous community that developed thousands of lines of improved beet varieties over the decades. Soviet beet varieties, also known as "mother beet seeds," were developed in an extensive network of experimental stations and achieved several important breeding aims, such as increased sugar content and increasing resistance to various environmental threats such as root rot, leaf spot, and storage rot, caused by various beet fungi.⁴⁶ Given the similarities in the history of wheat and beets, the divergent post-Soviet trajectories of wheat and beet were noted and a cause for concern. One Russian observer expresses particular concern about the reliance on foreign genetic material in a commodity as ostensibly Russian as the beet: "Almost all Russian agricultural products are grown from imported seeds. Take a beet grown on our soil—that would appear to be *nasha*, yet the seed for that beet is imported from abroad."⁴⁷ In fact, information on patent holders published by Gossortkommissiia suggests that 58 percent of patent holders for beet seeds registered in Russia are foreign. Table 4.3 provides an overview of whether patent holders are Russian or foreign (but note that the two columns of Russian patent holders include any company with an address or subsidiary in Russia). The share of Russian patent holders is high for wheat and a few other crops, such as sea buckthorn, or sandthorn (*oblepixa*), a popular Russian berry used for juice and jam. It is much lower for other industrial crops, such as sunflower, beets, corn, and the oilseed rape.⁴⁸ In 2020, the Russian government approved funding for a new large-scale research effort to support research and development of seed varieties to strengthen capabilities of domestic seed producers.

One of the peculiarities of crop genetic research and development in Russia is that Russia has banned the cultivation of genetically modified organisms since 2016.⁴⁹ The political reasoning for the law was that it would provide a basis for "clean" agricultural production. (As the law's provisions extend to imported products, critics of the law claimed that it was passed to shut out North American corn and soy from the Russian market.) The law allows for genetic modifications of plants for research purposes. Over the last few years, the Russian government has been supporting animal and crop genetic research and development, driven largely by fears of being dependent on foreign agrogenetic material. Among other measures, the Russian government has funded public research institutes and public-private joint ventures to develop new Russian varieties. An amendment to the tax code made in 2016 reduced the tax rate for "operations with purebred breeding agricultural animals" to 0 percent until 2020, a provision that has meanwhile been extended.⁵⁰ A 2018 decree laid the groundwork to strengthen genetic technologies in research, science, and agriculture.[51] This decree specifically addressed research and cultivation of gene-*edited* crops, maintaining the ban on genetically modified crops while carving out a space for CRISPR-Cas9 technologies, which have become increasingly common in US agro-genetic research. The decree walks a thin line between editing and modifying genetic material by prohibiting genetic modification "that cannot result from natural processes" while explicitly allowing for the reshuffling of genes with CRISPR–Cas9 technologies.[52] Russian scientists have long regarded the GMO ban as a political impediment to commercial and scientific use of new agro-genetic research; one commentator expressed relief about the new law as it would prevent Russia from being sidelined in the global "CRISPR bonanza."[53] A 2018 decree allocated funds to federal programs, specifically setting out the goal of developing at least thirty new crop and animal varieties over the next ten years and dedicating 111 billion rubles (US$1.7 billion) to agricultural genetic research to this effort. The decree lists four crops as priorities that should guide research: barley, sugar beets, wheat, and potatoes. Finally, in a move that is typical for Putin's technopolitics of agriculture, which enlists oligarchic corporate actors for political goals, the Russian government signed an agreement with the Rosneft oil company in March 2020 that devotes funds from oil profits to expediting the development of genetic technologies and genome editing.[54]

The post-Soviet shift in animal genetic resources more resembles the recent history of beets than that of wheat. With the advent of agroholdings, the growing conditions for livestock have been modified much more extensively than for field crops. New technologies have managed to target nutrient and pesticide application for crops, but in the end, weather conditions cannot be manipulated, and many pathogens are still largely beyond the control of agroholdings. The confinement conditions of pigs, chickens, and cows, however, have been extensively modified with the capital investments by agroholdings. These modifications are hugely important: new livestock confinement conditions have allowed agroholdings to use animal breeds that focus almost exclusively on economic criteria.

Livestock Breeding in Soviet and Post-Soviet Russia

Scientists and planners in the community of early Soviet-era livestock genetics and breeders have sought to bring science and technology to agriculture for the purpose of improving the characteristics of farm animals. Soviet animal breeding has also relied on an extensive and dispersed network of experimental breeding stations. Askaniia Nova, a nature preserve established in the 1880s and located in southern Ukraine, became one of the Soviet Union's first animal breeding research centers, renamed the Trofim Lysenko Station of Animal and Plant Hybridization in the late 1930s. When Soviet efforts to improve, rationalize, and reorganize collective animal husbandry intensified after World War II, this station became one of the most important centers for these efforts.[55] The scientists at this station focused on improving and breeding the Ukrainian White Steppe, a dual-purpose meat and lard pig breed. The fact that the Ukrainian White was native to southern Ukraine was specifically recognized and valued. Ecological specificity mattered to animal breeders as the basis for the recovery of the pig population in this part of the Soviet Union.[56] As in plant breeding, however, there was often a distinct difference between the health and quality of livestock on research stations and the less uniform, less well-fed herds on average collective farms.[57]

The difficulties in controlling conditions on collective farms also meant that the Soviet livestock sector relied on a remarkably large number of distinct animal breeds. The Ukrainian White was just one among many more pig species that were used on Soviet-era collective farms and on household farms. Overall, many more pig, cattle, chicken, and sheep breeds were raised in Soviet agriculture than in the industrial economies of the capitalist West. Russian agronomists and the geneticists of Russia's agriculture and livestock breeding institutes were of course well aware of this diversity; in fact, it was a conscious breeding strategy. For Western observers, the great variety of breeds appeared to be a failure to introduce the best and most efficient animal breeds. In the 1980s, though, the UN's Food and Agriculture Organization (FAO) and a group of international animal scientists started to pay attention to breed variety amid growing concerns that an increasing reliance on a small number of international breeds may have a detrimental impact on the diversity of animal species and plants. The FAO commissioned studies of the animal genetic resources of different countries; in 1989, the organization published a report titled *The Animal Genetic Resources of the USSSR*.[58] The introduction of the report states: "The Soviet Union features a great variety of breeds of farm animals with 52 breeds and breed groups of cattle, 30 of pigs, 90 of sheep and 50 of horses.... Although not noted for high performance, these animals showed good adaptation to local environmental and feed conditions."[59] The study is based on an extensive research project directed by N. K. Dmitriev and L. K. Ernst that surveyed a variety of livestock on collective farms that have been developed in breeding facilities controlled by the Ministry of Agriculture at the Union Republic level and a decentralized network of 93 breeding centers (*plemzavody*), 150 breeding state farms (*plemkhozy*), and 1257 breeding farms (*plemfermy*). For pigs specifically, Dmitriev and Ernst noted the presence of a large variety of breeds that had developed based on continuous adaptation to the local context. The authors also found that a large share of animals were not purebreds. While Soviet breeders valued purebreds for their performance, they also recognized that the vast majority of pigs on Soviet collective and backyard farms were in fact mixed-breed animals. The authors summarize these points as follows:

> In the USSR there are 32 breeds, breed groups and types of pigs.... The number includes 22 breeds that have been developed since the beginning of the Soviet-era or subjected to continuous acclimatization to become adapted to the conditions in the areas of their breeding. These 22 breeds account for 29 million out of the 73 million [pigs] in the Soviet Union. The rest are foreign breeds and 2- or 3-breed crosses.... Development of such a large number of breeds is justified by the diversity of natural and climatic zones in the country as well as by the need to have several contrasting breeds in each region for commercial crossbreeding.[60]

The report also clearly states that breed diversity was not accidental but the outcome of a deliberate breeding method and strategy pursued in Russia since the second half of the nineteenth century. Late imperial and Soviet scientists and animal breeders alike valued local adaptation alongside economic criteria. The FAO reports describes the method as follows: "[The breeding] technique ... was based on the following typical method: crossing of native animals distinguished by such assets as fitness, adaptation to the local climate, strong constitution and disease resistance, with highly productive, improved European breeds."[61] The reason for this strategy of preserving and relying on locally adapted breeds had to do with the in situ conditions of animal rearing. It was quite simply a necessity to breed animals not only for economically relevant traits but also for their adaptation to local climates across the vast expanse of the Russian empire and the Soviet Union. Livestock farms (collective farms starting in the 1930s) were spread far and wide across the country's diverse—and often harsh—climatic zones. The conditions of livestock rearing ranged from fully pasture-based models to "porous" confinement. In this latter model, animals were raised in dedicated facilities for some of their lives before slaughter, but animals spent only a limited time in these facilities; nor did they completely confine them from environmental conditions. The feed used was most often far from "optimal" from the perspective of a livestock farmer concerned with weight gain and fecundity. High-calorie and protein-rich livestock feed in particular was in short supply. Collective farms and households fed livestock whatever was available. Sometimes feed was brought in from other regions of the Soviet Union, but often it consisted of whatever was on hand in situ or on nearby farms, fields, and pastures. This is not to say that Soviet livestock production did not have confinement operations that separated animals from environmental conditions and optimized feed. Toward the late Soviet period, industrial pig and broiler operations were able to introduce more homogenous animals and had access to better feed.[62] Pork production intensified greatly in the 1980s, and many of the features of capitalist intensive confinement operations were adopted in the Soviet Union, including intensive employment of particular breeds, confinement with no access to outdoors, automation and mechanization, and specialized feed. But these kinds of intensive livestock conditions were novel in the seventies and eighties, and they were not the norm on most collective farms. For most of Soviet history, livestock rearing and feeding were closely related and tied to the varied environmental conditions of local environments.[63]

As in the case of crops, livestock breeding in the Soviet era was directed by union-level research institutions but relied on a decentralized network of research institutes and experimental stations. For each of the major livestock breeds, breed councils at the level of the Union Republics decided on directions for selection and breeding policies in specially designated regions. Pig breeding, for example, divided the country into 112 "breeding regions" in the fifteen Union Republics. Regional achievements and particular "champions" were displayed at annual exhibitions in Moscow and at the republic level and awarded with prizes. While the diversity of breeds was valued, their economic performance was nevertheless a central concern. Scientists and planners collected data on many of the same indicators that were (and remain) central to swine breeding in capitalist economies, such as the number of days to reach a particular body weight (100 kilograms in Soviet statistics), the average daily weight gain, and the percentage of meat on the carcass. What is interesting, though, is that Soviet swine breeds varied greatly along these indicators. Some Soviet pig breeds performed close to (though still lower than) breeds in capitalist economies. The most common Soviet swine breed was the Breitovskaya, developed from the Large White imported from Great Britain and the Landrace from Denmark, crossed with the "lop-eared" pigs from Latvia and Lithuania. The Breitovskaya was officially recognized as a distinct breed in 1948 and became more commonly used over the postwar decades. By the late eighties, the Breitovskaya was most common in the northwest and took, on average, 217 days to reach 100 kilograms. The assets of the breed are described as follows: "The renowned assets of the Breitovskaya are its hardiness, good adaptability to the climate in the northwest of the Russian Republic, ability to consume bulky feeds . . . and gain rapidly on low-concentrate feeding."[64] In short, this was a practical and common pig breed because it put on weight with feed that was not always perfect in protein content and because it could deal with the cold winters of northwestern Russia. It was one of a handful of breeds that were developed from international breeds common in Europe. The Soviet Large White, like the Breitovskaya, is closely related to the British Large White, first imported in the 1880s and later again in the 1920s and 1960s. The authors of the FAO report note that the Soviet Large White was the result of "many years' work by Russian and Soviet breeding experts to acclimatize the English Large White in varying climatic and feeding conditions" and was now "superior to the English Large White in many respects." It was a "general purpose breed" that could thrive across many climates of the Soviet Union.[65]

The balance between performance and local adaptation varied greatly across Soviet pig breeds. Some breeds performed well along the economically relevant indicators while also being specifically bred to thrive in the climate and with the feed of a particular environment. This was the case for the Semirechenskaya, for example: "This breed was developed specially for the climate of southeast Kazakhstan [to] combine the high productivity of an improved breed with the strong constitution of wild boar." Other breeds had few economically valuable traits, but they were still recognized for the traits they shared with local wild breeds. The Kakhetinskaya, at home in the Georgian Soviet Socialist Republic, is an example of this latter category: it is noted as being "a primate type close to the wild boar" that "cannot compete directly with improved breeds."[66] All of these breeds had geographically distinct distributions—the Breitovskaya was most common around Moscow, while the Kakhetian pig, as its name suggests, was a Georgian pig variety. Table 4.4 shows images of four

Table 4.4 Soviet pig breeds

	Breitovskaya	Soviet Large White	Semirechenskaya	Kakhetinskaya
Days to reach 100kg	217	192	198	"Not competitive" (85kg = 183 days)
Phenotype				

Source: N. K. Dmitriev and L. K. Ernst, "The Animal Genetic Resources of the USSSR" (1989).

breeds in terms of their economic performance. It is also noteworthy that the development of these breeds was not considered "complete" in the sense that they were not considered to have reached an ideal expression of their phenotypes. Soviet breeders did not consider one breed as universally optimal—breeding was essentially a work in progress, with further achievements in terms of performance and local adaptation always held up as future goals. Finally, given that diversity was valued and breeding was considered an ongoing process, the disappearance of breeds over time was considered a significant loss of genetic material that could have been used in the future. Soviet breeding institutions thus also considered the preservation of declining breeds an important task.

Soviet poultry breeding was in some ways similar to pork breeding in that it relied on a large variety of breeds used in state farms and reared in backyards for decades. The Russian White hen was one of the most common poultry breeds for much of Soviet history until the 1970s. While Nikita Khrushchev's attempts to bring corn to the Soviet Union are well known, he was also fascinated by American high-yield broilers and saw them as the way to scale up Soviet chicken production. In the 1960s, the Soviet Union was the world's largest egg and poultry producer, but the per-hen egg and meat production performance lagged behind Western Europe. Soviet animal genetics institutes developed new breeds with foreign genetic material, especially from Dutch breeds as well as the American Cobb broiler. Cobb, now a global animal genetics giant, was invited to the Soviet Union by Nikita Khrushchev, who encountered the marvels of the Cobb broiler at the British Agricultural Exhibit at VDNKh in Moscow.[67] Between 1964 and 1984, the Soviet Union's poultry farms intensified production, and between 1964 and 1984, the average annual egg yield per hen increased from 130 to 226.[68] This was largely the result of the adoption of new broiler types and a simultaneous departure from the historic reliance on dual-purpose breeds (those producing both eggs and meat) to dedicated egg and meat varieties. The Russian White hens were gradually displaced by crosses of imported grandparental lines.[69] Yet the Soviet Union never quite abandoned dual-purpose breeds. Despite the rise of special-purpose breeds on collective farms, the large chicken populations on household farms remained diverse and locally adapted. Overall, the genetic diversity of Soviet hens was always larger, and yields were lower, than in the US.

In the post-Soviet period, local adaptation and breed diversity became an obstacle to the aims of the technopolitical regime ushered in by the Putin administration and the agroholdings. The profound crisis of Russian agriculture in the nineties was largely perceived as stemming from the absence, or shortage, of the technological innovations that had spurred American agriculture in the second half of the twentieth century. Starting in the early 2000s, agroholdings directed immense resources to updating the technological tools used in newly acquired land assets and factories, as outlined in chapter 2. In this context, the most economically efficient pigs and broilers became valued. When Russian pork, chicken, and dairy farms and cattle ranchers started expanding production and updating facilities, they largely used imported purebred animals. Livestock traits that relate to local adaptation became all but irrelevant as new facilities were built to control the production environment. And even livestock breeds that had performed relatively well in the Soviet era, such as the Breitovskaya, did not compare favorably with the international purebreds. By 2014, the Breitovskaya accounted for a mere 0.19 percent of pork produced in Russia. Agroholdings thus looked abroad for high-performing animals for all sectors. In 2006, EkoNiva, for example, purchased 550 purebred Simmental heifers from Germany.[70] In 2010, a Voronezh cattle farm, the Sputnik-Stevenson ranch, imported 1,434 head of Black Angus cattle from Montana, bringing this sizable herd by cargo ship via the port of Novorossiysk.[71] Pork producers imported large numbers of live animals and genetic material for the Great White, Landrace, and Duroc varieties, and poultry producers largely used the Cobb, Ross, and Hubbard broilers.[72] Overall, hundreds of thousands of live purebred animals and genetic materials have been imported since the early 2000s. Table 4.5 shows the number of live cattle imported to Russia, for six years of intense growth in this sector, between 2011 and 2016. The seamless supply of these animals to domestic producers was clearly also a political concern: imported purebred cattle were exempt from import duties.[73] And while meat imports were banned after 2014 in Russia's response to Western sanctions, purebred live animals were excluded from the ban. As agroholdings fully embraced these new breeds, the livestock traits that relate to local adaptation, meanwhile, became all but irrelevant because new facilities were built to control the production environment.

The imports of live purebred animals declined over the years because purebred parent stock for high-performing animals became more available in Russia, not because commercial operations moved away from this kind of technology. Several transnational companies in the livestock genetic sector started producing in Russia. Also, Russian research institutes and breeding centers were rebuilt

Table 4.5 Russian imports of live cattle for purebred breeding, 2011–2016

2011	2012	2013	2014	2015	2016
86,534	136,982	96,894	41,958	33,065	30,402

Source: USDA FAS Gain Report No. RS1757, November 28, 2017.

and strengthened. With strong demand from agroholdings, staunch political support, and ongoing public funding, Russian livestock breeding institutes have been developing high-performance Russian animal breeds, such as the Libra piglet and the Smena chicken. In the pork sector, the most important institution in Russia today is the Znamensk Genetic Selection Center, created in 2006 and located in Orel.[74] The Znamensk Center was established through a partnership with the transnational company Hypor, which is a leading global supplier of pig genetics.[75] The Znamensk Center is a private holding company owned by Exima, which in turn has received investments from the two meat giants Miratorg and Cherkizovo. (Exima is one of the companies that explicitly aligns its own operations with the political goals of the Putin regime; see chapter 2.) The Znamensk Center has also developed a new, high-performance Russian big breed, known as Libra. The Libra pig, like its international cousins, is "highly adapted" to industrial livestock farming and maximizes economically relevant traits in both the maternal and paternal lines, as summarized in table 4.6. The Znamensk Center also specializes in raising the parent stock of four international breeds—Large White (originating in the UK), Landrace (from the Netherlands), Duroc (from the US), and Petren (from Belgium)—the four most commonly used breeds in commercial pig operations internationally. These pigs take an average of 142 to 145 days to reach 100 kilograms. This is more than two months less than the time needed to reach maturity for the Soviet-era Breitovskaya pig (it took an average of 217 days to reach the same weight). It is also notable that the international pork breeding community

Table 4.6 Breeding aims maximized in Libra/Svinka F-1

Maternal breeds	*Paternal breeds*
feed conversion	feed conversion
average daily gain; age attaining 100 kg in weight	average daily gain; age attaining 100 kg in weight
fertility index	meat quality and carcass index
total number of piglets born	the depth of the longest muscle
the number of live births	thickness of spinal fat
piglet weight at birth	meat percentage
survival / mortality	
age of first insemination	
spacing between weaning and insemination	

Source: Based on information provided by the Znamensk Genetic Selection Center, accessed June 2021, http://www.nsgc.ru/produkciya/roditelskaya-svinka-f1.

considers each of these breeds to have been "completed" in the 1980s and 1990s. Znamensk and Hypor thus state that production now seeks to remain as close as possible to the breed-specified phenotypes. Instead of being bred to do well in particular natural environments, they are bred to do well in typical confinement conditions. The Znamensk Center's description of the Petren and the Large White, for example, noted their ability to tolerate stress and crowding: "Despite the fact that the Large White pig breed was originally developed for free range conditions, pigs of this breed perform best while confined in cramped conditions"; of the Petren, it is noted, "Distinctive characteristic of this breed include ... the absence of a stress gene."[76]

Whether relying on the Libra or international breeds, Russia's meat industry and pork breeding center now focus on a much smaller number of breeds, virtually all of which are the product of breeding strategies that maximize economically relevant traits. This is possible because post-Soviet confinement facilities by design seal and cut off any interactions between the piglets and the local environment. Animal feed is composed of highly deliberate feed mixes finetuned to the particular breed based on the animal's function and life stage, containing various types of grains, proteins, micronutrients, and minerals. The bulk of feed, grain, is sourced from Russian producers, while soy proteins, micronutrients, and minerals in feed mixes are mostly imported. In the eyes of Russian veterinary authorities and agroholding veterinarians, industrial pigs needed to be sheltered from one further threat—the pigs from household farms. As these pigs were considered likely vectors for pathogens, extensive efforts were made to reduce the possibility of such contamination.

In the poultry sector—as on hog farms—locally adapted species and porous production facilities have been replaced by international breeds and modes of production that by design eliminate interaction with local environments. The most commonly used poultry breeds in Russia are Ross-308, Hubbard-F15, Arbor Acers, and Cobb-500. These hens are patent-protected products of two transnational companies that control the market for poultry genetic resources: the first three are Aviagen birds, and the latter are Cobb-Vantress.[77] As in the pork sector, the boom of Russian poultry production was initially largely dependent on imported purebred animals supplied by these companies. Russia imported between 600 and 700 million purebred poultry eggs per year in the middle of the first decade of the 2000s.[78] Russian livestock companies also bought around 23 million purebred chicks from the breeding centers that Cobb-Vantress and Aviagen operate in Russia; the year they were introduced, these chicks laid more than 4 billion eggs and yielded 4 million metric tons of chicken meat—the majority of Russia's chicken production.[79] The Russian government has funded research and development in poultry genetics, in particular the development of the Smena-8 (2011) and Smena-9 (2020) broiler—also known as the Russian "super chickens." The Smena broilers were developed at a state-funded research center, the All-Russian Poultry Science, Research and Technology Institute, which goes by the Russian acronym VNITIP (Vserossiiskii nauchno-issledovatel'skii institut ptitsevodstva), affiliated with the Russian Academy of Sciences and located in Sergiyev-Posad, a small town in Moscow oblast. The Soviet predecessor of the institute was founded in 1930 and has been producing genetic resources for industrial chicken production for decades. The first Smena broiler was developed in 1978 and was one of the more commonly used Soviet chicken breeds. VNITIP scientists recently turned to the Smena to transform it into Russia's new super chicken. The Smena-8 and 9 are "super" because they are bred specifically to compete with the existing global high-efficiency breeds, such as Cobb-500 and Ross-38. This is no small feat as the Cobb-500 is "the world's most efficient" broiler, bred for the following features: "lowest costs of live weight produced, superior performance on lower cost feed rations, best broiler uniformity for processing, competitive breeder," according to Cobb-Vantress.[80] The Ross-38 "is recognized globally as a broiler that will give consistent performance in the broiler house," according to Aviagen.[81] The Russian super-chicken breeds, the Smena-8 and 9, are attempting to compete on price, but they are also meant to be better "adapted to Russian conditions"—that is, feed and climate—than imported breeds. Yet, as has been the case with pigs, adaptation has meant suitability to the industry's confinement conditions: Smena-9 is said to be bred for "floor maintenance" and "cage maintenance," the two dominant models of confinement poultry operations.[82]

From a Focus on Yields to a Recognition of Vulnerabilities

The reliance on "capitalist" pigs and super chickens that maximize economic efficiency has allowed Russian meat producers to produce more meat at lower costs. The continued development of wheat seeds that are locally adapted has underpinned the success in the Russian wheat sector. The former has allowed Russians to eat more pork, and the latter has paved the way for Russia's ascent to the position of the world's largest wheat exporter. The success of domestic agricultural production—and livestock production in particular—has contributed to the perception that the Putin era has brought back more prosperity. At first glance, humans have scored a victory over nature.

At the same time, post-Soviet plant and livestock breeding communities are also acutely aware of vulnerabilities. In fact, different types of vulnerabilities are causing concern for bureaucrats, scientists, and veterinarians in Russia's livestock and crop genetic community. In Russian political discourse, a vulnerability that ensues from the reliance on imported genetic material took center stage around 2015. This perceived vulnerability was thought to stem from foreign powers' ability to threaten Russia's food supply, as discussed in chapter 1. Unpredictable and potentially hostile Western governments could curtail the flow of genetic technologies and genetic material to Russia. A concern with this kind of geopolitical vulnerability is imputed to V. V. Putin by a Russian observer: "For Putin, so much meat power in so few foreign hands is an unacceptable security risk."[83] Public investment in the domestic genetic resource industry is thus meant to shore up the resilience of Russian food security. Natalya Virchenko, a scientist working for the PRODO group, one of Russia's largest poultry producers, argued that it is "strategically important for Russia to maintain and promote its own type of broiler"—referring to the Smena chicken.[84] While Russian agroholdings thus rhetorically align their activities with political goals, as chapter 1 documented, their own corporate statements convey concern with economic viability. For a Russian agricultural consultant, the success of Smena is as much about the "economic security of enterprises" as it is about food security.[85] Agroholdings supported the development of Smena as a way to control the cost of inputs. With the Russian ruble's dependence on global oil markets and Western sanctions, currency fluctuations have been a persistent problem for agroholdings that depend on imports.

Concern about a third vulnerability, neither geopolitical nor economic but related to biosecurity and threats to human and public health, has received growing attention in Russia and elsewhere. In 2007, the WHO noted that global public health is at increasing risk from viral and bacterial threats, and that we are seeing an "alarming shift in the delicate balance between humans and microbes."[86] Industrial food systems are widely recognized to be one of the sources for the rising threat of disease outbreaks, caused by bacteria and viruses. In very general terms, smaller numbers of animal breeds and crop varieties lead to reduced biodiversity and make herds and harvests more vulnerable to these kinds of threats. The global pandemic caused by the COVID-19 virus perhaps largely obviates the need to establish why this kind of vulnerability deserves attention. Years before viral threats reached the notoriety of the COVID-19 virus, they alarmed veterinary authorities and operators of livestock confinement facilities across the world. Various strands of avian flu viruses were first reported in China in the late 1990s. A serious outbreak of the avian flu at the Smena poultry farm in March 2017 made it plainly clear to everyone in Russia that biosecurity and viral infections that might jump the species barrier were an important risk associated with the new kind of confinement farming practiced by agroholdings. On March 1, 2017, approximately 6,000 dead birds at the

Smena farm were registered as contaminated with the virus that causes avian flu—known as H5N8; by March 7, Rosselkhoznadzor culled the farm's entire flock of 250,000 birds. For chicken, the H5N8 virus is highly pathogenic (i.e., highly contagious and lethal). For humans it is less pathogenic, but there are concerns that it is becoming more so. At the Smena farm, fourteen farm workers were hospitalized with symptoms of avian flu in March 2017. Reports from the Russian Far East warned about a strain that was potentially harmful to humans at the time, even as Moscow oblast authorities stressed that the virus is not a threat to humans.[87] The outbreak was a serious blow to the development of Smena-9 and incurred enormous economic losses for the Smena farm. It also affected other farms in the Moscow region as well as poultry in household farms.[88]

At the moment of the H5N8 outbreak at the Smena farm, biosecurity was a more acute threat than foreign powers' possible intentions of cutting off the flow of genetic materials. Large-scale poultry producers were well aware of this: Aviagen, for example, strongly recommends stringent and demanding biosecurity protocols to all its clients. Biosecurity protocols are an umbrella term that includes knowledge and practices that are used to manage threats to biosecurity; they are as broad as the range of actors involved in managing these threats.[89] Pathogens are of course not new, and Soviet poultry breeders also worried about them. Yet the high degree of concentration of genetically identical birds in very large-scale facilities is new to twenty-first-century Russia. Both the technology of poultry production and the biosecurity protocols that they necessitate are attributes of the agro-technopolitical regimes created by the agroholdings and supported by the Putin government. The different vulnerabilities related to biosecurity, economic security, geopolitical factors, and human health are in fact more closely intertwined than ever. The Smena farm was at once the epicenter of the avian flu outbreak and the site where the gene pool of Russia's super chickens was developed with the intention of putting an end to Russia's dependence on foreign genetic material and securing Russia's food supply in the future.

Regardless of whether genetic material is Russian or foreign, the evidence in this chapter serves to draw attention to the interdependent vulnerabilities and costs that stem from narrowing the genetic pools of seeds and breeds. In the livestock sector, the most obvious costs and covulnerabilities are related to the confinement of animals that need to be isolated from their environment. The main and most immediate costs are thus borne by the animals—by design, their lives are separated from contact with the natural environment around them. Their only significant link to the outside world is their feed, the composition and administration of which is entirely controlled and mediated by the agroholdings. These types of pigs and chickens are highly susceptible to pathogens—especially the viruses that causes African Swine Fever and Avian flu. As a result, extensive efforts are made to eliminate the possibility of contagion. This has included costly routine biosecurity protocols at each plant, central to the elimination of contact with the natural environment of the production site. It has also included quarantines and "control measures" in case of disease outbreak—in other words, the slaughter of whole herds at affected plants as well as thousands of animals in noncorporate settings. In the case of the Swine Flu, this includes wild boar and pigs on household farms wherever even a small number of *asfarvidius* infections are reported, as noted in chapter 2. It is not proven that the virus responsible for the avian and swine flu can jump species barriers. However, not only are there many notorious historical cases of when livestock pathogens emerge as lethal causes of human diseases, such as influenza, measles, and smallpox, but this has also happened increasingly frequently over time.[90] Other impacts on human health from raising confinement livestock are being added to the list of similar vulnerabilities. The global rise in antimicrobial-resistant bacteria is widely understood to be related to the overuse of antibiotics in industrial livestock.[91]

Unlike livestock, wheat and other field crops cannot easily be contained. Even with precision agriculture and targeted nutrient applications, crops are always bound to be more exposed to environmental conditions and the spread of new pathogens. Wheat is by far Russia's most important field crop, and contemporary seed breeding institutions have treated Soviet-era research, knowledge, and cultivars as important vaults of genetic diversity that require care and resources to meet the challenges of the twenty-first century. Wheat breeding institutions are centrally concerned with historical and new vulnerabilities, and they actively work on strategies to address them. This is the case for a new fungus that causes stem rust, for example, which had not been considered a major risk in Russia until 2015, when a stem rust epidemic destroyed millions of hectares of wheat fields in Siberia.[92] Contemporary wheat breeding institutions are also making a concerted effort to breed varieties that are immune to new climatic/abiotic and biotic vulnerabilities. Russian seed breeders are keenly aware of the danger of losing inherited varieties. Many millions of acres of farmland in Russia are no longer cultivated, often in marginal areas with challenging climatic conditions. The varieties that had been bred and adapted to these regions are no longer in use and are no longer favored by breeders, who need to sell seeds to agroholdings. Given the new funding model of seed institutes, attempts to preserve them are subordinated to the research and development of seeds that are likely to be the most commercially viable.

What does this all mean for the human-nature nexus that twenty-first-century agriculture entails? William Cronon argued that the technologies introduced by American agribusiness corporations in the late nineteenth century—led by Swift and Armor—liberated meat from nature and geography.[93] Although liberation appears to give this historical trend a positive connotation, Cronon's account challenges readers to think of the role of capital and markets in the separation of production, markets, and animals from locally circumscribed, natural contexts. Is this what happened in Russia? Did the advent of capital "liberate" (or distance) production from nature? Again, at first glance, Russia's corporate agroholdings seem to have done precisely this. They introduced new technologies that led to a greater separation of production from the natural, social, and political geography of Soviet Russia: new animal breeds; new confinement conditions; new feed ingredients; new seeds; new agrochemicals; and new facilities where animals are hatched, grown, and slaughtered have loosened the ties to local geographies and natural conditions. Yet this distancing in some ways was just superficial. A technopolitical lens reveals the fragile interdependence of humans, animals, and seeds because it brings unforeseen consequences to our attention. It shows how new vulnerabilities take the place of old ones. It also reveals that many actors in the Russian political, scientific, and corporate worlds in fact operate, knowingly or not, in the third paradigm. Agroholdings' reliance on high-performance seeds and breeds is born from a wish to harness the power of nature, but at least in the case of field crops, this paradigm does not reign supreme. Those human actors who realize that even in a bio-secure facility, the spread of pathogens is a constant threat to animals and humans—and those who continue to breed new seed varieties and preserve old ones—understand that their agency is constrained and shaped by fragile interdependence and covulnerabilities. The contemporary technopolitical regime has brought new seed varieties and animal breeds to Russian soils and sites. It is, at this point, only very partially apparent what precisely the unintended effects and new vulnerabilities of this shift will turn out to be in the future.

Conclusion
Vulnerabilities

Solving the Grain Problem

Social discontent in Russia at the beginning of the twentieth century was fueled by the large gap between those who were hungry and those who were not.[1] Lenin's promise of peace, land, and bread gained critical support for the Bolshevik Revolution. This was no small feat for a group of urban revolutionaries in a predominantly rural empire. The resonance of the revolutionary promise was of course related to the fact that many Russian citizens did not have very much to eat. After the revolution, feudal land was nationalized by decree and from afar. How the newly minted government was to provide bread and basic staples for all turned out to be a much more protracted challenge. Bread was baked with flour, which required grain—grown in large quantities and delivered to newly constructed urban bread factories. Successive Soviet governments faced a version of what was known as the grain problem: how to convince or coerce Russian peasants to grow more crops, to sow seeds for plants that they would not eat, to use new technologies and cultivation methods that would raise yields and make harvests more plentiful, and to hand the grain over to government procurement agents.

In the eighty years of Soviet rule, the grain problem was never quite solved. Soviet collective farms were always less efficient and produced less in the way of grain, feed, and industrial crops than planners and party cadres hoped for. Only in the early 2000s, under Vladimir Putin's model of state capitalism, did Russian agricultural production soar to the levels the government planned for, though the main producers were now private agroholdings, who were making more grains, pulses, sugar beets, and other crops available for domestic processing, for livestock farms, and for exports. Russia has resumed its nineteenth-century role as the world's breadbasket. While Putin takes credit for putting food on Russian tables and for the rapid increase of Russian wheat exports, the success of his model of agricultural production owes much to Soviet-era rural policies and to wheat varieties cultivated for millennia across Eurasia. Putin's reforms would not have been possible without Stalin's brutal collectivization, which brought peasants under state control. Russia's recent rise as a grain power has also introduced new vulnerabilities and inequalities, and the country is now deeply integrated into volatile global food markets. A chicken nugget served at a Russian McDonald's relies on global proprietary technologies and imported soy and feed additives, even if it is made from broiler hens raised in Russia. This doesn't mean, though, that Russia's food system has simply "Americanized." The agricultural technologies, knowledge, and products involved are essentially global, but they also have local histories, and global seeds grow in local soils. In contemporary Russian agriculture, domestication and globalization have gone hand in hand.

Black Earth, White Bread details the transformation of Russia's food system over the past hundred years but also offers a way to think about change in food systems more generally. The chapters draw attention to a large and diverse group of actors and allow us to see critical relationships between agents of the state, producers, scientists, consumers, pigs, and wheat plants. Politics is about the questioning of privilege and suffering, and food systems distribute these unequally. Though Russian politics has a long history of heavy-handed paternalism and coercion, it also features its share of revolutionary upheavals, contestation, and gradual change. How can we think about food politics, in Russia as elsewhere? Much of the political science literature on agriculture treats governments, producers, and rural and urban voters as the protagonists and tells us how they shape institutions in their interests. Where does that leave two other powerful forces that drive food systems—consumers and nature? Agricultural practices are influenced just as much by the desires of consumers and by the biological makeup of plants and animals as they are by government policies and citizen preferences. Across other social sciences, it is no longer a radical move to consider nature's involvement in human political projects, but it is still one that is long overdue in political science. Novel technologies that modify the genetic makeup of plants raise new questions about the promise of science and new risks and vulnerabilities. The political agency of consumers unfolds in ways that are not limited to voting and protesting by citizens. Food consumption is tied up with national culture, desire, social status, and economic access in increasingly stratified societies. In Russia as elsewhere, economic, social, and cultural status is today under pressure and subject to intense debate: What precisely is a typical Russian diet? How can Russia carve out a particularly Russian path in global markets, and how can it reduce its dependency on foreign food imports?

Successive Russian governments have relied on technologies to realize changing political goals for agricultural production and food consumption. The technopolitics of agriculture brought about several waves of dramatic change throughout the twentieth and twenty-first centuries, from Lenin to Putin. As previous chapters have shown, Soviet and post-Soviet agriculture share several features with US capitalist agriculture. The US and Russia are among the world's largest agricultural producers, and both are highly industrialized. They both now produce large surpluses in a few commodities and have significant influence on global markets in agricultural commodities. American agriculture is a leading global exporter of corn and soy, and the Russian Federation supplies wheat to the Middle East and Africa. In both countries, state-sponsored efforts to increase yields have meant that synthetic fertilizer has accumulated in waterways, irrigation schemes have depleted water tables, and fragile soils have eroded over decades of intensive farming. Fundamental and important differences, of course, have always existed between the capitalist West and the socialist/postsocialist food systems. Stalin's collectivization was rapid and ruthless, while market consolidation of farming in the US was gradual. The Soviet Union relied on state-run collective farms and procurement systems. The US system is made up of private farms and agrifood corporations, input suppliers, and grain traders, albeit supported and fostered by a range of subsidies and publicly funded research. The American agrifood system was considered far more successful than Soviet agriculture if measured by the indexes of yields and total output. The capitalist system has long produced surpluses, while the communist system produced shortages. Of course, shortages are a problem and in many ways one of the main failures of the Soviet agro-technopolitical regime. And even if the US grain surpluses were a geopolitical asset during the Cold War, for domestic producers they were a decidedly mixed blessing—they are responsible for low farm-gate prices and declining farm incomes. Much of US food is produced, picked, or packed by vulnerable, undocumented workers, often both underpaid and exposed to dangerous work conditions.[2] Soviet collective farm workers lacked many things, but they were citizens, and in the postwar period, they were the intended beneficiaries of a slew of projects meant to improve rural standards of living.

Ironically, the most critical difference between the two systems—the fact that one is a surplus economy and the other is a shortage economy—turned out to be the basis for trade between them. This has shaped the fate of each and contributed to the increasing convergence and interactions between them in the long run. Bureaucrats, experts, and producers have exchanged ideas and learned from each other since the 1920s and throughout Russia's post-Soviet transition. Through visits by high-level Soviet delegations and waves of state-sponsored traineeships by US agronomists on collective farms, knowledge, skills, and technologies have made their way from the capitalist to the socialist planned context. These exchanges of knowledge, technology, and commodities have played a critical role in transforming the Russian and North American agrifood systems. The outcome of shared goals and cooperation was that there were indeed many parallels between Soviet and US postwar agriculture, mentioned previously. The US and Soviet technopolitical regimes coevolved in constant interactions with each other. When deciding which social organization and production technology to favor to realize their utopian goals, Russian leaders looked to the West and imported technologies that were deemed promising. The outcomes of these interactions—the respective modes of domestication—were not necessarily imitations and competitions to reach the same goals; they included rejections of some foreign technologies and adaptations of others to local conditions.

The remainder of the conclusion will recap and extend the discussion of the profound changes of the Russian food system that has taken place over the past fifteen to twenty years. Agrifood corporations are now important actors in the countryside and in the Russian economy as a whole. They are landowners, producers of vital food commodities, and financial backers of the technological transformation that has underpinned change. Large-scale capital investments in land and in processing industries have dramatically changed how, and how much, food is produced and processed. This transformation aligns with several political priorities of the Putin regime and in many ways was made possible through an array of public support measures, including subsidies, tax breaks, and trade measures. Private agroholdings have been the main actors and the privileged allies of the Russian government, enlisted in its political project to bring affordable food to Russian tables and export wheat across the world.

Globalization and Domestication

The agro-technopolitical regime created in the Putin era contains contradictory elements: on the one hand, production is "domesticated" as imports are significantly reduced and food is produced domestically, by local producers and with local inputs and natural resources. EkoNiva, Miratorg, Cherkizovo, Rusagro, Exima, and other similar companies are undoubtedly Russian, with Russian owners, operations based in Russia, and production focused on crops grown in Russia (e.g., winter and spring wheats, barley, sugar beets, oil seeds). They produce a majority of Russian foods, hire Russian employees, and have corporate social responsibility programs that build orthodox churches and help out local schools. At the same time, rural production has changed profoundly with the large-scale adoption of cutting-edge technologies and managerial practices imported from North America and Europe. How crops and animals are grown, raised, and processed in many instances closely resembles the modes of production in the highly competitive agrifood markets of late-modern capitalism in the US. Russia also exports wheat to more than a hundred countries. Over the past twenty years, then, the Russian food system has simultaneously globalized and domesticated. The diverse actors in the contemporary techno-political regime are both integrating into global systems and borrowing from abroad, while at the same time also seeking to create local versions of global technologies.

This multidimensional trajectory is important for Russia and for how we think of food systems elsewhere. The most common way of framing how food systems across the world have industrialized and integrated into global markets is to use the concept of "Americanization" or "Westernization." The changes in Russia's food system suggests that this framework only tells one side of the story. Agriculture has always been rooted in domestic soil, and political and cultural histories of place have an important role to play. What are the contours and consequences of Russia's simultaneous moves in the twenty-first century to integrate with global food commodity markets, while also insulating and distancing the domestic economy from them? The US is indeed the world's most powerful exporter of agrifood commodities, technologies, and food culture. There is no doubt that American actors involved in agriculture—the USDA, scientific experts, and US-based corporate actors—were influential in shaping agro-technopolitical regimes in Russia as they did elsewhere. During the Cold War, the US system served as the ultimate reference point for economic success. The Soviet Union's agrarian program was in large part understood as an enormous undertaking of catching up with the US and Western Europe. Proximity or distance, similarity and difference to Western models continue to inform debates about Russia's economic development in the post-Soviet period. Now the question of whether Russia is on a universal or unique path of socioeconomic development appears in the guise of assessments of whether or not Russia has a "normal" capitalist economy.[3] Over the past two decades, the vast majority of studies in political economy of the post-Soviet transition have stressed differences between mature capitalist economies and post-Soviet economies that are still "transitioning" from planned to market-based economic systems. Many accounts of the Russian economy in the post-Soviet period focus on corruption, the insecurity of property rights, the lack of due process, or other aspects of Russia's economy that emphasize just how distant Russian market institutions (still) are from Western models of capitalism.[4] This emphasis on differences reflects Cold War assumptions that the Soviet planned economy was the antithesis of capitalism and free markets. Yet the template of Americanization, or Westernization, does not do justice to these changing relationships between domestic and foreign actors.

New Vulnerabilities

Many features of Western or US food systems are now "produced" locally in Russia as elsewhere, and the boundaries between what is imported or foreign and what is Russian are exceedingly blurry. More important than judgment calls about whether a trend is foreign or domestic are accounts of the vulnerabilities created in Russia during the process of global integration. Three problems, or vulnerabilities, of food systems in the advanced capitalist West have appeared in Russia: inequality, obesity, and waste. They are introduced here in short summaries meant only as starting points for future research on these questions. The inventory of these issues highlights how Soviet-era history shaped post-Soviet trends. An obvious conclusion that emerges from this discussion is that markets have not solved the problems of the Soviet planned economy. They introduced new vulnerabilities, replicating some features of the capitalist West, but have also adapted and taken on particularly Russian features in post-Soviet political and economic life.

Inequality

Inequality in the US food system is closely tied to and implicated in class- and race-based differences that pervade the social and political fabric. Land occupancy and access to healthy foods are just two aspects of the US food system that are unequally distributed in ways that not only reflect but also produce stark and subtle differences between and within communities.[5] In the US as in Russia, land is valuable, and access to particular foods is a marker of status and wealth. Chapter 3 detailed how the Soviet technopolitical regime distributed different foods based on complex political, professional, and geographic hierarchies and social networks, even as the planned economy was meant to create universal access to foods identified by party elites and planners as essential elements of socialist modernity. The market reforms of the 1990s ostensibly produced many more choices, including retail stores fully stocked with a variety of food items.

Yet Yeltsin's and Putin's economic reforms also led to new forms of stratification. Unequal patterns of food consumption became linked to the monetary price of goods and household incomes rather than to the Soviet-era political hierarchies and social networks. Oligarchic elites' wealth afforded them access to whatever foods they prized. In the nineties, these were largely foreign and imported delicacies. Over time, in a shift that paralleled both the increasing nationalism in Russian political discourse and food trends among the upper middle class in other advanced industrialized countries, domestic, homegrown, and homemade products became sought after. Meanwhile, food consumption was changing among city and village residents with fewer resources. Among urbanites, those with the lowest incomes had the least choice about what foods they could consume. For those who were still employed by factories, employers continued to provide food in cafeterias, sometimes in lieu of unpaid wages. These fringe benefits of employment distributed at the workplace, however, were largely dependent on factories remaining in operation and employers being in a position to provide them.[6] This was the case in some sectors, in the hydrocarbon and metal industries, but in many cities, the factories that had provided meals shuttered. Unemployed, low-wage workers and pensioners in cities were largely unable to afford the novel processed foods that had appeared, even though since the early 2000s federal and regional authorities tried to keep prices for a few basic staples relatively stable. Those with little cash income in cities had fewer opportunities to grow their own food as the cost of maintaining a suburban vegetable plot and raising livestock increased in the post-Soviet period. In all regions, transport costs had risen, and in the most desirable regions around major cities, dacha land was sold to real estate developers.

Rural dispossession has looked different. Most villagers have scant or virtually no cash incomes. In Russia's remote and rural regions, the deterioration of public infrastructure, the devaluation of assets, and the erosion of state support have been far more severe than in urban centers.[7] Inputs that used to be funneled from collective farms to household farms are no longer available as agroholdings maintain much tighter control of inflows and outflows. At the same time, some villagers still have access to small plots of fertile land and valuable skills. During times of crisis, rural Russians have been able to grow produce and raise livestock, thereby controlling resources of considerable value. Having a family member in the countryside counts as an asset and a kind of insurance policy for children, nieces, nephews, and grandchildren who move to cities for jobs. In sum, the Soviet planned economy created inequality through political status and connections, which made choices possible for those at the center and marginalized those at the periphery of sociopolitical networks. In the post-Soviet period, choice is curtailed by cost and money, creating new patterns of post-Soviet inequality and byt.

Obesity

The American food system has many vulnerabilities, but obesity is the one that affects human and public health most directly. Since the early 1980s, public health experts—first in the US and later elsewhere—raised concerns about the link between high-calorie diets and being overweight. When obesity was first recognized as a disease, research considered it as a health condition affecting individuals. Initially the explanation for obesity was that it was caused by "inappropriate eating in the setting of attractive foods." By the mid-1980s, research had moved to acknowledge that it was a "complex disease."[8] Research continued to focus on individual health indicators, correlating obesity with individual behaviors and attributes, such as level of physical activity, caloric intake, and alcohol consumption. A major turn in obesity research was the realization that the disease was closely associated with what came to be called obesogenic environments, including food deserts and lack of safe outdoor spaces. By the 2000s, a growing body of research acknowledged that "patterns of body weight are influenced by the characteristics held by individuals (e.g., demographic, socio-cultural and economic) *and* the actual environments in which they live."[9] Obesity has become increasingly recognized as a global health problem; the WHO has considered obesity to be an epidemic at least since 1990. While the WHO stresses that obesity has social dimensions, the disease terminology and methodologies of obesity-related research still often privilege individual-level health indicators as the main contributing factors. A 2010 article in *The Lancet* notes that "the obesity epidemic is spreading to low-income and middle-income countries as a result of new dietary habits and sedentary ways of life, fueling chronic diseases and premature mortality."[10] This account portrays obesity as resulting from particular dietary and lifestyle habits. There are some observers who think of obesity from a political economy perspective: Kenneth Rogoff notes that Mexico's obesity rates soared after the country's 1993 adoption of NAFTA and argues that obesity is an American export. Rather than pinpoint individual behaviors, he finds that "post-NAFTA direct foreign investment in the processed food industry and a surge in advertising are important contributors."[11]

Obesity may be an epidemic, but it does not spread as a virus does—it is produced by a changing cast of actors. While Rogoff's account singles out American companies, in the Russian case, the cast involved in transforming the food system is diverse and includes global and Russian actors. In Russia, as elsewhere, obesity has rapidly increased over the past twenty years, and obesity is also implicated in increasing rates of diabetes and heart disease. Again, dietary changes, particularly "[a] change in the traditional dietary pattern to a more westernised diet," tend to be singled out as the main cause of these trends.[12] Public health and medical research on Russia also isolate the contributing factors at the level of the individual, largely because findings are based on multivariate analysis of survey evidence. A recent study on obesity in the countries of the former Soviet Union finds that for post-Soviet men, "factors associated with obesity were older age, increasing educational achievement, worse self-reported health, greater frequency of alcohol consumption and automobile ownership." By contrast, "males who were current smokers, not married and perceived physical activity to be important were less likely to be obese." For women the factors associated with obesity were the following: "greater age, worse health, . . . household economic situation, being married and completing secondary/some higher education." These factors were identified by the study's authors as "micro-level factors." As for "meso-level" (or social) factors, the multivariate analysis had a much harder time identifying the relevant community indicators for obesity. Finding that overall there was "strong evidence for variability in the prevalence of obesity between communities," the authors singled out only two meso-level conditions that seemed to predict obesity in the post-Soviet region: individuals living in communities with an "increased presence of garbage" were "30 percent more likely to be obese," and the "presence of graffiti was associated with a halving of the probability of being obese."[13] The presence of garbage in communities where individuals are more likely to be obese may well be an indicator for the increasing prevalence of processed foods (see below). Though what can we make of the puzzling finding that graffiti is negatively associated with obesity? Graffiti is a marker of urban living, though as urban and rural geographies in the post-Soviet region do not easily map onto expectations of urban and suburban living in the US and Europe, this finding does not appear to clarify the social context of obesity in a meaningful way.

The research on obesity's association with particular (obesogenic) environments suggests that the absence or presence of particular foods matters—that is, precisely the unequal patterns of consumption addressed in chapter 3. Michael Moss has pointed out that the foods that are the cheapest, most highly craved, and most readily available are also the most high-calorie foods with the lowest nutritive value. He points out that for food processing companies, these foods are cheap to produce and sold largely on the merits of their marketing appeal.[14] Yet, while such "attractive foods" have long been recognized as a problem for individual consumers, their abundant availability is clearly an element of a much larger socioeconomic story. Chapter 3 tracked changing availability, access, and allure of processed foods that took place during the shift from the Soviet to post-Soviet agro-technopolitical regime. Soviet citizens did have access to and did eat processed foods, such as pelmeni, macaroni, canned fish, and chocolates. At the same time, Soviet-era industrially processed foods were quite different from those available today, and they made up a much smaller part of Russian diets. Soviet food processing was not a priority sector in the planned economy, which did not provide the means and incentives to continuously reengineer, repackage, and churn out new and different products.

Foods lacked bright packaging and did without many of the micro-ingredients that today's processing innovations contain. What is more, because of recurring shortages in the planned system, entirely unprocessed, homegrown and home-processed foods were an important part of every citizen's diet. The post-Soviet system, in sharp contrast, has introduced a flood of highly processed and brightly packaged goods, and far fewer citizens now have the time or resources to grown their own food. The memory of an earlier, simpler food era remains appealing to many. Whether this memory is fleeting nostalgia for a bygone area, or whether it will prove to be a solid foundation for the resurgence of household gardening, is too early to tell.

The increasing ubiquity of processed food items is not just the adoption of foreign cultural habits and imported foods that have "westernized" the Russian diet. Instead, these trends follow from recent political priorities, the rise of agroholdings, the introduction of new technologies of production, and enormously important changes in land use and ownership. In other words, the profound changes to the Russian diet are the result of shifting agro-technopolitics. Dietary changes are just as much a Russian phenomenon as they are a foreign, or "Western," one. The creation and marketing of appealing foods that have fueled changes in consumer habits were initially imported from the US, but by now they have become part of a political project that is both global and genuinely Russian. As such, they are likely an enduring feature and vulnerability of the twenty-first-century Russian food system.

Waste

When obesity appeared to affect a growing share of US citizens, physicians, public health authorities, and health insurance companies were alarmed about vulnerable populations and rising health care costs. Environmental costs and vulnerabilities do not always have this kind of vocal and influential representation in food politics. One particular vulnerability illustrates this point well: waste and wastefulness. Waste is a by-product of production that is not reintegrated as an input, and wastefulness refers to unsustainable practices that deplete nonrenewable resources. Waste and wastefulness are characteristic of industrial agriculture and contemporary food processing, and different types of waste in industrial agrifood systems have been scrutinized. Critics of the US food system often point to the large quantities of food that are wasted by retailers and consumers who value only produce that conforms to standards of perfection that have little to do with the diversity of each plant or fruit. There are, of course, many other resources that are used in large quantities because they cost producers relatively little. The Soviet industrial food system produced waste both similar to and different from that of the US system. Food waste was a problem in the Soviet planned economy, but it was caused by an unwieldy transport system and damage caused en route to stores, not at the point of sale or in consumers' kitchens. In general, transport and storage were considered notoriously wasteful links in the Soviet-era agricultural system.[15] The Soviet planned economy was often described as inherently wasteful and inefficient, and that wastefulness was used to contrast it with capitalist economies. Janos Kornai held that socialism was "not capable of achieving a high level of efficiency" and that the "utilization of resources" is worse in a socialist planned economy than in capitalism.[16] A particular characteristic of planning was the inability to account for the "true" cost of inputs and outputs. Waste resulted from the mismatch between delivered and used inputs. Either too little of a particular input was delivered to a production site, which meant that other resources were wasted, or too much was delivered, which meant that this input went unused. The lack of cost accounting for inputs created other problems, too. Bread was so abundant and cheap that it was sometimes used to feed pigs—especially at times when dedicated livestock feed was in short supply. Considering the expense of producing and subsidizing bread, this was indeed a wasteful use of bread.

The problem of how prices reflect "true" costs, however, is not just a feature of socialist planned economies. In capitalist economies, the costs of energy, fuel, water, and agrochemicals for agricultural producers are kept low to make food affordable and encourage high levels of consumption. The price of foods then does not reflect the environmental and social costs of production. The widespread application of nitrogen fertilizer in agricultural production in the American Midwest has led to eutrophication, or algae blooms, in the Gulf of Mexico, for example. The judgment that capitalist allocation of resources is efficient while its socialist counterpart is inefficient largely ignores these and similar costs. A technopolitical lens traces the politics that keep the nominal costs of resources low, the resulting patterns of production and consumption, and the intended and unintended consequences of this way of governing the food system.

A glance at the use of fertilizer, herbicides, and pesticides in the Soviet era under a planned economy versus during the post-Soviet period illustrates the fact that contrasting a wasteful past with an efficient, market-driven present is misleading. Chapter 2 documented that agrochemicals were Brezhnev's answer to low farm productivity in the seventies and eighties. Applying fertilizers and pesticides allowed Soviet farms to increase overall production of grains and industrial crops. A significant share of the large quantity of fertilizer was lost on the way to collective farms because of transportation problems and diversions of various kinds, and in the end much of it was never applied to fields.[17]

Other farms overfertilized fields because the application of fertilizer was one of the plan targets that farms needed to meet. When Gorbachev's policy of glasnost encouraged more transparency and public debate, the Soviet media and scientists started drawing attention to problems of waste and environmental degradation. Scientific studies that indicated a link between high rates of agrochemical usage on state farms and above-threshold pesticide residue on foods came to the attention of the Soviet environmental movement.[18] With the introduction of post-Soviet markets, the use of agrochemicals dropped significantly: between 1990 and 1995, the application of nitrogen fertilizer dropped from 88 kilograms per hectare to 17 kilograms per hectare. This was not, however, due to the efficient allocation of these resources but rather to the collapse of agricultural production.[19] Fertilizer use increased again during the agricultural recovery since 2005 as Russian agroholdings once again started relying on agrochemicals. Yet contemporary Russia has few mechanisms in place to account for and respond to the environmental costs of fertilizer application. Political feedback mechanisms that would draw attention to complex environmental problems, such as eutrophication and pesticide residues, are largely absent in Putin's Russia. A recent study found that "the problem of eutrophication is widespread in Russia" and that "algal blooms attract considerable public attention in Russia," yet it is not likely that this attention and concern will translate into policy changes, or modified agricultural practices, in the near future.[20]

The overall point is that the shift from Soviet to post-Soviet wastefulness has not been a linear trend with predictable outcomes.[21] Even if Russian agriculture has to a significant degree been privatized, and the particular inefficiencies of the planned bureaucracy are confined to history, market prices for inputs still do not reflect social and environmental costs of the post-Soviet food system. Not only did waste not disappear; new forms of waste and wastefulness were created. Elaborate plastic packaging now clogs municipal waste systems that were built in the Soviet period and are unequipped to handle this new type of waste. Overflowing landfills and the need for new incinerators are impacting the economy and quality of life. Citizens have increasingly voiced their concerns over mounting heaps of waste through public demonstrations known as "garbage protests."[22] Yet few observers and analysts connect the problem with the wastefulness of new food production technologies that rely on a flood of plastic packaging.

New forms of inequality, obesity, and food packaging waste are just three of the vulnerabilities that have emerged during the shift from the Soviet to the post-Soviet technopolitical regime. The preceding chapters raised questions about whether new agricultural bio-technologies will strengthen the

Russian food system or whether they will make Russia's current and future agro-technopolitical regime more fallible and vulnerable. To a great extent, these and other vulnerabilities are still poorly understood. Political dynamics will determine which costs and vulnerabilities will actually be addressed. After all, in Russia as in the rest of the world, pigs threatened by *asfarvidiae* and eutrophic rivers cannot speak for themselves.

Politics of Agrifood Systems

How can we think about the politics of industrial agriculture? In Russia as elsewhere, the broader debates around food systems center on the desirability of global markets for food commodities and the relative value attached to efficiency versus local and domestic self-sufficiency. Market liberals favor free trade and global markets for food commodities. If American farms grow the best soy beans at the lowest costs, the rest of the world should procure soy protein from the US. If the world's most affordable high-quality wheat originates in Russia's Black Earth belt, bakeries across the world should use it to make bread and pasta. Others have stressed the need to think of domestic and local production of food commodities as a goal worth pursuing, largely for two reasons. First, local, native, and domestic foods have inherent value compared to food grown or processed in other parts of the world. Second, a globalized food system has many hidden costs incurred in part because of low-priced hydrocarbons that fuel the transport of food to and from far-flung locations. Both proponents and critics of contemporary global food systems tend to single out particular groups of actors as deliberate and rational architects of the current system. As noted in the introduction, many studies of the US industrial food system focus on the role of corporate actors and lobbies in shaping legislation in their favor. Corporate actors and global MNCs, such as Cargill, Nestle, and Pepsi, are indeed hugely influential in the US and elsewhere. Yet large producers and corporations are not the only forces shaping food systems. Collective farms in the Soviet era hardly wielded the power of US corporations, and while agroholdings do have financial clout and informal ties to political elites today, they hardly play a role in contemporary Russian politics. In large part, this is the case because in Putin's Russia, agroholdings operate in a statist economy and within a highly centralized political system. To be allowed to make profits, they need to demonstrate contributions to the political and developmental goals defined by federal and regional authorities.

Food studies, meanwhile, have often focused on the actions of individuals who "vote with their fork," that is, seek to influence food systems through their consumption choices.[23] Tracking the role of consumers is important as consumer choices and values are indeed crucial in contemporary food systems.

(Indeed, a growing set of studies in political economy has emphasized the role of consumers acting on their values, calling for changes in the labor laws and environmental standards, for example, or supporting private certification schemes.) Yet critics of "vote with your fork" logic have resisted its emphasis on choice, pointing instead to structural and institutional factors that leave many consumers with few or no choices.[24] The path to change for these scholars goes via citizen activism and voting behavior. Yet Russia's version of authoritarian governance shows that these channels of representative government cannot be taken for granted. Choice, consumer agency, and citizen activism are themselves part of the political economy of agrifood systems and they vary greatly across political and economic systems. Analyses of where they exist, and what the range of choices are, reveal more than studies that focus only on places and sectors where consumers and citizens are influential, and assume that this is the case across global food systems.

The book raises the question of whether the vulnerabilities of the contemporary agro-technopolitical regime may contribute to discontent with the political and economic order of the Putin government. Although the workings (and failings) of late Soviet agro-technopolitics did contribute to generating discontent in the 1980s, there is no way to predict whether the vulnerabilities of the contemporary food system contain the germ of instability that leads to a broader challenge to the contemporary political order. The history of Soviet and Russian agriculture and food does suggest more broadly that the citizens' byt, unequal consumption patterns, ill health, environmental damage, and garbage can be salient grievances and that they may feature in the future struggle between the opposition and the Putin regime.

A technopolitical lens does not assume that the influence of one type of actor can be transposed from one polity to another; rather, it reveals changing groups of relevant actors. Nor does it rely on intended and rational agency as the only force of change. Both intended and unintended consequences shape outcomes of food systems that have pasts, presents, and futures. Technopolitics shows how successes and failures, benefits and costs, and strengths and vulnerabilities of particular modes of domestication shaped outcomes just as much as the goal-oriented rational agency of particular groups. It can capture consumers' yearnings and the thriving or faltering of crops. Such a wide lens breaks open the silos of studies focused primarily on one of these realms—accounts of policy and institutional changes or ethnographies of consumer culture, for example. Recognizing these connections is vital because none of the realms of food systems are autonomous or dominant. Earlier chapters of the book emphasized Lenin's promise as an important driver of Russian history for well over a century. The campaigns of successive Soviet leaders, Vladimir

Putin, and the agents of the Soviet and Russian state mattered. But governments did not bring about change by themselves. Political promises and policies were enacted and farming was practiced by an evolving cast of actors, all of them following their own logic of agency and deeply influenced by success and failure, as Soviet and Russian industrial agriculture transformed the Eurasian steppe over the past hundred years. Technopolitics reveals change in food and agriculture by these actors who were deeply connected, codependent, and covulnerable within fragile webs of mutual sustenance.

NOTES

Introduction

Second chapter epigraph: "Kto khochet videt' kusok sotsializma, pust' idet na khlebozavod." "Khlebozavod-Avtomat," *Ogonek*, no. 1 (1952): 2.

1. Interview with Sergei Ivanov by Valerii Buldakov, "Gorod sozdaet ekstrennyi zapas zerna na zimu: Khvatit li khleba Moskve?," *Argumenty i fakty*, November 17, 1999.

2. Ibid.

3. See, for example, Deborah Fitzgerald, *Every Farm a Factory: The Industrial Ideal in American Agriculture* (New Haven, CT: Yale University Press, 2003), esp. chapter 6, "Collectivization and Industrialization: Learning from the Soviets." See also Jenny Leigh Smith, *Works in Progress: Plans and Realities on Soviet Farms, 1930–1963* (New Haven, CT: Yale University Press, 2014), esp. chapter 1, "Model Farms and Foreign Experts."

4. Lars Lih, *Bread and Authority in Russia, 1914–1921* (Berkeley: University of California Press, 1990). A hundred years later, Melissa Caldwell shows that Muscovites received more than bread when they visited soup kitchens during the turmoil of the 1990s. She documents how new post-Soviet identities took shape as bread and soup were shared in *Not by Bread Alone: Social Support in the New Russia* (Berkeley: University of California Press, 2004).

5. The Black Earth region, the Chernozem, has a dark or black color because of the high share of organic matter; soils are fertile because of the abundance of nutrients, such as phosphorus and ammonia. The Chernozem is legendary for "one of the most—if not *the* most—fertile soil(s) on earth," in the imaginaries of local and foreign observers. See Oane Visser, "Persistent Farmland Imaginaries: Celebration of Fertile Soil and the Recurrent Ignorance of Climate," *Agriculture and Human Values* 38 (2020): 313–26; and David Moon, *The Plough That Broke the Steppes: Agriculture and Environment on Russia's Grasslands, 1700–1914*, Oxford Studies in Modern European History (Oxford: Oxford University Press, 2013).

6. There are few historical monographs that focus on food in twentieth-century Russian history with an eye on both consumption and production. Jukka Gronow, *Caviar*

with Champagne: Common Luxury and the Ideals of the Good Life in Stalin's Russia, Leisure, Consumption, and Culture (New York: Berg, 2003); and Melissa Caldwell, *Dacha Idylls: Living Organically in Russia's Countryside* (Berkeley: University of California Press, 2011), are exceptions. Two notable edited volumes on food culture are Musya Glants and Joyce Toomre, eds., *Food in Russian History and Culture* (Bloomington: Indiana University Press, 1997); and Anastasia Lakhtikova, Angela Brintlinger, and Irina Glushchenko, eds., *Seasoned Socialism: Gender and Food in Late Soviet Everyday Life* (Bloomington: Indiana University Press, 2019). There are several books on Soviet and Russian agriculture that are mainly interested in production but do not examine the political and cultural functions of the food system as features in their own rights. For example, see Carol Leonard, *Agrarian Reform in Russia: The Road from Serfdom* (Cambridge, UK: Cambridge University Press, 2010); and Zhores Medvedev, *Soviet Agriculture* (New York: Norton, 1987). Stephen Wegren is the only political scientist with an extensive research agenda in Russian agriculture; his books have focused on institutions, policies, and economic outcomes. See, for example, Stephen Wegren, *Land Reform in Russia: Institutional Design and Behavioral Responses* (New Haven, CT: Yale University Press, 2009). Wegren's most recent book, written with Alexander Nikulin and Irina Trotsuk, combines a discussion of production, distribution, and consumption: *Russia's Food Revolution: The Transformation of the Food System*, Routledge Contemporary Russia and Eastern Europe Series (New York: Routledge, 2021).

7. Wegren, *Land Reform in Russia*, 35.

8. James Scott, *Against the Grain: A Deep History of the Earliest States* (New Haven, CT: Yale University Press, 2017), 3.

9. For detailed historical accounts of the state's role in US agriculture, see Fitzgerald, *Every Farm a Factory*; Monica Prasad, *The Land of Too Much: American Abundance and the Paradox of Poverty* (Cambridge, MA: Harvard University Press, 2013); and Shane Hamilton, *Supermarket USA: Food and Power in the Cold War Farms Race* (New Haven, CT: Yale University Press, 2018). For an account of industrial agriculture's rise in France, see Venus Bivar, *Organic Resistance: The Struggle over Industrial Farming in Postwar France* (Chapel Hill: University of North Carolina Press, 2018). For a comparative account, see Adam D. Sheingate, *The Rise of the Agricultural Welfare State: Institutions and Interest Group Power in the United States, France, and Japan* (Princeton, NJ: Princeton University Press, 2003).

10. I. Kogan, "V nogu s industriei," *Ogonek*, no. 28 (1930): 7.

11. Iurii Mikhailovich Lotman, *Besedy o russkoi kul'ture* (St. Petersburg, 1994). The conversations (*besedy*) were a series of popular TV interviews with Lotman recorded over a few years in the late 1980s; they were published after his death in 1994.

12. See, for example, Robert Conquest, *The Harvest of Sorrow: Soviet Collectivization and the Terror-Famine* (New York: Oxford University Press, 1986); Anne Applebaum, *Red Famine: Stalin's War on Ukraine* (New York: Anchor Books, 2017); Sarah Cameron, *The Hungry Steppe: Famine, Violence, and the Making of Soviet Kazakhstan* (Ithaca, NY: Cornell University Press, 2018).

13. The role of science in agriculture is emphasized in several histories of Soviet agriculture. See, for example, J. Smith, *Works in Progress*; Aaron Hale-Dorrell, *Corn*

Crusade: Khrushchev's Farming Revolution in the Post-Stalin Soviet Union (New York: Oxford University Press, 2018); and Nils Roll-Hansen, *The Lysenko Effect: The Politics of Science* (Humanity Books, 2005).

14. This is Karl-Eugen Wädekin's well-known assessment, in *The Private Sector in Soviet Agriculture* (Berkeley: University of California Press, 1973).

15. This was especially the case during wars and crises. See Alexander Shikov et al., "Traditional and Current Food Use of Wild Plants Listed in the Russian Pharmacopoeia," *Frontiers in Pharmacology* 8, no. 841 (November 21, 2017): 841.

16. This is a summary of the classical works of Janos Kornai and Gregory Grossman by Visser and Kalb; see Oane Visser and Don Kalb, "Financialised Capitalism Soviet Style? Varieties of State Capture and Crisis," *European Journal of Sociology / Archives Européennes de Sociologie / Europäisches Archiv für Soziologie* 51, no. 2 (2010): 173.

17. On this theme, Medvedev, in *Soviet Agriculture*, notes: "Although there was a vast variety of equipment available for larger farms, no implements or machinery are produced by the state industry which would be suitable for individuals. All kinds of traditional and hand implements must be made by local industry . . . not specified by the state plans" (377–78).

18. In the nineties, about 25 percent of the population was engaged in subsistence agriculture, according to Grigory Ioffe, Tatyana Nefedova, and Ilya Zaslavsky, *The End of Peasantry? The Disintegration of Rural Russia* (Pittsburgh, PA: University of Pittsburgh Press, 2006), 8. See also Judith Pallot and Tatyana Nefedova, *Russia's Unknown Agriculture: Household Production in Post-Socialist Rural Russia* (Oxford: Oxford University Press, 2007). For the history of private agriculture in earlier periods, see Wädekin, *The Private Sector in Soviet Agriculture*; and Stefan Hedlund, *Private Agriculture in the Soviet Union* (London: Routledge, 1989).

19. Stephen Wegren (with Alexander Nikulin and Irina Trotsuk) argues that recent changes amount to revolutionary change. See Wegren, *Russia's Food Revolution*.

20. For employment data, see International Labor Organization, "Employment by Sector—ILO Modelled Estimates," *ILOSTAT*, 2018; for discussion, see Richard Bell, *Comparison of Agriculture in the United States and the Soviet Union* (Washington, DC: USDA Economic Research Service, 1961), esp. 3.

21. Susanne Wengle, "The Domestic Effects of the Russian Food Embargo," *Demokratizatsiya* 24, no. 3 (2016): 281–89.

22. See, for example, the account by Roll-Hansen, *The Lysenko Effect*.

23. Sheila Jasanoff and Sang-Hyun Kim, *Dreamscapes of Modernity: Sociotechnical Imaginaries and the Fabrication of Power* (Chicago: University of Chicago Press, 2015).

24. Fitzgerald, *Every Farm a Factory*, 26.

25. This visit is recounted in Bob Belderok, Hans Mesdag, and Dingena Donner, *Bread-Making Quality of Wheat: A Century of Breeding in Europe* (Dordrecht, Netherlands: Kluwer Academic, 2000). The bread factory that Gorky visited in the 1920s continued to operate for nearly a hundred years; the building was torn down in 2016.

26. "Khlebozavod-Avtomat," 2 (as cited in second epigraph).

27. E. D. Tverdiukova, "Khlebopechenie v SSSR v 1960e–1980e gg.," *Voprosy istorii* 12 (2018): 42.

28. Alec Nove, "Soviet Agriculture under Brezhnev," *Slavic Review* 29, no. 3 (1970): 380.

29. For the source of the textbook quote, see the second epigraph to this introduction. See also the author's interview with Dmitry Rylko, agricultural consultant, Moscow, 2014.

30. *RIA Novosti*, "Putin posetil Samarskii bulochno-konditerskii kombinat," *RIA Novosti*, March 7, 2018. The visit was also reported in a Kremlin press release on March 7, 2018.

31. See Gronow, *Caviar with Champagne*.

32. Anastas Mikoyan, quoted by François-Xavier Nérard, "Variations on a *Shchi* Theme: Collective Dining and Politics in the Early USSR," *Gastronomica: The Journal for Food Studies* 17, no. 4 (November 1, 2017): 39.

33. For the realization of Soviet modernity in an urban setting, see Stephen Kotkin, *Magnetic Mountain: Stalinism as a Civilization* (Berkeley: University of California Press, 1995).

34. As the works by these theorists are extensive and have spawned entire schools of thought that debate its axiomatic claims about the dynamics linking politics, economics, and agriculture for well over a century, they are virtually impossible to summarize in a few paragraphs. Given that these debates were in fact also fundamental for the political imaginaries of rural modernization among Russian intellectual and political elites—especially in the 1920s, but also later—there is no way around a short, if incomplete summary here.

35. See Tilzey for a contrast between Marx and Polanyi's positions on the question of the peasantry: Mark Tilzey, "Reintegrating Economy, Society, and Environment for Cooperative Futures: Polanyi, Marx, and Food Sovereignty," *Journal of Rural Studies* 53 (January 2, 2017).

36. This view is based on Marx's reflection on the history of the French proletariat in the 18th Brumaire, chapter VII; it is developed more extensively by Lenin, who considered this one of the main social problems in the early years of the twentieth century.

37. Kautsky emphasizes this statement with a note that he had no doubts about the differences between industry and agriculture: "kein Zweifel . . . die Landwirtschaft entwickelt sich nicht nach derselben Schablone wie die Industrie; sie folgt eigenen Gesetzen." He concludes: "Die Streitfrage, ob große oder kleine Landgüter vorteilhafter sind beschäftige die Nationalökonomen seit mehr als einem Jahrhundert und es ist kein Ende des Streits abzusehen." Karl Kautsky, *Die Agrarfrage, eine Übersicht über die Tendenzen der modernen Landwirtschaft und die Agrarpolitik der Sozialdemokratie* (Hannover, Germany: Dietz, 1899), 5 and 6. Bertel Nygaard observes that Kautsky's writing presents a conflicted account of agency and structure; see Bertel Nygaard, "Constructing Marxism: Karl Kautsky and the French Revolution, History of European Ideas," *History of European Ideas* 35, no. 4 (December 1, 2009): 450–64.

38. Teodor Shanin, "Chayanov's Treble Death and Tenuous Resurrection: An Essay about Understanding, about Roots of Plausibility and about Rural Russia," *Journal of Peasant Studies* 36, no. 1 (2009): 89.

39. Karl Polanyi, *The Great Transformation: The Political and Economic Origins of Our Time* (Boston, MA: Beacon, 1944).

40. Harriet Friedmann and Philip McMichael, "Agriculture and the State System: The Rise and Decline of National Agricultures, 1870 to the Present," *Sociologia Ruralis* 29, no. 2 (1989): 93–117.

41. Ibid., 94. Friedmann and McMichael argued against the theories of mid-century modernization theorists, such as W. W. Rostow and others, who saw rural change in terms of national trajectories. This kind of pessimism about the state's ability to regulate neoliberal capitalism is also characteristic of recent work by political ecologists such as Mark Tilzey, who insists that the essence of capitalism shapes rural development everywhere. Tilzey accuses the Polanyians and Chayanovians of an overly romantic understanding of the conditions of small farms and a failure "to uncover the essence of capitalism." Tilzey, "Reintegrating Economy, Society, and Environment for Cooperative Futures," 53.

42. William Cronon, *Nature's Metropolis: Chicago and the Great West* (New York: W. W. Norton, 1991).

43. Shanin, "Chayanov's Treble Death and Tenuous Resurrection"; Henry Bernstein, "V. I. Lenin and A. V. Chayanov: Looking Back, Looking Forward," *Journal of Peasant Studies* 36, no. 1 (2009): 55–81. Karl Wittfogel, by contrast, focuses precisely on the role of authoritarian states, arguing that agricultural improvement projects are a chief rationale for authoritarian governments to control populations. Karl Wittfogel, *Oriental Despotism: A Comparative Study of Total Power* (New Haven, CT: Yale University Press, 1957).

44. Alan Olmstead and Paul Rhode, *Creating Abundance: Biological Innovation and American Agricultural Development* (New York: Cambridge University Press, 2008), 15.

45. Robert Bates, *Markets and States in Tropical Africa: The Political Basis of Agricultural Policies* (Berkeley: University of California Press, 1981).

46. For an account that emphasizes institutions, see John M. Hansen, *Gaining Access: Congress and the Farm Lobby, 1919–1981* (Chicago: University of Chicago Press, 1991). In studies of the US food system, corporations are often singled out as powerful actors. See Michael Moss, *Salt, Sugar, Fat: How the Food Giants Hooked Us* (New York: Random House, 2013); Marion Nestle, *Food Politics: How the Food Industry Influences Nutrition and Health* (Berkeley: University of California Press, 2002); and Phillip Howard, "Consolidation in the North American Organic Food Processing Sector, 1997 to 2007," *International Journal of Sociology of Agriculture and Food* 16, no. 1 (2009): 13–30.

47. Pollan's writing overall conveys this message; for his most forceful manifesto, see Michael Pollan, "Voting with Your Fork," *New York Times*, May 7, 2006, p. 5. Other observers have resisted this emphasis on choice, pointing instead to structural and institutional factors that leave many consumers with little or no choice; see Julie Guthman, "Can't Stomach It: How Michael Pollan et al. Made Me Want to Eat Cheetos," *Gastronomica* 7, no. 3 (2007): 75–79.

48. Fernand Braudel, *The Structures of Everyday Life: Civilization and Capitalism, 15th–18th Century*, vol. 1 (New York: Harper & Row, 1982); see chapters 5 and 6, esp. p. 334.

49. Lewis Mumford, "Authoritarian and Democratic Technics," *Technology and Culture* 5, no. 1 (1964): 5.

50. Langdon Winner, "Do Artifacts Have Politics?," *Daedalus* 109, no. 1 (1980): 135.

51. Susan Buck-Morss, *Dreamworld and Catastrophe: The Passing of Mass Utopia in East and West* (Cambridge, MA: MIT Press, 2000).

52. Gabrielle Hecht, *The Radiance of France: Nuclear Power and National Identity after World War II* (Cambridge, MA: MIT Press, 1998), 258. See also Michael Thad Allen and Gabrielle Hecht, eds., *Technologies of Power* (Cambridge, MA: MIT Press, 2001).

53. Hecht, *The Radiance of France*, 258.

54. Technopolitical regimes are contested because competing technopolitical regimes can coexist; ibid., 258.

55. Sheila Jasanoff, *States of Knowledge: The Co-Production of Science and Social Order* (London: Routledge, 2004), 2 and 3. Jasanoff argues that for the political realm, a coproduction lens draws attention to the roles of knowledge, expertise, and technologies in shaping relations of authority, and vice versa.

56. Timothy Mitchell, *Rule of Experts: Egypt, Techno-Politics, Modernity* (Berkeley: University of California Press, 2002); Hecht, *The Radiance of France*; Saara Matala, "Flashy Flagships of Cold War Cooperation: The Finnish-Soviet Nuclear Icebreaker Project," *Technology and Culture* 60, no. 2 (2019): 347–77; Chris Sneddon and Coleen Fox, "The Cold War, the US Bureau of Reclamation, and the Technopolitics of River Basin Development, 1950–1970," *Political Geography* 30, no. 8 (November 1, 2011): 450–60.

57. References to the work by Scott and Mitchell are in Sneddon and Fox, "The Cold War, the US Bureau of Reclamation, and the Technopolitics of River Basin Development, 1950–1970."

58. Freidberg's focus is on agrifood corporations (not on the state or empire) and on their use of footprinting as a tool or "technique to advance their political interests in the supply chains, industries and societies where they operate." Susanne Freidberg, "Footprint Technopolitics," *Geoforum* 55 (2014): 186. Tiago Saraiva relies on the concept of biopolitics; see chapter 4.

59. Susan E. Reid, "Cold War in the Kitchen: Gender and the de-Stalinization of Consumer Taste in the Soviet Union under Khrushchev," *Slavic Review* 61, no. 2 (2002): 211–52.

60. According to the authors, this means that consumers' relationship with food has "multiple entrance points" and is not a "commodity-defined and single-point (i.e., purchase)." Petr Jehlička et al., "Thinking Food Like an East European: A Critical Reflection on the Framing of Food Systems," *Journal of Rural Studies* 76 (2020): 286–95.

61. Soviet environmental historians who have stressed this include Stephen Brain, *Song of the Forest: Russian Forestry and Stalinist Environmentalism, 1905–1953* (Pittsburgh, PA: University of Pittsburgh Press, 2011); David Moon, *The Plough That Broke the Steppes: Agriculture and Environment on Russia's Grasslands, 1700–1914*; J. Smith, *Works in Progress*; Andy Bruno, *The Nature of Soviet Power: An Arctic Environmental History*, Studies in Environment and History (Cambridge, UK: Cambridge University Press, 2016); Bathsheba Demuth, *Floating Coast: An Environmental History of the Bering Strait* (New York: W. W. Norton, 2019).

62. Mark Tilzey, *Political Ecology, Food Regimes, and Food Sovereignty: Crisis, Resistance, and Resilience* (London: Palgrave Macmillan, 2018), 2.

63. Tilzey, "Reintegrating Economy, Society, and Environment for Cooperative Futures." The real logic of change, Tilzey argues, is shaped by "the drive to maximize profit, to accumulate, to compete with other capitalists . . . , and to keep social and environmental costs to a minimum" (318). See also John Bellamy Foster, "Marx's Theory of Metabolic Rift: Classical Foundations for Environmental Sociology," *American Journal of Sociology* 105, no. 2 (1999): 366–405.

64. Jehlička et al., "Thinking Food Like an East European," 76.

65. The consequences of individual actions are important for Dewey's notion of the public. See, for example, John Dewey, *The Public and Its Problems* (Athens: Ohio University Press, 1954), 54, emphasis added: "individuals . . . do the *thinking, desiring and purposing*, but what they think of *is the consequence of their behavior upon that of others* and *that of others upon themselves*." I draw on Dewey as well as on the recent revival of American pragmatist thought in sociology, political science, and history. See, for example, Christine Overdevest, "Towards a More Pragmatic Sociology of Markets," *Theory and Society* 40, no. 5 (2011): 533–52; Josh Withford, "Pragmatism and the Untenable Dualism of Means and Ends: Why Rational Choice Theory Does Not Deserve Paradigmatic Privilege," *Theory and Society* 31 (2002): 325–63.

66. According to Zhores Medvedev, in 1913, rye acreage covered 28.2 million hectares; by 1985, only a third of it remained, covering 9.4 million hectares; see Medvedev, *Soviet Agriculture*, 215–17.

67. M. Gessen, "Food Import Ban Means Russia Is at War with the West," *Washington Post*, August 12, 2014.

68. For a nuanced picture of successes and failures in the late Stalin and Khrushchev years, see Jenny Leigh Smith, "Agricultural Involution in the Postwar Soviet Union," *International Labor and Working-Class History*, no. 85 (2014): 59–74.

69. Contemporary agroholdings have not failed to notice these values, responding by trying to re-create them in advertising and branding for mass-produced dairy product and jams—for example, goods that tended to originate in the household sector in the Soviet Union; see the discussion in chapter 3.

70. Food studies is a growing interdisciplinary body of research that tracks the promises and failures of industrial agrifood systems. On the promise of industrial agriculture, see Robert Paarlberg, *Food Politics: What Everyone Needs to Know* (New York: Oxford University Press, 2013). On some of the perils, see Hamilton, *Supermarket USA*. There are by now many studies on the pathologies of food systems. See Nestle, *Food Politics*; Timothy Pachirat, *Every Twelve Seconds: Industrialized Slaughter and the Politics of Sight* (New Haven, CT: Yale University Press, 2013).

71. J. Smith, *Works in Progress*, 1.

72. Stephen Wegren's *Land Reform in Russia* (2009) did make this kind of judgment, arguing that the post-Soviet reforms have ultimately failed to achieve their stated objective. Wegren has meanwhile revised this call. See, for example, Stephen Wegren, "Private Farming in Russia: An Emerging Success?," *Post-Soviet Affairs* 27, no. 3 (July 1, 2011): 211–40.

73. Susanne Wengle, *Post-Soviet Power: State-Led Development and Russia's Marketization* (New York: Cambridge University Press, 2015).

74. Stephen Wegren is an exception to this trend as he has observed the transformation of Russian agriculture for years. His work is referenced throughout the book, and his most recent contribution is *Russia's Food Revolution*.

75. In histories of Russian agriculture, this question appeared, for example, in debates on prerevolutionary communal land ownership, the *obshchina*. Views differed as to whether the obshchina was a central, persistent, and unique communal arrangement critical for survival in a harsh climate, and thus a particularly Russian social form—or conversely, whether it was essentially similar to communal land management prevalent in other European preindustrial societies and only a transient stage in Russia's socioeconomic development. Noted in Ioffe, Nefedova, and Zaslavsky, *The End of Peasantry?*, 5, 10.

76. For assessments of US agriculture, see, for example, the accounts by Paarlberg, *Food Politics: What Everyone Needs to Know*; and John Fraser Hart, *The Changing Scale of American Agriculture* (Charlottesville: University of Virginia Press, 2003). For assessments of Soviet agriculture, see Hedlund, *Private Agriculture in the Soviet Union*; for the post-Soviet period, see Wegren, *Land Reform in Russia*.

77. James Scott, *Seeing Like a State* (New Haven, CT: Yale University Press, 1998), 193.

78. See chapters 1 and 2 for the eradicated small farms during Stalin's collectivization. For the US and the fate of "agriculture of the middle," see Thomas A. Lyson, G. W. Stevenson, and Rick Welsh, eds., *Food and the Mid-Level Farm: Renewing an Agriculture of the Middle* (Cambridge, MA: MIT Press, 2008).

79. For a fascinating discussion of the similarities between late-modern capitalism and late-socialist planning, see Visser and Kalb, "Financialised Capitalism Soviet Style?"

80. Melissa Caldwell, "Domesticating the French Fry: McDonald's and Consumerism in Moscow," *Journal of Consumer Culture* 4, no. 1 (2004): 6.

81. Karsten Lunze et al., "Food Security and Nutrition in the Russian Federation—a Health Policy Analysis," *Global Health Action* 8 (June 24, 2015); Adam Drewnowski and Nicole Darmon, "Food Choices and Diet Costs: An Economic Analysis," *Journal of Nutrition* 135, no. 4 (April 1, 2005): 900–904.

82. Thomas F. Remington, *The Politics of Inequality in Russia* (Cambridge, UK: Cambridge University Press, 2011), is a valuable exception. See also Bertram Silverman and Murray Yanowitch, *New Rich, New Poor, New Russia: Winners and Losers on the Russian Road to Capitalism* (New York: Routledge, 1997).

83. Income inequality is measured using the Gini coefficient. The Soviet Union's Gini coefficient stood roughly at around .23 during the late Soviet period, denoting a relatively equal distribution of family incomes. See Abram Bergson, "Income Inequality under Soviet Socialism," *Journal of Economic Literature* 22, no. 3 (1984): 1070. By the early nineties, Russia's Gini index had increased to .48, and by 2015, it was around .37—registering a sharp increase in family incomes.

84. Filip Novokmet, Thomas Piketty, and Gabriel Zucman, "From Soviets to Oligarchs: Inequality and Property in Russia 1905–2016," *Journal of Economic Inequality* 16, no. 1 (June 1, 2018): 190.

85. Elisabeth Schimpfössl, *Rich Russians: From Oligarchs to Bourgeoisie* (New York: Oxford University Press, 2018).

86. Ibid., 36.

87. Caroline Humphrey, *Unmasking of Soviet Life: Everyday Economies after Socialism* (Ithaca, NY: Cornell University Press, 2002).

88. In addition to the books cited above, see Jennifer Clapp, *Food* (Cambridge, UK: Polity, 2012). See also Pachirat, *Every Twelve Seconds*. Another recent exception is Henry Thomson, *Food and Power: Regime Type, Agricultural Policy, and Political Stability* (Cambridge, UK: Cambridge University Press, 2019).

89. However, consumers do feature as actors in recent political economy studies on the platform economy. See Sabeel Rahman and Kathleen Thelen, "The Rise of the Platform Business Model and the Transformation of Twenty-First-Century Capitalism," *Politics & Society* 47, no. 2 (2019): 177–204.

Chapter 1. Governance; or, How to Solve the Grain Problem

Chapter epigraphs: Nikolai Bukharin, *O novoi ekonomicheskoi politike i nashikh zadachakh: Doklad na sobranii aktiva moskovskoi organizatsii* (Moscow: Izdatel'stvo Proletarii, 1925); Kremlin, Office of the President of Russia, Vladimir V. Putin, Opening Remarks by President Putin during a Meeting in Belgorod to Address Russia's Problems of Agriculture, May 3, 2000, http://en.kremlin.ru/events/president/transcripts/24534.

1. For the "grain problem," see A. Mikoyan, *Prodovol'stvennoe snabzhenie i nashi zadachi* (Moscow: Gosizdat, 1930). Engels, Kautsky, Lenin, and Bukharin all wrote treaties on what they called the "rural problem" or the "peasant problem."

2. This is the assessment by Z. M. Fallenbuchl, "Collectivization and Economic Development," *Canadian Journal of Economics and Political Science* 33, no. 1 (1967): 1. The discussion here draws on James W. Heinzen, *Inventing a Soviet Countryside: State Power and the Transformation of Rural Russia, 1917–1929* (Pittsburgh, PA: University of Pittsburgh Press, 2004). The quotes are from the latter source (4). Heinzen also refers to a Gosplan report that remarked that Narkozem was "one of the most important commissariats" (89). A. Mikoyan also refers to the "grain problem" in A. Mikoyan, *The Food Supply and Our Tasks* (Moscow: Cooperative Publishing Society for Foreign Workers, 1931), 13.

3. Bukharin argued that good relations to peasants were necessary to solve the grain problem as the large-scale coercion of the peasantry would be ultimately unfeasible. Bukharin, *O novoi ekonomicheskoi politike i nashikh zadachakh*.

4. Heinzen reports that Narkozem commissars sent out young agronomists to replace religion with agronomic science.Heinzen, *Inventing a Soviet Countryside*, 142.

5. See Stephen Wheatcroft and R. W. Davies, *The Industrialisation of Soviet Russia*, vol. 5, *Soviet Agriculture 1931–1933* (London: Palgrave Macmillan, 2010).

6. The All-Union Exhibition of Achievements in Agriculture was built in 1948. See Medvedev, *Soviet Agriculture* (New York: W. W. Norton, 1987), 151.

7. Hale-Dorrell, *Corn Crusade*, 26.

8. Alec Nove, *An Economic History of the USSR: 1917–1991* (London: Penguin Books, 1992), 336 and 366.

9. See, for example, Werner Hahn, *The Politics of Soviet Agriculture, 1960–1970* (Baltimore, MD: Johns Hopkins University Press, 1972).

10. See, for example, Alec Nove, "Soviet Agriculture: The Brezhnev Legacy and the Gorbachev Cure" (RAND Corporation / UCLA Center for the Study of Soviet International Behavior, Santa Monica, CA, 1988).

11. Vladimir Uzun, "Large and Small Business in Russian Agriculture: Adaptation to Market," *Comparative Economic Studies* 47, no.1 (2005): 85–100; Svetlana Barsukova, "Dilemma 'Fermery-agrokholdingi' v kontekste importozameshcheniia," *Obshchestvennye nauki i sovremennost'* 5 (2016): 63–74. For an observation in a trade journal that small farmers do not receive support, see "Fermery: Bez pensii, bez prava na dom, eshche i zemliu otnimaiut," *Krest'ianskie vedomosti*, January 28, 2015.

12. See Hale-Dorrell, *Corn Crusade*; and Michaela Pohl, "From White Grave to Tselinograd to Astana," in *The Thaw: Soviet Society and Culture during the 1950s and 1960s*, ed. Denis Kozlov and Eleonory Gilburd (Toronto: University of Toronto Press, 2013), 269.

13. This question is at the core of the debate between Robert Allen and Michael Ellman. See Robert Allen, *Farm to Factory: Reinterpretation of the Soviet Industrial Revolution* (Princeton, NJ: Princeton University Press, 2003); Michael Ellman, "Soviet Industrialization: A Remarkable Success?," *Slavic Review* 63, no. 4 (2004): 841–49.

14. Nérard, "Variations on a Shchi Theme," 39.

15. See, for example, J. Smith, *Works in Progress*. For the nineteenth century, see also David Moon's work that emphasizes that agriculture on the Eurasian steppe was perennially insecure. Moon, *The Plough That Broke the Steppes*.

16. Peter Holquist, *Making War, Forging Revolution: Russia's Continuum of Crisis, 1914–1921* (Cambridge, MA: Harvard University Press, 2002), 12.

17. According to Lars Lih, a critical moment of the events of 1917 was the admission by the imperial food procurement minister that there was too little grain in government storage to feed the army and urban residents. See Lars Lih, *Bread and Authority in Russia, 1914–1921* (Berkeley: University of California Press, 1990).

18. Oscar Sanchez-Sibony, "Depression Stalinism: The Great Break Reconsidered," *Kritika: Explorations in Russian and Eurasian History* 15, no. 1 (2014): 25.

19. Heinzen, *Inventing a Soviet Countryside*, 47.

20. Ibid., 88.

21. Bukharin, *O novoi ekonomicheskoi politike i nashikh zadachakh*.

22. Medvedev, *Soviet Agriculture*, x.

23. Nove, "Soviet Agriculture under Brezhnev," 381.

24. J. Smith, *Works in Progress*, 60.

25. Fazil Iskander, *The Goatibex Constellations* (Ann Arbor, MI: Ardis, 1975).

26. For a detailed account of how these two factions were positioned within the Narkomzem (the Agriculture Ministry) in the Civil War years and the 1920s, see Heinzen, *Inventing a Soviet Countryside*.

27. See Hale-Dorrell, *Corn Crusade*, 11; Allen, *Farm to Factory*, 70.

28. The annual gross harvest of grains in 1913 was 765 million centners. In 1921 it was 362.6 million centners. Heinzen, *Inventing a Soviet Countryside*, 140.

29. Ibid., 52.

30. Ibid., 136–37.

31. This was the formulation of the rural future by Alexander P. Smirnov, People's Commissariat for Agriculture in the 1920s; paraphrased by Heinzen, ibid., 137.

32. Caroline Humphrey, *Marx Went Away—But Karl Stayed Behind* (Ann Arbor: University of Michigan Press, 1998), 75 and 93. Kolkhozy were initially meant to be transitional and to disappear once they evolved into more productive organizations—but they ended up persisting throughout the Soviet period, as the somewhat more autonomous and flexible version of a collective farm.

33. Sheila Fitzpatrick, *The Russian Revolution* (Oxford: Oxford University Press, 1982), 105.

34. Stefan Hedlund, *Crisis in Soviet Agriculture* (London: St. Martin's, 1984), 44.

35. Heinzen, *Inventing a Soviet Countryside*, 145.

36. Medvedev, *Soviet Agriculture*, 72.

37. "Bor'ba za khleb," *Ogonek*, no. 37 (1929): 6.

38. Heinzen, *Inventing a Soviet Countryside*, 137.

39. Leonard, *Agrarian Reform in Russia*, 69.

40. This was the position of E. A. Preobrazhenskii, who was later expelled from the party. See ibid., 143.

41. See Heinzen, *Inventing a Soviet Countryside*, esp. chapter 6, "Better Red than Bread." For specific reference to Chayanov, see 192. Chayanov was executed in 1937, after years in prison and exile.

42. Lynne Viola, *Peasant Rebels under Stalin: Collectivization and the Culture of Peasant Resistance* (New York: Oxford University Press, 1996).

43. Several important studies of collectivization detail these events. See Robert Conquest, *The Harvest of Sorrow: Soviet Collectivization and the Terror-Famine* (New York: Oxford University Press, 1986); Anne Applebaum, *Red Famine: Stalin's War on Ukraine* (New York: Anchor, 2018); Sarah Cameron, *The Hungry Steppe: Famine, Violence, and the Making of Soviet Kazakhstan* (Ithaca, NY: Cornell University Press, 2018); Viola, *Peasant Rebels under Stalin*. For collectivization in Kazakhstan, see also Niccolò Pianciola, "The Collectivization Famine in Kazakhstan, 1931–1933," *Harvard Ukrainian Studies* 25, nos. 3/4 (2001): 237–51.

44. On quotas, see Hale-Dorrell, *Corn Crusade*, 14. On taxes, see Allen, *Farm to Factory*, 102. On requisitions and taxes on private plots, see Medvedev, *Soviet Agriculture*, 155.

45. On political control through MTS, see Roy D. Laird, "Soviet Goals for 1965 and the Problems of Agriculture," *Slavic Review* 20, no. 3 (1961): 463; see also Nove, *An Economic History of the USSR*, 181–83.

46. Cynthia Buckley, "The Myth of Managed Migration: Migration Control and Market in the Soviet Period," *Slavic Review* 54, no. 4 (1995): 896–916.

47. Gronow, *Caviar with Champagne*.

48. Hale-Dorrell, *Corn Crusade*, 145 and 146.

49. Ibid. 11, 25, and 108.

50. Nove, *An Economic History of the USSR*, 336.

51. J. Smith, "Agricultural Involution in the Postwar Soviet Union."

52. Hale-Dorrell, *Corn Crusade*, chapter 6 (esp. the summary on 119).

53. Medvedev, *Soviet Agriculture*, 164.

54. Ibid., 166. Prices for other commodities also rose, though less significantly. See also Leonard, *Agrarian Reform in Russia*, 75.

55. Hale-Dorrell, *Corn Crusade*, 166.

56. Ioffe, Nefedova, and Zaslavsky, *The End of Peasantry?*, 27.

57. Brian Kuns, "'In These Complicated Times': An Environmental History of Irrigated Agriculture in Post-Communist Ukraine," *Water Alternatives* 11, no. 3 (2018): 874.

58. Leonard, *Agrarian Reform in Russia*, 215.

59. Nove, *An Economic History of the USSR*, 381.

60. Ioffe, Nefedova, and Zaslavsky, *The End of Peasantry?*, 28.

61. Samuel Baron, *Bloody Saturday in the Soviet Union: Novocherkassk, 1962* (Palo Alto, CA: Stanford University Press, 2001). See chapter 3 on retail prices.

62. For data on subsidies for basic foods, see Byung-Yeon Kim, "Causes of Repressed Inflation in the Soviet Consumer Market, 1965–1989: Retail Price Subsidies, the Siphoning Effect, and the Budget Deficit," *Economic History Review* 55 (2002): 109. On the growing magnitude of subsidies for livestock, see David J. Sedik, "A Note on Soviet Per Capita Meat Consumption," *Comparative Economic Studies* 35, no. 3 (September 1, 1993): 39–48; and Nove, *An Economic History of the USSR*, 370.

63. Heinzen, *Inventing a Soviet Countryside*, 15.

64. Corinne Gaudin, "'No Place to Lay My Head': Marginalization and the Right to Land during the Stolypin Reforms," *Slavic Review* 57, no. 4 (1998): 747–73.

65. Heinzen, *Inventing a Soviet Countryside*, 23.

66. Nove, *An Economic History of the USSR*.

67. Medvedev, *Soviet Agriculture*, 100.

68. Nove, *An Economic History of the USSR*, 373.

69. The discussion of this period during the war and immediate postwar period relies on the account of J. Smith, *Works in Progress*, 64–68.

70. Hale-Dorrell, *Corn Crusade*, 18 and 19. See also Medvedev, *Soviet Agriculture*, 130, for the famines of 1946–47.

71. Hale-Dorrell, *Corn Crusade*, 87. See 100–101 for corn as a "miracle" crop.

72. Hale-Dorrell, *Corn Crusade*; Nove, "Soviet Agriculture under Brezhnev."

73. Medvedev, *Soviet Agriculture*, 170.

74. Cameron, *The Hungry Steppe*.

75. Laird, "Soviet Goals for 1965 and the Problems of Agriculture"; Nove, *An Economic History of the USSR*, 364.

76. Leonard, *Agrarian Reform in Russia*, 75.

77. Nove, "Soviet Agriculture under Brezhnev," 380.

78. Central Intelligence Agency, *Intelligence Memorandum: Soviet Grain Supply, 1968*, Secret (Central Intelligence Agency, December 1968; approved for release December 6, 2009), 1.

79. Nove, "Soviet Agriculture under Brezhnev," 380.

80. Pohl, "From White Grave to Tselinograd to Astana," 269.

81. J. Smith, "Agricultural Involution in the Postwar Soviet Union."

82. Peter Craumer, "Agricultural Change, Labor Supply, and Rural Out-Migration in Soviet Central Asia," in *Geographic Perspectives on Soviet Central Asia*, ed. Robert Lewis (New York: Routledge, 1992), 138.

83. This is Gregory Grossman's summary of Wädekin's assessment in a foreword to the translation of Wädekin, *The Private Sector in Soviet Agriculture*, xv (originally published as *Privatproduzenten in der Sowjetischen Landwirtschaft*, Aktuelle Studien [Köln: Verlag Wissenschaft und Politik, 1967]).

84. Wädekin, *The Private Sector in Soviet Agriculture*, 69.

85. For example, he prohibited feeding bread to livestock. See John W. DePauw, "The Private Sector in Soviet Agriculture," *Slavic Review* 28, no. 1 (1969): 63–71.

86. Ibid. See also Hedlund, *Private Agriculture in the Soviet Union*, 24.

87. Wädekin, *Privatproduzenten in der Sowjetischen Landwirtschaft*, 173.

88. Hedlund, *Private Agriculture in the Soviet Union*, 32.

89. Wädekin, *Privatproduzenten in der Sowjetischen Landwirtschaft*, 85.

90. Ibid., 94.

91. Wegren, *Land Reform in Russia*.

92. Sanchez-Sibony, "Depression Stalinism"; Belderok, Mesdag, and Donner, *Bread-Making Quality of Wheat*, 361.

93. M. E. Falkus, "Russia and the International Wheat Trade, 1861–1914," *Economica* 33, no. 132 (1966): 416–29.

94. Fred R. Belk, "Migration of Russian Mennonites," *Social Science* 50, no. 1 (1975): 17–21. See also the account by Courtney Fullilove of Turkey Wheat's role in the development of American seed research: *The Profit of the Earth: The Global Seeds of American Agriculture* (Chicago: University of Chicago Press, 2017). David Moon's work examines seeds and other transfers from Russia to the Great Plains, in *The American Steppes: The Unexpected Russian Roots of Great Plains Agriculture, 1870s–1930s* (Cambridge, UK: Cambridge University Press, 2020).

95. Olmstead and Rhode, *Creating Abundance*, 3 and 30.

96. See Fitzgerald, *Every Farm a Factory*, 157; J. Smith, *Works in Progress*, chapter 1; for exchanges in the late nineteenth and early twentieth centuries, see Moon, *The American Steppes*.

97. Peggy Brown, "Diplomatic Farmers: Iowans and the 1955 Agricultural Delegation to the Soviet Union," *The Annals of Iowa* 72, no. 1 (January 1, 2013): 31–62. See also Aaron Hale-Dorrell, "The Soviet Union, the United States, and Industrial Agriculture," *Journal of World History* 26, no. 2 (2015): 295–324; and Jacqueline McGlade, "More a Plowshare than a Sword: The Legacy of US Cold War Agricultural Diplomacy," *Agricultural History* 83, no. 1 (2009): 79–102.

98. Andrei Markevich, "Russia in the Great War: Mobilisation, Grain, and Revolution," in *Economics of the Great War: A Centennial Perspective*, ed. Stephen Broadberry and Mark Harrison (London: Center for Economic Policy Research, 2018), 103–8.

99. Sanchez-Sibony, "Depression Stalinism."

100. Michael Dohan, "The Economic Origins of Soviet Autarky 1927/28–1934," *Slavic Review* 35, no. 4 (1976): 606. According to Robert Paarlberg, some exports continued even during years of grain shortages and famine in 1932 and 1946. See Robert Paarlberg, "Shifting and Sharing Adjustment Burdens: The Role of the Industrial Food Importing Nations," *International Organization* 32, no. 3 (1978): 671.

101. Joseph Berliner, "Soviet Economic Aid," *International Executive* 1, no. 2 (1959): 33.

102. Willard Radell, "Cuban-Soviet Sugar Trade, 1960–1970: How Great Was the Subsidy?," *Journal of Developing Areas* 17, no. 3 (1983): 365–82.

103. Central Intelligence Agency, *Intelligence Memorandum*.

104. Berliner, "Soviet Economic Aid," 33.

105. Paarlberg, "Shifting and Sharing Adjustment Burdens," 670. The Soviet Union had already imported grain from Canada since 1962, in the aftermath of protests that were caused by food supply problems. Although the 1972 deal with the US involved far more grain, the 1962 grain imports were the first big reversal of Soviet grain trade, according to Dan Morgan, *Merchants of Grain: The Power and Profits of the Five Giant Companies at the Center of the World's Food Supply* (New York: Viking, 1978).

106. David M. Schoonover, "Soviet Agricultural Policies from Development to Maturity," *Soviet and Post-Soviet Review* 4, no. 1 (1977): 271–96.

107. For bad harvests in the 1970s, see Leonard, *Agrarian Reform in Russia*, 79; and P. R. Chari, "US-USSR Grain-Oil Deal," *China Report* 11, nos. 5–6 (1975): 3–9.

108. Morgan, *Merchants of Grain*. For the development of global food commodity markets, see Friedmann and McMichael, "Agriculture and the State System," 93–117. For US prices, see Paarlberg, "Shifting and Sharing Adjustment Burdens," 672.

109. American criticism of the grain deal centered specifically around three points: First, taxpayer money was used to fund a short-term agricultural export subsidy of 47 cents per bushel. Second, the private companies involved in the deal hired highly ranked members of the Department of Agriculture after its completion. Finally, the Department of Agriculture deliberately limited knowledge of the Soviet Union's need for grain that would have allowed the farmers to benefit from higher prices. Chari, "US-USSR Grain-Oil Deal."

110. United States Government, "United States Grain and Oil Agreements with the Soviet Union," *Hearing before the Committee on International Relations, US House of Representatives, Ninety-Fourth Congress, First Session* (October 28, 1975); Chari, "US-USSR Grain-Oil Deal."

111. Nick Butler, "Soviet Agriculture and US-Soviet Grain Agreement," *Intereconomics* 17, no. 5 (1982): 211–16.

112. William Liefert and Olga Liefert, "Russian Agriculture during Transition: Performance, Global Impact, and Outlook," *Applied Economic Perspectives and Policy* 34, no. 1 (2012): 45.

113. Marilyn Podgainy, "Non-Violent Coercion: The 1980 Embargo of United States Grain to the Soviet Union," *Touro Journal of Transnational Law* 2, no. 1 (1991): 230.

114. Abraham Becker, *U.S.- Soviet Trade in the 1980s*, RAND Publication Series (Santa Monica, CA: RAND Corporation, 1987); Karl-Eugen Wädekin, "Soviet Agriculture's Dependence on the West," *Foreign Affairs*, no. 60 (1982): 882–903; "Russians Are Reported Concerned about the EDB in US Grain," *New York Times*, January 11, 1984, p. 13.

115. See, for example, "Krome togo," *Kommersant*, October 27, 1992; and "I ne sprashivai, pochem zvonit kolokol. Vse ochen' dorogo," *Kommersant*, September 2, 1991, section "Vlast'."

116. Mark Kramer, *Food Aid to Russia*, PONARS Policy Memo (PONARS, 1999). At the nadir of the Russian crisis in the nineties, the EU supplemented US aid. Kramer concludes that food aid in such large quantities was a misguided policy in many ways; in addition to the cost to the US taxpayer, "US food aid has inadvertently undercut private farmers and propped up the old state-controlled grain monopolies." Ibid., 2. Media reports at the time note that Russians were ashamed to rely on foreign food; see, for example, "Novaia eda Rossii," *Kommersant*, February 2, 2010.

117. Wegren, *Land Reform in Russia*, 38–40.

118. Ibid., 42.

119. Ibid., 70.

120. K. Brooks, E. Krylatykh, Zvi Lerman, and Vasily Uzun, *Agricultural Reform in Russia: A View from the Farm Level*, World Bank Discussion Paper (Washington, DC: World Bank, 1996).

121. This is an observation by Grigory Ioffe and Tatyana Nefedova, "Russian Agriculture and Food Processing: Vertical Cooperation and Spatial Dynamics," *Europe-Asia Studies* 53, no. 3 (May 1, 2001): 389–418.

122. Wegren, *Land Reform in Russia*.

123. This is the assessment by Stephen Wegren, David O'Brien, and Valeri Patsiorkovski, "Why Russia's Rural Poor Are Poor," *Post-Soviet Affairs* 19, no. 30 (2003): 266.

124. Wegren, introduction to *Land Reform in Russia*.

125. Jessica Allina-Pisano, *The Post-Soviet Potemkin Village: Politics and Property Rights in the Black Earth* (Cambridge, UK: Cambridge University Press, 2007).

126. Sanchez-Sibony, "Depression Stalinism," 23 and 24, notes that Polanyi already described this problem.

127. Ioffe, Nefedova, and Zaslavsky, *The End of Peasantry?*, 38; Wegren, *Land Reform in Russia*, 51.

128. Leo Granberg and Ann-Mari Sätre, *The Other Russia: Local Experience and Societal Change*, Studies in Contemporary Russia (New York: Routledge, 2017), 17.

129. Liefert and Liefert, "Russian Agriculture during Transition," 46.

130. Petr Jehlička et al., "Thinking Food Like an East European," 286–95.

131. On state withdrawal, see Alexander Vorbrugg, "Not About Land, Not Quite a Grab: Dispersed Dispossession in Rural Russia," *Antipode* 51, no. 3 (2019): 1011–31; and Stephen Wegren, "State Withdrawal and the Impact of Marketization on Rural Russia," *Policy Studies Journal* 28, no. 1 (February 1, 2000): 46–67.

132. David Sedik, Sergey Sotnikov, and Doris Wiesman, *Food Security in the Russian Federation* (Rome: FAO, 2003).

133. Liefert and Liefert, "Russian Agriculture during Transition," 47.

134. See Clapp, *Food*.

135. Comment by Agriculture Minister Gordeev, in a Federation Council Session on March 7, 2007. See Kremlin, Office of the President of Russia, Vladimir V. Putin, "Stenograficheskii otchet o zasedanii soveta pri prezidente Rossii po realizatsii prioritetnykh natsional'nykh proektov i demograficheskoi politike," March 7, 2007, http://

kremlin.ru/events/president/transcripts/24074. The 2010 Food Security Doctrine singled out meat production as a priority.

136. Stephen Wegren points out that a speech by Mikhail Gorbachev in 1987 made similar points. See Wegren, *Land Reform in Russia*, 35. See also Svetlana Barsukova, "Agricultural Policy in Russia," *Social Sciences* 48, no. 4 (2017): 3–18.

137. Osnovnye napravleniia agroprodovol'stvennoi politiki pravitel'stva Rossiiskoi Federatsii na 2001–2010 gody, July 27, 2000.

138. Liefert and Liefert, "Russian Agriculture during Transition," 50. On public support and the increase in production, see, for example, Steven J. Main, "Food Policy and Food Security: Putting Food on the Russian Table," *Europe-Asia Studies* 71, no. 2 (2019): 331–32; and Ekaterina Diatlovskaia and Tat'iana Kulistikova, "Vladimir Putin: 'Razmery podderzhki APK izmeriaiutsia sotniami milliardov rublei,'" *Agroinvestor*, December 20, 2018.

139. Food and Agriculture Organization, "FAO Agriculture and Trade Policy Background Note: Russia," 2013, p. 2.

140. See Kremlin, Office of the President of Russia, Vladimir V. Putin, "Utverzhdena Doktrina prodovol'stvennoi bezopasnosti Rossiiskoi Federatsii," February 1, 2010, http://www.kremlin.ru/events/president/news/6752.

141. Erik Hansen, *Russian Food Ban Extended until August 2016*, GAIN Report (USDA Foreign Agriculture Service, Moscow, June 25, 2015).

142. Reported by *Itar-Tass*, September 2012.

143. Dmitry Prikhodko and Albert Davleyev, *Russian Federation: Meat Sector Review* (Rome: United Nations Food and Agriculture Organization, 2014), 33.

144. Russian comments at a G8 meeting reflect concerns about raising global prices for food. See Kremlin press release titled "Global'naia prodovol'stvennaia bezopasnost'," July 8, 2008.

145. Andrew Kramer, "Russia's Collective Farms: Hot Capitalist Property," *New York Times*, August 30, 2008.

146. Critics rejected the possibility that Russia would control enough of the world market for wheat to play an important role; see World Bank, *A State Trading Enterprise for Grains in Russia? Issues and Options*, Policy Note (Washington, DC: World Bank, October 1, 2009). Aside from questions about whether post-Soviet countries would control enough global market shares, the cooperation between Russia, Ukraine, and Kazakhstan was also an absolute prerequisite for the cartel's viability. The conflict between Russia and Ukraine that erupted after the annexation of Crimea made this kind of cooperation all but impossible.

147. Susanne Wengle, "Local Effects of the New Land Rush: How Capital Inflows Transformed Rural Russia," *Governance* 31, no. 2 (2018): 259–77.

148. Kremlin, "Stenograficheskii otchet."

149. Michele Crumley, *Sowing Market Reforms: The Internationalization of Russian Agriculture* (New York: Palgrave Macmillan, 2013), 113.

150. The mixed track record of these programs led the government to create UGC/OZK, Ob"edinennaia zernovaia kompaniia, a state-controlled grain trading company that came to control port infrastructure and storage facilities. See Janetta Azarieva,

Grain and Power in Russia 2001–2011 (Jerusalem, Israel: Hebrew University of Jerusalem, 2014), esp. chapter 3 for more details on UGC.

151. Cherkizovo, *One Big Family*, 2015 Annual Report, 6, accessed July 2020 from Cherkizovo website, https://cherkizovo.com/.

152. Food and Agriculture Organization, *Russian Federation: Analysis of the Agribusiness Sector in Southern Russia* (Rome: UN FAO Investment Centre, January 2009).

153. This information was obtained from the RusAg/Rossel'khozbank website, accessed January 2021, http://www.rshbins.ru/. A special section outlines the bank's role in implementing state programs: https://www.rshb.ru/gosprograms/.

154. Crumley, *Sowing Market Reforms*, 113.

155. See, for example, Irina Granik, "Dmitrii Medvedev zalivaet zasukhu den'gami; a zhivotnovodstvo dolzhno prevratit'sia v eksportnuiu otrasl'," *Kommersant*, July 14, 2010.

156. Prikhodko and Davleyev, *Russian Federation*; Holly Higgens, *2014 Livestock and Products Semi-Annual Report*, GAIN Report (Washington, DC: USDA Foreign Agriculture Service, March 17, 2014). This modernization was clearly supported by the highest rung of the government. Morgan Haas and Mikhail Maximenko, *Russian Federation Livestock and Products Semi-Annual*, GAIN Report (Washington, DC: USDA Foreign Agriculture Service, 2012).

157. Robin Gray, *Russian Federation: Sugar Annual Sugar Update 2017*, GAIN Report (Washington, DC: USDA Foreign Agriculture Service, April 14, 2017).

158. Miratorg, *Miratorg Annual Report 2013* (Moscow: Miratorg Agribusiness Holding, 2013), 13. Note: 24 bln rubles were approximately $580 million at that time.

159. Viktor Andreev, "Korruptsiia ili biznes? Kak zemli i molochnye predpriiatiia rossiiskikh regionov otkhodiat Shtefanu Diurru—Novosti sel'skogo khoziaistva," *Moscow Post*, July 1, 2019.

160. "Interview with Adrian Schairer, Head of Investor Relations at Ekosem-Agrar: EkoNiva Is Taking Advantage of the Window of Opportunity," May 2, 2019, https://www.largescaleagriculture.com/home/news-details/adrian-schairer-m-sc-head-of-investor-relations-at-ekosem-agrar-ekoniva-is-taking-advantage-of/.

161. Wegren, "Russia's Food Policies and Foreign Policy."

162. The disappearance of babushki selling produce on street corners was obvious to anybody who has visited Russia during these years. This was noted, for example, in Melissa L. Caldwell, ed., *Food and Everyday Life in the Post-Socialist World* (Bloomington: Indiana University Press, 2009), 121.

163. Andrew Scott Barnes, *Owning Russia: The Struggle over Factories, Farms, and Power* (Ithaca, NY: Cornell University Press, 2006), 199.

164. Dmitri Rylko, interview with author, Moscow, July 2014. The Russian government has not published data on the NAOs, and they are not a category in official statistics; Rylko has also published estimates of NAO landholdings, for example in Dmitri Rylko and Robert Jolly, "Russia's New Agricultural Operators: Their Emergence, Growth and Impact," *Comparative Economic Studies* 47 (2005): 115–26. See also the annual calculations of agroholding land assets calculated by the consulting company BEFL, published in the trade journal *Agroinvestor*.

165. While many agroholdings do not have a public presence, Rusagro has over the years published information about the size of its land bank. See http://www.rusagro group.ru/.

166. Oane Visser, Natalia Mamonova, and Max Spoor, "Is Russia the Emerging Global 'Breadbasket'? Re-Cultivation, Agroholdings and Grain Production," *Europe- Asia Studies* 66, no. 10 (2014): 1589–1610.

167. The largest sovkhozy were roughly 15,000 hectares. See Dmitri Rylko in Csaba Csáki, Gershon Feder, and Zvi Lerman, *Agriculture in Transition: Land Policies and Evolving Farm Structures in Post-Soviet Countries* (Lanham, MD: Lexington Books, 2004).

168. In these regions, Rylko estimated that agroholdings hold between 25 and 50 percent of arable land; they hold less than 10 percent of the arable land in the Urals and Siberia and are virtually absent in the less productive agricultural regions of Russia. Rylko et al., "Agroholdings." See also Thomas Fellmann and Olexandr Nekhay, *Agricultural Sector and Market Developments: A Special Focus on Ukraine, Russia and Kazakhstan* (Kiev: European Commission Joint Research Centre and the Institute for Prospective Technological Studies, January 1, 2012). The Far East is often noted as a region of potential development for agroholdings, but the extent of their presence there is not clear. This was also noted by a Rusagro representative in interview with author, Moscow, July 2014.

169. Jiayi Zhou, "Chinese Agrarian Capitalism in the Russian Far East," *Third World Thematics: A TWQ Journal* 1, no. 5 (September 2, 2016): 612–32.

170. This was a cause of protests over land rights violations. See Natalia Mamonova, "Rethinking Rural Politics in Post-Socialist Settings: Rural Communities, Land Grabbing and Agrarian Change in Russia and Ukraine" (PhD diss., International Institute of Social Studies, Erasmus University, Rotterdam, Netherlands, 2016). See also Alexander Vorbrugg about the absence of a "grab" in Russia's recent land consolidation.

171. Miratorg has many of its original production facilities in Bryansk. Irina Skrynnik, "The Pork Offensive: How Miratorg Won over the Russian Product Market," *Forbes Business*, October 16, 2014; Alexander Nikulin, Irina Trotsuk, and Stephen Wegren, "The Importance of Strong Regional Leadership in Russia: The Belgorod Miracle in Agriculture," *Eurasian Geography and Economics* 58, no. 3 (May 4, 2017): 316–39. See also Oane Visser, Alexander Kurakin, and Alexander Nikulin, "Corporate Social Responsibility, Coexistence and Contestation: Large Farms' Changing Responsibilities vis-à-vis Rural Households in Russia," *Canadian Journal of Development Studies / Revue Canadienne d'études Du Développement* 40, no. 4 (October 2, 2019): 580–99.

172. A. Yakovlev and O. Balaeva, "'Good Governor' or Institution Building: What Can Explain the Success Story of Voronezh after 2009?" (working paper in progress shared by authors).

173. Christopher Gaudoin, "The Sugar Policy in Russia: An Import Substitution Strategy," *Agriculture Stratégies* (blog), November 13, 2018, https://www.agriculture -strategies.eu/en/2018/11/the-sugar-policy-in-russia/. Over the last few years, the share of imported sugar has dropped below 10 percent.

174. It was contested because it clearly hurt domestic grain producers. But the fact that proponents of the ban prevailed made clear that "Putin chose to sacrifice exports

for domestic stability"—that is, that domestic goals of food sovereignty trumped external ones. See Mary Ellen Smith and Yelena Vassilieva, *Ban on Grain Exports from Russia Comes to Force on August 15*, GAIN Report (Moscow: USDA Foreign Agriculture Service, August 6, 2010). The ban was based on the Government Resolution #599 of August 5, 2010, "About Introduction of the Temporary Ban on Exports of Certain Agricultural Commodities from Russia." It was also widely commented upon in Russia and abroad. See Sergei Minaev, "Suverennyi Karavai," *Kommersant*, August 16, 2010, 32 edition, sec. Vlast'; see also Stephen K. Wegren, "The Development of Agrarian Capitalism in Post-Soviet Russia," *Journal of Agrarian Change* 11, no. 2 (April 1, 2011): 138–63.

175. Mariia Zheleznova, "Zhizn' na bezryb'e," *Vedomosti*, May 24, 2016.

176. Decree No. 778 of 7 August 2014. For the full text in English, see E. Hansen, *Russian Food Ban Extended until August 2016*.

177. "Postavki v Rossiiu produktov iz nakhodiashchikhsia pod sanktsiiami stran snizilis' v 100 Raz," *Vedomosti*, September 27, 2019, sec. Business.

178. For the effects on the EU of the sanctions and countersanctions, see Marcin Szczepański, *Economic Impact on the EU of Sanctions over Ukraine Conflict*, EPRS_BRI Report (European Parliamentary Research Service, October 2015).

179. *RBC News*, "Medvedev poruchil gotovit'sia k prodleniiu antisanktsii do kontsa 2017 goda," *RBC News*, May 27, 2016. See also E. Hansen, *Russian Food Ban Extended until August 2016*; and William Liefert et al., "The Effect of Russia's Economic Crisis and Import Ban on Its Agriculture and Food Sector," *Journal of Eurasian Studies* 10, no. 2 (2019): 119–35. On effects of the food ban, see Wengle, "The Domestic Effects of the Russian Food Embargo," 281–89.

180. Don Van Atta, *Russian Food Supplies in 1992 and Prospects for 1993* (Durham, NC: National Council for Soviet and East European Research, Duke University, April 7, 1993). Since the late 1990s, though, studies documenting the role of vested interests in the post-Soviet context have generally highlighted the influence of oligarchic conglomerates on reform trajectories, deemphasizing parties and interest groups. See Joel Hellman, "Winners Take All: The Politics of Partial Reform in Postcommunist Transitions," *World Politics* 50, no. 3 (1998): 203–34.

181. The agrarian party eventually merged with United Russia in 2008. Interestingly, the party was revived in 2012, although it is unclear and perhaps unlikely that it can play a role as an independent political actor in the current political order dominated by United Russia. Oane Visser and Natalia Mamonova also documented that a few grassroots organizations were formed in the middle of the first decade of the 2000s to coordinate their demands vis-à-vis the NAOs, although only one of them, the Krestyansky Front, was independent of the government. See Oane Visser and Natalia Mamonova, *Large-Scale Land Acquisitions in the Former Soviet Union*, IS Land Academy Report (Utrecht: Utrecht University, April 2012), 21.

182. Chapter 2 will provide more detailed corporate histories of the agroholdings.

183. The National Meat Association (Natsional'naia miasnaia assotsiiatsiia; see http://www.natmeat.ru/) and the National Union of Poultry Producers (Rosptitsesoiuz; see http://www.rps.ru/) formed in 2003 and 2001, respectively. See their websites for information about these associations. See also the National Swine Breeder's Association

(http://www.nssrf.ru/about.php?action=history) and the Union of Milk Producers (Soiuzmoloko; http://www.souzmoloko.ru).

184. Howard Amos, "The True Tale of Russia's German Dairy King," *Moscow Times*, November 23, 2015.

185. These goals are apparent in several public venues and in media appearances by Stefan Dürr; see also an entry in the corporate history on the company website, EkoNiva-APK-Holding, "History," accessed 2020, https://www.ekoniva-apk.ru/en/company/history.

186. Ekaterina Diatlovskaia, "'EkoNiva' vlozhit do 2 mlrd rublei v agrokompleks, sozdannyi Luzhkovym," *Agroinvestor*, October 24, 2017; see also "Nemetskii biznesmen i rossiiskii grazhdanin Shtefan Diurr pokazal svoi vladeniia Olegu Kharseevu i Olegu Mukhinu," *Ogonek*, February 13, 2017, p. 10.

Chapter 2. Production

Chapter epigraphs: I. Kogan, "V nogu s industriei," *Ogonek*, no. 28 (1930): 7; D. Iu. Katalevskii and A. Iu. Ivanov, eds., *Sovremennye agrotekhnologii: Ekonomiko-pravovye i reguliatornye aspekty* (Moscow/Skolkovo: Institute for Law and Development, Higher School of Economics at Skolkovo, 2018).

1. Cherkizovo, *Delicious Story*, 2017 Annual Report, https://cherkizovo.com/.

2. Denis Kolbasov et al., "African Swine Fever Virus, Siberia, Russia, 2017," *Emerging Infectious Diseases* 24, no. 4 (April 2018): 796–98.

3. Viola, *Peasant Rebels under Stalin*, 68; Sheila Fitzpatrick, *Stalin's Peasants: Resistance and Survival in the Russian Village after Collectivization* (Oxford, UK: Oxford University Press, 1994), 66.

4. Viola, *Peasant Rebels under Stalin*, 71; Nove, *An Economic History of the USSR*, 176.

5. Joseph Berliner, *The Innovation Decision in Soviet Industry* (Cambridge, MA: MIT Press, 1976), 437. Berliner is quoted in Allen, *Farm to Factory*, 207.

6. Nove, *An Economic History of the USSR*, 365.

7. Loren Graham, *Lonely Ideas: Can Russia Compete?* (Cambridge, MA: MIT Press, 2013), 123.

8. Ibid., 73.

9. See Allen, *Farm to Factory*, 209, for a refutation of Berliner. Christine Evans and Lars Lundgren show how innovation in satellite technology revolutionized civilian broadcasting starting in the 1960s. Christine Evans and Lars Lundgren, "Geographies of Liveness: Time, Space, and Satellite Networks as Infrastructures of Live Television in the Our World Broadcast," *International Journal of Communication* 10 (January 1, 2016): 5362–80. An interesting aspect of these revisions is that they mirror studies on innovation in capitalist economies that have increasingly stressed the role of the state in fostering innovation.

10. See, for example, Heinzen, *Inventing a Soviet Countryside*.

11. Allen, *Farm to Factory*, 48.

12. Markevich, "Russia in the Great War."

13. Fitzpatrick, *Stalin's Peasants*, 66.

14. Viola, *Peasant Rebels under Stalin*, 71; Nove, *An Economic History of the USSR*, 176.

15. Quoted and discussed by Roy D. Laird, "Kolkhozy, the Russian Achilles Heel: Failed Agrarian Reform," *Europe-Asia Studies* 49, no. 3 (May 1, 1997): 469–78.

16. For Soviet fisheries, see Andrey Bogeruk, *National Aquaculture Sector Overview—Russian Federation* (Rome: FAO, 2005).

17. Based on data by the Gosudarstvennyi komitet SSSR po statistike, *Narodnoe khoziaistvo SSSR v 1989* (Moscow: Goskomstat, 1989).

18. Alexey Morgunov, *Wheat and Wheat Breeding in the Former USSR* (Texcoco, Mexico: CIMMYT Wheat, November 1992), 4.

19. Medvedev, *Soviet Agriculture*, 221.

20. For the Soviet history of collectivizing and settling reindeer herds in the Russian Far East, see Demuth, *Floating Coast*.

21. Richard Bell, *Comparison of Agriculture in the United States and the Soviet Union*, 8.

22. Leonard, *Agrarian Reform in Russia*, 249.

23. J. Smith, *Works in Progress*.

24. See Buckley, "The Myth of Managed Migration," 896–916.

25. Moshe Lewin, *Russian Peasants and Soviet Power: A Study of Collectivization* (New York: W. W. Norton, 1975), 514.

26. Fitzpatrick, *Stalin's Peasants*, 136.

27. Laird, "Soviet Goals for 1965 and the Problems of Agriculture," 454–64.

28. Leonard, *Agrarian Reform in Russia*, 7.

29. Soviet agriculture also had less capital and technology than the US. See Richard Bell, "Comparison of Agriculture in the United States and the Soviet Union," 4.

30. Fitzgerald, *Every Farm a Factory*, chapter 6.

31. J. Smith, *Works in Progress*, 8.

32. Leonard, *Agrarian Reform in Russia*, 201–4.

33. Medvedev, *Soviet Agriculture*, 217.

34. Ioffe, Nefedova, and Zaslavsky, *The End of Peasantry?*, 25.

35. Cameron, *The Hungry Steppe*, 237–51.

36. Medvedev, *Soviet Agriculture*, 173.

37. Morgunov, "Wheat and Wheat Breeding in the Former USSR," 1.

38. Nove, *An Economic History of the USSR*, 376.

39. Morgunov, "Wheat and Wheat Breeding in the Former USSR."

40. Nove, *An Economic History of the USSR*, 365.

41. Medvedev, *Soviet Agriculture*, 225.

42. Wädekin, *Privatproduzenten in der Sowjetischen Landwirtschaft*, 92.

43. For the US experience with these efforts, see Deborah Fitzgerald, "World War II and the Quest for Time-Insensitive Foods," *Osiris* 35, no. 1 (August 1, 2020): 291–309.

44. J. Smith, *Works in Progress*; J. Smith, "Agricultural Involution in the Postwar Soviet Union."

45. Jan Solecki, "A Review of the USSR Fishing Industry," *Ocean Management* 5 (1979): 97–123.

46. Fish was subsidized with 2.6 billion rubles in 1988, compared to 26.8 for meat and 16.1 for milk, according to Kim, "Causes of Repressed Inflation in the Soviet Consumer Market," 109.

47. Jenny Leigh Smith, "Empire of Ice Cream: How Life Became Sweeter in the Postwar Soviet Union," in *Food Chains: From Farmyard to Shopping Cart*, ed. Warren Belasco and Roger Horowitz (Philadelphia: University of Pennsylvania Press, 2009), 142–57.

48. Exhibit at the St. Petersburg Bread Museum on the Bakery Karavai. Since the Leningrad bakery seems not to have influenced the bakery design elsewhere, this architectural innovation might be an example of a utopian food processing scheme that never made it far beyond the model stage.

49. For example, Nove, *An Economic History of the USSR*, 365.

50. Olga Syutkin and Pavel Syutkin, *CCCP Cook Book: True Stories of Soviet Cuisine* (London: FUEL, 2015), 10.

51. United State Congress and Senate Committee on Finance, *Background Materials Relating to the United States-Soviet Union Commercial Relations* (Washington, DC: US Congress Printing Office, 1974), 14.

52. On champagne, see Gronow, *Caviar with Champagne*; on canning, see Syutkin and Syutkin, *CCCP Cook Book*, 38; on the canning industry, see J. Smith, *Works in Progress*, 157.

53. Tverdiukova, "Khlebopechenie v SSSR v 1960e–1980e gg."

54. Leonard, *Agrarian Reform in Russia*, 79.

55. Hedlund, *Crisis in Soviet Agriculture*, 17.

56. Medvedev, *Soviet Agriculture*, 386.

57. Ethel Dunn, *Perestroika of Soviet Agriculture: The Peasant View* (Washington, DC: National Council for Soviet and East European Research, July 5, 1991).

58. Ioffe, Nefedova, and Zaslavsky, *The End of Peasantry?*, 80.

59. Ibid., 80.

60. Hedlund, *Private Agriculture in the Soviet Union*, 9; Nove, *An Economic History of the USSR*. See also Humphrey, *Unmasking of Soviet Life*, 134.

61. Wädekin, *Privatproduzenten in der Sowjetischen Landwirtschaft*, 83.

62. Brandon M. Schechter, "The State's Pot and the Soldier's Spoon," in *Hunger and War: Food Provisioning in the Soviet Union during World War II*, ed. Wendy Z. Goldman and Donald A. Filtzer (Bloomington: Indiana University Press, 2015), 98–157.

63. Wädekin, *Privatproduzenten in der Sowjetischen Landwirtschaft*, 52.

64. Hedlund, *Private Agriculture in the Soviet Union*, 95.

65. Wädekin, *The Private Sector in Soviet Agriculture*, 20, 23, 26, and 39.

66. See, for example, Ioffe, Nefedova, and Zaslavsky, *The End of Peasantry?*; Pallot and Nefedova, *Russia's Unknown Agriculture*, 109; and Stephen Wegren, *Agriculture and the State in Soviet and Post-Soviet Russia* (Pittsburgh, PA: University of Pittsburgh Press, 1998).

67. Nove, *An Economic History of the USSR*.

68. Wädekin, *Privatproduzenten in der Sowjetischen Landwirtschaft*; Hedlund, *Private Agriculture in the Soviet Union*, 106.

69. Several authors have stressed the symbiotic relationship between collective and large-scale farms and small-scale household plots. See Hedlund, *Private Agriculture in the Soviet Union*; and Pallot and Nefedova, *Russia's Unknown Agriculture*. The most recent studies show how this symbiosis changed over time. See Visser, Kurakin, and Nikulin, "Corporate Social Responsibility, Coexistence and Contestation," 580–99; and Jehlička et al., "Thinking Food Like an East European," 286–95.

70. Wädekin, *Privatproduzenten in der Sowjetischen Landwirtschaft*, 20. See pages 53 for data and 170 for labor implications.

71. Ibid., 18.

72. Hedlund, *Crisis in Soviet Agriculture*, 105.

73. For regional data on private agriculture, see Wädekin, *Privatproduzenten in der Sowjetischen Landwirtschaft*, 50.

74. Ibid., 75. Wädekin also estimates overall volumes for harvests by such urban farmers in 1956, a relatively good year for collective production: 3,740,000 tons of potatoes; 935,000 tons of vegetables; 425,000 tons of meat (of which 325,000 was pork); 2,200,000 tons of milk.

75. Ibid., 75, emphasis added.

76. Hedlund, *Private Agriculture in the Soviet Union*.

77. A. A. Mokrushin, "Nedostatki finansovo ustoichivykh predpriiatii (organizatsii), sposobnykh na krupnye kapital'nye vlozheniia v modernizatsiiu sel'skokhoziaistvennogo proizvodstva," *Nauchnyi zhurnal KubGAU* 24, no. 8 (2006): 2.

78. Grigory Ioffe, "The Downsizing of Russian Agriculture," *Europe-Asia Studies* 57, no. 2 (March 1, 2005): 179–208. Alexander Nikulin calls them "post-kolkhozes." Alexander M. Nikulin, "From Post-Kolkhoz to Oligarkhoz," *RUDN Journal of Sociology*, no. 2 (June 15, 2011): 56–68.

79. Ioffe, "The Downsizing of Russian Agriculture," 182.

80. Allina-Pisano, *The Post-Soviet Potemkin Village*, 139.

81. Alexander Prishchepov et al., "Determinants of Agricultural Land Abandonment in Post-Soviet European Russia," *Land Use Policy* 30, no. 1 (2013): 873.

82. Sedik, Sotnikov, and Wiesman, *Food Security in the Russian Federation*.

83. This observation refers to trends in 2000; see Ioffe, Nefedova, and Zaslavsky, *The End of Peasantry?*, 185.

84. Kazbek Toleubayev, Kees Jansen, and Arnold Huis, "Knowledge and Agrarian De-Collectivisation in Kazakhstan," *Journal of Peasant Studies* 37, no. 2 (April 1, 2010): 367.

85. The abandonment of agricultural land in post-Soviet Russia was rapid and extensive, affecting particularly regions with less fertile land. Prishchepov et al., "Determinants of Agricultural Land Abandonment in Post-Soviet European Russia," 881.

86. Granberg and Sätre, *The Other Russia*, 16.

87. Ioffe, Nefedova, and Zaslavsky, *The End of Peasantry?*, 15.

88. For example, Granberg and Sätre, *The Other Russia*, 20. See also Ann-Mari Sätre, *The Politics of Poverty in Contemporary Russia* (New York: Routledge, 2019); and Niobe Thompson, *Settlers on the Edge* (Vancouver: University of British Columbia Press, 2009).

89. Nancy Ries, "Potato Ontology: Surviving Postsocialism in Russia," *Cultural Anthropology* 24, no. 2 (May 1, 2009): 181–212.

90. Recounted by visiting researcher; interview with author, 2019. See also Thompson, *Settlers on the Edge*, 92; and Yulian Konstantinov, *Conversations with Power: Soviet and Post-Soviet Developments in Reindeer Husbandry of the Kola Peninsula*, Uppsala Studies in Cultural Anthropology 56 (Uppsala, Sweden: Uppsala Universitet, 2015).

91. Shikov et al., "Traditional and Current Food Use of Wild Plants Listed in the Russian Pharmacopoeia."

92. Barnes, *Owning Russia*.

93. See Oane Visser and Max Spoor, "Land Grabbing in Post-Soviet Eurasia: The World's Largest Agricultural Land Reserves at Stake," *Journal of Peasant Studies* 38, no. 2 (2011): 299–323; and Wengle, "Local Effects of the New Land Rush," 259–77.

94. Pallot and Nefedova, *Russia's Unknown Agriculture*, 123.

95. Eugenia Serova, "Farm Restructuring in Transition: Land Distribution in Russia," chapter 17 in *Food Policy for Developing Countries: Case Studies*, ed. Per Pinstrup-Andersen and Fuzhi Cheng (Ithaca, NY: Cornell University Press, 2007), 207.

96. "Oligarchs Eating Up $8 Bln Meat Market," *Moscow Times*, July 25, 2002.

97. Visser and Spoor's careful analysis documents regional trends: European investors were mainly interested in the Russian Black Earth, while China pursued opportunities in Siberia as well as Kazakhstan. Visser and Spoor, "Land Grabbing in Post-Soviet Eurasia."

98. Ibid., 311.

99. See Brian Kuns, Oane Visser, and Anders Wästfelt, "The Stock Market and the Steppe: The Challenges Faced by Stock-Market Financed, Nordic Farming Ventures in Russia and Ukraine," *Journal of Rural Studies* 45 (June 1, 2016): 199–217; and Oane Visser, "Running Out of Farmland? Investment Discourses, Unstable Land Values and the Sluggishness of Asset Making," *Agriculture and Human Values* 34, no. 1 (March 1, 2017): 185–98.

100. Sources for information related to Rusagro and Prodimex were corporate reports, corporate histories, and industry association reports, such as "Russia's Agricultural Giant—Prodimex," *Manufacturing Journal*, 2019; Rusagro, *Growth Drivers—Annual Report 2018* (Moscow: Rusagro Group, 2018).

101. Sources for information related to Miratorg and Cherkizovo were annual reports, company press releases, industry reporting, and information by technology suppliers. See also Irina Skrynnik, "Nastuplenie svin'ei: Kak 'Miratorg' zavoeval Rossiiskii produktovyi rynok," *Forbes Business*, October 16, 2014; and Aleksander Levinsky, "Kak 'Miratorg' s pomoshch'iu gosudarstva stal prodovol'stvennym gigantom," *Forbes Business*, April 7, 2019.

102. Rachel Vanderberg, *2017 Poultry and Products: Growth through Integration* GAIN Report (USDA Foreign Agriculture Service, Washington, DC, August 18, 2017).

103. Miratorg, *Asian Catalogue* (Moscow: Miratorg Agribusiness Holding, 2019).

104. These maps were compiled based on data provided by the annual reports by the five largest agroholdings in the south and west and the twelve largest agroholdings in Siberia and the Far East, as ranked by *Agroinvestor* in 2018.

105. Despite having brought enormously valuable assets under the umbrella of one organization, the government refrained from placing government representatives on the UGC board; the statist faction of Putin's government criticized this move, as did

the Ministry of Agriculture. See "Pochemu v rukovodstve OZK net predstavitelei Minsel'khoza?," *Krest'ianskie vedomosti*, March 13, 2014.

106. The winning bidder was Summa Group, which paid 5.951 billion rubles ($198 million) for UGC shares in what appeared to have been a competitive tender. See Yelena Vassilieva, *Russian Federation: Agriculture Development Program 2013–2020*, GAIN Report (Washington, DC: USDA Foreign Agriculture Service, 2012).

107. The full quote on the Cherkizovo corporate website (https://cherkizovo.com/, section on corporate history) reads as follows: "Realizing the need for import substitution in the food market, Mr. Babaev and his team acquired and modernized poultry farms, pig farms, feed mills and meat processing plants."

108. Statement by Aleksandr Vinokurov, the president of Summa Group, quoted in Vassilieva, *Russian Federation: Agriculture Development Program 2013–2020*.

109. Information retrieved from Exima website, accessed June 2019, http://www.exima.ru/company/. Full quote: "Kompaniia prinimaet aktivnoe uchastie v realizatsii Gosudarstvennoi programmy razvitiia sel'skogo khoziaistva Rossii do 2020 goda."

110. See Miratorg website, accessed June 2020, https://miratorg.ru/en/about/.

111. Interview by author with Dmitri Rylko, Moscow, July 2014.

112. Arup Banerji, "Food Shortages in Russia," *Economic and Political Weekly* 29, no. 19 (May 7, 1994): 1148.

113. Ioffe, Nefedova, and Zaslavsky, *The End of Peasantry?*

114. See product catalogs available on the Russian corporate websites for these companies. For example, Bayer Agroscience, *Katalog produktsii*, available at https://www.cropscience.bayer.ru/; and Corteva Agriscience (Pioneer/DuPont), Katalog 2019, each listing dozens of herbicides, pesticides, retardants, and seed treatments.

115. In map 2.4, the data for technology are compiled by the author; for the origins of financial investment, see Visser and Spoor, "Land Grabbing in Post-Soviet Eurasia." Table 2.4 is compiled using several sources of information from agroholding corporate reports and exhibitors at Russia's agricultural fairs.

116. See Claas website, section "Overview," accessed June 2021, https://www.claas-group.com/the-group/about-claas/overview.

117. See Mondi Group website, "Our History," accessed June 2021, https://www.mondigroup.com/en/about-mondi/our-history/.

118. Ibid.; Mondi Group, "Mondi Syktyvkar: A Russian Success Story Turns 50" (press release, July 19, 2019). For background on the packaging industry, see United States Government, International Trade Administration, *Russia—Food Processing and Packaging* (Washington, DC: ITO, August 14, 2019).

119. Interview by author with Andrey Lyan, Cargill Moscow government relations office, May 19, 2016.

120. Susanne Wengle, "When Experimentalist Governance Meets Science-Based Regulations; the Case of Food Safety Regulations," *Regulation & Governance* 10, no. 3 (2016): 262–83.

121. Interview by the author with Musheg Mamykonyan, director of the Russian Meat Association, Moscow, May 2016. See also Dmitrii Katalevskii and Aleksei Iu. Ivanov, *Sovremennye agrotekhnologii: Ekonomiko-pravovye i reguliatornye aspekty* (Moscow: Institute for Law and Development, Higher School of Economics / Skolkovo, 2018), 375.

122. Christopher D. Lander, "Foreign Investment Adaptations to the Changing Political and Economic Environments of the Agro-Food Sector," *Problems of Post-Communism* 65, no. 3 (May 4, 2018): 201–19.

123. Ekaterina Diatlovskaia, "Pravitel'stvo obsuzhdaet novuiu sistemu otneseniia sel'khoztekhniki k rossiiskoi," *Agroinvestor*, January 23, 2019; Katalevskii and Ivanov, *Sovremennye agrotekhnologii*.

124. The knowledge dimension of farming is explicitly examined by a study on farming in Kazakhstan, by Kazbek Toleubayev and coauthors, addressing this question: "Has farming knowledge developed in the Soviet era become irrelevant or is it still being used and adapted in the recent period?" They observe a "loss of knowledge and the disrupt[ion of] knowledge structure" as well as a "scarcity of agro-technicians." See Toleubayev, Jansen, and Huis, "Knowledge and Agrarian De-Collectivisation in Kazakhstan." For a study of knowledge specific to a particular region in Russia, see Insa Theesfeld and Ladislav Jelinek, "A Misfit in Policy to Protect Russia's Black Soil Region: An Institutional Analytical Lens Applied to the Ban on Burning of Crop Residues," *Land Use Policy* 67 (September 1, 2017): 517–26. Oane Visser, a leading expert on post-Soviet agriculture, reports in communication with the author that Western consultants are sometimes frustrated that Russian agroholdings are willing to pay for machines but not for training and knowledge components.

125. Insa Theesfeld and Ladislav Jelinek observe, for example, that a traditional Russian practice—that of burning crop residues on fields—has persisted, despite an international consensus that tilling crop residues is environmentally more sustainable and even domestic legislation that mandates conservation tillage. Theesfeld and Jelinek, "A Misfit in Policy to Protect Russia's Black Soil Region."

126. Katalevskii and Ivanov, *Sovremennye agrotekhnologii*.

127. This is evident in data by the Russian government and FAO; see also Raushan Bokusheva, Heinrich Hockman, and Subal Kumbakhar, "Dynamics of Productivity and Technical Efficiency in Russian Agriculture," *European Review of Agricultural Economics* 39, no. 4 (2012): 611–37.

128. Russia harvested about 83 million metric tons of wheat in 2017. For comparison with 1978, see "Russian Federation: Grain and Feed Update" (USDA FAS, October 27, 2017). The high yield estimates are from the Russian Ministry of Agriculture, quoted by USDA: "According to the Ministry of Agriculture, Russia's harvest of grain is estimated at 105 MMT, 30 MMT less than its record high crop of 135.4 MMT in MY2017/18." United States Department of Agriculture, *Russian Federation: Grain and Feed Update* (Washington, DC: USDA FAS, October 10, 2018).

129. United States Department of Agriculture, *Russian Federation: Grain and Feed Update* (Washington, DC: USDA FAS, October 27, 2017).

130. Data retrieved from the UN Food and Agriculture database FAO STAT, accessed June 2021, http://www.fao.org/faostat/en/.

131. Different sources quote different yields. According to FAO STAT, Russian wheat yields in 2017 were 3.1 MT/ha; see http://www.fao.org/faostat/en/.

132. Robin Gray, *Russian Federation: Sugar Annual Sugar Update 2017*, GAIN Report (Washington, DC: USDA Foreign Agriculture Service, April 14, 2017). For a more detailed report on the sugar industry, see Food and Agriculture Organization,

Sugar Sector Review: Russian Federation, Report on Sugar Industry in Russia (Rome: UN FAO, 2013).

133. Goskomstat Rossii, *Sel'skoe khoziaistvo v Rossii* (Moscow: Goskomstat Rossii, 2013, 1995). Industry reports by the major meat industry associations attest to these trends. Finally, successive USDA FAS GAIN Reports are also good resources for tracking consolidation.

134. A growing number of studies on food systems in Western capitalist economies track the negative externalities of this kind of mass production; see the introduction and conclusion of this book for discussion and references.

135. Allina-Pisano, *The Post-Soviet Potemkin Village*, 52.

136. Vorbrugg, "Not About Land, Not Quite a Grab," 1011–31.

137. Ioffe, Nefedova, and Zaslavsky, *The End of Peasantry?*, 18. The authors referred to villagers as "de facto" social outcasts.

138. A Rusagro representative, in a 2014 interview with the author in Moscow, was skeptical about the qualities of the rural local labor force. See also the interview with Adrian Schairer, head of investor relations at Ekosem-Agrar, in "EkoNiva Is Taking Advantage of the Window of Opportunity," published by LaScalA, the Competence Center on Large Scale Agriculture at the Leibniz Institute for Agricultural Development, Germany, February 5, 2019. "EkoNiva: In general, it is difficult to find good staff with reasonable compensation conditions. Therefore, we have been training our own specialists at our academy for several years. At the EkoNiva academy, experienced employees teach prospective specialists. In addition, we work with universities throughout Russia, offer a large internship program with nearly 1,000 student participants in 2018, and promote so-called agricultural classes in schools. With these measures, we have sufficient qualified personnel for our current growth strategy." Andrey Lyan, a representative for Cargill, by contrast argued that Cargill has relied on good workers (interview with author, Cargill Moscow government relations office, 2016). See also the discussion of agroholdings and their relationship to rural workers in Ioffe, Nefedova, and Zaslavsky, *The End of Peasantry?*, 92.

139. Serova, "Farm Restructuring in Transition." For research on these interactions between NAOs and local residents, see Alexander Nikulin, "The Kuban Kolkhoz between a Holding and a Hacienda," *Focaal Journal of Global and Historical Anthropology*, no. 41 (2003): 137–52; Pallot and Nefedova, *Russia's Unknown Agriculture*; and Max Spoor and Oane Visser, "Restructuring Postponed? Large Russian Farm Enterprises' Coping with the Market," *Journal of Peasant Studies* 31, nos. 3–4 (2004): 515–51. I also relied on author's interview with Rusagro representative, Moscow, July 2014. See also Azarieva, *Grain and Power in Russia 2001–2011*.

140. Ioffe, Nefedova, and Zaslavsky, *The End of Peasantry?*, 103. See Jiayi Zhou for Chinese farms in the Russian Far East: Zhou, "Chinese Agrarian Capitalism in the Russian Far East," 612–32.

141. Oane Visser, Natalia Mamonova, and Max Spoor, "Oligarchs, Megafarms and Land Reserves: Understanding Land Grabbing in Russia," *Journal of Peasant Studies* 39, no. 3 (2012): 899–932. Pallot and Nefedova and Nikulin reported that NAOs invest in churches and schools; Nikulin observed that one NAO manager collected funds to build a church and hire a priest. See Nikulin, "From Post-Kolkhoz to Oligarkhoz." On

the corporate social responsibility programs of large farms, see also Visser, Kurakin, and Nikulin, "Corporate Social Responsibility, Coexistence and Contestation."

142. Visser and Mamonova, *Large-Scale Land Acquisitions in the Former Soviet Union*; Miroslava Bavorová, Zuzana Bednarikova, Elena V. Ponkina, and Oane Visser, "Agribusiness Social Responsibility in Emerging Economies: Effects of Legal Structure, Economic Performance and Managers' Motivations," *Journal of Cleaner Production* 289 (March 2021).

143. Pallot and Nefedova, *Russia's Unknown Agriculture*.

144. Prikhodko and Davleyev, *Russian Federation*, 25.

145. According to data by the Federal'naia sluzhba gosudarstvennoi statistiki, *Osnovnye pokazateli sel'skogo khoziaistva v Rossii* (Moscow: Rosstat, 1995–2013). See also Michael Smith and Mikhail Maximenko, *Russian Federation: Poultry and Products*, GAIN Report (Washington, DC: USDA Foreign Agriculture Service, 2000).

146. Goskomstat data in *Sel'skoe khoziaistvo v Rossii* (multiple years). For the estimate by the Russian Union of Poultry Producers, see Holly Higgens, *Poultry Products Semi-Annual*, GAIN Report (Washington, DC: USDA Foreign Agriculture Service, 2014).

147. The 70 percent in 2005 is an official estimate by the Union of Pork Producers, quoted in Higgens, *2014 Livestock and Products Semi-Annual Report*. See also data in *Sel'skoe khoziaistvo v Rossii*, esp. tables on "Livestock Inventory by Types of Enterprises."

148. This is an assessment by Musheg Mamykonyan, director of the Russian Meat Association, interview with author, Moscow, May 2016. Vladislav Vorotnikov, "Large Avian Flu Outbreak Hits Moscow Oblast," *Global Meat News*, March 7, 2017, estimates the number at 23,000–27,000 destroyed head of pork for 2014; see also Haas and Maximenko, *Russian Federation Livestock and Products Semi-Annual*. In a recent case, in March 2017, ASF was reported in one small-scale farm near Irkutsk. The reaction that was thought to be required was swift and extensive: "In a 5-km risk zone established around the affected farm, 1,327 pigs were slaughtered within 3 days." Kolbasov et al., "African Swine Fever Virus, Siberia, Russia, 2017." See also Bloomberg News, "Can China Learn from Russia and Save Its Pigs from African Swine Fever?," *South China Morning Post*, December 7, 2018.

149. Oane Visser, Natalia Mamonova, Max Spoor, and Alexander Nikulin, "'Quiet Food Sovereignty' as Food Sovereignty without a Movement? Insights from Post-Socialist Russia," *Globalizations* 12, no. 4 (July 4, 2015): 518.

150. Peter Hobson, "Russian Pig Cull Leaves Farmers Facing Ruin," *The Independent*, August 30, 2015.

151. Author interviews with Russian journalists covering agriculture, Moscow, 2016. This is also noted by Jehlička et al., "Thinking Food Like an East European."

152. Visser et al., "'Quiet Food Sovereignty' as Food Sovereignty without a Movement?" The continuation of some subsistence practices, though in a new context, is not an overt resistance movement or an explicit struggle for rights and land-claims but a "quiet food sovereignty" that deserves attention as such.

153. This is documented by a study on farming in Kazakhstan: Toleubayev, Jansen, and Huis, "Knowledge and Agrarian De-Collectivisation in Kazakhstan," 367.

154. See information on vendors published on Lavka Lavka websites, https://lavka lavka.rest/project/nina-kozlova/ and https://lavkalavka.rest/project/ruslan-zheltenko/.

155. Wengle, "The Domestic Effects of the Russian Food Embargo," 281–89.

156. Natalia Shagaida and Vasily Uzun, "The Agriculture and Food: Does Import Substitution Take Place?," *Russian Economic Developments*, no. 11 (2015): 52.

157. Chris Harris, "Is Russia Nearing Self-Sufficiency in Meat?," *Farm Gate to Fork*, May 12, 2016.

158. Rachel Vanderberg, *Russian Federation Livestock and Products Semi-Annual 2016 Report*, GAIN Report (Washington, DC: USDA Foreign Agriculture Service, March 3, 2016), 12. Imports of live swine declined by 68 percent, from 8,000 head in January 2014 to only 1,000 head in January 2015 and January 2016.

159. Stephen K. Wegren and Christel Elvestad, "Russia's Food Self-Sufficiency and Food Security: An Assessment," *Post-Communist Economies* 30, no. 5 (September 3, 2018): 565–87.

160. Interview by the author with Sergey Yushin, head of the National Meat Association, Moscow, May 2016.

161. This is according to press releases by the respective companies. See http://www.miratorg.ru/ and http://cherkizovo.com/. Increased sales already started in 2014; see Sam Skove, "Despite Kremlin's Promises, Russian Food Ban Fails to Deliver," *Moscow Times*, June 30, 2015.

162. C. Harris, "Is Russia Nearing Self-Sufficiency in Meat?"

163. Vanderberg, *Russian Federation Livestock and Products Semi-Annual 2016 Report*.

164. Data by Federal Customs Service, cited in Shagaida and Uzun, "The Agriculture and Food."

165. Marina Obrazkova, "Russian Fishing Industry Witnesses Stable Growth," *Russia beyond the Headlines*, June 29, 2015.

166. Vanderberg, *Russian Federation Livestock and Products Semi-Annual 2016 Report*, 20.

167. Zheleznova, "Zhizn' na bezryb'e," 2016.

168. Ekaterina Burlakova, "Proizvodstvo syrnykh produktov s zameniteliami zhira upalo vpervye za deviat' let," *Vedemosti*, December 24, 2019.

169. Elizaveta Vereykina, "Sanctions Spark Russian Cheese Industry Boom," *Moscow Times*, June 1, 2015.

170. This trend was noted in the author's interview with a representative of Damate, a dairy and poultry agroholding, Moscow, 2016. EkoNiva was an exception to this trend.

171. Natalia Karlova, Vasily Uzun, and Natalia Shagaida, "Russian Agriculture: The Impact of Sanctions," Published Research Paper no. 212 (Moscow: Gaidar Institute for Economic Policy, 2015), 3.

172. Schairer, "EkoNiva Is Taking Advantage of the Window of Opportunity." For a comparison: this is roughly the size of a very large US dairy farm. FairOaks Farms, located in the state of Indiana in the US, milks roughly the same number of cows.

173. This information is gathered from the company's corporate newsletter, EkoNiva Novosti.

Chapter 3. Consumption; or, Perestroika of the Quotidian

Chapter epigraphs: Sergei Grammatin, teacher, January 28, 1951, Prozhito Archive; Erkin Zholdasov, artist, June 30, 1983, Prozhito Archive; oligarch quoted in Schimpfössl, *Rich Russians*, viii.

1. Historians and anthropologists such as Susan Reid, Caroline Humphrey, and Catriona Kelly have tracked the role of consumption and consumers in the radical transformations of the socialist and post-socialist social order; see Reid, "Cold War in the Kitchen"; Humphrey, *Unmasking of Soviet Life*; Catriona Kelly and David Shepherd, *Constructing Russian Culture in the Age of Revolution, 1881–1940* (Oxford: Oxford University Press, 1998); and Elizabeth Cullen Dunn, *Privatizing Poland: Baby Food, Big Business, and the Remaking of Labor* (Ithaca, NY: Cornell University Press, 2004).

2. Vladimir Vernadskii, "25 ianvaria 1938," Prozhito, January 25, 1938.

3. Sergei Grammatin, "28 ianvaria 1951," Prozhito, January 28, 1951, remembering a meal with family and neighbors.

4. Boris Vronskii, "10 fevralia 1961," Prozhito, February 10, 1961.

5. Iurii Lapshin, "25 avgusta 1988," Prozhito, August 25, 1988.

6. Tat'iana Korob'ina, "17 ianvaria 1991," Prozhito, January 17, 1991.

7. Lev Osterman, "2 iiunia 1992," Prozhito, June 2, 1992.

8. Stephen Wegren, *Russia's Food Policies and Globalization* (Lanham, MD: Lexington Books, 2005), 7.

9. Notably, both Soviet and post-Soviet regimes tried to define norms of consumption. In the 1960s, they were called "normative consumption budgets." See Reid, "Cold War in the Kitchen," 214 and 219. In the Putin era, they have been defined as "rational norms of consumption."

10. Yuri Slezkine, *The House of Government* (Princeton, NJ: Princeton University Press, 2017), 192, 220, and 225.

11. Schimpfössl, *Rich Russians*, viii.

12. Reid, "Cold War in the Kitchen," 211. See also Gail Lapidus, *Women, Work and Family in the Soviet Union* (London: Routledge, 1982). The fact that subsistence farming was mostly woman's work is noteworthy in this context. See chapter 2.

13. Emmanuel Skoufias, "Consumption Smoothing in Russia," *Economics of Transition and Institutional Change* 11, no. 1 (2003): 67–91.

14. Gronow, *Caviar with Champagne*.

15. Moss, *Salt, Sugar, Fat*; Michael Pollan, *The Omnivore's Dilemma: A Natural History of Four Meals* (New York: Penguin, 2006).

16. Moss, *Salt, Sugar, Fat*. For a discussion of obesity, see chapter 6.

17. Ronald LeBlanc, "The Ethics and Politics of Diet: Tolstoy, Pilnyak, and the Modern Slaughterhouse," *Gastronomica: The Journal of Critical Food Studies* 17, no. 4 (November 1, 2017): 9–25.

18. Halina Rothstein and Robert A. Rothstein, "Beginnings of Soviet Culinary Arts," in *Food in Russian History and Culture*, ed. Musya Glants and Joyce Toomre (Bloomington: Indiana University Press, 1997), 184.

19. Gronow, *Caviar with Champagne*, 4.

20. Schechter, "The State's Pot and the Soldier's Spoon." See also Brandon Schechter, *The Stuff of Soldiers: A History of the Red Army in World War II through Objects* (Ithaca, NY: Cornell University Press, 2019).
21. Gronow, *Caviar with Champagne*.
22. Olga Syutkin and Pavel Syutkin, *CCCP Cook Book*, 44.
23. J. Smith, "Empire of Ice Cream."
24. Laura Goering, "Marketing Soviet Nostalgia: The Many Faces of Buratino," *Gastronomica* 17, no. 4 (November 1, 2017): 88–101.
25. J. Smith, "Empire of Ice Cream."
26. Gronow, *Caviar with Champagne*.
27. Syutkin and Syutkin, *CCCP Cook Book*, 36.
28. Ibid., 154.
29. Crumley, *Sowing Market Reforms*, 64.
30. J. Smith, "Empire of Ice Cream."
31. Syutkin and Syutkin, *CCCP Cook Book*.
32. Medvedev, *Soviet Agriculture*, 219.
33. J. Smith, "Empire of Ice Cream."
34. The famous Stalin-era cookbook the *Book of Tasty and Healthy Food* was largely aspirational in the sense that it assumed that sophisticated ingredients and fabulous dinnerware were available to all. Later editions admit to some of the scarcities and suggest ways for the home cook to work around them. See Edward Geist, "Cooking Bolshevik: Anastas Mikoian and the Making of the 'Book about Delicious and Healthy Food,'" *Russian Review* 71, no. 2 (April 2012): 295–313.
35. For a description of family food procurement as a "group effort," see Sarah Moir, "The People's Phenomenon: 'Author's Song' in Khrushchev's Soviet Union," *Constructing the Past* 13, no. 1 (2012).
36. Humphrey, *Unmasking of Soviet Life*, 52.
37. Wegren, *Russia's Food Policies and Globalization*, 37.
38. Caldwell, *Food and Everyday Life in the Post-Socialist World*; Syutkin and Syutkin, *CCCP Cook Book*, 16.
39. PepsiCo entered a deal with the Soviet government in 1972: in exchange for distributing Stolichnaya Vodka in the US, Pepsi could produce, market, and distribute Pepsi in the Soviet Union starting in 1974.
40. See ethnographies of consumption, especially Humphrey, *Unmasking of Soviet Life*, 40.
41. Ries, "Potato Ontology."
42. LeBlanc, "The Ethics and Politics of Diet." LeBlanc argues that proponents of vegetarian diets ran afoul of the political regimes that felt threatened by their critiques.
43. Rothstein and Rothstein, "Beginnings of Soviet Culinary Arts."
44. Konstantin Izmailov, "2 iiunia," Prozhito, June 2, 1933.
45. Jenny Leigh Smith, "Tushonka: Cultivating Soviet Postwar Taste," *Media/Culture Journal* 13, no. 5 (October 17, 2010).
46. Filadel'f Parshinskii, "4 noiabria 1941," Prozhito, November 4, 1941.
47. Sergei Grammatin, "10 dekabria 1951," Prozhito, December 10, 1951.
48. Syutkin and Syutkin, *CCCP Cook Book*, 22.

49. J. Smith, "Tushonka."
50. Syutkin and Syutkin, *CCCP Cook Book*, 122.
51. See chapter 4 for a discussion of Soviet animal breeds and animal genetics.
52. Josef C. Brada, Karl-Eugen Wädekin, and Ihor Stebelsky, *Socialist Agriculture in Transition: Organizational Response to Failing Performance* (Boulder, CO: Westview, 1988), 75.
53. Data by the UN Food and Agriculture Organization, FAO STAT. See also "Meat Consumption per Capita," *The Guardian*, September 2, 2009.
54. Central Intelligence Agency, *Nutrient Content of Soviet Food Supply* (Washington, DC: Directorate of Intelligence, US Government Central Intelligence Agency, 1984), 14.
55. Lev Levitskii, "14 sentiabria 1978," Prozhito, September 14, 1978.
56. Syutkin and Syutkin, *CCCP Cook Book*, 36 and 38.
57. Anton Masterovoy, "Eating Soviet: Food and Culture in the USSR, 1917–1991" (PhD diss., City University of New York, 2013). This source refers to the kinds of jokes circulating at the time.
58. Korob'ina, "17 ianvaria 1991."
59. Wegren, *Russia's Food Policies and Globalization*, 13.
60. Prikhodko and Davleyev, *Russian Federation*, 18.
61. Ibid., 64.
62. See Miratorg's product catalog *Frozen Convenience Food and Ready Meals* (Moscow: Miratorg Agribusiness Holding, 2017), 6.
63. Rothstein and Rothstein, "Beginnings of Soviet Culinary Arts." See chapter 11, esp. 177.
64. Mauricio Borrero, "Communal Dining and State Cafeterias in Moscow and Petrograd, 1917–1921," in *Food in Russian History and Culture*, ed. Musya Glants and Joyce Toomre (Bloomington: Indiana University Press, 1997), 162–76.
65. According to N. A. Semashko, commissar of health, quoted in Rothstein and Rothstein, "Beginnings of Soviet Culinary Arts," 178.
66. Ibid.
67. Ibid., 169. See also Nérard, "Variations on a Shchi Theme."
68. Gronow, *Caviar with Champagne*, 35.
69. Syutkin and Syutkin, *CCCP Cook Book*.
70. There are many sources for the role of the communal kitchen. See, for example, Steven E. Harris, *Communism on Tomorrow Street: Mass Housing and Everyday Life after Stalin* (Baltimore, MD: Johns Hopkins University Press, 2013); and Anya von Bremzen, *Mastering the Art of Soviet Cooking: A Memoir of Food and Longing* (London: Doubleday, 2013). For images, see Ilya Utekhin, Alice Nakhimovsky, Slava Paperno, and Nancy Ries, *Communal Living in Russia: A Virtual Museum of Everyday Life*, Colgate University, accessed May 2021, https://russlang.as.cornell.edu/komm/.
71. Reid, "Cold War in the Kitchen," 227.
72. Ibid., 228.
73. Adrianne Jacobs, "The Many Flavors of Socialism: Food Culture in Late Soviet Russia, 1965–1985" (PhD diss., University of North Carolina, Chapel Hill, 2015).

74. George Cohon and David Macfarlane, *To Russia with Fries: My Journey from Chicago's South Side to Moscow's Red Square* (Toronto, Canada: McClelland & Stewart, 1999).

75. Deanna Ayala and Alla Putiy, *Food Service-Hotel Restaurant Institutional*, GAIN Report (Moscow: USDA Foreign Agriculture Service, March 3, 2011); Andrew E. Kramer, "Russia Becomes a Magnet for US Fast-Food Chains," *New York Times*, August 3, 2011.

76. Erik Hansen, *Fast Food Sector Keeps Expanding, As Economy Cools*, GAIN Report (Washington, DC: USDA Foreign Agriculture Service, November 13, 2014)

77. Vanderberg, *Poultry and Products*.

78. Erik Hansen, *Franchise Restaurants Doing Well Despite Slowing Economy*, GAIN Report (Washington, DC: USDA Foreign Agriculture Service, May 18, 2015).

79. Vanderberg, *Poultry and Products*. This report quotes research by a Russian consulting firm that found 70 percent of Russian residents of large cities eat at fast food restaurants several times a month, spending between 150 and 300 rubles per visit.

80. Author's interview with Andrey Lyan, Cargill Moscow government relations office, Moscow, May 19, 2016. See also Crumley, *Sowing Market Reforms*.

81. "Edim Doma" has a web presence. See *Ofitsial'nyi sait kulinarnykh retseptov Iulii Vysotskoi*, https://www.edimdoma.ru/.

82. Miratorg, *Frozen Convenience Food and Ready Meals*, 19.

83. Caldwell, *Dacha Idylls*.

84. Wegren, *Russia's Food Policies and Globalization*, 4.

85. Syutkin and Syutkin, *CCCP Cook Book*, 186.

86. Crumley, *Sowing Market Reforms*, 71.

87. Lunze et al., "Food Security and Nutrition in the Russian Federation."

88. Svetlana Barsukova, "Mobilizing Patriotism in Russia," *Russian Analytical Digest*, no. 207 (Center for Security Studies at ETH Zürich, October 2, 2017); Svetlana Barsukova, "Ekonomicheskii patriotizm na prodovol'stvennykh rynkakh: Importozameshchenie i realizatsiia eksportnogo potentsiala," *Zhurnal institutsional'nykh issledovanii* 2, no. 2 (2010): 118–34.

89. For example, Crumley, *Sowing Market Reforms*, 120.

90. Wengle, "The Domestic Effects of the Russian Food Embargo," 281–89.

91. Gronow, *Caviar with Champagne*, 13.

92. Ibid., 122.

93. Jacobs, "The Many Flavors of Socialism"; Syutkin and Syutkin, *CCCP Cook Book*, 186.

94. Crumley notes that this was the case despite fluctuations in prices for imported goods; Soviet consumers were thus shielded from international price fluctuations. See Crumley, *Sowing Market Reforms*, 16.

95. Kim, "Causes of Repressed Inflation in the Soviet Consumer Market,"109. For higher prices on kolkhoz markets, see Wädekin, *Privatproduzenten in der Sowjetischen Landwirtschaft*, 95.

96. These black-market venues were semi-tolerated during some periods but at other times experienced crackdowns. Borrero, "Communal Dining and State Cafeterias in

Moscow and Petrograd," 172; Cathy Young, *Growing Up in Moscow: Memories of a Soviet Girlhood* (New York: Ticknor & Fields, 1989).

97. Gronow, *Caviar with Champagne*, 124.

98. On food provisions in Soviet and post-Soviet Kamchatka, see Thompson, *Settlers on the Edge*.

99. Nérard, "Variations on a Shchi Theme."

100. Young, *Growing Up in Moscow*.

101. New York Public Library Menu Collection, NYPL Labs, http://menus.nypl.org/.

102. See Humphrey, *Unmaking of Soviet Life*, 45 and 44: "there used to be an underlying sense that for the most part goods were not really bought by choice but allocated."

103. See the discussion of starvation and hunger in the twenties and thirties in chapters 1 and 2 of this book.

104. Mikhail Grobman, "12 iiulia 1969," Prozhito, July 12, 1969.

105. Brada, Wädekin, and Stebelsky, *Socialist Agriculture in Transition*, 72.

106. Kenneth R. Gray, *Soviet Agriculture: Comparative Perspectives* (Iowa City: Iowa State University Press, 1990), 68.

107. Wädekin, *Privatproduzenten in der Sowjetischen Landwirtschaft*, 95.

108. Caldwell, *Food and Everyday Life in the Post-Socialist World*; Humphrey, *Unmaking of Soviet Life*, 45.

109. Syutkin and Syutkin, *CCCP Cook Book*, 171.

110. Gronow, *Caviar with Champagne*, 123.

111. In fact, the name of the chain stems from its origin as a network of souvenir stores serving foreign tourists.

112. Anna Ivanova, "Shopping in Beriozka: Consumer Society in the Soviet Union," *Zeithistorische Forschungen* 10, no. 2 (2013): 243–63; Tommy O'Callaghan, "Beryozka Shops: How Soviet Citizens Bought Scarce Goods with Foreign Currency," *Russia Beyond the Headlines*, April 29, 2018. See also Humphrey, *Unmaking of Soviet Life*, 41. On special "hard currency stores" called "Torgsin" that were set up in the 1920s, see Gronow, *Caviar with Champagne*, 33.

113. Humphrey, *Unmaking of Soviet Life*, 55.

114. Lisa Jahns, Alexander Baturin, and Barry Popkin, "Obesity, Diet, and Poverty: Trends in the Russian Transition to Market Economy," *European Journal of Clinical Nutrition* 57, no. 10 (2003): 1295–1302.

115. Melissa L. Caldwell, "The Taste of Nationalism: Food Politics in Postsocialist Moscow," *Ethnos* 67, no. 3 (January 1, 2002): 295–319.

116. Banerji, "Food Shortages in Russia."

117. Wegren, *Russia's Food Policies and Globalization*, 18. For a reference to elderly pensioners, see p. 12.

118. Lunze et al., "Food Security and Nutrition in the Russian Federation."

119. Ibid., 18, 12. For an ethnography of Chukotka and poverty in the remote north, see Thompson, *Settlers on the Edge*.

120. Wegren, *Russia's Food Policies and Globalization*.

121. Gessen, "Food Import Ban Means Russia Is at War with the West."

122. Leo Tolstoy, *Anna Karenina*, trans. Richard Pevear and Larissa Volokhonsky (Netherlands: Penguin, 2002), 35. See the discussion by Ronald LeBlanc, *Slavic Sins of the Flesh: Food, Sex, and Carnal Appetite in Nineteenth-Century Russian Fiction* (Durham, NH: University of New Hampshire Press, 2009). That the Oblonsky-Levin contrast serves as a metaphor for cultural battles in contemporary Russia is noted by Ivan Nechepurenko in "You Are What You Eat: Why Food, Culture and Politics Go Hand in Hand in Russia," *Calvert Journal*, September 3, 2014.

123. Gronow, *Caviar with Champagne*, 9.

124. "USSR Pavilion Restaurant: Menus: What's on the Menu?," New York Public Library Menus Collection, accessed June 2020, http://menus.nypl.org/menu_pages/59129.

125. Adrianne Jacobs, "V. V. Pokhlëbkin and the Search for Culinary Roots in Late Soviet Russia," *Cahiers Du Monde Russe* 54, nos. 1–2 (2013): 165–86.

126. Syutkin and Syutkin, *CCCP Cook Book*.

127. Ibid., 108. See also Jacobs, "The Many Flavors of Socialism."

128. For the history of Korean food in the Soviet Union since the late-imperial era, see Changzoo Song, "Kimchi, Seaweed, and Seasoned Carrot in the Soviet Culinary Culture: The Spread of Korean Food in the Soviet Union and Korean Diaspora," *Journal of Ethnic Foods* 3, no. 1 (March 1, 2016): 80.

129. Barsukova, "Mobilizing Patriotism in Russia," 8.

130. This is the statement by the founder of Teremok, one of Russia's most successful fast-food chains; see Talia Lavin, "A Russian Fast-Food Chain Tries Its Luck in America," *New Yorker*, April 13, 2017. On the "imaginary West," see Alexei Yurchak, *Everything Was Forever, until It Was No More: The Last Soviet Generation* (Princeton, NJ: Princeton University Press, 2006).

131. Caldwell, "The Taste of Nationalism."

132. Barsukova, "Mobilizing Patriotism in Russia."

133. Sergey Chernov, "Spreading It on Thick: Russia's Latest Supermarket Substitutes," RadioFreeEurope/RadioLiberty, January 22, 2015; Barsukova, "Mobilizing Patriotism in Russia." See also Barsukova, "Ekonomicheskii patriotizm na prodovol'stvennykh rynkakh."

134. Melinda Joe, "Dining under Putin: How Sanctions Are Fueling a Russian Food Revolution," *CNN*, November 29, 2016. See White Rabbit's menus: https://wrh.su.

135. Lavka Lavka's founder argues that "we believe that food isn't just food," and that "we are what we eat." See Lavka Lavka's website, accessed May 2021, https://lavkalavka.com/.

136. Keith Livers, "From Fecal Briquettes to Candy Kremlins: The Edible Ideal in Sorokin's Prose," *Gastronomica* 17, no. 4 (November 1, 2017): 26–35.

137. Caldwell, *Dacha Idylls*.

138. Ibid.; Humphrey, *Unmaking of Soviet Life*, 56.

139. For example, *Afisha Eda*, a popular print and online lifestyle publication, runs master classes on classics of Russian cuisine. One example of a contribution is Marina Shakleina's "How to make soup from white mushrooms" (Kak varit' sup iz belykh gribov).

140. Masterovoy, "Eating Soviet," 81.

141. Goering, "Marketing Soviet Nostalgia."
142. Barsukova calls this "gastronomic patriotism." Barsukova, "Mobilizing Patriotism in Russia."
143. Teremok website, *Nashe meniu*, accessed May 2021, http://teremok.ru/menu/.

Chapter 4. Nature

Chapter epigraphs: Fyodor Kirichenko, Soviet geneticist, 1920, quoted by Belderok, Mesdag, and Donner, *Bread-Making Quality of Wheat*, 371; Znamensk Genetic Selection Center, on the Libra/Svinka F1 parent stock pig, "Roditel'skaia svinka (F1)," 2020, http://nsgc.ru/produkciya/roditelskaya-svinka-f1.

1. Richard Bell, *Comparison of Agriculture in the United States and the Soviet Union*.
2. Florian Schierhorn et al., "Quantifying Yield Gaps in Wheat Production in Russia," *Environmental Research Letters* 9, no. 8 (2014): 9. Droughts are reflected in recurring years of bad harvests—in the Soviet period, the years 1965, 1967, 1972, 1975, and 1979 were all known to be catastrophically bad. Nove, *An Economic History of the USSR*, 379.
3. This is a central argument by J. Smith, *Works in Progress*, 12.
4. Moon, *The Plough That Broke the Steppes*. See also Johannes Kamp et al., "Agricultural Development and the Conservation of Avian Biodiversity on the Eurasian Steppes: A Comparison of Land-Sparing and Land-Sharing Approaches," *Journal of Applied Ecology* 52, no. 6 (2015): 1578–87.
5. See Billie L. Turner et al., eds., *The Earth as Transformed by Human Action: Global and Regional Changes in the Biosphere over the Past 300 Years* (Cambridge, UK: Cambridge University Press, 1990), 12.
6. Scott, *Against the Grain*. Scott argues that the process of domestication, in which "humans have intervened to gain more control of the reproductive functions of the plants and animals that interest us," was more gradual and lasted much longer than is generally assumed (12).
7. Fullilove, *The Profit of the Earth*, 1.
8. Winner, "Do Artifacts Have Politics?," 135, emphasis added.
9. Bruno, *The Nature of Soviet Power*, 9.
10. J. Smith, *Works in Progress*, 60.
11. Bruno, *The Nature of Soviet Power*; B. Demuth, *Floating Coast*. In *Works in Progress*, Jenny Smith calls for a focus on nature's resistance as another way to think about why Soviet-era collective farms produced less efficiently than Western counterparts. This allows her to revise the narrative on the question of who is to blame for the apparently low performance of Soviet farms: it was not the peasants' backwardness, as Stalin claimed, or the wastefulness of the planned economy, as Western historians argue.
12. Bruno, *The Nature of Soviet Power*, 125; Demuth, *Floating Coast*, 138.
13. Stephen Brain, "The Great Stalin Plan for the Transformation of Nature," *Environmental History* 15, no. 4 (2010): 673. I borrow the label "promethean" in the discussion here from Bain's work.
14. See Bruno, *The Nature of Soviet Power*, 12 for an imperial-era official's comparison of nature with a treasure chest.

15. This dichotomy is remarkably reminiscent of the contemporary debate about whether "green" and sustainable economic growth is possible.

16. Bruno, *The Nature of Soviet Power*, 21.

17. Scott, *Against the Grain*. See references on pages 104, 108, and 109.

18. Peter Pringle, *The Murder of Nikolai Vavilov: The Story of Stalin's Persecution of One of the Great Scientists of the Twentieth Century* (New York: Simon & Schuster, 2008). See chapters 11–14 for Vavilov's struggle to reconcile with the increasingly hostile political environment in the 1930s.

19. Ann-Mari Sätre, *Environmental Problems in the Shortage Economy: The Legacy of Soviet Environmental Policy*, New Horizons in Environmental Economics (Cheltenham, UK: Edward Elgar, 1994), 21.

20. Scott, *Against the Grain*, 104.

21. Michael Pollan and before him Evans Pritchard called attention to the symbiosis between men and domesticated plants and animals and the mutual dependence of humans and nonhumans throughout their lives. Michael Pollan, *The Botany of Desire: A Plant's-Eye View of the World* (New York: Random House, 2001); Evans-Pritchard, cited in Scott, *Against the Grain*, 87.

22. Gary N. Atlin, Jill E. Cairns, and Biswanath Das, "Rapid Breeding and Varietal Replacement Are Critical to Adaptation of Cropping Systems in the Developing World to Climate Change," *Global Food Security* 12 (March 1, 2017): 31–37.

23. Abby Kinchy, *Seeds, Science, and Struggle: The Global Politics of Transgenic Crops* (Cambridge, MA: MIT Press, 2012).

24. Tiago Saraiva, *Fascist Pigs: Technoscientific Organisms and the History of Fascism* (Cambridge, MA: MIT Press, 2018), 13.

25. J. L. Anderson, "Lard to Lean: Making the Meat-Type Hog in Post–World War II America," in *Food Chains*, ed. Warren Belasco and Roger Horowitz (Philadelphia: University of Pennsylvania Press, 2009), 29–46. Thomas Fleischman's history of farm animals in East Germany by contrast argues that the "communist" pigs of East Germany converged with the capitalist pig, as "agriculture under communism came to be indistinguishable from capitalist agriculture." Thomas Fleischman, *Communist Pigs: An Animal History of East Germany's Rise and Fall* (Seattle: University of Washington Press, 2020), 4.

26. The life and work of N. I. Vavilov is documented by several authors, including Nils Roll-Hansen, "Wishful Science: The Persistence of T. D. Lysenko's Agrobiology in the Politics of Science," *Osiris* 23, no. 1 (February 1, 2008): 166–88; Pringle, *The Murder of Nikolai Vavilov*; and James F. Crow, "N. I. Vavilov, Martyr to Genetic Truth," *Genetics* 134, no. 1 (May 1993): 1–4.

27. Graham, *Lonely Ideas*, 72.

28. J. Smith, *Works in Progress*, 126.

29. Ibid., 122–29.

30. Hale-Dorrell, *Corn Crusade*, 180.

31. Karl S. Quisenberry and L. P. Reitz, "Turkey Wheat: The Cornerstone of an Empire," *Agricultural History* 48, no. 1 (January 1974): 98–110. See also Fullilove, *The Profit of the Earth*, 115.

32. Alan Olmstead and Paul Rhode, *The Red Queen and the Hard Reds: Productivity Growth in American Wheat, 1800–1940*, NBER Working Paper (Washington, DC: National Bureau of Economic Research, March 2002).

33. Belderok, Mesdag, and Donner, *Bread-Making Quality of Wheat*, 388.

34. For Soviet-era wheat breeding, see ibid., esp. 388.

35. Ibid.

36. See the account of the history of the NIISKh Iugo-vostoka, Nauchno-issledovatel'skii institut sel'skogo khoziaistva Iugo-Vostoka, https://www.arisersar.ru/.

37. Morgunov, *Wheat and Wheat Breeding in the Former USSR*, 10.

38. Ibid., 19.

39. This program was later widely criticized. See United States Congress, Government Accountability Office, *Foreign Assistance: Donation of US Planting Seed to Russia in 1999; Report by Subcommittee on Agriculture, Rural Development and Related Agencies, House of Representatives* (Washington, DC: GAO, March 2000).

40. Ibid., 10.

41. See Belderok, Mesdag, and Donner, *Bread-Making Quality of Wheat*, 383, on the historical varieties of the Nemchinovka. See the institute website for current seed varieties, accessed June 2020, https://www.ficnemchinovka.ru/seeds.

42. Evgenii Zuev, curator of spring bread wheat collection, N. I. Vavilov All-Russian Institute of Plant Genetic Resources (VIR), interview with author, St. Petersburg, October 2019.

43. Hans-Jürgen Wittmann, "Russland forciert Lokalisierung von Saatgut; Branchenbericht, Russland" (Germany Trade & Invest [GTAI], February 14, 2020).

44. Alexander Archimowitsch, "Selective Breeding of Sugar-Beets in Russia and the USSR," *Botanical Review* 22, no. 1 (1956): 1–37.

45. Ibid., 17.

46. Ibid., 21, 30. Russian climatic challenges, especially harsh winters, were an issue for breeders as they required particular storage qualities.

47. Marina Tretiakova, "Chto proiskhodit s rossiiskimi semenami," *Parliamentskaia gazeta*, April 27, 2018.

48. Note that the share of Russian and foreign patent holders is calculated using the addresses the patentholders provide to Gossortkommissiia. The share of Russian patent holders thus also includes foreign and transnational companies with Russian subsidiaries. See also Olga P. Mitrofanova, "Wheat Genetic Resources in Russia: Current Status and Preceding Studies," *Russian Journal of Genetics: Applied Research* 2, no. 4 (2012): 277–85.

49. Peter Roudik, "Russia: Full Ban on Food with GMOs," Law Library of Congress: Global Legal Monitor, 2016; Federation Council of the Russia Federation, "Ustanovlen zapret na vyrashchivanie i razvedenie genno-inzhenerno-modifitsirovan nykh organizmov na territorii Rossii" (press release, June 29, 2016), http://council.gov.ru/events/news/69701/.

50. David Leishman and FAS Moscow Staff, *Russia 2017 Livestock and Products Annual*, GAIN Report (Washington, DC: USDA Foreign Agriculture Service, November 28, 2017).

Notes to Pages 198–204

51. Decree #680 "On development of genetic technologies in the Russian Federation." See, for example, Kremlin, "Meeting on Developing Genetic Technology in Russia" (press release, May 14, 2020).
52. Olga Dobrovidova, "Russia Joins in Global Gene-Editing Bonanza," *Nature* 569, no. 7756 (May 14, 2019): 319–20.
53. Comment by Konstantin Severinov, a molecular geneticist, quoted in ibid.
54. Deanna Ayala, *Russian Genetic Technologies Accelerate*, GAIN Report (Moscow: USDA Foreign Agricultural Service, March 19, 2020).
55. J. Smith, *Works in Progress*, 114.
56. Ibid., 136.
57. Ibid., 117.
58. N. G. Dmitriev and L. K. Ernst, *Animal Genetic Resources of the USSR* (Rome: Food and Agriculture Organization of the United Nations, 1989).
59. Ibid., ix.
60. Ibid., 104.
61. Ibid., 105.
62. Kenneth R. Gray, A. V. Uvrkin, and Anthony J. Biddlestone, "Purification of Wastewater from Industrial Pig Farms in the USSR," *Journal of Agricultural Engineering Research* 49 (1991): 21–31.
63. Kenneth R. Gray, *Soviet Livestock Cycles with United States Comparisons* (Final Report to the National Council for Soviet and East European Research, 1980). This is documented for the period of 1930–63 by J. Smith, *Works in Progress*, as well as by Dmitriev and Ernst, *Animal Genetic Resources of the USSR*. For these reasons, then, the Soviet communist pig was still distinct from the "capitalist" pig, even if some degree of convergence did happen, as Fleischman observed in East Germany. Fleishman, *Communist Pigs*.
64. Dmitriev and Ernst, *Animal Genetic Resources of the USSR*, 110.
65. Ibid., xx.
66. Ibid., 149.
67. Though Cobb is an American company, it had a British subsidiary and for that reason is present at the British Exhibition. See Andrew Godley, "The Emergence of Agribusiness in Europe and the Development of the Western European Broiler Chicken Industry, 1945 to 1973," *Agricultural History Review* 62, no. 2 (2014): 315–36.
68. Dmitriev and Ernst, *Animal Genetic Resources of the USSR*, 437.
69. Ibid., 437.
70. As noted in the company newsletter by EkoNiva, "Eko-Niva Novosti," *Corporate Journal of the EkoNiva Group* 2 (October 6, 2006); and "Eko-Niva Novosti," *Corporate Journal of the EkoNiva Group* 3 (December 21, 2006).
71. Interview by the author with Darrell Stevenson, by phone, 2016. See also Ryan Bell, "Comrade Cowboy," *Western Horseman*, November 29, 2011.
72. Prikhodko and Davleyev, *Russian Federation*, 132–33.
73. Leishman, *Russia 2017 Livestock and Products Annual*. The support given to the pork industry was particularly robust in the second half of the first decade in the 2000s. Between 2006 and 2011, for example, $8 billion of state support flowed to the update of pork production facilities, according to the Russian Union of Swine Breeders.

In 2014, pork producers received 75 billion rubles (slightly more than $2 billion) in government support payments from the state program on "Pork Production Development in 2013–2015." See Higgens, *2014 Livestock and Products Semi-Annual Report*.

74. See website for Znamensk Genetic Resource Center, Znamenskii selektsionno-geneticheskii tsentr, "Glavnaia," accessed 2020, http://www.nsgc.ru/.

75. Russian originals: "Nesmotria na to, chto plemennye svin'i porody Krupnaia Belaia iznachal'no vyvodilis' dlia soderzhaniia na svobodnom vygule, ee predstaviteli pokazyvaiut ves'ma khoroshie pokazateli, brebyvaia v stesnennykh usloviiakh" and "Otlichitel'nye kharakteristiki porody iavliaetsia . . . otsutstvie gena stressa." See statement about these breeds on dedicated Hypor website, https://www.hypor.com/.

76. See Znamensk Genetic Resource Center website, Znamenskii selektsionno-geneticheskii tsentr, "Glavnaia," http://www.nsgc.ru/porody.

77. Katalevskii and Ivanov, *Sovremennye agrotekhnologii*, 373. The same degree of concentration holds for pork: the largest producers of pig genetics resources are Hypor and Topigs (both Dutch companies) and PIC (in the UK).

78. Inga Sysoeva, "V Rossii ispytyvaiut novyi otechestvennyi kross broilera. Na ego sozdanie pravitel'stvo vydeliaet 5,1 mlrd rublei," *Agroinvestor*, March 14, 2020.

79. Stepan Kravchenko, Anatoly Medetsky, and Evgenia Pismennaya, "Putin Resurrects the Soviet Super Chicken. And It's Not Just Poultry the Kremlin Is Worried About," *Bloomberg News*, November 9, 2018; Alena Belaia, "Vazhnaia ptitsa. Zachem Rossii sobstvennyi kross broilera," *Agroinvestor*, October 4, 2019.

80. See the corporate website: https://www.cobb-vantress.com/en_US/products/cobb500/.

81. See the corporate website: http://en.aviagen.com/brands/ross/.

82. This is according to Zhanna Emanuilova. Sysoeva, "V Rossii ispytyvaiut novyi otechestvennyi kross broilera."

83. Belaia, "Vazhnaia ptitsa."

84. Ibid.

85. Comment by Albert Davleev, agricultural consultant, quoted in Sysoeva, "V Rossii ispytyvaiut novyi otechestvennyi kross broilera."

86. Andrew Lakoff and Stephen J. Collier, eds., *Biosecurity Interventions: Global Health and Security in Question* (New York: Columbia University Press, 2008).

87. Victoria Kulagina, "Ptichii gripp v Podmoskov'e v 2017 godu: Est' li predposylki dlia epidemii i kak sebia obezopasit'," *Pravitel'stvo Moskovskoi Oblasti*, March 6, 2017.

88. Ibid.; Vorotnikov, "Large Avian Flu Outbreak Hits Moscow Oblast."

89. Lakoff and Collier, *Biosecurity Interventions*.

90. Scott, *Against the Grain*, 104–5.

91. Thomas P. Van Boeckel et al., "Global Trends in Antimicrobial Use in Food Animals," *Proceedings of the National Academy of Sciences of the United States of America* 112, no. 18 (May 5, 2015): 5649–54.

92. Vladimir Shamanin et al., "Genetic Diversity of Spring Wheat from Kazakhstan and Russia for Resistance to Stem Rust Ug99," *Euphytica* 212, no. 2 (November 1, 2016): 287.

93. Cronon, *Nature's Metropolis*, 259.

Conclusion

1. Drawing on the account of Nicholas Riasanovsky, "Afterworld: The Problem of the Peasant," in *The Peasant in Nineteenth-Century Russia*, ed. Wayne S. Vucinich (Stanford: Stanford University Press, 1968), 265; and Lih, *Bread and Authority in Russia, 1914–1921*.

2. See, for example, Barry Estabrook, *Tomatoland: How Modern Industrial Agriculture Destroyed Our Most Alluring Fruit* (Kansas City: Andrews McMeel, 2011).

3. These studies implicitly or explicitly rely on stylized templates of capitalism as a presumed end point of the transition; this point is made by Stephen Collier and Lucan Way, "Beyond the Deficit Model: Social Welfare in Post-Soviet Georgia," *Post-Soviet Affairs* 20, no. 3 (2004): 258–84.

4. Landmark studies that stress differences are Hellman, "Winners Take All"; and Timothy Frye, "The Perils of Polarization: Economic Performance in the Post-Communist World," *World Politics* 54, no. 3 (2002): 308–37. See also Sergei Guriev and Ekaterina Zhuravskaya, "Why Russia Is Not South Korea," *Journal of International Affairs* 63, no. 2 (2010): 125–39. Jordan Gans-Morse, *Property Rights in Post-Soviet Russia: Violence, Corruption, and the Demand for Law* (Cambridge, UK: Cambridge University Press, 2017); and Stanislav Markus, *Property, Predation, and Protection: Piranha Capitalism in Russia and Ukraine* (New York: Cambridge University Press, 2015), both focus on threats to property rights.

5. See the introduction and case studies in Alison Hope Alkon and Julian Agyeman, eds., *Cultivating Food Justice: Race, Class, and Sustainability* (Cambridge, MA: MIT Press, 2011).

6. Remington, *The Politics of Inequality in Russia*. See pages 35 and 41 for food as a workplace benefit and 55 for food as part of wage bargaining between unions and employers.

7. See chapter 2 of this book for a more detailed account. See also Humphrey, *Marx Went Away*; and Vorbrugg, "Not about Land, Not Quite a Grab."

8. United States Department of Health and Human Services, "Health Implications of Obesity," vol. 9:5 (National Institutes of Health, Consensus Development Conference Statement, 1985).

9. Kaitlyn Watson et al., "Micro- and Meso-Level Influences on Obesity in the Former Soviet Union: A Multi-Level Analysis," *European Journal of Public Health* 23, no. 2 (April 1, 2013): 291, emphasis added.

10. Michele Cecchini et al., "Tackling of Unhealthy Diets, Physical Inactivity, and Obesity: Health Effects and Cost-Effectiveness," *The Lancet* 376, no. 9754 (November 20, 2010): 1775.

11. Kenneth Rogoff, "The US Is Exporting Obesity—and Trump Is Making the Problem Worse," *The Guardian*, December 4, 2017.

12. Ketevan Rtveladze et al., "Obesity Trends in Russia: The Impact on Health and Healthcare Costs," *Health* 4, no. 12 (December 31, 2012): 1472.

13. Watson et al., "Micro- and Meso-Level Influences on Obesity in the Former Soviet Union," 294.

14. Julie Guthman, *Weighing In: Obesity, Food Justice, and the Limits of Capitalism* (Berkeley: University of California Press, 2011); Moss, *Salt, Sugar, Fat*. See also C. A.

Monteiro et al., "Ultra-Processed Products Are Becoming Dominant in the Global Food System," *Obesity Reviews* 14, no. 2 (2013): 21–28.

15. For reference to wasted agricultural products in storage and transport, see Toleubayev, Jansen, and Huis, "Knowledge and Agrarian De-Collectivisation in Kazakhstan," 365.

16. Janos Kornai, *The Socialist System: The Political Economy of Communism* (Oxford, UK: Clarendon, 1992), 293.

17. See the discussion in Nove, *An Economic History of the USSR*, 381. For environmental consequences, see Sätre, *Environmental Problems in the Shortage Economy*, 19.

18. Sätre, *Environmental Problems in the Shortage Economy*.

19. Schierhorn et al., "Quantifying Yield Gaps in Wheat Production in Russia," 4. Fertilizer use increased again in the 2000s, though technologies of application have changed dramatically and become more targeted to increase yields.

20. Zorigto Namsaraev et al., "Algal Bloom Occurrence and Effects in Russia," *Water* 12, no. 1 (January 2020): 285.

21. Brian Kuns shows that irrigation practices in post-Soviet Ukraine were sustainable and used less water than similar practices in the US Great Plains. See Kuns, "'In These Complicated Times.'"

22. See, for example, Ravil Mukmenov and Tony Wesolowsky, "An Incinerator in Tatarstan Is the Latest Battleground in Russia's Garbage Wars," *RadioFreeEurope / RadioLiberty*, March 17, 2019.

23. Those who emphasize the power of consumers draw on and reinforce the argument proposed by the food movement. The slogan "vote with your fork" is from Pollan, "Voting with Your Fork."

24. See, for example, Julie Guthman, *Agrarian Dreams: The Paradox of Organic Farming in California* (Berkeley: University of California Press, 2004); and Howard, "Consolidation in the North American Organic Food Processing Sector."

BIBLIOGRAPHY

Alanen, Ilkka, ed. *Mapping the Rural Problem in the Baltic Countryside: Transition Processes in the Rural Areas of Estonia, Latvia, and Lithuania*. Perspectives on Rural Policy and Planning. Burlington, VT: Ashgate, 2004.

Alkon, Alison Hope, and Julian Agyeman, eds. *Cultivating Food Justice: Race, Class, and Sustainability*. Cambridge, MA: MIT Press, 2011.

Allen, Robert. *Farm to Factory: Reinterpretation of the Soviet Industrial Revolution*. Princeton, NJ: Princeton University Press, 2003.

Allen, Michael Thad, and Gabrielle Hecht, eds. *Technologies of Power*. Cambridge, MA: MIT Press, 2001.

Allina-Pisano, Jessica. *The Post-Soviet Potemkin Village: Politics and Property Rights in the Black Earth*. Cambridge, UK: Cambridge University Press, 2007.

Amos, Howard. "The True Tale of Russia's German Dairy King." *Moscow Times*, November 23, 2015.

Anderson, J. L. "Lard to Lean: Making the Meat-Type Hog in Post–World War II America." In *Food Chains*, edited by Warren Belasco and Roger Horowitz, 29–46. Philadelphia: University of Pennsylvania Press, 2009.

Andreev, Viktor. "Korruptsiia ili biznes? Kak zemli i molochnye predpriiatiia rossiiskikh regionov otkhodiat Shtefanu Diurru—Novosti sel'skogo khoziaistva." *Moscow Post*, July 1, 2019.

Applebaum, Anne. *Red Famine: Stalin's War on Ukraine*. New York: Anchor Books, 2017.

Archimowitsch, Alexander. "Selective Breeding of Sugar-Beets in Russia and the USSR." *Botanical Review* 22, no. 1 (1956): 1–37.

Atlin, Gary N., Jill E. Cairns, and Biswanath Das. "Rapid Breeding and Varietal Replacement Are Critical to Adaptation of Cropping Systems in the Developing World to Climate Change." *Global Food Security* 12 (March 1, 2017): 31–37.

Ayala, Deanna. *Russian Genetic Technologies Accelerate*. GAIN Report. Moscow: USDA Foreign Agriculture Service, March 19, 2020.

Ayala, Deanna, and Alla Putiy. *Food Service-Hotel Restaurant Institutional*. GAIN Report. Moscow: USDA Foreign Agriculture Service, March 3, 2011.

Azarieva, Janetta. *Grain and Power in Russia 2001–2011*. Jerusalem: Hebrew University of Jerusalem, 2014.
Banerji, Arup. "Food Shortages in Russia." *Economic and Political Weekly* 29, no. 19 (May 7, 1994): 1147–54.
Barnes, Andrew Scott. *Owning Russia: The Struggle over Factories, Farms, and Power*. Ithaca, NY: Cornell University Press, 2006.
Baron, Samuel. *Bloody Saturday in the Soviet Union: Novocherkassk, 1962*. Palo Alto, CA: Stanford University Press, 2001.
Barsukova, Svetlana. "Agricultural Policy in Russia." *Social Sciences* 48, no. 4 (2017): 3–18.
———. "Dilemma 'Fermery-agrokholdingi' v kontekste importozameshcheniia." *Obshchestvennye nauki i sovremennost'* 5 (2016): 63–74.
———. "Ekonomicheskii patriotizm na prodovol'stvennykh rynkakh: Importozameshchenie i realizatsiia eksportnogo potentsiala." *Zhurnal institutsional'nykh issledovanii* 2, no. 2 (2010): 118–34.
———. "Mobilizing Patriotism in Russia." *Russian Analytical Digest*, no. 207. Center for Security Studies at ETH Zürich, October 2, 2017.
Bates, Robert. *Markets and States in Tropical Africa: The Political Basis of Agricultural Policies*. Berkeley: University of California Press, 1981.
Bavorová, Miroslava, Zuzana Bednarikova, Elena V. Ponkina, and Oane Visser. "Agribusiness Social Responsibility in Emerging Economies: Effects of Legal Structure, Economic Performance and Managers' Motivations." *Journal of Cleaner Production* 289 (March 2021).
Becker, Abraham. *U.S.-Soviet Trade in the 1980s*. RAND Publication Series. Santa Monica, CA: RAND Corporation, 1987.
Belaia, Alena. "Vazhnaia ptitsa. Zachem Rossii sobstvennyi kross broilera." *Agroinvestor*, October 4, 2019.
Belderok, Bob, Hans Mesdag, and Dingena Donner. *Bread-Making Quality of Wheat: A Century of Breeding in Europe*. Dordrecht, Netherlands: Kluwer Academic, 2000.
Belk, Fred R. "Migration of Russian Mennonites." *Social Science* 50, no. 1 (1975): 17–21.
Bell, Richard. *Comparison of Agriculture in the United States and the Soviet Union*. Washington, DC: USDA Economic Research Service, 1961.
Bell, Ryan. "Comrade Cowboy." *Western Horseman*, November 29, 2011.
Bergson, Abram. "Income Inequality Under Soviet Socialism." *Journal of Economic Literature* 22, no. 3 (1984): 1070.
Berliner, Joseph. *The Innovation Decision in Soviet Industry*. Cambridge, MA: MIT Press, 1976.
———. "Soviet Economic Aid." *International Executive* 1, no. 2 (1959): 33–34.
Bernstein, Henry. "V. I. Lenin and A. V. Chayanov: Looking Back, Looking Forward." *Journal of Peasant Studies* 36, no. 1 (2009): 55–81.
Bivar, Venus. *Organic Resistance: The Struggle over Industrial Farming in Postwar France*. Chapel Hill: University of North Carolina Press, 2018.
Bloomberg News. "Can China Learn from Russia and Save Its Pigs from African Swine Fever?" *South China Morning Post*, December 7, 2018.
Bogeruk, Andrey. *National Aquaculture Sector Overview—Russian Federation*. FAO, Rome, 2005.

Bokusheva, Raushan, Heinrich Hockman, and Subal Kumbakhar. "Dynamics of Productivity and Technical Efficiency in Russian Agriculture." *European Review of Agricultural Economics* 39, no. 4 (2012): 611–37.

"Bor'ba za khleb." *Ogonek*, no. 37 (1929).

Borrero, Mauricio. "Communal Dining and State Cafeterias in Moscow and Petrograd, 1917–1921." In *Food in Russian History and Culture*, edited by Musya Glants and Joyce Toomre, 162–76. Bloomington: Indiana University Press, 1997.

Brada, Josef C., Karl-Eugen Wädekin, and Ihor Stebelsky. *Socialist Agriculture in Transition: Organizational Response to Failing Performance*. Boulder, CO: Westview, 1988.

Brain, Stephen. "The Great Stalin Plan for the Transformation of Nature." *Environmental History* 15, no. 4 (2010): 670–700.

———. *Song of the Forest: Russian Forestry and Stalinist Environmentalism, 1905–1953*. Pittsburgh, PA: University of Pittsburgh Press, 2011.

Braudel, Fernand. *The Structures of Everyday Life: Civilization and Capitalism, 15th–18th Century*. Vol. 1. New York: Harper & Row, 1982.

Bremzen, Anya von. *Mastering the Art of Soviet Cooking: A Memoir of Food and Longing*. London: Doubleday, 2013.

Brooks, K., E. Krylatykh, Zvi Lerman, and Vasily Uzun. *Agricultural Reform in Russia: A View from the Farm Level*. World Bank Discussion Paper. Washington, DC: World Bank, 1996.

Brown, Peggy. "Diplomatic Farmers: Iowans and the 1955 Agricultural Delegation to the Soviet Union." *Annals of Iowa* 72, no. 1 (January 1, 2013): 31–62.

Bruno, Andy. *The Nature of Soviet Power: An Arctic Environmental History*. Studies in Environment and History. Cambridge, UK: Cambridge University Press, 2016.

Buckley, Cynthia. "The Myth of Managed Migration: Migration Control and Market in the Soviet Period." *Slavic Review* 54, no. 4 (1995): 896–916.

Buck-Morss, Susan. *Dreamworld and Catastrophe: The Passing of Mass Utopia in East and West*. Cambridge, MA: MIT Press, 2000.

Bukharin, Nikolai Ivanovich. *O novoii ekonomicheskoi politike i nashikh zadachakh: Doklad na sobranii aktiva moskovskoi organizatsii*. Moscow: Izdatel'stvo Proletarii, 1925.

Buldakov, Valeri. "Gorod sozdaet ekstrennyi zapas zerna na zimu. Khvatit li khleba Moskve?" *Argumenty i fakty*, November 17, 1999.

Burlakova, Ekaterina. "Proizvodstvo syrnykh produktov s zameniteliami zhira upalo vpervye za deviat' let." *Vedemosti*, December 24, 2019.

Butler, Nick. "Soviet Agriculture and US-Soviet Grain Agreement." *Intereconomics* 17, no. 5 (1982): 211–16.

Caldwell, Melissa. *Dacha Idylls: Living Organically in Russia's Countryside*. Berkeley: University of California Press, 2011.

———. "Domesticating the French Fry: McDonald's and Consumerism in Moscow." *Journal of Consumer Culture* 4, no. 1 (2004): 5–26.

———, ed. *Food and Everyday Life in the Post-Socialist World*. Bloomington: Indiana University Press, 2009.

———. *Not by Bread Alone: Social Support in the New Russia*. Berkeley: University of California Press, 2004.

———. "The Taste of Nationalism: Food Politics in Postsocialist Moscow." *Ethnos* 67, no. 3 (January 1, 2002): 295–319.

Cameron, Sarah. *The Hungry Steppe: Famine, Violence, and the Making of Soviet Kazakhstan*. Ithaca, NY: Cornell University Press, 2018.

Cecchini, Michele, Franco Sassi, Jeremy A. Lauer, Yong Y. Lee, Veronica Guajardo-Barron, and Daniel Chisholm. "Tackling of Unhealthy Diets, Physical Inactivity, and Obesity: Health Effects and Cost-Effectiveness." *The Lancet* 376, no. 9754 (November 20, 2010): 1775–84.

Central Intelligence Agency. *Intelligence Memorandum: Soviet Grain Supply, 1968*. Washington, DC: Directorate of Intelligence Central Intelligence Agency, December 1968.

———. *Nutrient Content of Soviet Food Supply*. Washington, DC: Directorate of Intelligence Central Intelligence Agency, 1984.

Chari, P. R. "US-USSR Grain-Oil Deal." *China Report* 11, no. 5–6 (1975): 3–9.

Cherkizovo. *Delicious Story*. 2017 Annual Report. https://cherkizovo.com/.

Cherkizovo. *One Big Family*. 2015 Annual Report. https://cherkizovo.com/.

Chernov, Sergey. "Spreading It on Thick: Russia's Latest Supermarket Substitutes." RadioFreeEurope / RadioLiberty, January 22, 2015.

Clapp, Jennifer. *Food*. Cambridge, UK: Polity, 2012.

Cohon, George, and David Macfarlane. *To Russia with Fries: My Journey from Chicago's South Side to Moscow's Red Square*. Toronto, Canada: McClelland & Stewart, 1999.

Collier, Stephen, and Lucan Way. "Beyond the Deficit Model: Social Welfare in Post-Soviet Georgia." *Post-Soviet Affairs* 20, no. 3 (2004): 258–84.

Conquest, Robert. *The Harvest of Sorrow: Soviet Collectivization and the Terror-Famine*. New York: Oxford University Press, 1986.

Craumer, Peter. "Agricultural Change, Labor Supply, and Rural Out-Migration in Soviet Central Asia." In *Geographic Perspectives on Soviet Central Asia*, edited by Robert Lewis, 132–74. New York: Routledge, 1992.

Cronon, William. *Nature's Metropolis: Chicago and the Great West*. New York: W. W. Norton, 1991.

Crow, James F. "N. I. Vavilov, Martyr to Genetic Truth." *Genetics* 134, no. 1 (May 1993): 1–4.

Crumley, Michele. *Sowing Market Reforms: The Internationalization of Russian Agriculture*. New York: Palgrave Macmillan, 2013.

Csáki, Csaba, Gershon Feder, and Zvi Lerman. *Agriculture in Transition: Land Policies and Evolving Farm Structures in Post-Soviet Countries*. Lanham, MD: Lexington Books, 2004.

Demuth, Bathsheba. *Floating Coast: An Environmental History of the Bering Strait*. New York: W. W. Norton, 2019.

DePauw, John W. "The Private Sector in Soviet Agriculture." *Slavic Review* 28, no. 1 (1969): 63–71.

Dewey, John. *The Public and Its Problems*. Athens: Ohio University Press, 1954.

Diatlovskaia, Ekaterina. "'EkoNiva' vlozhit do 2 mlrd rublei v agrokompleks, sozdannyi Luzhkovym." *Agroinvestor*, October 24, 2017.

———. "Pravitel'stvo obsuzhdaet novuiu sistemu otneseniia sel'khoztekhniki k rossiiskoi." *Agroinvestor*, January 23, 2019.
Diatlovskaia, Ekaterina, and Tat'iana Kulistikova. "Vladimir Putin: 'Razmery podderzhki APK izmeriaiutsia sotniami milliardov rublei.'" *Agroinvestor*, December 20, 2018.
Dmitriev, N. G., and L. K. Ernst. *Animal Genetic Resources of the USSR.* Room: Food and Agriculture Organization of the United Nations, 1989.
Dobrovidova, Olga. "Russia Joins in Global Gene-Editing Bonanza." *Nature* 569, no. 7756 (May 14, 2019): 319–20.
Dohan, Michael. "The Economic Origins of Soviet Autarky 1927/28–1934." *Slavic Review* 35, no. 4 (1976): 603–35.
Drewnowski, Adam, and Nicole Darmon. "Food Choices and Diet Costs: An Economic Analysis." *Journal of Nutrition* 135, no. 4 (April 1, 2005): 900–904.
Dunn, Elizabeth Cullen. *Privatizing Poland: Baby Food, Big Business, and the Remaking of Labor.* Ithaca, NY: Cornell University Press, 2004.
Dunn, Ethel. *Perestroika of Soviet Agriculture: The Peasant View.* Washington, DC: National Council for Soviet and East European Research, July 5, 1991.
Ellman, Michael. "Soviet Industrialization: A Remarkable Success?" *Slavic Review* 63, no. 4 (2004): 841–49.
Estabrook, Barry. *Tomatoland: How Modern Industrial Agriculture Destroyed Our Most Alluring Fruit.* Kansas City: Andrews McMeel, 2011.
Evans, Christine, and Lars Lundgren. "Geographies of Liveness: Time, Space, and Satellite Networks as Infrastructures of Live Television in the Our World Broadcast." *International Journal of Communication* 10 (January 1, 2016): 5362–80.
Falkus, M. E. "Russia and the International Wheat Trade, 1861–1914." *Economica* 33, no. 132 (1966): 416–29.
Fallenbuchl, Zbigniew M. "Collectivization and Economic Development." *Canadian Journal of Economics and Political Science* 33, no. 1 (1967): 1–15.
Federal'naia sluzhba gosudarstvennoi statistiki. *Osnovnye pokazateli sel'skogo khoziaistva v Rossii.* Moscow: Rosstat (annual publication; multiple years referenced), 1995–2013.
Federation Council of the Russia Federation. "Ustanovlen zapret na vyrashchivanie i razvedenie genno-inzhenerno-modifitsirovannykh organizmov na territorii Rossii." Press release, June 29, 2016. http://council.gov.ru/events/news/69701/.
Fellmann, Thomas, and Olexandr Nekhay. *Agricultural Sector and Market Developments: A Special Focus on Ukraine, Russia and Kazakhstan.* Kiev: European Commission Joint Research Centre and the Institute for Prospective Technological Studies, January 1, 2012.
"Fermery: Bez pensii, bez prava na dom, eshche i zemliu otnimaiut." *Krest'ianskie vedomosti*, January 28, 2015.
Fitzgerald, Deborah. *Every Farm a Factory: The Industrial Ideal in American Agriculture.* New Haven, CT: Yale University Press, 2003.
———. "World War II and the Quest for Time-Insensitive Foods." *Osiris* 35, no. 1 (August 1, 2020): 291–309.
Fitzpatrick, Sheila. *The Russian Revolution.* Oxford, UK: Oxford University Press, 1982.

———. *Stalin's Peasants: Resistance and Survival in the Russian Village after Collectivization.* Oxford, UK: Oxford University Press, 1994.

Fleischman, Thomas. *Communist Pigs: An Animal History of East Germany's Rise and Fall.* Seattle: University of Washington Press, 2020.

Food and Agriculture Organization. *FAO Agriculture and Trade Policy Background Note: Russia.* Rome: UN Food and Agriculture Organization, 2013.

———. FAO STAT. http://www.fao.org/faostat/en/.

———. *Russian Federation: Analysis of the Agribusiness Sector in Southern Russia.* Rome: UN FAO Investment Centre, January 2009.

———. *Sugar Sector Review: Russian Federation.* Report on Sugar Industry in Russia. Rome: UN FAO, 2013.

Foster, John Bellamy. "Marx's Theory of Metabolic Rift: Classical Foundations for Environmental Sociology." *American Journal of Sociology* 105, no. 2 (1999): 366–405.

Freidberg, Susanne. "Footprint Technopolitics." *Geoforum* 55 (2014): 178–89.

Friedmann, Harriet, and Philip McMichael. "Agriculture and the State System: The Rise and Decline of National Agricultures, 1870 to the Present." *Sociologia Ruralis* 29, no. 2 (1989): 93–117.

Frye, Timothy. "The Perils of Polarization: Economic Performance in the Post-Communist World." *World Politics* 54, no. 3 (2002): 308–37.

Fullilove, Courtney. *The Profit of the Earth: The Global Seeds of American Agriculture.* Chicago: University of Chicago Press, 2017.

Gans-Morse, Jordan. *Property Rights in Post-Soviet Russia: Violence, Corruption, and the Demand for Law.* Cambridge, UK: Cambridge University Press, 2017.

Gaudin, Corinne. "'No Place to Lay My Head': Marginalization and the Right to Land during the Stolypin Reforms." *Slavic Review* 57, no. 4 (1998): 747–73.

Gaudoin, Christopher. "The Sugar Policy in Russia: An Import Substitution Strategy." *Agriculture Strategies* (blog), November 13, 2018. https://www.agriculture-strategies.eu/en/2018/11/the-sugar-policy-in-russia/.

Geist, Edward. "Cooking Bolshevik: Anastas Mikoian and the Making of the 'Book about Delicious and Healthy Food.'" *Russian Review* 71, no. 2 (April 2012): 295–313.

Gessen, Masha. "Food Import Ban Means Russia Is at War with the West." *Washington Post*, August 12, 2014.

Godley, Andrew. "The Emergence of Agribusiness in Europe and the Development of the Western European Broiler Chicken Industry, 1945 to 1973." *Agricultural History Review* 62, no. 2 (2014): 315–36.

Goering, Laura. "Marketing Soviet Nostalgia: The Many Faces of Buratino." *Gastronomica* 17, no. 4 (November 1, 2017): 88–101.

Goskomstat Rossii. *Sel'skoe khoziaistvo v Rossii.* Moscow: Goskomstat Rossii, 1995–2013.

Gosudarstvennyi komitet SSSR po statistike. *Narodnoe khoziaistvo SSSR v 1989.* Moscow: Goskomstat, 1989.

Graham, Loren. *Lonely Ideas: Can Russia Compete?* Cambridge, MA: MIT Press, 2013.

Granberg, Leo, and Ann-Mari Sätre. *The Other Russia: Local Experience and Societal Change.* Studies in Contemporary Russia. New York: Routledge, 2017.

Granik, Irina. "Dmitrii Medvedev zalivaet zasukhu den'gami; a zhivotnovodstvo dolzhno prevratit'sia v eksportnuiu otrasl'." *Kommersant*, July 14, 2010.
Gray, Kenneth R. *Soviet Agriculture: Comparative Perspectives*. Iowa City: Iowa State University Press, 1990.
———. *Soviet Livestock Cycles with United States Comparisons*. Final Report to the National Council for Soviet and East European Research, 1980.
Gray, Kenneth R., A. V. Uvrkin, and Anthony J. Biddlestone. "Purification of Wastewater from Industrial Pig Farms in the USSR." *Journal of Agricultural Engineering Research* 49 (1991): 21–31.
Gray, Robin. *Russian Federation: Sugar Annual Sugar Update 2017*. GAIN Report. Washington, DC: USDA Foreign Agriculture Service, DC, April 14, 2017.
Gronow, Jukka. *Caviar with Champagne: Common Luxury and the Ideals of the Good Life in Stalin's Russia*. Leisure, Consumption, and Culture. New York: Berg, 2003.
Guriev, Sergei, and Ekaterina Zhuravskaya. "Why Russia Is Not South Korea." *Journal of International Affairs* 63, no. 2 (2010): 125–39.
Guthman, Julie. *Agrarian Dreams: The Paradox of Organic Farming in California*. Berkeley: University of California Press, 2004.
———. "Can't Stomach It: How Michael Pollan et al. Made Me Want to Eat Cheetos." *Gastronomica* 7, no. 3 (2007): 75–79.
———. *Weighing In: Obesity, Food Justice, and the Limits of Capitalism*. United Kingdom: University of California Press, 2011.
Haas, Morgan, and Mikhail Maximenko. *Russian Federation Livestock and Products Semi-Annual*. GAIN Report. Washington, DC: USDA Foreign Agriculture Service, 2012.
Hahn, Werner. *The Politics of Soviet Agriculture, 1960–1970*. Baltimore, MD: Johns Hopkins University Press, 1972.
Hale-Dorrell, Aaron. *Corn Crusade: Khrushchev's Farming Revolution in the Post-Stalin Soviet Union*. New York: Oxford University Press, 2018.
———. "The Soviet Union, the United States, and Industrial Agriculture." *Journal of World History* 26, no. 2 (2015): 295–324.
Hamilton, Shane. *Supermarket USA: Food and Power in the Cold War Farms Race*. New Haven, CT: Yale University Press, 2018.
Hansen, Erik. *Fast Food Sector Keeps Expanding as Economy Cools*. GAIN Report. Washington, DC: USDA Foreign Agriculture Service, November 13, 2014.
———. *Franchise Restaurants Doing Well Despite Slowing Economy*. GAIN Report. Washington, DC: USDA Foreign Agriculture Service, May 18, 2015.
———. *Russian Food Ban Extended until August 2016*. GAIN Report. Washington, DC: USDA Foreign Agriculture Service, June 25, 2015.
Hansen, John M. *Gaining Access: Congress and the Farm Lobby, 1919–1981*. Chicago: University of Chicago Press, 1991.
Harris, Chris. "Is Russia Nearing Self-Sufficiency in Meat?" *Farm Gate to Fork*, May 12, 2016.
Harris, Steven E. *Communism on Tomorrow Street: Mass Housing and Everyday Life after Stalin*. Baltimore, MD: Johns Hopkins University Press, 2013.

Hart, John Fraser. *The Changing Scale of American Agriculture.* Charlottesville: University of Virginia Press, 2003.
Hecht, Gabrielle. *The Radiance of France: Nuclear Power and National Identity after World War II.* Cambridge, MA: MIT Press, 1998.
Hedlund, Stefan. *Crisis in Soviet Agriculture.* London: St. Martin's, 1984.
———. *Private Agriculture in the Soviet Union.* London: Routledge, 1989.
Heinzen, James W. *Inventing a Soviet Countryside: State Power and the Transformation of Rural Russia, 1917–1929.* Pittsburgh, PA: University of Pittsburgh Press, 2004.
Hellman, Joel. "Winners Take All: The Politics of Partial Reform in Postcommunist Transitions." *World Politics* 50, no. 3 (1998): 203–34.
Higgens, Holly. *Poultry Products Semi-Annual.* GAIN Report. Washington, DC: USDA Foreign Agriculture Service, March 17, 2014.
Higgens, Holly. *2014 Livestock and Products Semi-Annual Report.* GAIN Report. Washington, DC: USDA Foreign Agriculture Service, March 17, 2014.
Hobson, Peter. "Russian Pig Cull Leaves Farmers Facing Ruin." *The Independent*, August 30, 2015.
Holquist, Peter. *Making War, Forging Revolution: Russia's Continuum of Crisis, 1914–1921.* Cambridge, MA: Harvard University Press, 2002.
Howard, Phillip. "Consolidation in the North American Organic Food Processing Sector, 1997 to 2007." *International Journal of Sociology of Agriculture and Food* 16, no. 1 (2009): 13–30.
Humphrey, Caroline. *Marx Went Away—But Karl Stayed Behind.* Ann Arbor: University of Michigan Press, 1998.
———. *Unmaking of Soviet Life: Everyday Economies after Socialism.* Ithaca, NY: Cornell University Press, 2002.
"I ne sprashivai, pochem zvonit kolokol. Vse ochen' dorogo." *Kommersant*, September 2, 1991.
International Labor Organization. "Employment by Sector—ILO Modelled Estimates." *ILOSTAT*, 2018.
Ioffe, Grigory. "The Downsizing of Russian Agriculture." *Europe-Asia Studies* 57, no. 2 (March 1, 2005): 179–208.
Ioffe, Grigory, and Tatyana Nefedova. "Russian Agriculture and Food Processing: Vertical Cooperation and Spatial Dynamics." *Europe-Asia Studies* 53, no. 3 (May 1, 2001): 389–418.
Ioffe, Grigory, Tatyana Nefedova, and Ilya Zaslavsky. *The End of Peasantry? The Disintegration of Rural Russia.* Pittsburgh, PA: University of Pittsburgh Press, 2006.
Iskander, Fazil. *The Goatibex Constellations.* Ann Arbor, MI: Ardis, 1975.
Ivanova, Anna. "Shopping in Beriozka. Consumer Society in the Soviet Union." *Zeithistorische Forschungen* 10, no. 2 (2013): 243–63.
Jacobs, Adrianne. "The Many Flavors of Socialism: Food Culture in Late Soviet Russia, 1965–1985." PhD diss., University of North Carolina, Chapel Hill, 2015.
———. "V. V. Pokhlëbkin and the Search for Culinary Roots in Late Soviet Russia." *Cahiers Du Monde Russe* 54, no. 1–2 (2013): 165–86.
Jahns, Lisa, Alexander Baturin, and Barry Popkin. "Obesity, Diet, and Poverty: Trends in the Russian Transition to Market Economy." *European Journal of Clinical Nutrition* 57, no. 10 (2003): 1295–1302.

Jasanoff, Sheila, ed. *States of Knowledge: The Co-Production of Science and Social Order.* London: Routledge, 2004.

Jasanoff, Sheila, and Sang-Hyun Kim. *Dreamscapes of Modernity: Sociotechnical Imaginaries and the Fabrication of Power.* Chicago: University of Chicago Press, 2015.

Jehlička, Petr, Miķelis Grīviņš, Oane Visser, and Bálint Balázs. "Thinking Food Like an East European: A Critical Reflection on the Framing of Food Systems." *Journal of Rural Studies* 76 (2020): 286–95.

Joe, Melinda. "Dining under Putin: How Sanctions Are Fueling a Russian Food Revolution." *CNN*, November 29, 2016.

Kamp, Johannes, Ruslan Urazaliev, Andrew Balmford, Paul F. Donald, Rhys E. Green, Anthony J. Lamb, and Ben Phalan. "Agricultural Development and the Conservation of Avian Biodiversity on the Eurasian Steppes: A Comparison of Land-Sparing and Land-Sharing Approaches." *Journal of Applied Ecology* 52, no. 6 (2015): 1578–87.

Karlova, Natalia, Vasily Uzun, and Natalia Shagaida. "Russian Agriculture: The Impact of Sanctions." Published Research Paper no. 212. Moscow: Gaidar Institute for Economic Policy, 2015.

Katalevskii, Dmitrii Iu., and Aleksei Iu. Ivanov, eds. *Sovremennye agrotekhnologii: Ekonomiko-pravovye i reguliatornye aspekty.* Moscow/Skolkovo: Institute for Law and Development, Higher School of Economics at Skolkovo, 2018.

Kautsky, Karl. *Die Agrarfrage, eine Übersicht über die Tendenzen der modernen Landwirtschaft und die Agrarpolitik der Sozialdemokratie.* Hannover, Germany: Dietz, 1899.

Kelly, Catriona, and David Shepherd. *Constructing Russian Culture in the Age of Revolution, 1881–1940.* New York: Oxford University Press, 1998.

"Khlebozavod-Avtomat." *Ogonek*, no. 1 (1952).

Kim, Byung-Yeon. "Causes of Repressed Inflation in the Soviet Consumer Market, 1965–1989: Retail Price Subsidies, the Siphoning Effect, and the Budget Deficit." *Economic History Review* 55 (2002): 105–27.

Kinchy, Abby. *Seeds, Science, and Struggle: The Global Politics of Transgenic Crops.* Cambridge, MA: MIT Press, 2012.

Kolbasov, Denis, Ilya Titov, Sodnom Tsybanov, Andrey Gogin, and Alexander Malogolovkin. "African Swine Fever Virus, Siberia, Russia, 2017." *Emerging Infectious Diseases* 24, no. 4 (April 2018): 796–98.

Konstantinov, Yulian. *Conversations with Power: Soviet and Post-Soviet Developments in Reindeer Husbandry of the Kola Peninsula.* Uppsala Studies in Cultural Anthropology 56. Uppsala, Sweden: Uppsala Universitet, 2015.

Kornai, Janos. *The Socialist System: The Political Economy of Communism.* Oxford, UK: Clarendon Press, 1992.

Kotkin, Stephen. *Magnetic Mountain: Stalinism as a Civilization.* Berkeley: University of California Press, 1995.

Kramer, Andrew E. "Russia Becomes a Magnet for US Fast-Food Chains." *New York Times*, August 3, 2011, sec. Business.

———. "Russia's Collective Farms: Hot Capitalist Property." *New York Times*, August 30, 2008.

Kramer, Mark. *Food Aid to Russia.* PONARS Policy Memo. Washington, DC: PONARS, 1999.

Kravchenko, Stepan, Anatoly Medetsky, and Evgenia Pismennaya. "Putin Resurrects the Soviet Super Chicken. And It's Not Just Poultry the Kremlin Is Worried About." *Bloomberg News*, November 9, 2018.

Kremlin, Office of the President of Russia, Vladimir V. Putin. "Opening Remarks by President Putin during a Meeting in Belgorod to Address Russia's Problems of Agriculture." Press release, Moscow, May 3, 2000. http://en.kremlin.ru/events/president/transcripts/24534.

———. "Meeting on Developing Genetic Technology in Russia." Press release, Moscow, May 14, 2020. http://www.en.kremlin.ru/events/president/transcripts/deliberations/63350.

———. "Stenograficheskii otchet o zasedanii soveta pri prezidente Rossii po realizatsii prioritetnykh natsional'nykh proektov i demograficheskoi politike," March 7, 2007. http://kremlin.ru/events/president/transcripts/24074.

———. "Utverzhdena Doktrina prodovol'stvennoi bezopasnosti Rossiiskoi Federatsii." February 1, 2010. http://www.kremlin.ru/events/president/news/6752.

"Krome togo." *Kommersant*, October 27, 1992.

Kogan, I. "V nogu s industriei." *Ogonek*, no. 28 (1930): 5 and 16.

Kulagina, Victoria. "Ptichii gripp v Podmoskov'e v 2017 godu: Est' li predposylki dlia epidemii i kak sebia obezopasit'." *Pravitel'stvo Moskovskoi oblasti*, March 6, 2017.

Kuns, Brian. "'In These Complicated Times': An Environmental History of Irrigated Agriculture in Post-Communist Ukraine." *Water Alternatives* 11, no. 3 (2018): 866–92.

Kuns, Brian, Oane Visser, and Anders Wästfelt. "The Stock Market and the Steppe: The Challenges Faced by Stock-Market Financed, Nordic Farming Ventures in Russia and Ukraine." *Journal of Rural Studies* 45 (June 1, 2016): 199–217.

Laird, Roy D. "Kolkhozy, the Russian Achilles Heel: Failed Agrarian Reform." *Europe-Asia Studies* 49, no. 3 (May 1, 1997): 469–78.

———. "Soviet Goals for 1965 and the Problems of Agriculture." *Slavic Review* 20, no. 3 (1961): 454–64.

Lakhtikova, Anastasia, Angela Brintlinger, and Irina Glushchenko, eds. *Seasoned Socialism: Gender and Food in Late Soviet Everyday Life*. Bloomington: Indiana University Press, 2019.

Lakoff, Andrew, and Stephen J. Collier, eds. *Biosecurity Interventions: Global Health and Security in Question*. New York: Columbia University Press, 2008.

Lander, Christopher D. "Foreign Investment Adaptations to the Changing Political and Economic Environments of the Agro-Food Sector." *Problems of Post-Communism* 65, no. 3 (May 4, 2018): 201–19.

Lapidus, Gail. *Women, Work and Family in the Soviet Union*. London: Routledge, 1982.

Lavin, Talia. "A Russian Fast-Food Chain Tries Its Luck in America." *New Yorker*, April 13, 2017.

LeBlanc, Ronald. "The Ethics and Politics of Diet: Tolstoy, Pilnyak, and the Modern Slaughterhouse." *Gastronomica: The Journal of Critical Food Studies* 17, no. 4 (November 1, 2017): 9–25.

———. *Slavic Sins of the Flesh: Food, Sex, and Carnal Appetite in Nineteenth-Century Russian Fiction*. Durham, NH: University of New Hampshire Press, 2009.

Leishman, David. *Russia 2017 Livestock and Products.* Annual GAIN Report. Washington, DC: USDA Foreign Agricultural Service, November 28, 2017.
Leonard, Carol. *Agrarian Reform in Russia: The Road from Serfdom.* Cambridge, UK: Cambridge University Press, 2010.
Levinsky, Aleksander. "Kak 'Miratorg' s pomoshch'iu gosudarstva stal prodovol'stvennym gigantom." *Forbes Business*, April 7, 2019. https://www.forbes.ru/biznes/374459-kak-miratorg-s-pomoshchyu-gosudarstva-stal-prodovolstvennym-gigantom
Lewin, Moshe. *Russian Peasants and Soviet Power: A Study of Collectivization.* New York: W. W. Norton, 1975.
Liefert, William, and Olga Liefert. "Russian Agriculture during Transition: Performance, Global Impact, and Outlook." *Applied Economic Perspectives and Policy* 34, no. 1 (2012): 37–75.
Liefert, William, Olga Liefert, Ralph Seeley, and Tani Lee. "The Effect of Russia's Economic Crisis and Import Ban on Its Agriculture and Food Sector." *Journal of Eurasian Studies* 10, no. 2 (2019): 119–35.
Lih, Lars. *Bread and Authority in Russia, 1914–1921.* Berkeley: University of California Press, 1990.
Livers, Keith. "From Fecal Briquettes to Candy Kremlins: The Edible Ideal in Sorokin's Prose." *Gastronomica* 17, no. 4 (November 1, 2017): 26–35.
Lotman, Iurii Mikhailovich. *Besedy o russkoi kul'ture.* St. Petersburg, 1994.
Lunze, Karsten, Elena Yurasova, Bulat Idrisov, Natalia Gnatienko, and Luigi Migliorini. "Food Security and Nutrition in the Russian Federation—a Health Policy Analysis." *Global Health Action* 8 (June 24, 2015).
Lyson, Thomas A., G. W. Stevenson, and Rick Welsh, eds. *Food and the Mid-Level Farm: Renewing an Agriculture of the Middle.* Cambridge, MA: MIT Press, 2008.
Main, Steven J. "Food Policy and Food Security. Putting Food on the Russian Table." *Europe-Asia Studies* 71, no. 2 (2019): 331–32.
Mamonova, Natalia. "Rethinking Rural Politics in Post-Socialist Settings: Rural Communities, Land Grabbing and Agrarian Change in Russia and Ukraine." PhD diss., International Institute of Social Studies, Erasmus University, Rotterdam, Netherlands, 2016.
Markevich, Andrei. "Russia in the Great War: Mobilisation, Grain, and Revolution." In *Economics of the Great War: A Centennial Perspective*, edited by Stephen Broadberry and Mark Harrison, 103–8. London: Center for Economic Policy Research, 2018.
Markus, Stanislav. *Property, Predation, and Protection: Piranha Capitalism in Russia and Ukraine.* New York: Cambridge University Press, 2015.
Masterovoy, Anton. "Eating Soviet: Food and Culture in the USSR, 1917–1991." PhD diss., City University of New York, 2013.
Matala, Saara. "Flashy Flagships of Cold War Cooperation: The Finnish-Soviet Nuclear Icebreaker Project." *Technology and Culture* 60, no. 2 (2019): 347–77.
McGlade, Jacqueline. "More a Plowshare than a Sword: The Legacy of US Cold War Agricultural Diplomacy." *Agricultural History* 83, no. 1 (2009): 79–102.
"Meat Consumption per Capita." *The Guardian*, September 2, 2009.
Medvedev, Zhores. *Soviet Agriculture.* New York: W. W. Norton, 1987.

Mikoyan, A. *The Food Supply and Our Tasks*. Moscow: Cooperative Publishing Society for Foreign Workers, 1931. Originally published as *Prodovol'stvennoe snabzhenie i nashi zadachi* (Moscow: Gosizdat, 1930).

Minaev, Sergei. "Suverennyi Karavai." *Kommersant*, August 16, 2010.

Miratorg. *Asian Catalogue*. Moscow: Miratorg Agribusiness Holding, 2019. Copy in author's possession.

———. *Frozen Convenience Food and Ready Meals*. Moscow: Miratorg Agribusiness Holding, 2017. Copy in author's possession.

———. *Miratorg Annual Report 2013*. Moscow: Miratorg Agribusiness Holding, 2013. Copy in author's possession.

Mitchell, Timothy. *Rule of Experts: Egypt, Techno-Politics, Modernity*. Berkeley: University of California Press, 2002.

Mitrofanova, Olga P. "Wheat Genetic Resources in Russia: Current Status and Preceding Studies." *Russian Journal of Genetics: Applied Research* 2, no. 4 (2012): 277–85.

Moir, Sarah. "The People's Phenomenon: 'Author's Song' in Khrushchev's Soviet Union." *Constructing the Past* 13, no. 1 (2012).

Mokrushin, A. A. "Nedostatki finansovo ustoichivykh predpriiatii (organizatsii), sposobnykh na krupnye kapital'nye vlozheniia v modernizatsiiu sel'skokhoziaistvennogo proizvodstva." *Nauchnyi zhurnal KubGAU* 24, no. 8 (2006).

Mondi Group, "Mondi Syktyvkar: A Russian Success Story Turns 50." Press release, July 19, 2019. https://www.mondigroup.com/en/newsroom/press-release/2019/mondi-syktyvkar-a-russian-success-story-turns-50/.

Monteiro, C. A., et al. "Ultra-Processed Products Are Becoming Dominant in the Global Food System." *Obesity Reviews* 14, no. 2 (2013): 21–28.

Moon, David. *The American Steppes: The Unexpected Russian Roots of Great Plains Agriculture, 1870s–1930s*. Cambridge, UK: Cambridge University Press, 2020.

———. *The Plough That Broke the Steppes: Agriculture and Environment on Russia's Grasslands, 1700–1914*. Oxford Studies in Modern European History. Oxford: Oxford University Press, 2013.

Morgan, Dan. *Merchants of Grain: The Power and Profits of the Five Giant Companies at the Center of the World's Food Supply*. New York: Viking, 1978.

Morgunov, Alexey. *Wheat and Wheat Breeding in the Former USSR*. Texcoco, Mexico: CIMMYT Wheat, November 1992.

Moss, Michael. *Salt, Sugar, Fat: How the Food Giants Hooked Us*. New York: Random House, 2013.

Mukmenov, Ravil, and Tony Wesolowsky. "An Incinerator in Tatarstan Is the Latest Battleground in Russia's Garbage Wars." RadioFreeEurope / RadioLiberty, March 17, 2019.

Mumford, Lewis. "Authoritarian and Democratic Technics." *Technology and Culture* 5, no. 1 (1964): 1–8.

Namsaraev, Zorigto, Anna Melnikova, Anastasia Komova, Vasily Ivanov, Anastasia Rudenko, and Evgenii Ivanov. "Algal Bloom Occurrence and Effects in Russia." *Water* 12, no. 1 (January 2020): 285.

Nechepurenko, Ivan. "You Are What You Eat: Why Food, Culture and Politics Go Hand in Hand in Russia." *Calvert Journal*, September 3, 2014.

"Nemetskii biznesmen i rossiiskii grazhdanin Shtefan Diurr pokazal svoi vladeniia Olegu Kharseevu i Olegu Mukhinu." *Ogonek*, February 13, 2017.

Nérard, François-Xavier. "Variations on a Shchi Theme: Collective Dining and Politics in the Early USSR." *Gastronomica: The Journal for Food Studies* 17, no. 4 (November 1, 2017): 36–47.

Nestle, Marion. *Food Politics: How the Food Industry Influences Nutrition and Health*. Berkeley: University of California Press, 2002.

Nikulin, Alexander. "From Post-Kolkhoz to Oligarkhoz." *RUDN Journal of Sociology*, no. 2 (June 15, 2011): 56–68.

———. "The Kuban Kolkhoz between a Holding and a Hacienda." *Focaal Journal of Global and Historical Anthropology*, no. 41 (2003): 137–52.

Nikulin, Alexander, Irina Trotsuk, and Stephen Wegren. "The Importance of Strong Regional Leadership in Russia: The Belgorod Miracle in Agriculture." *Eurasian Geography and Economics* 58, no. 3 (May 4, 2017): 316–39.

"Novaia eda Rossii." *Kommersant*, February 2, 2010.

Nove, Alec. *An Economic History of the USSR: 1917–1991*. London: Penguin Books, 1992.

———. "Soviet Agriculture: The Brezhnev Legacy and the Gorbachev Cure." RAND Corporation / UCLA Center for the Study of Soviet International Behavior, Santa Monica, CA, 1988.

———. "Soviet Agriculture under Brezhnev." *Slavic Review* 29, no. 3 (1970): 379–410.

Novokmet, Filip, Thomas Piketty, and Gabriel Zucman. "From Soviets to Oligarchs: Inequality and Property in Russia 1905–2016." *Journal of Economic Inequality* 16, no. 1 (June 1, 2018): 189–223.

Nygaard, Bertel. "Constructing Marxism: Karl Kautsky and the French Revolution." *History of European Ideas* 35, no. 4 (December 1, 2009): 450–64.

Obrazkova, Marina. "Russian Fishing Industry Witnesses Stable Growth." *Russia beyond the Headlines*, June 29, 2015.

O'Callaghan, Tommy. "Beryozka Shops: How Soviet Citizens Bought Scarce Goods with Foreign Currency." *Russia Beyond the Headlines*, April 29, 2018.

"Oligarchs Eating Up $8 Bln Meat Market." *Moscow Times*, July 25, 2002.

Olmstead, Alan, and Paul Rhode. *Creating Abundance: Biological Innovation and American Agricultural Development*. New York: Cambridge University Press, 2008.

———. *The Red Queen and the Hard Reds: Productivity Growth in American Wheat, 1800–1940*. NBER Working Paper. Washington, DC: National Bureau of Economic Research, March 2002.

Overdevest, Christine. "Towards a More Pragmatic Sociology of Markets." *Theory and Society* 40, no. 5 (2011): 533–52.

Paarlberg, Robert. *Food Politics: What Everyone Needs to Know*. New York: Oxford University Press, 2013.

———. "Shifting and Sharing Adjustment Burdens: The Role of the Industrial Food Importing Nations." *International Organization* 32, no. 3 (1978): 655–77.

Pachirat, Timothy. *Every Twelve Seconds: Industrialized Slaughter and the Politics of Sight*. New Haven, CT: Yale University Press, 2013.

Pallot, Judith, and Tatyana Nefedova. *Russia's Unknown Agriculture. Household Production in Post-Socialist Rural Russia*. Oxford: Oxford University Press, 2007.

Pianciola, Niccolò. "The Collectivization Famine in Kazakhstan, 1931–1933." *Harvard Ukrainian Studies* 25, no. 3/4 (2001): 237–51.
"Pochemu v rukovodstve OZK net predstavitelei Minsel'khoza?" *Krest'ianskie vedomosti*, March 13, 2014.
Podgainy, Marilyn. "Non-Violent Coercion: The 1980 Embargo of United States Grain to the Soviet Union." *Touro Journal of Transnational Law* 2, no. 1 (1991): 221–42.
Pohl, M. "From White Grave to Tselinograd to Astana." In *The Thaw: Soviet Society and Culture during the 1950s and 1960s*, edited by Denis Kozlov and Eleonory Gilburd, 269–307. Toronto: University of Toronto Press, 2013.
Polanyi, Karl. *The Great Transformation: The Political and Economic Origins of Our Time*. Boston, MA: Beacon, 1944.
Pollan, Michael. *The Botany of Desire: A Plant's-Eye View of the World*. New York: Random House, 2001.
———. *The Omnivore's Dilemma: A Natural History of Four Meals*. New York: Penguin, 2006.
———. "Voting with Your Fork." *New York Times*, May 7, 2006.
"Postavki v Rossiiu produktov iz nakhodiashchikhsia pod sanktsiiami stran snizilis' v 100 raz." *Vedomosti*, September 27, 2019.
Prasad, Monica. *The Land of Too Much: American Abundance and the Paradox of Poverty*. Cambridge, MA: Harvard University Press, 2013.
Prikhodko, Dmitry, and Albert Davleyev. *Russian Federation: Meat Sector Review*. Rome: United Nations Food and Agriculture Organization, Rome, 2014.
Pringle, Peter. *The Murder of Nikolai Vavilov: The Story of Stalin's Persecution of One of the Great Scientists of the Twentieth Century*. New York: Simon & Schuster, 2008.
Prishchepov, Alexander, Daniel Müller, Maxim Dubinin, Matthias Baumann, and Volker Radeloff. "Determinants of Agricultural Land Abandonment in Post-Soviet European Russia." *Land Use Policy* 30, no. 1 (2013): 873–84.
Quisenberry, Karl S., and L. P. Reitz. "Turkey Wheat: The Cornerstone of an Empire." *Agricultural History* 48, no. 1 (January 1974): 98–110.
Radell, Willard. "Cuban-Soviet Sugar Trade, 1960–1970: How Great Was the Subsidy?" *Journal of Developing Areas* 17, no. 3 (1983): 365–82.
Rahman, Sabeel, and Kathleen Thelen. "The Rise of the Platform Business Model and the Transformation of Twenty-First-Century Capitalism." *Politics & Society* 47, no. 2 (2019): 177–204.
RBC News. "Medvedev poruchil gotovit'sia k prodleniiu antisanktsii do kontsa 2017 goda." *RBC News*, May 27, 2016.
Reid, Susan E. "Cold War in the Kitchen: Gender and the de-Stalinization of Consumer Taste in the Soviet Union under Khrushchev." *Slavic Review* 61, no. 2 (2002): 211–52.
Remington, Thomas F. *The Politics of Inequality in Russia*. Cambridge, UK: Cambridge University Press, 2011.
RIA Novosti. "Putin posetil Samarskii bulochno-konditerskii kombinat." *RIA Novosti*, March 7, 2018.
Riasanovsky, Nicholas. "Afterword: The Problem of the Peasant." In *The Peasant in Nineteenth-Century Russia*, edited by Wayne S. Vucinich, 263–84. Stanford: Stanford University Press, 1968.

Ries, Nancy. "Potato Ontology: Surviving Postsocialism in Russia." *Cultural Anthropology* 24, no. 2 (May 1, 2009): 181–212.
Rogoff, Kenneth. "The US Is Exporting Obesity—and Trump Is Making the Problem Worse." *The Guardian*, December 4, 2017.
Roll-Hansen, Nils. "Wishful Science: The Persistence of T. D. Lysenko's Agrobiology in the Politics of Science." *Osiris* 23, no. 1 (February 1, 2008): 166–88.
———. *The Lysenko Effect: The Politics of Science*. New York: Humanity Books, 2005.
Rothstein, Halina, and Robert. A. Rothstein. "Beginnings of Soviet Culinary Arts." In *Food in Russian History and Culture*, edited by Musya Glants and Joyce Toomre, 162–76. Indiana University Press, 1997.
Roudik, Peter. "Russia: Full Ban on Food with GMOs." Law Library of Congress: Global Legal Monitor, 2016.
Rtveladze, Ketevan, Tim Marsh, Laura Webber, Fanny Kilpi, Yevgeniy Goryakin, Anna Kontsevaya, Antonina Starodubova, Klim McPherson, and Martin Brown. "Obesity Trends in Russia. The Impact on Health and Healthcare Costs." *Health* 4, no. 12 (December 31, 2012): 1471–84.
Rusagro. *Growth Drivers—Annual Report 2018*. Moscow: Rusagro Group, 2018.
Rylko, Dmitri, and Robert Jolly. "Russia's New Agricultural Operators: Their Emergence, Growth and Impact." *Comparative Economic Studies* 47 (2005): 115–26.
Rylko, Dmitri, Robert Jolly, Irina Khramov, and Vasilii Uzun. "Agroholdings: Russia's New Agricultural Operators." In *Russia's Agriculture in Transition: Factor Markets and Constraints on Growth*, edited by Zvi Lerman, 95–133. Lanham, MD: Lexington Books, 2008.
Sanchez-Sibony, Oscar. "Depression Stalinism: The Great Break Reconsidered." *Kritika: Explorations in Russian and Eurasian History* 15, no. 1 (2014): 23–49.
Saraiva, Tiago. *Fascist Pigs: Technoscientific Organisms and the History of Fascism*. Cambridge, MA: MIT Press, 2018.
Sätre, Ann-Mari. *Environmental Problems in the Shortage Economy: The Legacy of Soviet Environmental Policy*. New Horizons in Environmental Economics. Cheltenham, UK: Edward Elgar, 1994.
———. *The Politics of Poverty in Contemporary Russia*. New York: Routledge, 2019.
Schechter, Brandon M. "The State's Pot and the Soldier's Spoon." In *Hunger and War: Food Provisioning in the Soviet Union during World War II*, edited by Wendy Z. Goldman and Donald A. Filtzer, 98–157. Bloomington: Indiana University Press, 2015.
———. *The Stuff of Soldiers: A History of the Red Army in World War II through Objects*. Ithaca, NY: Cornell University Press, 2019.
Schierhorn, Florian, Monireh Faramarzi, Alexander Prishchepov, Friedrich Koch, and Daniel Müller. "Quantifying Yield Gaps in Wheat Production in Russia." *Environmental Research Letters* 9, no. 8 (2014): 4.
Schimpfössl, Elisabeth. *Rich Russians: From Oligarchs to Bourgeoisie*. New York: Oxford University Press, 2018.
Schoonover, David M. "Soviet Agricultural Policies from Development to Maturity." *Soviet and Post-Soviet Review* 4, no. 1 (1977): 271–96.
Scott, James. *Against the Grain: A Deep History of the Earliest States*. New Haven, CT: Yale University Press, 2017.

———. *Seeing Like a State*. New Haven, CT: Yale University Press, 1998.
Sedik, David J. "A Note on Soviet Per Capita Meat Consumption." *Comparative Economic Studies* 35, no. 3 (September 1, 1993): 39–48.
Sedik, David, Sergey Sotnikov, and Doris Wiesman. *Food Security in the Russian Federation*. Rome: FAO, 2003.
Serova, Eugenia. "Farm Restructuring in Transition: Land Distribution in Russia." In *Food Policy for Developing Countries: Case Studies*, edited by Per Pinstrup-Andersen and Fuzhi Cheng, 207-16. Ithaca, NY: Cornell University Press, 2007.
Shagaida, Natalia, and Vasily Uzun. "The Agriculture and Food: Does Import Substitution Take Place?" *Russian Economic Developments*, no. 11 (2015): 51–54.
Shamanin, Vladimir, Elena Salina, Ruth Wanyera, Yuriy Zelenskiy, Pablo Olivera, and Alexey Morgounov. "Genetic Diversity of Spring Wheat from Kazakhstan and Russia for Resistance to Stem Rust Ug99." *Euphytica* 212, no. 2 (November 1, 2016): 287–96.
Shanin, Teodor. "Chayanov's Treble Death and Tenuous Resurrection: An Essay about Understanding, about Roots of Plausibility and about Rural Russia." *Journal of Peasant Studies* 36, no. 1 (2009): 83–101.
Sheingate, Adam D. *The Rise of the Agricultural Welfare State: Institutions and Interest Group Power in the United States, France, and Japan*. Princeton, NJ: Princeton University Press, 2003.
Shikov, Alexander, Andrey Tsitsilin, Olga Pozharitskaya, Valery Makarov, and Michael Heinrich. "Traditional and Current Food Use of Wild Plants Listed in the Russian Pharmacopoeia." *Frontiers in Pharmacology* 8, no. 841 (November 21, 2017).
Silverman, Bertram, and Murray Yanowitch. *New Rich, New Poor, New Russia: Winners and Losers on the Russian Road to Capitalism*. New York: Routledge, 1997.
Skoufias, Emmanuel. "Consumption Smoothing in Russia." *Economics of Transition and Institutional Change* 11, no. 1 (2003): 67–91.
Skove, Sam. "Despite Kremlin's Promises, Russian Food Ban Fails to Deliver." *Moscow Times*, June 30, 2015.
Skrynnik, Irina. "Nastuplenie svin'ei: Kak 'Miratorg' zavoeval rossiiskii produktovyi rynok." *Forbes Business*, October 16, 2014.
Slezkine, Yuri. *The House of Government*. Princeton, NJ: Princeton University Press, 2017.
Smith, Jenny Leigh. "Agricultural Involution in the Postwar Soviet Union." *International Labor and Working-Class History*, no. 85 (2014): 59–74.
———. "Empire of Ice Cream: How Life Became Sweeter in the Postwar Soviet Union." In *Food Chains: From Farmyard to Shopping Cart*, edited by Warren Belasco and Roger Horowitz, 142–57. Philadelphia: University of Pennsylvania Press, 2009.
———. "Tushonka: Cultivating Soviet Postwar Taste." *Media/Culture Journal* 13, no. 5 (October 17, 2010).
———. *Works in Progress: Plans and Realities on Soviet Farms, 1930–1963*. New Haven, CT: Yale University Press, 2014.
Smith, Mary Ellen, and Yelena Vassilieva. *Ban on Grain Exports from Russia Comes to Force on August 15*. GAIN Report. Washington, DC: USDA Foreign Agriculture Service, August 6, 2010.

Smith, Michael, and Mikhail Maximenko. *Russian Federation: Poultry and Products*. USDA-FAS/GAIN Report. Washington, DC: Foreign Agriculture Service, 2000.

Sneddon, Chris, and Coleen Fox. "The Cold War, the US Bureau of Reclamation, and the Technopolitics of River Basin Development, 1950–1970." *Political Geography* 30, no. 8 (November 1, 2011): 450–60.

Solecki, Jan. "A Review of the USSR Fishing Industry." *Ocean Management* 5 (1979): 97–123.

Song, Changzoo. "Kimchi, Seaweed, and Seasoned Carrot in the Soviet Culinary Culture: The Spread of Korean Food in the Soviet Union and Korean Diaspora." *Journal of Ethnic Foods* 3, no. 1 (March 1, 2016): 78–84.

Spoor, Max, and Oane Visser. "Restructuring Postponed? Large Russian Farm Enterprises' Coping with the Market." *Journal of Peasant Studies* 31, no. 3–4 (2004): 515–51.

Sysoeva, Inga. "V Rossii ispytyvaiut novyi otechestvennyi kross broilera. Na ego sozdanie pravitel'stvo vydeliaet 5,1 mlrd rublei." *Agroinvestor*, March 14, 2020.

Syutkin, Olga, and Pavel Syutkin. *CCCP Cook Book: True Stories of Soviet Cuisine*. London: FUEL, 2015.

Szczepański, Marcin. *Economic Impact on the EU of Sanctions over Ukraine Conflict*. EPRS_BRI Report. European Parliamentary Research Service, October 2015.

Theesfeld, Insa, and Ladislav Jelinek. "A Misfit in Policy to Protect Russia's Black Soil Region. An Institutional Analytical Lens Applied to the Ban on Burning of Crop Residues." *Land Use Policy* 67 (September 1, 2017): 517–26.

Thompson, Niobe. *Settlers on the Edge*. Vancouver: University of British Columbia Press, 2009.

Thomson, Henry. *Food and Power: Regime Type, Agricultural Policy, and Political Stability*. Cambridge, UK: Cambridge University Press, 2019.

Tilzey, Mark. *Political Ecology, Food Regimes, and Food Sovereignty: Crisis, Resistance, and Resilience*. London: Palgrave Macmillan, 2018.

———. "Reintegrating Economy, Society, and Environment for Cooperative Futures: Polanyi, Marx, and Food Sovereignty." *Journal of Rural Studies* 53 (January 2, 2017): 317–34.

Toleubayev, Kazbek, Kees Jansen, and Arnold Huis. "Knowledge and Agrarian De-Collectivisation in Kazakhstan." *Journal of Peasant Studies* 37, no. 2 (April 1, 2010): 353–77.

Tolstoy, Leo. *Anna Karenina*. Translated by Richard Pevear and Larissa Volokhonsky. Netherlands: Penguin Books, 2002.

Tretiakova, Marina. "Chto proiskhodit s rossiiskimi semenami." *Parliamentskaia gazeta*, April 27, 2018.

Turner, Billie L., William Clark, Robert Kates, Jessica Mathews, John Richards, and William Meyer, eds. *The Earth as Transformed by Human Action: Global and Regional Changes in the Biosphere over the Past 300 Years*. Cambridge, UK: Cambridge University Press, 1990.

Tverdiukova, E. D. "Khlebopechenie v SSSR v 1960e–1980e gg." *Voprosy istorii* 12 (2018): 42–54.

United States Congress, Government Accountability Office. *Foreign Assistance: Donation of US Planting Seed to Russia in 1999; Report by Subcommittee on Agriculture,*

Rural Development and Related Agencies, House of Representatives. Washington, DC: GAO, March 2000.
United States Congress and Senate Committee on Finance. *Background Materials Relating to the United States-Soviet Union Commercial Relations*. Washington, DC: US Congress Printing Office, 1974.
United States Department of Agriculture. *Russian Federation: Grain and Feed Update*. Washington, DC: USDA FAS, October 27, 2017.
United States Department of Agriculture. *Russian Federation: Grain and Feed Update*. Washington, DC: USDA FAS, Washington, DC, October 10, 2018.
United States Department of Health and Human Services. "Health Implications of Obesity." Vol. 9:5. National Institutes of Health, Consensus Development Conference Statement, 1985.
United States Government, International Trade Administration. *Russia—Food Processing and Packaging*. Washington, DC: ITO, August 14, 2019.
United States Government. "United States Grain and Oil Agreements with the Soviet Union." *Hearing before the Committee on International Relations, US House of Representatives, Ninety-Fourth Congress, First Session* (October 28, 1975).
"USSR Pavilion Restaurant: Menus: What's on the Menu?" New York Public Library Menus Collection. Accessed June 2020. http://menus.nypl.org/menu_pages/59129.
Utekhin, Ilya, Alice Nakhimovsky, Slava Paperno, and Nancy Ries. *Communal Living in Russia: A Virtual Museum of Everyday Life*. Colgate University. Accessed June 2021. https://russlang.as.cornell.edu/komm/.
Uzun, Vladimir. "Large and Small Business in Russian Agriculture: Adaptation to Market." *Comparative Economic Studies* 47, no.1 (2005): 85–100
Van Atta, Don. *Russian Food Supplies in 1992 and Prospects for 1993*. Durham, NC: National Council for Soviet and East European Research, Duke University, April 7, 1993.
Van Boeckel, Thomas P., Charles Brower, Marius Gilbert, Bryan T. Grenfell, Simon A. Levin, Timothy P. Robinson, Aude Teillant, and Ramanan Laxminarayan. "Global Trends in Antimicrobial Use in Food Animals." *Proceedings of the National Academy of Sciences of the United States of America* 112, no. 18 (May 5, 2015): 5649–54.
Vanderberg, Rachel. *2017 Poultry and Products: Growth through Integration*. GAIN Report. Washington, DC: USDA Foreign Agriculture Service, August 18, 2017.
———. *Russian Federation Livestock and Products Semi-Annual 2016 Report*. GAIN Report. Washington, DC: USDA Foreign Agriculture Service, March 3, 2016.
Vassilieva, Yelena. *Russian Federation: Agriculture Development Program 2013–2020*. Washington, DC: USDA Foreign Agriculture Service, 2012.
Vereykina, Elizaveta. "Sanctions Spark Russian Cheese Industry Boom." *Moscow Times*, June 1, 2015.
Viola, Lynne. *Peasant Rebels under Stalin: Collectivization and the Culture of Peasant Resistance*. New York: Oxford University Press, 1996.
Visser, Oane. "Persistent Farmland Imaginaries: Celebration of Fertile Soil and the Recurrent Ignorance of Climate." *Agriculture and Human Values* 38 (2020): 313–26.
———. "Running Out of Farmland? Investment Discourses, Unstable Land Values and the Sluggishness of Asset Making." *Agriculture and Human Values* 34, no. 1 (March 1, 2017): 185–98.

Visser, Oane, and Don Kalb. "Financialised Capitalism Soviet Style? Varieties of State Capture and Crisis." *European Journal of Sociology / Archives Européennes de Sociologie / Europäisches Archiv für Soziologie* 51, no. 2 (2010): 171–94.

Visser, Oane, Alexander Kurakin, and Alexander Nikulin. "Corporate Social Responsibility, Coexistence and Contestation: Large Farms' Changing Responsibilities vis-à-vis Rural Households in Russia." *Canadian Journal of Development Studies / Revue Canadienne d'études Du Développement* 40, no. 4 (October 2, 2019): 580–99.

Visser, Oane, and Natalia Mamonova. *Large-Scale Land Acquisitions in the Former Soviet Union*. IS Land Academy Report. Utrecht: Utrecht University, April 2012.

Visser, Oane, Natalia Mamonova, and Max Spoor. "Is Russia the Emerging Global 'Breadbasket'? Re-Cultivation, Agroholdings and Grain Production." *Europe-Asia Studies* 66, no. 10 (2014): 1589–1610.

———. "Oligarchs, Megafarms and Land Reserves: Understanding Land Grabbing in Russia." *Journal of Peasant Studies* 39, no. 3 (2012): 899–932.

Visser, Oane, Natalia Mamonova, Max Spoor, and Alexander Nikulin. "'Quiet Food Sovereignty' as Food Sovereignty without a Movement? Insights from Post-Socialist Russia." *Globalizations* 12, no. 4 (July 4, 2015): 513–28.

Visser, Oane, and Max Spoor. "Land Grabbing in Post-Soviet Eurasia: The World's Largest Agricultural Land Reserves at Stake." *Journal of Peasant Studies* 38, no. 2 (2011): 299–323.

Vorbrugg, Alexander. "Not About Land, Not Quite a Grab: Dispersed Dispossession in Rural Russia." *Antipode* 51, no. 3 (2019): 1011–31.

Vorotnikov, Vladislav. "Large Avian Flu Outbreak Hits Moscow Oblast." *Global Meat News*, March 7, 2017.

Wädekin, Karl-Eugen. *Privatproduzenten in der Sowjetischen Landwirtschaft*. Aktuelle Studien. Köln: Verlag Wissenschaft und Politik, 1967. Translated as *The Private Sector in Soviet Agriculture* (Berkeley: University of California Press, 1973).

———. "Soviet Agriculture's Dependence on the West." *Foreign Affairs*, no. 60 (1982): 882–903.

Watson, Kaitlyn, Bayard Roberts, Clara Chow, Yevgeniy Goryakin, David Rotman, Alexander Gasparishvili, Christian Haerpfer, and Martin McKee. "Micro- and Meso-Level Influences on Obesity in the Former Soviet Union: A Multi-Level Analysis." *European Journal of Public Health* 23, no. 2 (April 1, 2013): 291–98.

Wegren, Stephen. *Agriculture and the State in Soviet and Post-Soviet Russia*. Pittsburgh, PA: University of Pittsburgh Press, 1998.

———. "The Development of Agrarian Capitalism in Post-Soviet Russia." *Journal of Agrarian Change* 11, no. 2 (April 1, 2011): 138–63.

———. *Land Reform in Russia: Institutional Design and Behavioral Responses*. New Haven, CT: Yale University Press, 2009.

———. "Private Farming in Russia: An Emerging Success?" *Post-Soviet Affairs* 27, no. 3 (July 1, 2011): 211–40.

———. "Russia's Food Policies and Foreign Policy." *Demokratizatsiia* 18, no. 3 (2012): 189–207.

———. *Russia's Food Policies and Globalization*. Lanham, MD: Lexington Books, 2005.

———. *Russia's Food Revolution: The Transformation of the Food System.* Routledge Contemporary Russia and Eastern Europe Series. New York: Routledge, 2021.

———. "State Withdrawal and the Impact of Marketization on Rural Russia." *Policy Studies Journal* 28, no. 1 (February 1, 2000): 46–67.

Wegren, Stephen, and Christel Elvestad. "Russia's Food Self-Sufficiency and Food Security: An Assessment." *Post-Communist Economies* 30, no. 5 (September 3, 2018): 565–87.

Wegren, Stephen K., David J. O'Brien, and Valeri V. Patsiorkovski, "Why Russia's Rural Poor Are Poor." *Post-Soviet Affairs* 19, no. 30 (2003): 264–87.

Wengle, Susanne. "The Domestic Effects of the Russian Food Embargo." *Demokratizatsiya* 24, no. 3 (2016): 281–89.

———. "Local Effects of the New Land Rush: How Capital Inflows Transformed Rural Russia." *Governance* 31, no. 2 (2018): 259–77.

———. *Post-Soviet Power: State-Led Development and Russia's Marketization.* New York: Cambridge University Press, 2015.

———. "When Experimentalist Governance Meets Science-Based Regulations; the Case of Food Safety Regulations." *Regulation & Governance* 10, no. 3 (2016): 262–83.

Wheatcroft, Stephen, and R. W. Davies. *The Industrialisation of Soviet Russia.* Vol. 5, *Soviet Agriculture 1931–1933.* London: Palgrave Macmillan, 2010.

Winner, Langdon. "Do Artifacts Have Politics?" *Daedalus* 109, no. 1 (1980): 121–36.

Withford, Josh. "Pragmatism and the Untenable Dualism of Means and Ends: Why Rational Choice Theory Does Not Deserve Paradigmatic Privilege." *Theory and Society* 31 (2002): 325–63.

Wittfogel, Karl. *Oriental Despotism: A Comparative Study of Total Power.* New Haven, CT: Yale University Press, 1957.

Wittmann, Hans-Jürgen. "Russland forciert Lokalisierung von Saatgut." Germany Trade & Invest (GTAI), February 14, 2020.

World Bank. *A State Trading Enterprise for Grains in Russia? Issues and Options.* Policy Note. Washington, DC: World Bank, October 1, 2009.

Young, Cathy. *Growing Up in Moscow: Memories of a Soviet Girlhood.* New York: Ticknor & Fields, 1989.

Yurchak, Alexei. *Everything Was Forever, until It Was No More: The Last Soviet Generation.* Princeton, NJ: Princeton University Press, 2006.

Zheleznova, Mariia. "Zhizn' na bezryb'e." *Vedomosti*, May 24, 2016.

Zhou, Jiayi. "Chinese Agrarian Capitalism in the Russian Far East." *Third World Thematics: A TWQ Journal* 1, no. 5 (September 2, 2016): 612–32.

PROZHITO, ARCHIVE OF PERSONAL DIARIES, EUROPEAN UNIVERSITY OF ST. PETERSBURG

Grammatin, Sergei. "10 dekabria 1951." Prozhito, December 10, 1951. https://prozhito.org/note/220352.

———. "28 ianvaria 1951." Prozhito, January 28, 1951. https://prozhito.org/note/220040.

Grobman, Mikhail. "12 iiulia 1969." Prozhito, July 12, 1969. https://prozhito.org/note/83648.

Izmailov, Konstantin. "2 iiunia 1933." Prozhito, June 2, 1933. https://prozhito.org/note/317192.
Korob'ina, Tat'iana. "4 ianvaria 1992." Prozhito, January 4, 1992. https://prozhito.org/note/247584.
———. "17 ianvaria 1991." Prozhito, January 17, 1991. https://prozhito.org/note/247475.
Lapshin, Iurii. "25 avgusta 1988." Prozhito, August 25, 1988. https://prozhito.org/note/72742.
Levitskii, Lev. "14 sentiabria 1978." Prozhito, September 14, 1978. https://prozhito.org/note/75673.
Osterman, Lev. "2 iiunia 1992." Prozhito, June 2, 1992. https://prozhito.org/note/206325.
Parshinskii, Filadel'f. "4 noiabria 1941." Prozhito, November 4, 1941. https://prozhito.org/note/87782.
Vernadskii, Vladimir. "25 ianvaria 1938." Prozhito, January 25, 1938. https://prozhito.org/note/111170.
Vronskiii, Boris. "10 fevralia 1961." Prozhito, February 10, 1961. https://prozhito.org/note/292062.
Zholdasov, Erkin. "30 iiunia 1983." Prozhito, June 30, 1983. https://prozhito.org/note/399218.

INDEX

Page numbers followed by letters *f*, *m*, and *t* refer to figures, maps, and tables, respectively.

access to food: and consumption patterns, 36; geographical variation in, 164, 165–66, 168; market liberalization and changes in, 167–70; post-Soviet inequalities in, 33–34, 139, 141, 176; Soviet-era inequalities in, 33, 139–40, 163–67, 164, 165, 166; strategies for obtaining, 166–67

African Swine Fever (ASF): household farms targeted for, 84, 131; vulnerability of food production to, 30, 84, 210

agency: in agrifood systems, technopolitical lens on, 24–27, 37, 225; unintentional consequences of, 23–24, 26–28

Agricultural Research Institute of the Non-Chernozem Zone (Nemchinovka), 191, 194; seed varieties developed and sold by, 194, 195*t*

Agricultural Research Institute of the Southeast (Saratov Institute), 191

agriculture: and human-nature nexus, 178; and political power/legitimacy, 5, 13, 31, 39, 83, 135; political science literature on, 37, 213. *See also under* change

agriculture, Russian: major episodes of change in, 4–5, 29, 214; as political and technological project, 13, 17, 39; precision, 120; under Putin, 4, 5, 12, 13, 42–43, 69–83, 198; during World War I, 45–46

agriculture, Soviet: Bolshevik government and, 46–49, 55; under Brezhnev, 52–54, 58, 59, 60, 63; under Gorbachev, 59–60; under Khrushchev, 51–52, 56–58, 59, 60, 62–63, 97–98; shortages and inefficiencies plaguing, 11, 28, 36, 45, 163, 214; under Stalin, 49–52, 55–56, 60, 96–97; successes of, 28, 44–45; transformation in 1990s, 4–5, 29; two forms of production in, 85–86; US agriculture compared to, 31, 214; under Yeltsin, 66–69

agrochemicals: environmental costs of, 214, 223; use in Brezhnev era, 53, 54, 222; use in post-Soviet era, 120–23, 223

agroholdings, 78*t*, 112; activities by region, 115, 116*m*, 117*m*; as agents of change, 42–43, 215; and breeding strategies, 124–25, 181, 203–5; capital investments by, 111–12, 112*t*, 119, 120; collective farms compared to, 29, 77; and confinement farming practices,

291

agroholdings (*continued*)
198, 208; corporate social responsibility programs of, 128–29, 134, 215; as dominant actors in Russian agriculture, 29, 35, 215; employment levels at, 12, 30, 128, 129*t*; and food embargo, 82; and global integration, 89, 91, 123, 135; government's political goals and, 82, 118, 208, 224; and grain surpluses, 12, 212; and human-nature nexus, changes in, 89, 211; joint ventures with foreign companies, 123; land acquisition by, 12, 77–79, 78*t*, 115, 119; and livestock production, 115, 126, 198, 203–5; policies supporting growth of, 72–76, 78–79, 81–82; in primary production, 114; and productivity, increase in, 125–27, 126*t*; Putin's regime and, 5, 29, 35, 42–43, 72–76, 82, 83, 85, 112, 118–19, 124, 135, 215; regional administrations and, 78–79; rise of, 82, 89, 111–14; and rural residents, relationship with, 127–28; and rural transformation, 5, 78–79, 111; state-owned corporations, 115–18; and subsistence farming, sidelining of, 113, 135; and technological modernization, 85, 89, 91, 112, 119, 120–24, 121*t*, 122*m*, 135; types of, 113–18; US corporate lobbies compared to, 81; Yeltsin-era privatization and, 77

Agrokultura, 78*t*, 114

agro-technopolitics, 8; and changes in diet, 27, 36, 137–38, 221; and flow of state-controlled resources, 43; and four realms of food systems, 17, 24. *See also* technopolitics

Allen, Richard, 90

Allina-Pisano, Jessica, 67, 109

All-Russian Poultry Science Research and Technology Institute (VNITIP), 207; logo of, 13

allure of food, 170–76; authentically Russian, 172, 173–74; and consumption patterns, 36; local/homemade, 173, 175; nostalgia for Soviet-era products and, 36, 175–76; processed, 142; technopolitics and, 175; Western, 172

Altai Agricultural Research Institute, seed varieties developed and sold by, 195*t*

Anderson, Joseph, 187

Anna Karenina (Tolstoy), 170

Aral Sea basin, demise of, 28, 58, 60, 186

Argentina, food imports from, 64, 162

Asfivirus, 30, 84. *See also* African Swine Fever (ASF)

Askaniia Nova (nature preserve), 198–99

availability of food: and consumption patterns, 36, 146–47; crisis of 1991–92 and, 66, 68–69; Putin regime and, 149–50, 163, 170, 176, 212–13; Soviet-era shortages, 11, 28, 36, 144, 146–47, 152, 153, 214

Aviagen, 206, 207

Avian flu: confinement farming practices and threat of, 208–9; household farms targeted for, 131; vulnerability of food production to, 30, 210

Babaev, Igor, 115
banks, subsidized credits by, 75, 76
barley, 26, 93, 125
Barnes, Andrew, 67
Barsukova, Svetlana, 172, 173
Baskin-Robbins, 159, 160
Bates, Robert, 21
Bayer, 120
beef: food embargo of 2015 and, 132, 133–34; imports in post-Soviet era, 162; Putin-era subsidies to producers of, 76; in Soviet diet, 151; suggested substitutes for, Soviet planners and, 152. *See also* livestock production
Belarus: challenges of planned agriculture in, 99–100; foods imported from, 80, 133, 162; pork exports to, 133; seasonal migrant labor from, 128
Belgorod, agroholdings in, 78
Beriozka stores, 166–67

Berliner, Joseph, 90, 91
Bernstein, Henry, 20
biosecurity, threats to, 208–9
Black Earth Farming, 114
Black Earth region (Chernozem), 5; agroholdings' land ownership in, 12, 77, 115, 128; collectivization and loss of livestock in, 92; grains grown in, 93; subsistence farming in, 107
black markets, in Soviet era, 164
"black repartition," 55
black rye bread, white bread replacing, 26, 138
Blue Noses Art Collective, 173
Bolshevik government: agricultural policies of, 46–49, 55; and communal dining halls, 154; grain problem and, 35, 46, 47–49; land use policies of, 55, 91; political goals for agriculture under, 39; and rural modernization, 38, 39–40
Bolshevik Revolution: grain shortage and promise of bread, 5, 9–10, 14, 16–17, 46, 212; Russian grain exports during, 62; and transformation of existing order and diet, 6, 55, 136, 142–43
Book of Tasty and Healthy Food (*Kniga o vkusnoi i zdorovoi pishche*), 141–42, 161, 171
Brain, Stephen, 182
Braudel, Fernand, 21
Brazil, food imports from, 110, 133, 162
bread: Bolshevik Revolution and promise of, 5, 9–10, 14, 16–17, 46, 212; centrality to Russian diet and cultural identity, 3; cost in Soviet era, 163; Leningrad bakeries and, 102; as marker of diet changes, 136–37; material reality and symbolic value of, 9, 17; rising prices of, Yeltsin's reforms and, 3–4, 168; Soviet production and, 10; state monopoly on production of, 68; wasteful use in Soviet era, 222; white, black rye bread replaced with, 26, 138; white, symbolic value of, 17

bread factories (*khlebozavody*): as essential manifestation of Soviet socialism, 14, 15f; excluded from privatization of 1990s, 3; Gorky's visit to, 14; Putin's visit to, 16, 16f

breeding, plant and animal: agroholdings and, 125, 181, 203–4; as artificial selection, 186; climate change and, 194–95; diversity as strategy in, 199–200, 201, 203; fundamental rationales for, 179; global giants and, 186; human-nature nexus and, 179; hybrid seed technology and, 189; investment in, in Brezhnev era, 53; local context and, 179–80, 184, 200, 202; political projects and, 187; in post-Soviet era, 180, 193–98, 203–7; in Soviet era, 179–80, 187–93, 198–203; vernalization (*iarovisatsiia*) theory of, 188; vulnerabilities associated with, 30, 186, 207–11

Breitovskaya pig breed, 201–2, 202*t*, 204, 205

Brezhnev, Leonid: agricultural imports under, 27, 63–64, 103; agricultural policies under, 52–54, 58, 59, 60, 63–64; chemicalization of agriculture under, 103, 134, 222; fishing fleet expansion under, 26, 138; promise of more meat, 17, 103; rural modernization under, 39, 42; subsistence farming under, 59

broilers, high-efficiency: in post-Soviet era, 26, 205, 206–7; in Soviet era, 63, 203

Bruno, Andy, 181, 182–83
Bryansk, agroholdings in, 78
Buck-Morss, Susan, 21–22
Bukharin, Nikolai, 38, 46, 48
Butz, Earl, 63
byt. *See* everyday life; transformation of everyday life

cabbage: as authentically Russian food, 173; collective sector production and, 99; fermented (*kvashenaia kapusta*), 147; in Russian diet, 140, 143, 147, 151, 155, 170

cafés: in post-Soviet era, 159; in Soviet era, 154, 156, 157f

cafeterias, Soviet-era, 154–55

Caldwell, Melissa, 32, 173, 174

Cambodia, Soviet aid to, 62, 64

Canada, Russian wheat seeds in, 61, 189

canteens (*stolovye*): factory, 164; fast-food restaurants compared to, 159; in post-Soviet era, 159; in Soviet era, 154–55

capital: availability of, and food sovereignty agenda, 72; lack of, and failure of Yeltsin's reforms, 72, 109; state and, coproduction in technopolitics, 22–23. *See also* investments

Cargill, 123, 124, 127, 160, 224

Carter, Jimmy, 64

Caterpillar, 96

cattle, "dual purpose" breeds of, 151. *See also* livestock production

Caucasus region: agroholdings' operations in, 128; famines in, 50; food consumption in, 166; fruits and vegetables from, 162; subsistence farming in, 107; wheat exports from, 61

Central Asia: agriculture schemes in, environmental consequences of, 28, 58, 60, 98–99, 186; food consumption in, 166; forced settling and collectivization of nomadic societies in, 97; seasonal labor from, 120, 128. *See also* Kazakhstan; Uzbekistan

champagne, industrial production of, 51, 102–3, 139, 144

change, 7; agricultural, extant theories of, 17–20, 21; in agrifood systems, broader perspective on, 8, 24, 36, 37, 213; in diet, shifting agro-technopolitics and, 27, 36, 137–38, 221; dramatic episodes of, in Russia's history, 5, 87, 89, 214; food as tool to track, 6, 9; technopolitical lens on, 23, 24, 225–26; unintentional consequences of agency and, 23–24, 26–28; vulnerabilities as triggers of, 28, 225. *See also* rural change; technological change

Chayanov, Alexander, 18, 48, 50, 131; theory of rural change, 18–19

Chechnya, subsidies to farmers in, 75

Cherkizovo, 115, 215; charitable projects of, 128; demand for feed grain, 126; export markets sought by, 124; favorable regulatory environment and, 74–75; food embargo of 2015 and, 132; land holdings of, 115; and livestock breeding research, 205; pork production by, 84, 115; support for government's agenda, 118

Chernozem. *See* Black Earth region

chicken: "dual purpose" breeds of, 151; on fast-food menus, 160; imports from US, 69, 16279; in post-Soviet diet, 26, 153, 169; suggested substitutes for, Soviet planners and, 152. *See also* broilers; poultry production

China: agricultural exports to, 114, 124; avian flu in, 208; seasonal labor from, 113

chocolates, industrial production of, 51, 144

CIMMYT germplasm, 193

Civil War: agriculture during, 48, 59; forced requisitions during, 91; grain exports during, 62

Claas, 120, 123

climate: and Russian agriculture, 177, 185. *See also* drought(s)

climate change: and plant breeding strategies, 194–95; response to, 186

Cobb-Vantress, 206, 207; broiler developed by, 203

collective dining establishments, Soviet, 154–56. *See also* canteens; restaurants

collective farms (*kolkhozy*), 48–49, 92; agroholdings compared to, 29, 77; as backbone of Soviet industrial agriculture, 10, 86; catastrophic beginnings of, 92; commodities produced by, 93, 94*m*; consolidation and modernization of, 54; expansion under Khrushchev, 97; Gorbachev's reforms and, 108–10; grain problem and, 212; important role of, 87, 93; labor-intensive production practices of, 52, 95, 95*f*; labor shortages affecting, 103–4; LPKh farms and, 11, 59, 104, 106, 127, 129; Machine Tractor Stations (MTS) and, 50–51, 56, 57, 96; mechanization of, 96; political control over, 50–51, 56, 92–93, 98; "price scissor" problem affecting, 68, 109; problems plaguing, 68, 87, 99–102, 212; and rural residents, relationship of, 127; and scientists, idealized alliance between, 13, 13*f*; social functions of, 127; and social organization of production, 92–93; after Soviet Union's collapse, 11, 119–20; wheat varieties used on, 191; workers at, undocumented workers in US compared to, 214; Yeltsin's reforms and breakup of, 66–68, 109, 110, 110*f*

collectivization, 41, 50, 55–56, 92, 214; grain problem and, 41, 50; human cost of, 10, 28, 35; Khrushchev's position on, 51; and loss of livestock herds, 85, 92, 96; "middle" producers eliminated during, 31; and modernization of production, 35; peasant resistance to, 49, 50; and Putin's reforms, 213; and social organization of production, 92–93; subsistence farming during, 104

combine harvesters: German, exports to Russia, 120; introduction of, and decline in rye cultivation, 26, 97, 138

ComEcon, 62

communal apartments, kitchens in, 156, 158*f*

communal dining, in Soviet era, 154–56

confinement farming practices, 198, 201, 206, 207; vulnerabilities associated with, 208–10

consumers: and change in agrifood systems, 24, 36, 37, 213, 224–25; rising expectations of, 103

cookbook(s), official Soviet, 141–42, 146, 161, 171; portions of meat and fish in, 150

cooking shows, Russian, 160

corn: agroholdings and production of, 114, 115; canned, in Stalin era, 51; GMO ban and, 197; imported seeds for, 125, 196; Khrushchev's policies on, 15, 41, 57–58, 63, 98, 189; Soviet production of, 93, 184, 185; Soviet vs. US yields of, 185; US exports of, 27, 214; vulnerability to pathogenic agents, 184

cotton production, Soviet, 93; irrigation schemes and environmental consequences of, 28, 58

Crimean annexation, trade regimes after, 80–81

CRISPR-Cas9 technology, as political tool, 8, 198

Cronon, William, 19–20, 211

dachas (suburban garden plots), 11, 104, 105*f*. *See also* LPKh farms; subsistence farming

dairy: consumer expectations regarding, 171; factory farms and supply of, 164; fermented milk products, in Russian diet, 32, 33, 139, 146, 147; food embargo of 2015 and, 132, 133–34; perishability problem and, 100–102; Putin-era subsidies for production of, 76; reliance on foreign parent stock for, 125; Russian imports of, under Brezhnev, 63, 64; subsistence farming and, 105, 107, 147. *See also* milk; yogurt

Danone, 113, 168

Demuth, Bathsheba, 182

Dewey, John, 25–26

diet, Russian: agroholdings and changes in, 89, 135; authentic, quest for, 172, 173–74, 175; baked goods in, 148; Bolshevik Revolution and transformation of, 142–43; bread in, 3, 136–37; Brezhnev-era policies and, 26, 103; changes in, shifting agro-technopolitics and, 27, 36, 137–38, 221; changing expectations and, 16–17; communal dining and, 154–56; early socialist utopian thinking on, 171; fast-food restaurants and, 32, 149, 159–60; fermented milk products in, 32, 33, 139, 146, 147; fish in, 152–53; food embargo of 2015 and, 132–33; geographical variations in, 139, 166; homegrown and home-processed foods in, 140, 149, 153–56, 174; imported vs. domestic food in, 161–62; meat in, 150–53, 152*t*; pensioners', 34, 168, 169*f*; in post-Soviet era, 12, 26, 33, 140–41, 148–50, 169–70, 221; in prerevolutionary era, 5; processed foods in, 148–50; shortages and, 36, 146–47; in Soviet era, 10, 32–33, 140, 143–44, 220–21; subsistence agriculture and, 147–48; unequal access to food and, 139, 141, 162–70; of urban vs. rural residents, 10, 164, 165; vegetarian, advocates of, 143, 150, 171; Western influences on, 150, 172, 219; during World War II, 143
DLF Seeds, 196
Dmitriev, N. K., 199–200
Dow Chemical, 120
drought(s): climate change and, 194; export embargo following, 79; persistent problem of, 41, 177; plant breeding for resistance to, 184, 189, 190, 191, 194; US irrigation systems adopted in response to, 53
DuPont, 120
Dürr, Stefan, 74, 82

Eastern European states, foods imported from, 62, 64, 80, 94*m*, 133, 162

eggs: collective farm production of, 93; factory farms and supply of, 164; in fast-food breakfast sandwiches, 160; genetic research and production of, 203; household farm production of, 105, 107*t*, 108, 147; shortages in Soviet era, 107, 146
Egypt: Russian wheat exports to, 72; Soviet aid to, 62
EkoNiva, 215; charitable projects of, 128, 134; demand for feed grain, 126; food embargo and growth of, 134; jobs created by, 128; land holdings and main commodities of, 78*t*; regional administrations' support for, 79; special relationship with the state, 74, 76, 82
employment, agricultural: agroholdings and decline in, 12, 30, 128, 129*t*; collective farms and, 52, 95, 95*f*, 103–4; seasonal migrant, 113, 120, 128; in US, 95, 214
environmental costs: of fertilizer application, 214, 223; of Soviet agricultural policies, 28, 58, 60, 186, 214
Ernst, L. K., 199–200
Eskimo bars, 144. *See also* ice cream
Estonia: fish collective farm in, 101*f*; meat consumption in, 152
European Union (EU)/Western Europe: ban on imports from, 80–81; food aid to Russia, 66; imperial Russia as breadbasket for, 61; knowledge exchange with, 45. *See also* West
everyday life (*byt*), Russian: communal eating and, 154–56; post-Soviet, 176; Soviet, shortage economy as hallmark of, 140, 146–47; Western influences on, 31–32. *See also* transformation of everyday life
Exima, 118, 205, 215
exports, Russian: agroholdings and, 124, 135; during Bolshevik Revolution, 62; as foreign policy tool, 72; and global integration, 113; impact on

countryside, 61–62; in imperial era, 61; infrastructure investments under Putin, 127; in post-Soviet era, 12, 27, 70, 70*f*, 72, 79, 89, 127, 127*t*; during World War I, 61, 62. *See also* grain exports; wheat exports

famines: in 1920s, 48; in 1940s, 56; forced collectivization and, 50

Far East: agricultural production in, 78; agroholdings' activities in, 117*m*; food consumption in, 166; subsistence farming in, 107

fast-food restaurants: arrival of, 149, 159–60; and revaluation of local food, 161; Russian, branding of, 175–76; and transformation of *byt*, 32

feed, livestock: imports of, 103; increased demand for, 64, 126; in post-Soviet era, 126, 206; shortages in Soviet era, 200; Soviet vs. US, 185

fertilizers: agroholdings' use of, 120–23; environmental costs of, 214, 223; use in Brezhnev era, 53, 54, 222; use in post-Soviet era, 223; wasteful use of, 222–23

fish, in Soviet diet, 26, 138, 140, 144, 145, 151, 152–53, 168

fishing industry: food embargo of 2015 and, 133; Soviet, 26, 93, 100, 101*f*

Fitzgerald, Deborah, 96

flax, Soviet production of, 93

food: material reality and symbolic properties of, 6, 9; and political power/legitimacy, 5, 6–7; tracking of change through, 6, 9

food consumption: Bolshevik party and, 139; determinants of, 36, 138, 147, 176; evolution from Soviet to post-Soviet period, 140–41; and national culture, 213; and social status, 33–34, 213. *See also* diet

food embargo of 2015, 12, 80–81; and agricultural production, 112; agroholdings' support for, 82; effects of, 132–34; as resistance against Western forces, 173

food futurists, 143

food nationalism, 173–74

food processing: capital investment in 2000s, 111, 112*t*; in post-Soviet era, 113; in Soviet era, 102; and waste/wastefulness, 221. *See also* processed foods

food safety standards: impact on household farms, 130–31; imported technologies and, 123–24; Soviet vs. Western, 123–24

food security: doctrine of, 70–72; imported genetic material and issues of, 208

food sovereignty: meaning in Russian context, 43; Putin's agenda of, 42, 43, 69–72, 80, 82; trade policies as tools for, 79

Food Supply Commissariat, 48

food system(s)/agrifood system(s): agency in, technopolitical lens on, 24–27, 37; change in, broader perspective on, 8, 24, 36, 37, 213; four realms of, 17, 24; modes of production and domestication and, 85; politics of, 224–26

food system, Russian: compared to US agrifood system, 30–31, 214–15, 221–22; contemporary, 31–32; convergence with Western food system, 12, 31–32; global integration and domestication of, 213, 215–17; global integration of, vulnerabilities associated with, 213, 217–24; international context and changes in, 45; political dimensions of, 5, 6–7; science and changes in, 12–13, 13*f*; in Soviet era, 10–11, 31, 36; waste and wastefulness in, 221–24

Ford, Henry, 96

Ford Motor Company, 96

Fosters, John B., 25

Fox, Coleen, 23

France, agricultural imports from, 162, 196

Freidberg, Susanne, 23–24
Friedmann, Harriet, 19
fruits: household farms and production of, 147; imports of, in post-Soviet era, 162; per-capita consumption of, decrease in 1990s, 162; planned economy and challenges of production, 99–100
Fullilove, Courtney, 178–79

garden plots (*usad'by*), 54
Gazprom, arable land holdings of, 77
gene-edited crops, 198. *See also* CRISPR-Cas9 technology
General Electric, 96
genetically modified organisms (GMOs), Russia's ban on, 187, 197, 198
genetic diversity: lack of, and vulnerability to viral threats, 30; in Soviet breeding strategies, 199–200, 201, 203
geneticists, Russian, 180, 184, 186, 187–88, 190; purges under Stalin, 90, 188
genetic resources, foreign, Russian agriculture's dependence on, 125, 180–81, 204, 204*t*, 206, 208
Georgian cuisine, 172
Germany, trade with, 61, 120, 125
Gessen, Masha, 27, 169
global food regimes, 19; technopolitical regimes and, 27
global integration: agroholdings and, 89, 91, 123, 135; capital investments in Russian agriculture and, 113–14, 122*m*; collective farms' inability to grow enough feed grains and, 103; and domestication, Russia's simultaneous moves of, 213, 215–17; post-Soviet, 69, 113, 161–62; seed and animal genetic material and, 125, 180–81; Soviet, 64, 65*m*, 86; technology transfers and, 113; timeline of, 88*t*; vulnerabilities associated with, 213, 217–24
GMO crops, Russia's ban on, 187, 197, 198
Goatibex, 47

goats, backyard, 107
Gorbachev, Mikhail: decentralization under, 42; land use policies under, 59, 60; rural reforms under, 108
Gordeev, Alexey, 69, 71, 72, 74, 79, 82
Gordeev, Nikita, 82
Gorky, Maxim, visit to Leningrad bakery, 14
Gossortkommissia, 195
GOST (Soviet-era food safety standards), 123
GPS data, use in agriculture, 120
Graham, Loren, 90, 91, 188
grain(s): agrochemicals used in production of, 120; agroholdings focusing on, 114; imports of, under Brezhnev, 27, 63–64, 103; as most important Soviet commodity, 93; Putin-era policies to encourage production of, 118. *See also* wheat
grain exports: agroholdings and, 135; during Bolshevik Revolution, 62; as foreign policy tool, 72; and global integration, 113; impact on countryside, 61–62; under Putin, 12, 27, 70, 70*f*, 72, 79, 89, 127, 127*t*. *See also* wheat exports
grain problem, 35, 39–40; Bolshevik government's response to, 35, 46, 47–49; collectivization in response to, 41, 50; Khrushchev's approach to, 51, 57–58; nature and persistence of, 41, 47, 177–78; New Economic Policy's failure to solve, 35; Putin's success in solving, 12, 82–83, 212–13; social resistance and persistence of, 41, 46–47; Soviet efforts to solve, 10, 40–42, 47–48, 212; Soviet governments' inability to solve, 40–41, 212; Stalin's approach to, 41, 50, 83
Granberg, Leo, 68
greens (*zelen'*), household farm production of, 147
grocery stores: agroholdings and, 115; changes in post-Soviet era, 36, 110,

130, 137, 140–41, 150, 160, 168, 169, 217; imported foods in, 172; inefficiencies of planned economy and, 99–100; processed goods in, in 1990s, 149; Soviet-era shortages and, 11, 28, 107, 144, 146–47, 152, 164–67; special, for Soviet-era political elites, 33, 161, 164, 166–67

Gronow, Jukka, 102, 144, 164

H5N8: vulnerability of food production to, 30. *See also* Avian flu
HACCP (hazard analysis and critical control points) food safety regulations, 123–24
Hale-Dorrell, Aaron, 41, 189
Hecht, Gabrielle, 22, 23
Heinzen, James, 39–40
Holodomor, 50
Holquist, Peter, 45
home cooking: in communal kitchens, 156, 158*f*; vs. eating out, 153–56; in post-Soviet era, 160; Soviet government's suspicion of, 154
home production of food, nostalgia for, 12, 28, 174, 221. *See also* subsistence farming
human-nature nexus: agriculture and, 178; agroholdings and changes in, 89, 211; and breeding strategies, 179; harmonious paradigm of, 182–83; interdependent vulnerability paradigm of, 37, 183–84, 209–10, 211; Promethean paradigm of, 182, 183, 184; technopolitical lens on, 8–9, 37
Humphrey, Caroline, 34, 147, 165, 167
Hungary, foods imported from, 62, 94*m*
hunger: market transition of 1991–92 and, 66, 68, 168; in prerevolutionary Russia, 5, 10, 212. *See also* famines
Hypor, 205, 206

ice cream, in Soviet era, 144, 145*f*, 146, 160

imperial Russia: land ownership in, 55; trade policies in, 61
imports: of agro-technologies, 63, 90, 96, 102, 134; under Brezhnev, 27, 63–64, 103; food embargo of 2015 and, 12, 80–81, 132, 133, 162; Food Security Doctrine and limits on, 71–72; under Khrushchev, 63; of processed foods, 148–49; under Putin, 126; of Western foods, in 1970s and 1980s, 64, 65*m*; of Western foods, in post-Soviet era, 140, 161–62
India: foods imported from, 161; Soviet aid to, 62, 64
industrial agriculture: and convergence between US and Russian food systems, 31, 214; politics of, 224; Soviet, collective farms as backbone of, 10, 86; and waste and wastefulness, 221; Western, critiques of, 131
inequality, food-related, 32–34, 162–63; global integration and, 217–18; in post-Soviet era, 33–34, 141, 167–70; in Soviet era, 33, 139, 163–67
infrastructure, rural: disintegration in post-Soviet era, 68; investments under Putin, 127
investments, in Russian agriculture: agroholdings and, 111–12, 112*t*; foreign, 113–14, 122*m*; Putin and, 127
Ioffe, Grigory, 11, 109, 111, 120
irrigation systems, Soviet: Brezhnev-era policies and, 58; environmental consequences of, 28, 58, 60, 186; US technology and, 53
Iskander, Fazil, 47

Jacobs, Adrienne, 171
Jasanoff, Sheila, 13, 22
Jasny, Naum, 93
John Deere, 120

Kakhetinskaya pig breed, 202, 202*t*
kasha, in Russian diet, 33, 140, 168, 170
Kautsky, Karl, 18

Kazakhstan: agricultural schemes and environmental consequences in, 58, 60, 178; famines in, 50, 56; Virgin Lands campaign in, 57, 58, 97. *See also* Central Asia

Khrushchev, Nikita: agricultural diplomacy with US, 61, 189; agricultural policies under, 51–52, 56–58, 59, 60, 62–63, 97–98; breeding strategies under, 189; on collectivization, 51; corn crusade of, 15, 41, 57–58, 63, 98, 189; and crackdown on subsistence farming, 59, 106, 107; fall from power, 27, 58, 135; focus on consumption and *byt*, 143–44; grain problem and, 51, 57–58; and Nixon, kitchen debate between, 156; and poultry production, 63, 203; rural modernization under, 39, 41, 42, 52, 58, 97–98; Virgin Lands campaign of, 5, 27, 35, 44, 57–58, 97, 134–35; visit to Moskovsky State Farm, 52, 53*f*

Khudokormov, Igor, 114

Kiev cake, 144, 161, 166

Kirichenko, Fyodor, 177, 179

kitchens, in communal apartments, 156, 158*f*

Kitchen Suprematism, 173

kolkhoz markets (*kolkhoznyi rynok*), 59–60; closure under Putin, 77

kolkhozy, 48, 92. *See also* collective farms

Korea: foods from, adoption in Russia, 172; foreign seasonal labor from, 113

Kornai, Janos, 222

Krasnodar Agricultural Research Institute, 193, 194; seed varieties developed and sold by, 194, 195*t*

Krasnoufimsk Breeding Station, 193

Krymka wheat variety, 184, 189

kulaks, targeted under Stalin, 38, 49, 50

kumys (fermented mare's milk), 139

labor. *See* employment

labor shortages, in agriculture, 103–4; Soviet policies addressing, 52, 53

Ladoga wheat variety, 189

Lander, Chris, 124

land ownership: agroholdings and, 12, 77–79, 78*t*, 115, 119; in imperial Russia, 55

Land Rush, 112

land use policies, 54–61; and agricultural production, 43; Bolshevik regime and, 55, 91; under Brezhnev, 58; under Gorbachev, 59, 60; in imperial Russia, 55; under Khrushchev, 56–58, 59; lasting impact of, 60; New Economic Policy (NEP) and, 55; privatization of 1990s and, 29; under Putin, 74, 77–79; under Stalin, 55–56; and subsistence farming (LPKh), 58–59; under Yeltsin, 60–61, 66–68, 108

Large White pig variety, 205, 206

Lavka Lavka, 131–32, 174

Lenin, Vladimir: promise of bread and land, 5, 9–10, 91, 212; on transformation of everyday life (*perestroika byta*), 136

Libra pig variety, 177, 181, 205, 205*t*

Linnik, Victor and Aleksandr, 115

Lithuania, food imports from, 133, 162

Livers, Keith, 174

livestock herds, loss of: collectivization and, 85, 92, 96; reforms of 1990s and, 109

livestock production: agroholdings and, 115, 126, 198, 203–5; by agroholdings vs. small household farms, 84; breeding strategies in, 184, 198–207; Brezhnev's efforts to increase, 17, 53, 103; on collective farms, 93; confinement operations in, 198, 201, 206, 207, 208–10; decline in 1990s, 68–69; "dual purpose" breeds in, 151; factory farms and, 164; Khrushchev's efforts to increase, 98; public subsidies for, in Soviet era, 54; Putin-era policies regarding, 69, 76, 126; reliance on imported parent stock in, 125, 204, 204*t*; in Soviet era, 200–201;

subsistence farming and, 105, 107–8, 107*t*, 147, 151; viral threats in, 30, 84, 208–9, 210. *See also* meat; *specific types of meat*
local food movement, 12, 131–32, 161, 173, 175
Lotman, Yuri, 9
LPKh farms (private subsidiary farms), 11, 104–5; role in Soviet agricultural production, 86, 87, 104; share of total production, 106–8, 107*t*; Soviet state's policies regarding, 54–55, 56, 58–59, 98. *See also* subsistence farming
luxury goods, in Soviet era: affordability of, 51, 144, 145, 171; limited availability of, 166
Luzhkov, Yuri, 4, 82
Lysenko, Trofim, 90, 187, 188

Machine Tractor Stations (MTS), 50–51, 56, 96; abolition of, 57; inefficiencies of, 56
Mamonova, Natalia, 128, 131
markets: black, in Soviet era, 164; kolkhoz (*kolkhoznyi rynok*), 59–60, 77; outdoor, 147–48, 148*f*
Marx, Karl, 18
Matala, Saara, 23
McDonald's: arrival in Russia, 149, 159; global integration and, 213; menu of, 160; in Russians' daily lives, 32; supplier for, 115
McMichael, Philip, 19
meal(s), Russian: aspirational, 170–71; typical, 140, 144, 145, 168. *See also* diet
meat: consumer expectations regarding, 171; cost in Soviet era, 163; food embargo of 2015 and, 132; imports of, 62, 69, 110, 162; Putin's promise of, 17, 27; in Russian diet, 150–53, 152*t*; shortages of, 68–69, 152, 153, 165. *See also* livestock production; meat consumption; *specific types of meat*
meat consumption: in 1970s Soviet Union, 64; democratization of, as vision of good life, 17; Food Security Doctrine on, 71; increase in, 151, 152*t*; as marker of political success, 139–40, 150; in post-Soviet Russia, 26, 153; in postwar decades, 144
Medvedev, Dmitry, 80, 81
Medvedev, Zhores, 20, 46
Mikoyan, Anastas, 16–17; on affordable luxuries, 51, 144, 145, 171; cookbook endorsed by, 141; and food processing innovations, 102, 142
milk: increase in consumption of, 151; logistical challenges associated with, 145–46. *See also* dairy
millet, Soviet production of, 93
Miratorg, 115, 215; demand for feed grain, 126; export markets sought by, 124; food embargo of 2015 and, 132; government agenda and, 119; land holdings of, 78*t*, 115; and livestock breeding research, 205; products of, 78*t*, 115, 153, 160; state subsidies and growth of, 76
Mironovskaya winter wheat, 191, 192*f*, 193
Mitchell, Timothy, 23
Moir, Sarah, 147
Monsanto, 120, 186
Moskovich, Vadim, 114
Moskovskaya wheat variety, 191, 194
Moss, Michael, 220
multicrop rotation, 49
Mumford, Lewis, 21

Narkozem (People's Commissariat of Agriculture), 46; approach to grain problem, 47–48, 49; purges of, 50
National Food Security Doctrine, 70–72
nature: as actor in agrifood systems, 24–25, 36–37, 58, 177–78, 213; and humans, covulnerabilities of, 37, 183–84, 209–10, 211; and Russia's "grain problem," persistence of, 41, 47, 177–78; Soviet modernization project and, 181–82; technologies as weapons

nature (*continued*)
against, 36. See also human-nature nexus
Nefedova, Tatyana, 11, 109, 111, 120
Nemchinovka, 191, 194; seed varieties developed and sold by, 194, 195*t*
Nérard, François-Xavier, 44
new agricultural operators (NAOs), 112. See also agroholdings
New Economic Policy (NEP), 48, 91–92; failure to solve grain problem, 35; international context and, 62; land use during, 55
New Zealand, food imports from, 64, 80, 162
Nikulin, Alexander, 131
Nixon, Richard, 156, 165
Norway: food imports from, 80, 133, 162; genetic material from, 193
nostalgia: for home-produced food, in contemporary Russia, 12, 28, 174, 221; for Soviet-era products, and contemporary consumption patterns, 36, 175–76
Nove, Alec, 46, 57, 90
Novocherkassk, food riots in, 54
Novokmet, Filip, 32

obesity: in contemporary Russia, 32, 219–20; environments associated with, 219, 220; as global health problem, 219; in US, 218
ogorody (rural household farms), 11, 104
oil revenues, and subsidies to agriculture, 54, 198
Olmstead, Alan, 20
outdoor markets: disappearance of, 175; and Russian diet, 147–48, 148*f*

packaging: imported processed foods and, 149; in Soviet era, 145–46; suppliers of, in post-Soviet era, 123
palm oil, imports of, 133
pasta (*makarony*), 145, 146

pathogens, vulnerability of food production to, 30, 84, 210
peasants, future of, classical political economists on, 18–19
peasants, Russian: collectivization and, 10, 49, 92; Khrushchev's policies on, 52; "peasant problem" and, 39–40; resistance to Bolshevik campaigns, 46–47, 49, 50; restrictions on movement of, 95; Stalin's policies on, 38, 49, 50; state control over, 50–51. See also rural residents
pelmeni: packaging of, 145, 146, 150; in Russian diet, 151
PepsiCo, 102, 148, 224
perestroika byta. See transformation of everyday life
perishability, problem of, 99–102, 107, 149
Petren pig variety, 205, 206
Piketty, Thomas, 32
planned economy, Soviet: shortages associated with, 11, 28, 36, 45, 163, 214; successes of, 28, 44–45; waste and inefficiency associated with, 222
Pokhlebkin, Vil'iam V., 172
Poland: food imports from, 162; grain exports to, 62; meat consumption in, 152; riots over food prices in, 63
Polanyi, Karl, 18, 19
political elites, Soviet, access to privileged foods, 33, 140, 163, 164, 165, 166
political power/legitimacy: agriculture and, 5, 13, 31, 39, 83, 135; food and, 5, 6–7; technologies and, 7–8, 14–17, 35
politics: of agrifood systems, 224–26; agroholdings and, 82, 118, 208, 224; Russian agrifood system and, 5, 6–7, 13, 17, 39. See also technopolitics
Pollan, Michael, 21
pork: canned (*tushonka*), 151, 175; import restrictions on, under Putin, 79, 80; in post-Soviet diet, 153; in Soviet diet, 151

pork production: African Swine Fever (ASF) scare and, 84, 131; by agroholdings, 84, 115, 206; breeding strategies, 199–203, 202t, 205–6, 205t; confinement operations in, 201, 206; food embargo of 2015 and, 132, 133; government subsidies for, in Putin era, 75–76; by household farms, 84, 130, 130t; parent stock in, 125, 180–81, 204, 205–6; post–World War II increases in, 100; Stalin regime and increase in, 51

potatoes: collective farms and challenges of growing, 99; fertilizers used in production of, 120; household farm production of, 105, 107, 107t, 108, 111, 135, 147, 149; in Russian diet, 140, 144, 168

poultry production: agroholdings and, 115; and biosecurity threats, 208–9; confinement operations in, 207; decline in 1990s, 109; dual-purpose breeds in, 203; food embargo of 2015 and, 132, 133; genetic diversity of Soviet hens, 203; genetic research and, 205, 206–7; government subsidies for, in Putin era, 75; high-efficiency broilers in, 26, 63, 203, 205, 206–7; household, decline in, 129, 130; imported purebred parent stock in, 206; in post-Soviet era, 26, 75, 115, 206–7; in Soviet era, 63, 203

poverty: everyday lived experience of, 32; increase in 1990s, 34, 67, 167, 168; in prerevolutionary Russia, 10

precision agriculture, 120

prices, consumer: artificial suppression in Soviet era, 54, 163; Putin's regime and control of, 71; Yeltsin's reforms and rise in, 3–4, 168

prices, procurement: as central governance tool of Soviet regime, 43, 47; efforts to solve grain problem and, 49; under Khrushchev, 52; "scissor" problem affecting collective farms, 68, 109

privatization of 1990s, 3, 5, 29; agroholdings as beneficiaries of, 77; bread factories (*khlebozavody*) excluded from, 3; failure of, factors contributing to, 72; Gorbachev's failed reforms and, 70–71; impact on farmland, 60–61, 66–67; international economic policy consensus and, 71; and transformation of farming, 87–89; unintended consequences of, 29, 35, 42, 44

processed foods: appeal of, 142; consumer expectations regarding, 171; fast-food restaurants and, 159; history in Russia, 142, 144; and obesity, 220; packaging issues associated with, 145–46; in post-Soviet era, 138, 148–50, 153, 160, 221; Russian, branding of, 175–76; in Soviet era, 31, 102–3, 140, 144–46, 220–21; symbolic value of, 139, 172

Prodimex, 78t, 114

public, Dewey's notion of, 25–26

Putin, Vladimir: agricultural policies of, 4, 5, 12, 13, 42–43, 69–83, 198; and agroholdings, 5, 29, 35, 42–43, 72–76, 82, 83, 85, 112, 118–19, 124, 135, 215; agro-technopolitical regime under, contradictory elements of, 215–17; availability of food under, 149–50, 163, 170, 176, 212–13; and domestication of food production, 29, 215; failure of Yeltsin's reforms and, 71; and food embargo, 12, 80–81, 112; food sovereignty agenda of, 42, 43, 69–72, 80, 82; and foreign imports, decreased reliance on, 126; grain exports under, 12, 27, 70, 70f, 72, 79, 89, 127, 127t; grain purchasing programs under, 118; and high-efficiency poultry broilers, 26; land use policies under, 74, 77–79; on main problem for agriculture, 38; and political goals for agriculture, 39, 198; and promise of better life, 15, 17, 27; resurgence of nationalism under, 173–74; rural recovery programs

Putin, Vladimir (*continued*)
under, 69–70, 71, 87, 111; state capitalism under, 69, 82, 212; state support for agriculture under, 69–70, 74–76; subsidies for agriculture under, 69, 74–76, 138; success of agricultural production under, 212–13; and technological modernization of agriculture, 15, 38, 39, 134; trade policies under, 69, 74, 79–81; transformation of agriculture under, 5, 213, 215; visit to bread factory, 16, 16*f*; vulnerabilities of contemporary agro-technopolitical regime and, 225; wheat production under, 4

Reagan, Ronald, 64
Red Army (Soviet Army): challenge of feeding, 39, 46, 48, 87; food grown by, 104, 105, 108; meals for soldiers in, 143, 151
refrigeration: invention of, and US development, 19–20; investment in, agroholdings and, 120, 121*t*; Soviet-era challenges of, 102, 146
Reid, Susan, 138, 156
reindeer herds, and reindeer farming, 93, 182
research, agronomy: agroholdings and, 124–25, 181, 203–5; Brezhnev-era investment in, 53; importance of, 125; in post-Soviet era, 193–98; in Soviet era, 187–93, 198–99. *See also* breeding
restaurants: "democratic" (*demokratichnyi*), 169; fast-food, 149, 159–60; food nationalism and, 173–74; local food movement and, 173; in post-Soviet era, 159–60; in Soviet era, 154, 155–56; underground, in Soviet era, 164, 165
Rhode, Paul, 20
Ries, Nancy, 149
roadside stands: disappearance of, 175; and Russian diet, 147–48, 148*f*
Rogoff, Kenneth, 219
Romania, foods imported from, 62

Rosneft oil company, 198
Rossel'khozbank (RusAg), subsidized credits by, 75, 76
Rosselkhoznadzor: food embargo and, 80, 133; household farms targeted by, 131
rural change: agroholdings and, 5, 78–79; Brezhnev and, 39, 42; classical political economists on, 18–19; crisis of 1990s and, 168; grain exports and, 61–62; international context and, 62; Khrushchev and, 39, 41, 42, 52, 97–98; North American scholarship on, 19–20; outmigration and, 103–4, 128; as prerequisite for construction of socialism, 38, 39–40; Putin and, 69–70, 71, 87, 111; role of state in, 20; Stalin and, 20, 38, 51, 55–56, 87, 96–97; technologies employed to achieve, 5, 12–13, 39, 86
rural labor force: in post-Soviet era, agroholdings and reduction in, 12, 30, 128, 129*t*; in Soviet era, labor-intensive production practices and, 52, 95, 95*f*
rural residents: and agroholdings, relationship of, 127–28; and collective farms, relationship of, 127; dispossession in post-Soviet era, 34, 218; outmigration in late 20th–early 21st century, 103–4, 128; restrictions on movement of, 95; unequal access to food, in Soviet era, 10, 164, 165
RusAg. *See* Rossel'khozbank
Rusagro, 215; corporate charitable projects of, 128; export markets sought by, 124; land holdings of, 77, 78*t*; main commodities of, 78*t*, 114
Russian White hen, 203
ryazhenka (fermented milk product), 33
rye, decline in cultivation of, 93; technological change and, 26, 97, 138

Samara Agricultural Research Institute, 193, 194; seed varieties developed and sold by, 194, 195*t*

Sanchez-Sibony, Oscar, 62
Saraiva, Tiago, 187
Saratov Institute, 191
Saratovskaya spring wheat, 191–93
Sätre, Ann-Mari, 68
Savchenko, Yevgeny, 78–79
SberBank, 76
Schechter, Brandon, 143
science: and changes in Russia's agrifood system, 12–13, 13f; and society, coproduction of, 22–23; as weapon against nature, 36. *See also* research
Scott, James, 7, 23, 31, 186
seeds: hybrid, endorsement by Khrushchev, 189; imported, reliance on, 125, 189, 194, 196, 197; Russian, US imports of, 61, 189; as "technologies," 178; varieties developed and sold by Russia, 194, 195t; wheat, 125, 183, 184, 189–95, 192f. *See also* breeding
seed vault, Soviet, 187
Semirechenskaya pig breed, 202, 202t
Shanin, Theodor, 20
shortages: foreign consumer goods in context of, 172; as hallmark of Soviet *byt*, 28, 140, 146–47; in Khrushchev era, 52; of meat, 68–69, 152, 153; rising expectations and, 103; Soviet planned agriculture and, 11, 28, 36, 45, 163, 214; in Yeltsin era, 66, 68–69. *See also* labor shortages
Siberia: agroholdings' activities in, 117m; food consumption in, 166; subsistence farming in, 107; Virgin Lands campaign in, 57, 97
Siberian Agricultural Research Institute, 193, 194; seed varieties developed and sold by, 194, 195t
Smena chicken, 205, 207, 208
Smith, Jenny Leigh, 20, 28, 47, 95, 100, 181, 188
Sneddon, Chris, 23
social organization of production: changes in, 85, 87–89, 88t; collectivization and, 92–93; definition of, 85

Sorokin, Vladimir, 174
soup kitchens, 168
Soviet Army. *See* Red Army
Soviet Large White pig breed, 202, 202t
sovkhozy (state farms), 48, 92. *See also* collective farms
soy: agroholdings and production of, 78, 78t, 114, 115; GMO ban and, 197; Russian imports of, 132, 206, 213; seeds for, 125, 195t, 196; Soviet production of, 185; US exports of, 214, 224
Spoor, Max, 113, 131
Sputnik-Stevenson ranch, 204
Stalin, Joseph: and affordable luxuries, 51, 145, 171; agricultural policies of, 49–52, 55–56, 60; collectivization under, 5, 35, 41, 50, 55–56, 85, 92, 214; grain problem and, 41, 50, 83; and Lysenko, 90, 188; mechanization of farming under, 56, 96–97, 134; purges under, 90, 188; and rural transformation, 20, 38, 51, 55–56, 87, 96–97; and shift to autarky, 62
state(s): and agricultural production, 31, 43; and agricultural technologies, 20, 134; and capital, coproduction in technopolitics, 22–23; marketization and new role of, 29; policy tools to change agricultural production, 43; role in rural modernization, 20; as source of inefficiencies, international economic policy consensus on, 71; support for agriculture, under Putin, 69–70; unintended effects of, technopolitical lens on, 23–24, 26–27
state capitalism, under Putin, 69, 82, 212
state-owned corporations, 115–18
status, food consumption as marker of, 33–34, 213
steppe, expansion of field-crop farming to, 178; environmental impact of, 98–99, 186
Stolichnaya Vodka, distribution in US, 102
stolovye. *See* canteens

Stolypin, Pyotr, 42, 55
street food, Soviet, 148
subsidies: to private farmers, in post-Soviet era, 43, 69, 74–76; to state farmers, in Soviet era, 54
subsistence farming, 104–5; agroholdings and sidelining of, 113, 135; and collective farming, mutual dependence of, 11, 59, 104, 106, 127, 129; Khrushchev's crackdown on, 59, 106, 107; and livestock production, 107–8, 107*t*, 151; local knowledge and domestic technologies and, 90–91, 135; as percentage of arable land, 105; in post-Soviet era, 129–32; Putin-era policies and, 76; during reforms of 1980s and 1990s, 108–9, 111; role in Soviet agricultural production, 86, 87, 106–8, 107*t*; and Russian diet, 147–48; Soviet policies on, 54–55, 56, 58–59, 106; timeline of, 88*t*; types of, 11; variations across regions, 107; women and, 104; during World War II, 56. *See also* LPKh farms
sugar: consumption of, steady increase in, 144; foreign imports of, in 1990s, 110; import restrictions on, under Putin, 79; sourced from beets vs. sugar cane, 149; unequal access to, in Soviet era, 165; uneven availability of, in Soviet era, 144, 166
sugar beets: agroholdings and production of, 114, 126; breeding of, Soviet history of, 196–97; fertilizers used in production of, 120–23; imported seeds for, 196, 197; new technologies to refine, 100; Putin government's support for growers of, 76; Russian exports of, during World War I, 61; Soviet production of, 93
sunflower seeds: agroholdings and production of, 78*t*, 114; procurement price for, Khrushchev's reforms and, 52; seeds for, 125, 196*t*; Soviet production of, 93

sweets: in new processed foods, 138, 150; in Soviet diet, 39, 140, 144, 150, 155. *See also* chocolates; ice cream; sugar
Syngenta, 120, 186

tax exemptions, and agricultural policy under Putin, 74–75
Taylor, Frederick, 96
technological change: classical political economists on, 18, 19; North American scholarship on, 19–20
technologies, food and agriculture: agroholdings and modernization of, 85, 89, 91, 112, 119, 120–24, 121*t*, 122*m*, 135; under Brezhnev, 103, 134; changes in 20th and 21st centuries, 10, 14–16, 88*t*; foreign, late adoption on Russian farms, 96–97; and global integration, 113; imported, and food safety standards, 123–24; imports from US, 63, 90, 96, 102, 134; inherited from Soviet collective farms, 119–20; local, 90–91; as political instruments, 7–8, 14–17, 35; under Putin, 31–32, 38, 39, 122*m*, 123, 134; and rural transformation, 5, 12–13, 39, 86; and social organization of production, 85; Soviet political priorities and adoption of, 89–90; under Stalin, 56, 96–97, 134; state and, 20, 134; subsidized credits supporting, in Putin era, 75, 76; subsistence farming and, 90–91, 135; unintended consequences of, 26, 29–30, 97, 134–35, 186; as weapons against nature, 36
technopolitics, 6; and agency in agrifood systems, 24–27, 37, 225–26; as conceptual device, 8–9, 14, 17–18, 37; coproduction in, 22–23; definition of, 8; Hecht's formulation of, 22; and large producers, advantages for, 31; on state's unintended effects, 23–24, 26–27; studies employing, 23. *See also* agro-technopolitics
Teremok (fast-food chain), 175–76
Tilzey, Mark, 25

Tkachov, Alexander, 74
Tolstoy, Lev, 150, 170, 171
tractor(s): and land use practices, 56; Stalin-era "tractorization" and reliance on, 7–8, 96
trade, external, Russian policies on: and agricultural production, 43, 61–64; with Eastern European satellite states, 62, 64; in imperial era, 61; under Khrushchev, 62–63; in late 1980s, 65*m*; under Putin, 69, 74, 79–81; with US, in 1970s and 1980s, 63–64. *See also* exports; imports
transformation of everyday life (*perestroika byta*): Bolshevik Revolution and, 6, 136; fast-food restaurants and, 32; political and technological change and, 6; post-Soviet markets and, 136, 176
treats, Soviet-era, 51, 102, 103, 139, 144, 145*f*. *See also* chocolates; ice cream; sweets
Turkey: combine harvesters rented from, 120; foreign seasonal labor from, 113; grain exports to, 72, 127
Turkey Red Wheat, 61, 189
tvorog (fermented milk product), 32, 34, 147

Ukraine: challenges of planned agriculture in, 99; famines in, 50, 56; fruits and vegetables from, 93, 99, 162; grain exports by, 72; Holodomor in, 50; livestock breeding research center in, 198–99; pork exports to, 133; seasonal migrant labor from, 128; transformation of steppes of, 178; wheat production in, 61
Ukrainian White Steppe pig breed, 199
United Grain Company (UGC), 43, 115–18, 127
United States: agricultural order in, pivotal role in 20th century, 31, 216; agrifood system in, commonalties with Russian agrifood system, 30–31, 214–15, 221–22; fast-food restaurants' operations in Russia, 149, 159–60; food aid to Russia, in 1991–92, 66; grain surpluses in, mixed blessing of, 214; high-efficiency broilers developed in, 203; imports of grains from, in 1970s, 27, 63–64; imports of meat from, in 1990s, 69, 110; imports of seeds from, 189, 194; income inequality in, 32; inequality in food system of, 217; influences on Russian diet and *byt*, 31–32; irrigation systems in, import and replication of, 53; Khrushchev's agricultural diplomacy with, 61, 189; Khrushchev's visit to, 57; knowledge exchange with Soviet Union, 214–15; market consolidation of farming in, 214; meat consumption in, 152; Mikoyan's visit to, 102, 142; "miracle kitchen" in, 156; obesity in, 218; politics of agrifood system in, 31, 224; rural labor force in, 95, 214; Russian wheat seeds imported in, 61, 189; small farmers in, crisis of late 1980s–early 1990s, 66; technological change in, scholarship on, 19–20; technology transfers from, 63, 90, 96, 102, 134; vulnerabilities associated with capitalist agriculture of, 214; waste in food system of, 221; wheat yields in, vs. Soviet yields, 185, 185*t*
United States Department of Agriculture (USDA): and grain exports to Soviet Russia, in 1970s, 63; role in industrialization of farming, 20; and wheat varieties adopted from Russia, 61
urban residents, access to food among: in post-Soviet era, 34, 140–41, 168, 218; in Soviet era, 10, 103, 138, 164
usad'by (garden plots), 54. *See also* LPKh farms; subsistence farming
Uzbekistan: irrigation schemes in, 82; meat consumption in, 152. *See also* Central Asia

Vavilov, Nikolai I., 180, 184, 186, 187–88, 190
Vavilov Institute of Plant Genetic Resources (VIR), 187
vegetable oils: agroholdings and production of, 114; consumption of, steady increase in, 144; Russian imports of, under Brezhnev, 63
vegetables: consumption in Soviet era, 140; household farm production of, 107t, 108, 147; imports in post-Soviet era, 161–62; per-capita consumption of, decrease in 1990s, 162; planned economy and challenges of production, 99–100
vegetarian diet, advocates of, 143, 150, 171
vernalization (*iarovisatsiia*), 188
viral threats: confinement farming practices and, 208–9, 210; genetic uniformity and vulnerability to, 30; impact on humans, 210; impact on small-scale farmers, 84, 131
Virgin Lands campaign, 5, 27, 35, 44, 57–58, 97–98; failure of, 27, 44; impact of, 35, 134–35
Visser, Oane, 113, 128, 131
vodka: debates about origins of, 172, 175; marketing in US, 102; potatoes used in production of, 99; in Soviet diet, 140, 143, 151
Volga basin: agroholdings in, 78; Virgin Lands campaign in, 57; wheat production in, 61
Vorbrugg, Alexander, 68
Voronezh, agroholdings in, 78, 79
vulnerabilities: confinement farming practices and, 208–10; global integration of food systems and, 213, 217–24; human-nature nexus and, 37, 183–84, 209–10, 211; plant and animal breeding and, 30, 186, 207–11; as triggers of change, 28, 225; of US capitalist agriculture, 214. *See also* environmental costs

Wädekin, Karl-Eugen, 20, 59, 60, 104, 108
waste and wastefulness: in post-Soviet food system, 223; in Soviet food system, 221–23; in US food system, 221
Wegren, Stephen, 67, 161, 168
West: industrial agriculture in, criticism of, 131; local food movement in, 131–32; technology-intensive farming in, agroholdings adopting, 120. *See also* European Union; United States
Western consumer goods, cult of, 172
Western foods, backlash against, 173
Western technologies, 5, 90; agroholdings adopting, 120
wheat: genetic vulnerabilities of, 210; increased production under Khrushchev, 98; increased yields of, agroholdings and, 125–27, 126t; as most common Soviet field crop, 93; revival of production under Putin, 4; rye replaced by, 26, 97; seed breeding for, 125, 183, 184, 189–95, 192f; seeds used for, 181; strength of Russian varieties of, 195, 196t; yields in Soviet Union vs. US, 185, 185t
wheat exports: as foreign policy tool, 72; in imperial era, 61; main destinations for, 72, 73m; in post-Soviet era, 12, 27, 70, 72, 127, 127t
Wimm-Bill-Dann, 113
Winner, Langdon, 21, 179
Witte, Sergey, 61
women, Soviet: and meal preparation, 156; and procurement of food items, 167; and subsistence farming, 104
World Trade Organization (WTO), Russia's accession to, 79–80; negotiations leading to, 79, 82
World War I: Russian agriculture during, 45–46; Russian grain exports during, 62; Russian sugar beet seeds exports during, 61

World War II: diet during, 143; impact on agriculture, 56; Soviet rural planning after, 51; subsistence farming during, 59

Yeltsin, Boris: agricultural policies under, 66–69, 108, 109; failure of reforms of, 70–71; international economic policy consensus and, 71; land use policies under, 60–61, 66–68, 108; market liberalization/privatization under, 3, 5, 29, 35, 42, 44, 70–71, 87–89; new forms of stratification under, 33–34

yields, 185–86; push for higher, unintended consequences of, 186; in US vs. Soviet Union, 185, 185*t*, 214

yogurt, in Soviet vs. post-Soviet food system, 32–33, 34, 142, 150, 168

Zaslavsky, Ilya, 11, 109, 111, 120

zelen' (greens), household farm production of, 147

Znamensk Genetic Selection Center, 205, 206

Zucman, Gabriel, 32

www.ingramcontent.com/pod-product-compliance
Lightning Source LLC
Chambersburg PA
CBHW052231230426
43666CB00035B/2611